W9-BDQ-751

THE AUTOBIOGRAPHY OF
Benjamin Franklin

Sponsored by
The American Philosophical Society
and Yale University

THE AUTOBIOGRAPHY OF

Benjamin Franklin

SECOND EDITION

EDITED BY LEONARD W. LABAREE,
RALPH L. KETCHAM, HELEN C. BOATFIELD,
AND HELENE H. FINEMAN

WITH A NEW FOREWORD
BY EDMUND S. MORGAN

Yale Nota Bene

YALE UNIVERSITY PRESS

New Haven & London

First published as a Yale Nota Bene book in 2003.
First published by Yale University Press in 1964.

For information about this and other
Yale University Press publications, please contact:
U.S. office sales.press@yale.edu
Europe office sales@yaleup.co.uk

Printed in the United States of America.

Library of Congress Control Number: 2002114383
ISBN 0-300-09858-8 (pbk.)
A catalogue record for this book
is available from the British Library.

10 9 8 7 6 5 4 3 2

Contents

Acknowledgments vii
Foreword by Edmund S. Morgan 1
Editorial Note 9
Introduction 11

The Autobiography
Part One 43
Two Letters 133
Part Two 141
Part Three 161
Part Four 261

Franklin's Outline 267
Biographical Notes 273
Franklin Chronology 303
Selected Bibliography 323
Index 327

Acknowledgments

The editors are most grateful to The Trustees of the Henry E. Huntington Library and Art Gallery for permission to print Franklin's Autobiography from the original manuscript in their possession; to the University of California Press for permission to use *Benjamin Franklin's Memoirs Parallel Text Edition* in preparing copy for the printer; and to The Trustees of the Pierpont Morgan Library for permission to print Franklin's Outline from the manuscript in their possession. We appreciate the interest and help of John E. Pomfret and Frederick B. Adams, Jr., in making these arrangements. We wish also to express our warm thanks to Harriet R. Tremaine and to Dale Hershey, members of the editorial staff while this book was in preparation; to Mrs. Tremaine for the many hours she spent in typing our introduction and annotation, often working under great difficulties; and to Mr. Hershey for the substantial part he took in preparing the index.

Foreword to the Second Edition

EDMUND S. MORGAN

When people reach a certain age, they often become interested in tracking down their ancestors. Benjamin Franklin felt the urge when the opportunity presented itself on his trip to England as agent of the Pennsylvania legislative Assembly in 1758. He was then fifty-one. He and his son William traveled to the village of Ecton in Northamptonshire, where his father had lived before coming to America. There they found a host of welcoming collateral relatives as well as memorials of their direct forbears. Franklin valued the experience. By seeing at first hand where his family came from, tracing the chain of men and women responsible for his existence, he was learning something about himself, about the English implications of being American.

Thirteen years later, when he began writing the autobiography, he was less certain than he had been at Ecton about the significance of his English ancestry, and he was wrestling with the uncertainty. Writing about himself in an earlier time may have been part of an effort to dispel it. He did not say so. Instead he dismissed his writing as "the inclination so natural in old men, to be talking of themselves." And he offered a number of other explanations: to give his posterity examples of conduct that had worked well for him and might for them, to gratify his vanity in recounting his successes, to enjoy reliving a life that had left him with few regrets. He would perhaps be pleased to know that his telling of his own early story became itself the most widely read autobiography ever written by an American. It has served many Americans as it may have served Franklin—to define what it meant, what it had meant, and what it ought to mean to be an American. Among later readers the definition has evoked admiration, imitation, anger, and disgust. For him it may have been an act of defiance, a celebration of himself and his country as they had been before a heedless set of British officials tried to change them.

The autobiography is the story of a young man living in the British Empire at a time when the difference between being American and being English was more the result of geography than of politics. In 1771 Franklin had spent six years in London trying to keep it that way, but he had begun to doubt the possibility of doing so. Since 1764 the men who sat in the British Parliament and the offices in Whitehall had been set on politicizing the difference. They had decided to impose direct taxes on Americans without asking for the kind of consent that British subjects in England enjoyed through representation in Parliament. For that body, with no American representative, to levy taxes on Americans was to make the Englishmen who *were* represented in it the sovereign lords of every American. And that was the way the English had begun to talk and write in the public press. "Every Man in England," Franklin wrote to his friend Lord Kames in 1767, "seems to consider himself as a Piece of a Sovereign over America; seems to jostle himself into the Throne with the King, and talks of OUR *Subjects in the Colonies.*"

Franklin was proud to be an American, an English American, and proud to be a subject of England's king. Before the king's English government began its taxing campaign he and other Americans were content to let it supervise many of their activities, as it had done in the years Franklin wrote about (the autobiography itself did not get beyond the year 1757). Before 1764 acquiescence in the government's supervision had worked well. The island and the continent had both prospered under British direction. There was no need for a conflict between the two, a conflict in which British statesmen ought to have recognized that a continent would eventually prevail over an island. It should have been British policy to avoid alienating a people whose submission to British direction depended only on their satisfaction with it. The Americans had been so content with British control, Franklin told the members of Parliament in 1766, that "They were governed by this country at the expence only of a little pen, ink and paper. They were led by a thread. They had not only a respect, but an affection, for Great Britain." The attempt to tax them broke the thread and changed affection to anger.

Franklin hated conflict. From the beginning he urged the Americans to moderate their resistance and the British Parliament to back away from taxation. Instead, both sides escalated the conflict by making it a matter of principle. The amount of taxation and the capacity of Americans to bear it were never serious issues. The dispute was about Parliament's *right* to tax and raised at once the question of its right to do anything to Americans. Franklin was convinced it had none, that the system which had worked so well before Parliament began to fix it rested entirely on the voluntary acquiescence of the Americans. In 1771 he was still doing what he could to promote that acquiescence and to discourage British measures that threatened it. He loved England and the English, and as late as 1772 would have considered moving there permanently, he wrote his son William, if it were not for "the indelible Affection I retain for that dear Country, from which I have so long been in a State of Exile." What he dreaded was the possibility that he would be obliged to choose between two countries that ought to be one country.

Franklin foresaw as early as 1751 that American natural resources and exponential population growth could make it eventually the center of the empire. His opinions of America's growing strength were so well known that in 1767 the dean of Gloucester, a habitual critic of Franklin's, was heard to say that "Dr. Franklin wanted to remove the seat of government to America; that, says he, is his constant plan." Franklin had no such plan, but it could easily have been his prediction. And it certainly was his opinion, expressed to Lord Kames in the same year, that America "must become a great Country, populous and mighty; and will in a less time than is generally conceiv'd be able to shake off any Shackles that may be impos'd on her, and perhaps place them on the Imposers."

Franklin was shaking off the shackles when he sat down to begin the autobiography during a two-week visit with his friend Jonathan Shipley, Bishop of St. Asaph, at Shipley's country home, Twyford. Franklin's attachment to the empire was fading before his recognition that a continued attempt to tax Americans could and ought to result in "a total disunion of the two countries, though, as yet, that event may be at a considerable distance." A few days before he left for Twyford, he wrote a long letter to Thomas Cushing, Speaker of the Massachusetts House of Representatives, which exhibits the conflict in his own mind about the larger conflict. He asks Cushing, "whether it will not be better gradually to wear off the assum'd Authority of Parliament over America . . . than by a general open Denial and Resistance to it, bring on prematurely a Contest, to which, if we are not found equal, that Authority will by the Event be more strongly establish'd." If, on the other hand, Americans succeeded in the contest and left the empire, "yet by the Division the general Strength of the British Nation must be greatly diminished," an outcome that Franklin apparently considered equally undesirable. He suggests moderation but does not actually advise it "because I see, in this seemingly prudent Course, some Danger of a diminishing Attention to our Rights, instead of a persevering Endeavour to recover and establish them." Even in his hesitant endorsement of moderation, he now accepts the fact that the contest has become inescapably one of principle, and he advises continued declarations of American rights "in occasional solemn Resolves and other publick Acts . . . avoiding even the slightest Expressions that seem confirmatory of the Claim that has been set up against them." At the same time he wished to "see a steady dutiful Attachment to the King and his Family maintained among us." He does not say what duties might be involved in such a dutiful attachment.

Franklin struggled with his dual allegiance until 1775. The two weeks he spent in the "sweet air of Twyford," where the Shipleys gave him a secluded nook for his writing, must have been a welcome relief from dealing with feckless politicians, infatuated with a right that did not exist and would not have been exercised by any sane statesman if it had existed. Was the autobiography that he began in those two weeks (he must have come prepared to write it) the most effective relief, a journey back to a time when there was no doubt about who he was and where he belonged? Was it an oblique indictment of the changes he was trying so hard to reverse?

Franklin took those changes personally, as a betrayal of the empire he had grown up in. In casting the autobiography as a letter to his son William, his constant companion in the years he writes about, he was perhaps inviting William to join him in opposing the changes. In 1762, just before those changes began, Franklin had pulled strings to get William appointed royal governor of New Jersey. Since then the two had carried on a cordial correspondence, William in Burlington, Franklin in London. On the surface neither of them seems to have been inhibited by the fact that William was so immediately at the call of a ministry which by 1771 his father was doing his best to bring down. Nevertheless, the fact of William's courtly connections, initiated by Franklin himself, must have added to his inner turmoil, especially when it became apparent that William did not share his father's political views. Franklin continued to write to him with fatherly advice about his health, his farm, his conduct of the New Jersey government, and their common investment in a proposed new colony in the Ohio country. And aboard ship in 1775, after turning his back on England, Franklin addressed to William a long account of the fruitless last-minute negotiations in which the unbending ministry had sought to bend him and his countrymen through him. The letters and the account can be read as a plea and an expectation that William would join him as an American. In addressing the autobiography to him, was Franklin making a similar plea?

Franklin took the whole political contest personally, and the British placed him personally at the center of it. When he gave up on them and returned to America, he was severing a personal connection, declaring independence more than a year sooner than his countrymen were ready to but no sooner than he expected William to do. When the two met for the first time in many years after Franklin's return, William demurred. Franklin promptly disowned him and scarcely spoke to him again, even after the Revolutionary War was over. Writing his will in 1788 he left William virtually nothing that he did not already have (books and papers, land claims) because of "the part he acted against me in the late war." Acting "against me" was Franklin's way of saying that William had become a loyalist. American independence was as personal a matter for Franklin as his ten-year effort to prevent it had been.

Historians argue about the extent to which the events of their own time affect their views of the past. It would be difficult to find in Franklin's account of his youth any shadow of the combat that occupied him before and after his stay at Twyford. Readers have gone to the autobiography for what it tells us about Franklin's view of himself, for its embodiment of American values, for its homely admonitions, its deceptively simple style. They have not found in it a reflection of the political contest that dominated his private as it did his public life when he was writing the first part. The very absence of such a reflection challenges us to ask whether that is part of the message. If the autobiography was intended for eventual publication, as seems possible, was it a way of telling not only William but the English public what they were in danger of losing, particularly the opportunities in America open to ordinary people? Franklin was never the simple man he enjoyed appearing to be. In describing the successes of his youth in an old empire, was he appealing over the heads of the statesmen who stood in the way of restoring it?

He had a long history of appealing to the public in political contests. If what he first addressed to William at Twyford, defining himself and his country, was intended to bring the English public to his support, it did not reach them in time. But its posthumous publication and popularity have made him an American founding father in a more intimate fatherly way than the others who earned that title. At the Constitutional Convention of 1787 the others rejected his favorite political proposals: a plural executive, a unicameral legislature, a limit on salaries of public officials. But the autobiography, retaining its appeal after two centuries, has given him an immediate personal presence at the family table. It still provokes adolescent rebellion and adult imitation. The book he wrote in search of his own and his country's identity continues to tell Americans something special about who they are.

Editorial Note

When the first editors of *The Papers of Benjamin Franklin* prepared their edition of the autobiography in 1964, they had completed the first seven volumes of the *Papers*, the same span of years (1706–57) covered by the autobiography. They could thus draw on their unique experience in preparing those volumes. Their introduction and annotation, reflecting that experience, retain a lasting authority. The introduction included sections on the reputation of the autobiography among public figures and critics as it stood in 1964. Rather than attempt to bring those sections up to date, this edition simply omits them, retaining the rest of the introduction intact. The bibliography has been updated. A new foreword by Edmund S. Morgan, chairman of the Administrative Board of *The Papers of Benjamin Franklin*, takes advantage of what the *Papers* have now made available. It suggests what may have been going on in Franklin's mind when he began the autobiography in 1771.

In the years since the 1964 edition appeared, a succession of editors has carried publication of Franklin's *Papers* to August 1782, in thirty-seven volumes. The current editorial team is presently at work on Volume 38, in which Abel James sends Franklin the outline of the autobiography and urges him to resume work. (Franklin inserted that letter in the autobiography, before Part Two.) We have just reached, in other words, the moment when Franklin will begin once again to think about completing the story of his life. As we trace that life—transcribing, dating, and annotating the thousands of papers that will fill another ten volumes—our readers will be able to place the last three parts of the autobiography in the context of Franklin's rich and productive final years.

Editorial Note

Standards of textual reproduction have changed since 1964. At that time, the transcription reprinted here was the most accurate ever produced. The text is based closely on the original while being eminently readable, and the editorial methodology (while differing slightly from our present one) is clearly stated in the introduction. As the introduction also makes clear, the manuscript is a heavily edited draft whose cancellations, interlineations, and additions were made over a period of eighteen years and are often difficult to decipher. For readers interested in analyzing these emendations we recommend the *Genetic Text* produced by J. A. Leo Lemay and Paul Zall. When the present editors complete their examination of the material from the year 1784, during which Franklin wrote Part Two of the autobiography, we will issue a revised edition whose introduction will reflect four more decades of editorial experience and whose text will be based on a fresh reading of the manuscript at the Henry E. Huntington Library and Art Gallery.

Ellen R. Cohn
Editor

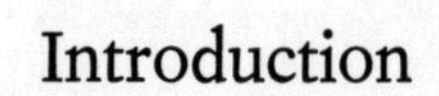

Introduction

Introduction

Franklin's autobiography has been admired both as representative eighteenth-century literature and as a revolutionary document belonging to a new era. Though the kind of story it tells and the unpretentious manner of telling it were unprecedented, its moralizing intent and literary mode were common enough. Readers of Xenophon's *Memorabilia* and Aristotle's *Ethics* were familiar with lists of virtues and how to encourage them. Plutarch's *Lives,* known to Franklin from boyhood, furnished abundant examples of teaching morality by recounting the lives of great men. He knew the Bible and admired its lessons: the moral system of Jesus, recorded in the beatitudes and parables, he said was "the best the World ever saw, or is likely to see."[1] In the two hundred years before Franklin's birth, the English press issued countless self-help tracts, evidence of the spread of commercial, bourgeois mores and values. One of them, William Perkins' *A Treatise Of The Vocations, Or, Callings of men, with the sorts and kindes of them, and the right use thereof* (1603), has been suggested as "the corner stone of that American faith in the virtues of industry and thrift which found supreme expression in Benjamin Franklin."[2] Such moral guides and tracts were no less popular in America; Franklin must have known, for example, Cotton Mather's *Corderius Americanus. An Essay upon the Good Education of Children* (1708), and William Penn's *Fruits of a Father's Love* (1727).

Besides the "conduct books," dozens of people, especially noblemen, soldiers, statesmen, and clergymen, wrote memoirs, occasion-

1. To Ezra Stiles, March 9, 1790.

2. Louis B. Wright, *Middle-Class Culture in Elizabethan England* (Chapel Hill, 1935), pp. 170–1.

ally addressed to their posterity.[3] Benvenuto Cellini (1500–1571), often regarded as the first modern autobiographer, wrote that "all men of whatsoever quality they be, who have done anything of excellence . . . ought, if they are persons of truth and honesty, to describe their life with their own hand."[4] The autobiography of Lord Herbert of Cherbury (1583–1648), first published by Horace Walpole in 1764, may have had a direct influence on Franklin when he began his memoirs seven years later. Lord Herbert commented: "I have thought fit to relate to my posterity those passages of my life, which I conceive may best declare me, and be most useful to them."[5] So when Franklin sat down to "do a little Scribbling in the Garden Study" at Twyford in 1771,[6] he wrote in respected traditions as a moralist and as an autobiographer.

The style and outlook of the autobiography are further evidence of Franklin's debt to major traditions of English letters and thought. It has been compared repeatedly to the writings of Bunyan and Addison; and its simplicity, clarity, and objective pose mirror the methods of Bacon and Newton in prose as does Pope's work in poetry. Franklin's curiosity about the motives and circumstances of his life was as natural and characteristic as his interest in lightning or street cleaning. He was, as Carl Becker has said, "a true child of the Enlightenment, not indeed of the school of Rousseau, but of Defoe and Pope and Swift, of Fontenelle and Montesquieu and Voltaire. He spoke their language, although with a homely accent, a tang of the

3. William Matthews, comp., *British Autobiographies* (Berkeley, 1955).

4. *The Autobiography of Benvenuto Cellini* (N.Y., Modern Library, n.d.), p. 3.

5. Sidney L. Lee, ed., *The Autobiography of Edward, Lord Herbert of Cherbury* (London, 1886), p. 2; quoted in Jack C. Barnes, "Benjamin Franklin's Memoirs" (unpublished dissertation, University of Maryland, 1954), pp. 8–9.

6. To Jonathan Shipley, Sept. 13, 1775.

soil, that bears witness to his lowly and provincial origin. . . . He accepted without question and expressed without effort all the characteristic ideas and prepossessions of the century—its aversion to "superstition" and "enthusiasms" and mystery; its contempt for hocus-pocus and its dislike of dim perspectives; its healthy, clarifying scepticism; its passion for freedom and its humane sympathies; its preoccupation with the world that is evident to the senses; its profound faith in common sense, in the efficacy of Reason for the solution of human problems and the advancement of human welfare."[7]

The autobiography also reflects the limitations of its times. Most of the literature of Georgian England lacked spiritual quality; Milton and Donne had gone before and Wordsworth and Coleridge were yet to come. Eighteenth-century writers in English were giving their talent most fruitfully to the building of strong, clean, polished prose, and in general their poetry is impressive more for style than for substance. Matthew Arnold has observed that as a result the poetry of the eighteenth century is "often eloquent, and always in the hands of such masters as Dryden and Pope, clever; but it does not take us much below the surface of things. . . . [Poets] conceived and composed in their wits; genuine poetry is conceived and composed in the soul."[8] This same distinction separates Franklin from two more "poetical" contemporaries who also wrote about themselves, John Woolman (1720–1772) and Jean Jacques Rousseau (1712–1778).[9] They do plumb the depths of the soul and one would not call either

7. "Benjamin Franklin," *Dictionary of American Biography.*

8. Matthew Arnold, *Essays in Criticism, Second Series* (London, 1921), pp. 95–6.

9. Amelia Mott Gummere, ed., *The Journal and Essays of John Woolman* (N.Y., 1922); *The Confessions of Jean-Jacques Rousseau, Translated from the French,* with a preface by Edmund Wilson (N.Y., 1923).

of them clever or witty. Beside them Franklin seems reserved, impersonal, even artful.

AN AMERICAN DOCUMENT

The autobiography is also a uniquely American book. After a life like Franklin's had become possible and could be described matter-of-factly, the Declaration of Independence seems understandable and much less revolutionary. In England, at the time of Franklin's birth, Daniel Defoe, a journalist of humble origins and at least as gifted a writer as Franklin, lived hazardously in the midst of imprisonments, ministerial alliances, and threats of treason, and his life ended in obscurity. There was in America a society which valued the things Franklin could do well: work hard, write effectively, plan improvements, conciliate differences, and conduct public affairs with popular needs and interests in view.[1] His autobiography records these achievements and the values and habits which made them possible, and tells how a remarkable human being used his heritage and created a life on a new, revolutionary model.

Comparison of the autobiography with the elegant, verbose work of university-trained scholars who wrote to please the critics underscores its unique quality. Franklin had no place or reputation to maintain in the complicated verbal battles carried on in the English reviews. Though known and sometimes present in the clubs and circles which dominated the literary scene, his writing had not been molded by their disputes and his career did not depend upon their approval or upon "victories" gained in exchange of words. In 1806 an English critic, disgusted with the prevailing fashions, pointed out Franklin's exceptional qualities: had he "been bred in a college, he would have contented himself with expounding the merits of Pin-

1. Vernon L. Parrington, *Main Currents in American Thought* (N.Y., 1927), I, 166–8, 180–1.

dar. . . . If Boston had abounded with men of letters, he would never have ventured to come forth from his printinghouse, or [he would have] been driven back to it, at any rate, by the sneers of the critics. . . . Since he had no chance of being admired for the beauty of his [early] composition, it was natural for him to aim at making an impression by the force and clearness of his statements. . . . As a writer on morality and general literature, the merits of Dr. Franklin cannot be estimated properly, without taking into consideration the peculiarities . . . of his early history and situation. . . . He endeavoured with . . . appropriate eloquence to impress upon [the mechanics and traders of Boston and Philadelphia] the importance of industry, sobriety, and economy, and to direct their wise and humble ambition to the attainment of useful knowledge and honourable independence. That morality, after all, is certainly the most valuable, which is adapted to the circumstances of the greater part of mankind."[2]

One hundred years later Woodrow Wilson also emphasized the indigenous character of Franklin and his book: "He is racy of the soil and institutions . . . of the English colonies in America. In England . . . he might have been such another as his uncle Thomas, the 'ingenious' scrivener . . . but hardly the chief figure of a whole nation for sagacity and for all the thoughts that make for enlighten-

2. [Francis Jeffrey], review of *The Complete Works . . . of . . . Benjamin Franklin . . . With Memoirs of his Early Life, written by Himself* (3 vols., London, 1806), in *The Edinburgh Review,* VIII (1806), 330, 340–1. Though Jeffrey has his sharp knife turned mainly against the academic critics of his own country, he is also condescending about American culture, observing, for example, that Franklin wrote simply and directly because "his countrymen had no relish for fine writing, and could not easily be made to understand a deduction depending on a long or elaborate power of reasoning" (p. 330). The compliments to Franklin throughout are edged with hostility toward the former colonies.

ment and quiet progress. Such a career bespeaks a country in which all things are making and to be made. . . . [The Autobiography] is letters in business garb, literature with its apron on, addressing itself to the task, which in this country is every man's, of setting free the processes of growth, giving them facility and speed and efficacy."[3] However conventional Franklin may have been in his devotion to the school of Addison and Pope, and however commonplace his didactic intent, the life he led and the story he told about it shattered precedent and stimulated new ideas and habits. Franklin's life and autobiography had meaning for a changing, not a static, world; they were "connected with the detail of the manners and situation of *a rising* people."[4]

LITERARY ARTISTRY

The autobiography, however, was not a rich source of "new facts" which revised or added very much to the history of Franklin's day. It is not notably accurate; Franklin frequently misremembered public and private details, and occasionally even distorted versions of important events in his life. He gave the wrong date for the beginning of his interest in electricity, he obscured some of the circumstances of Braddock's arrival in America, and he gave partisan accounts of his political activity in Pennsylvania and of his dealings with Lord

3. Introduction to *The Autobiography of Benjamin Franklin* (The Century Classics, N.Y., 1901), pp. vi, x.

4. From Benjamin Vaughan's letter, Jan. 31, 1783, urging Franklin to complete the autobiography; see below, p. 135. F. L. Lucas has suggested that Franklin's style also differs significantly from that of his European models: it "seems more virile [than Addison's]; and though at times it shows a likeness to Swift or Voltaire, it is to a kindlier Swift, a more staid Voltaire. Franklin has not their brilliance; but he remains always human, where Swift becomes at moments a hyena, Voltaire a monkey." *The Art of Living. Four Eighteenth-Century Minds: Hume, Horace Walpole, Burke, and Benjamin Franklin* (N.Y., 1959), p. 210.

Loudoun—deficiencies perhaps, but insignificant beside the autobiography's superb revelation of human qualities. Franklin's father and brother James spring to life from its pages, the quarrels with Keimer ring as true as the best description by Balzac or Mark Twain, and the account of the Quaker objections to war is a brilliant treatment of those earnest people. Scenes and personages can be pictured as readily as those in Genesis, Shakespeare, *Pilgrim's Progress*, and Sir Walter Scott.[5] Franklin makes you see.

His own qualities emerge with equal clarity. Phillips Brooks wrote that "he who has read this book has always afterward the boy-man who wrote it clear and distinct among the men he knows."[6] Theodore Parker found abundant material from which to fashion epigrams about Franklin's character: on his moral growth, for example, "he stumbled many times in learning to walk, and, as he was a tall youth, and moved fast, so he fell hard"; and on his remarkable practicality: "his powers of molding matter into machines, of organizing men into companies and institutions."[7] According to the English historian Lecky, Franklin was "one of the very small class of men who can be said to have added something of real value to the art of living. Very few writers have left so many profound and original observations on the causes of success in life, and on the best means of cultivating the intellect and the character."[8]

Lecky also admired Franklin's style: it "was always terse, luminous, simple, pregnant with meaning, eminently persuasive. There

5. William C. Bruce, *Benjamin Franklin Self-Revealed* (N.Y., 1917), II, 503.

6. Phillips Brooks, *Biography* (Boston, 1893), The Phillips Exeter Lectures, p. 195.

7. Theodore Parker, *Historic Americans* (Boston, 1908), pp. 27, 38 (essay on Franklin written in 1858 and first published in 1870).

8. William E. H. Lecky, *A History of England in the Eighteenth Century*, III (London, 1887), 375–6.

is scarcely an obscure or superfluous sentence, scarcely an ambiguous term in his works." Few things would have pleased Franklin as much as this praise. He explains at length in the autobiography how he imitated the best English authors, heeded his father's advice to be clear, and practiced good English usage with his friends. He outlined the key precepts of good writing in *The Pennsylvania Gazette:* it "should proceed regularly from things known to things unknown, distinctly and clearly without confusion. The words used should be the most expressive that the language affords, provided that they are the most generally understood. Nothing should be expressed in two words that can be as well expressed in one; that is, no synonymes should be used, or very rarely, but the whole should be as short as possible, consistent with clearness; the words should be so placed as to be agreeable to the ear in reading; summarily it should be *smooth, clear,* and *short,* for the contrary qualities are displeasing."[9] Herman Melville considered Franklin's writing "only surpassed by the unimprovable sentences of Hobbes of Malmsbury, the paragon of perspicuity."[1] Another reviewer wrote that "the fierce but clouded reasoning of Junius, the rude splendor of Johnson, the thoughtful verbiage of Burke, grow feeble and overstrained" when compared with Franklin.[2]

To readers used to James Joyce and William Faulkner, such high praise of order and perspicuity may seem strange. Just as Franklin

9. From Franklin's draft notes; Jared Sparks, ed., *The Works of Benjamin Franklin,* II (Boston, 1836), 553. The whole essay, printed Aug. 2, 1733, is in *Papers,* I, 328–31.

1. Herman Melville, *Israel Potter, His Fifty Years of Exile* (N.Y., 1924), p. 72. (First published in 1855.)

2. Eugene Lawrence, *A Primer of American Literature* (N.Y., 1880), p. 32; quoted in Charles W. Moulton, ed., *The Library of Literary Criticism,* IV (Buffalo, 1902), 102.

reflected the Newtonian world-view in exalting these qualities,[3] many modern writers follow Freud and others into dark regions where clear, simple words and sentences would perhaps mock the substance of their work. *Ulysses* or *The Sound and the Fury* can scarcely be imagined in Franklin's idiom. Similarly, what becomes of his lucid, luminous commentary on human nature and society in an era accustomed to the opacity of Karl Marx and Talcott Parsons? Whatever the need to seek language suited to complex subjects, this model for revealing a versatile and subtle man remains a valuable one, in the midst of obscurity and irrationality, for those who want to read and see and understand.

WRITING THE MEMOIRS

Franklin worked on his autobiography at four different times during a period of nearly nineteen years. He began it in August 1771 while on a visit of about two weeks at Twyford, the country home of his friend Jonathan Shipley, Bishop of St. Asaph. The house, which is still standing, is near the southern coast of England, about six miles south of Winchester and nine miles from Southampton. The bishop was politically a liberal. Probably influenced in part by Franklin, he became an outspoken defender of the American colonies in the House of Lords, and after the war began he vigorously opposed the British ministry for continuing it. The friendship between the two men continued until the bishop's death in 1788. His wife, Anna Maria Mordaunt, was a niece of the third Earl of Peterborough; their family consisted of one son (away from home at the time of Franklin's visit) and five girls ranging in age from twenty-three to eleven. There is a tradition that while at Twyford Franklin wrote for several hours each day and then during the evening the family gathered

3. Frank L. Mott and Chester E. Jorgenson, eds., *Benjamin Franklin, Representative Selections* (N.Y., 1936), pp. xlvi–lvii.

around and listened with delight while he read aloud what he had put down about his boyhood and early career in America, a setting so different from the comfortable English country house the Shipleys called their home.

If Franklin completed all of Part I of the autobiography during these two weeks he must have written very rapidly; possibly he added some of the last pages when he was back in London and before he became absorbed again in other activities. In any case, about thirteen years passed before he resumed this account of his life, and much had happened to Franklin personally and to the English-speaking world during that interval. He was now in France, the world-famous minister of the newly independent United States, waiting for orders that would permit him to return to spend his last years in his Philadelphia home. The tone and purpose of his writing in the rest of the autobiography reflect that change. The first part—begun in the form of a long letter to his son William (then royal governor of New Jersey), but actually addressed to all his "Posterity"—is an highly personal account of the first twenty-five years or so of his life: his humble beginnings, his progress down to the firm establishment of his printing business, his marriage, and the formation of his club of like-minded fellow tradesmen. In it he reveals a good deal—but by no means all—of what the distinguished scientist and political leader of sixty-five thought of the boy and young man he had been.

In the remaining three installments that he succeeded in writing before his final illness, he was consciously addressing a much wider public than his own descendants. He was no longer, even in form, writing to his son. William and he were now completely estranged, for the younger man had supported the British cause during the Revolution, while the father was giving every effort to help win American independence. These three parts of the work deal almost exclusively with Franklin's external, rather than his inner, life. The one important exception is in Part Two, where he included a description of his project for attaining "moral Perfection." He had long planned to give it a more extended treatment in a separate book to be called *The Art of Virtue*, which he had promised his friends to write but never did. An urgent reminder of this intention by Benjamin Vaughan perhaps explains why he devoted so much space to the subject when he resumed writing. With this exception, the last three parts reveal little of the inner man; the "private Franklin" virtually disappears as he becomes in the continuing narrative more and more the public figure, concerned with civic and political affairs and with his scientific pursuits.

Public service so completely engaged Franklin's thought and energies between 1771 and 1784 that it was not until the end of the Revolutionary War that he found time to resume work on the autobiography. And even then it took the stimulus of two friends to set him writing again. Meanwhile he had lost possession of the part he had already set down. When he was preparing to set sail in October 1776 as one of the American commissioners to France, he packed many of his papers in a trunk which he placed for safekeeping at Trevose, the country home of his trusted friend Joseph Galloway a few miles outside Philadelphia. To Franklin's distress, Galloway soon went over to the British; and during the enemy occupation of the city, 1777–78, Trevose was raided, the trunk was broken into, the papers were scattered, and many were lost.

When the British evacuated Philadelphia, Mrs. Galloway remained in the city, where she died in 1782. Whether the sheets containing the completed section of the autobiography had been in the trunk at Trevose or were in her personal possession is not certainly known. In either case, a well-known Philadelphia Quaker merchant, Abel James, who was one of the executors of her estate, wrote Franklin some time in 1782 a letter (printed here between Parts One and Two, as Franklin desired) telling him that the manuscript and the original outline for the whole had come into his hands. He enclosed a copy of the outline and begged his friend to complete the memoirs if he had not already done so. He did not send the manuscript itself to France but evidently returned it to its writer after Franklin came back to Philadelphia in 1785.

On receiving James's letter, Franklin sent a copy of the outline to his friend Benjamin Vaughan, who had published in London in 1779 the first extensive edition of his nonscientific writings, and asked for advice on whether to continue the autobiography. Vaughan was then in Paris; his reply (printed here as Franklin planned, directly following the letter from James) was an enthusiastic and urgent recommendation that Franklin take "the work most speedily into hand." Negotiation of the definitive treaty of peace with Great Britain and other public business kept him for a while from adopting these recommendations, but in 1784 he found time to write a second, much shorter, section, designated here as Part Two.

Soon after reaching Philadelphia in September 1785, Franklin was elected president of the Supreme Executive Council of Pennsylvania and served for three years in this post, which corresponded in a general way to that of governor in the other states. This and other responsibilities, such as membership in the Federal Constitutional Convention of 1787, together with poor health, explain why he was unable to go on vigorously with the autobiography until 1788, although he may have spent some time in 1786 going over the first part and making some changes and additions at various points. At last in August 1788 he settled down to work and wrote Part Three. This section, about the same length as the first, carries the narrative to Franklin's arrival in England in July 1757.

The fourth part is very short and describes only his negotiations with the Proprietors as agent of the Pennsylvania Assembly. Except for the very last pages, which briefly mention incidents in 1759 and 1760, the account stops in 1758. He probably composed this section in the winter of 1789–90, and the manuscript shows, as do his letters of that time, that his hand was losing some of its firmness and control, though the writing remains perfectly legible. By early 1790 he was dictating nearly all his correspondence to his grandson Benjamin Franklin Bache, and it is doubtful that he was strong enough to write even these last few pages any later than January or February. A few short additions and corrections elsewhere in the manuscript, written in a very shaky hand, suggest that he may also have made some final revisions during these last few months before his death on April 17, 1790.

THE MANUSCRIPT AND ITS PUBLICATION

Franklin wrote the autobiography on large folio sheets, two leaves or four pages to a sheet. In initial composition he used only one vertical half of each page, leaving the other temporarily blank. As he later reviewed what he had written, he canceled words or phrases in the first draft, inserted between the lines new or revised phraseology, or, if more room was necessary, used the space in the adjoining blank column, noting by means of a caret or other symbol just where he wanted the addition to go. Sometimes he jotted down opposite a line in the text a reminder to himself of a topic he wanted to discuss or of a document or quotation he planned to insert at that point. Since the writing was spread over nearly nineteen years, both his handwriting and the color of his ink changed somewhat, so it is often (though not invariably) possible to determine about when he made any particular change. After Le Veillard had acquired the manuscript (see below, p. 28), either he or one of his heirs had it bound in red pasteboard covers with a red morocco spine and green vellum corners. Using a common French spelling, the binder labeled the spine: THE LIFE / OF / FRANCKLIN.

The vicissitudes of the Franklin manuscript and the account of its publication make a strange and complicated story—too complicated, in fact, to be repeated here in full detail. What follows deliberately omits several particulars not essential to the narrative as a whole.[4]

In 1789 Franklin had his grandson Benjamin Franklin Bache prepare two copies of the three parts he had then completed. One of these he sent to England with a covering letter, Nov. 2, 1789, to Benjamin Vaughan with instructions to show it also to Dr. Richard Price. The other he sent to France with similar letters, both dated November 13, to Louis Guillaume Le Veillard, mayor of Passy, and to the Duc de La Rochefoucauld d'Enville.[5] He asked that all four men give him their opinions whether it should be published and, if so, what parts should be altered or omitted. He added an emphatic request not to permit the whole or any part to be copied "for any purpose whatsoever."

In his last will Franklin bequeathed all his "Books, Manuscripts and Papers" (with a few exceptions) to his eldest grandson William Temple Franklin, who had served as his secretary during the Paris years. About a month after Franklin's death Temple wrote Le Veillard a rather tactlessly worded letter telling of this legacy, assuring him that it was intended for Temple's profit, and asking Le Veillard earnestly not to show the copy of the autobiography in his possession to anyone (except for use in preparing a eulogy for the Academy), but to seal it up and label it with Temple's name on the envelope "in case of accident." He indicated that he planned to publish as soon as possible the complete life and his grandfather's other works. Probably he wrote Vaughan to the same effect, though that letter has not survived. Within a year Temple had settled his

4. The editors will present a more detailed discussion of the autobiography's bibliographical history and of their views on some of the conflicting points of evidence at the appropriate place in a future volume of *The Papers of Benjamin Franklin.*

5. This copy was actually sent to La Rochefoucauld for delivery to Le Veillard.

affairs in America, sorted out those of Franklin's papers he thought he might use in his edition, and taken them, including the manuscript of the autobiography, to England, where he proposed to live and work. He was, however, in no great hurry to get on with his task.

He must have suffered a rude shock when he learned that a Paris publisher named Jacques Buisson had brought out early in 1791 a French translation of Part One of his grandfather's memoirs.[6] In the preface Buisson stated blandly that he would not enter into the detail, of little importance to his readers, as to how he had procured a copy of the manuscript, but he did add in a footnote that he would also print the English original if he could get 400 subscribers. This offer he never carried out. The finger of suspicion naturally pointed to Le Veillard as the source of Buisson's text, but that gentleman promptly issued a public statement denying any connection with the matter, and the available evidence seems to support his innocence. Other suggestions as to Buisson's source have been made, but without any substantial basis. Yet, since no copies of the autobiography other than those sent to Le Veillard in France and Vaughan in England are known to have been in Europe until Temple brought the original manuscript over with him, it seems virtually certain that the Buisson translation must have been based on one of these two or at least on a further copy of the first part of one of them. The matter still remains a mystery.

Temple Franklin was naturally displeased at this French publication and he wrote Le Veillard that he had taken what he hoped were effectual steps to prevent an English retranslation from appearing in

6. *Mémoires de la vie privée de Benjamin Franklin, écrits par lui-même, et adresses a son fils, suivis d'un précis historique de sa vie politique, et de plusieurs pièces, relatives à ce père de la liberté*. Paris, Chez Buisson, 1791. The translation has been attributed to Dr. Jacques Gibelin.

London. He apparently realized that the manuscript in his grandfather's handwriting was too full of additions and corrections to be used as printer's copy and he knew that Le Veillard had one of the two copies Benny Bache had made. Possession of it might save having the original copied again for use in his own contemplated edition. Sometime later then, probably toward the end of 1791, he went to Paris and made an exchange, giving Le Veillard his grandfather's original manuscript and receiving the Frenchman's copy. Apparently Temple never realized that the last short installment (Part Four) existed only in the manuscript he was giving up. Why he thought it necessary to exchange with Le Veillard in Paris rather than with Benjamin Vaughan right there in London, and further, what became of Vaughan's copy, which has never been traced, are two more mysteries.

Temple's hope that he had prevented retranslation of Buisson's French text was dashed in 1793, when two English versions appeared. One, published by J. Parsons, is a very literal rendering of the French.[7] It did little to familiarize the reading public with Franklin's account of his life.

The other retranslation appeared in installments in *The Lady's Magazine; or Entertaining Companion of the Fair Sex*, beginning with January 1793,[8] and was also issued in that year by the same publishers, G. G. J. and J. Robinson, as the most important part of a long-famous two-volume book with the intriguing title *Works of the late Doctor Benjamin Franklin: Consisting of His Life Written by Him-*

7. *The Private Life of the Late Benjamin Franklin . . . Originally Written by Himself, and Now Translated from the French. To Which Are Added, Some Account of His Public Life, a Variety of Anecdotes Concerning Him, by M. M. Brissot, Condorcet, Rochefoucault, Le Ray, &c. &c. and the Eulogium of M. Fauchet*. London, Printed for J. Parsons, 1793.

8. XXIV (London, 1793), 27–36, [59]–64, 139–46, 409–15, 462–7, 516–22, 578–83, 632–4.

self, together with Essays, Humorous, Moral & Literary, Chiefly in the Manner of the Spectator. Apparently this work had been projected in 1791 with Richard Price as the proposed editor, but, following his death in April of that year, Benjamin Vaughan almost certainly assumed the responsibility, made the retranslation, and assembled the other materials to be included. The fact that he printed only Part One of the autobiography and used the Buisson publication as his source is nearly conclusive evidence that the copy of the first three parts Franklin had sent him in 1789 was no longer in his possession.

With a justifiable slap at Temple Franklin for his dilatoriness the translator declared in the preface with reference to the French edition that "There can be no sufficient reason, that what has thus been submitted to the perusal of Europe, should not be made accessible to those to whom Dr. Franklin's language is native." He went on to explain that he had "endeavoured, as he went along, to conceive the probable manner in which Dr. Franklin expressed his ideas in his English manuscript, and he hopes to be forgiven if this enquiry shall occasionally have subjected him to the charge of a style in any respect bald or low: to imitate the admirable simplicity of the author, is no easy task." Naturally it was impossible for Vaughan to reproduce Franklin's exact words, even though the two men had been good friends, yet there is no question but that his translation is much more satisfactory than that in the Parsons edition.

The editor compensated to some extent for the fact that the portion of the autobiography available to him stopped at about 1731 by reprinting the latter part of a short life of Franklin by Dr. Henry Stuber which had been published serially in Philadelphia in *The Universal Asylum, and Columbian Magazine* beginning with the issue for May 1790. Internal evidence shows that Stuber had been allowed access to the original manuscript of the memoirs before Temple Franklin took it to England. This combination of autobiography and biography comprises the first volume of the work; the second contains, as the general title suggests, a wide variety of Franklin's shorter writings.

In the absence of adequate copyright laws, this collection was printed and reprinted in English in Great Britain, Ireland, the United States, and Canada, and translated into Danish, Dutch, French, German, Polish, Spanish, altogether more than 150 times during the next seventy years. A surprising number of the imprints represent obscure printers in small towns scattered throughout the English-speaking world.[9] Many of the later issues added other Franklin selections, including his most often reprinted single piece, "The Way to Wealth," not contained in the original edition of 1793. For the great majority of "general readers" during these years, this collection served as the chief source of their knowledge of Franklin's life and writings.

For reasons best known to himself Temple Franklin failed to bring out his edition of the papers until 1817–18. He was severely criticized for his delay and defended himself in his preface merely by saying "that there are *times* and *seasons* when prudence imposes the restriction of silence in the gratification of even the most laudable curiosity." Perhaps these words refer to the general distractions caused by the French Revolution and the series of wars which culminated only with the final overthrow of Napoleon in 1815. Volume II of the quarto edition, containing the private correspondence, was published first in 1817, followed in 1818 by Volume I containing the life and then in the same year by Volume III, "Select Political, Philosophical and Miscellaneous Writings."[1] The volume containing

9. Examples: Fairhaven, Vt., Auburn and Peekskill, N.Y., Huntingdon and Easton, Pa., and Bungay, Suffolk, England. A disproportionately large number of all these editions were published in Scotland.

1. General title: *Memoirs of the Life and Writings of Benjamin Franklin, LL.D. F.R.S. &c.* . . . London: Printed for Henry Colburn, British and

the life—the only one which concerns us here—is in five sections which Temple called "Parts." The first of these is the portion his grandfather wrote in England in 1771 and corresponds to what in the present publication we have likewise called Part One. Temple's Part Two includes the letters from Abel James and Benjamin Vaughan urging Franklin to continue his memoirs, and the two installments we have called Parts Two and Three, written respectively in Passy, 1784, and Philadelphia, 1788. Since Temple was using the Bache manuscript sent to Le Veillard in 1789 and had long since given the original manuscript to the Frenchman, he had no text of the short final installment (our Part Four); therefore he ended his version with his grandfather and father's arrival in London, July 27, 1757. His Parts Three, Four, and Five were his own continuation of the life, in which he inserted many documents bearing on the events described.[2]

Temple's version was regarded for half a century as the "standard" and only complete text. Yet when the original manuscript became available in 1867 differences between the two became quickly apparent. Quite apart from the fact that Temple had modernized spelling, capitalization, and punctuation and failed to include the final section found only in the original, his text showed many divergences in wording. Some were obvious efforts on somebody's part to correct awkwardly phrased or clumsy sentences; others substituted more "dignified" language for the manuscript's

---

Foreign Public Library, Conduit Street. The work also appeared in a six-volume octavo edition, 1817–18, and there were three later octavo editions, ending in 1833, each with additional materials. The bibliographical details of this work are highly complex and need not be discussed here.

2. He also made extensive use of Stuber's life of Franklin. A "Supplement to the Memoirs: comprising Characters, Eulogiums, and Anecdotes of Dr. Franklin, selected from Various Writers" and nine documentary appendices occupy the remainder of this volume.

colloquial or inelegant expressions. For example, Watts's printers, who in the manuscript were described as "great Guzzlers of Beer," had become merely "great drinkers of beer"; Collins' explanation to the ship's captain that Franklin wished to leave Boston because he "had got a naughty Girl with Child" read in Temple's version that he "had had an intrigue with a girl of bad character." A few of the changes had introduced downright errors, as when "the Quarrel of Geo. Keith" became in Temple's text "a quarrel with the governor, Geo. Keith," thereby confusing a famous but controversial evangelist with the unprincipled Pennsylvania official Sir William Keith. A question immediately arose which has vexed students of the autobiography ever since: Who made these many revisions?

As printed, Temple's version was at least two removes from the original manuscript. First, there were Benny Bache's copies of 1789, one sent to Le Veillard in France, the other to Vaughan in England, neither of which is known to survive. The Buisson translation of 1791 reflects many, perhaps most, of the changes in Part One that appeared later in the Temple Franklin edition, indicating that these must have been already present in the Bache copies.[3] In addition to the number of copyist's errors that might normally be expected in a composition of this length, Franklin may have authorized Bache to make various changes in the course of the copying. Some students agree, too, that the twenty-year-old copyist—a brash young man, as his later career amply demonstrates—probably took it upon himself to "improve" the wording of some passages without his grandfather's knowledge.

Second, Temple Franklin himself almost certainly made changes and "corrections" before sending the Le Veillard text, or a fresh copy

3. The best treatment of this matter is in Jack C. Barnes, "Benjamin Franklin's Memoirs" (unpublished dissertation, University of Maryland, 1954).

of it, to the printer. Ample evidence exists in other parts of his edition that he sometimes used an editorial pen rather freely on his grandfather's papers, and there is no reason to believe that he acted with more restraint in this instance than in others. Yet, since Buisson's translation shows that many of the revisions in Part One had been made in Philadelphia before Temple began to work on his edition and so must have appeared in the Le Veillard copy Temple used, he can be held responsible at very most for the rest of the changes in Part One and the proportionately much smaller number that appear in Parts Two and Three.

No documentary evidence has been found to prove precisely who made all the changes. Many, including the most important ones in Part One, had been made before 1791, but in other instances the translation offers no clue; its "de grands buveurs de bière," for example, might represent either "great Guzzlers" or the later, more refined, "great drinkers." The fact that Temple seems to have inherited no revised copy with his grandfather's other papers is strong negative evidence that Franklin himself probably had little to do with the changes; if he had written or dictated them, it is highly likely that a revised manuscript would have been found among his papers after his death, along with, or perhaps in place of, the earlier version. It is still possible, of course, that he was responsible for all the changes made in the Bache copies; but the more plausible hypothesis is that Benny undertook to "improve" his grandfather's text, perhaps with Franklin's permission or even encouragement, though probably without his subsequent inspection and approval. Franklin's declining health in 1789 would very likely have prevented his careful attention to proofreading the copies sent to Europe.[4]

4. As early as June 3, 1789, Franklin wrote to Vaughan expressing a wish that "I may be able to complete what you so earnestly desire, the Memoirs of my life. But of Late I am so interrupted by extreme pain, which obliges

Since Temple's collection of Franklin manuscripts contains no version of the autobiography, his part in the final revision must remain undetermined.

For the last chapters of this story we must return to France and to Louis Guillaume Le Veillard. While Franklin's old friend still held possession of the 1789 copy, he undertook a careful translation. After he had exchanged his copy for the original manuscript, he not only completed his own version but went back and revised it in many places by reference to the original. A clean copy, partly in the hand of a clerk, partly in his own, suggests that he expected some day to publish it. But those expectations were all too literally cut short by Le Veillard's death on the guillotine in 1794 during the Reign of Terror. The translation passed to his daughter's keeping; after undetermined wanderings it was bought from a bookseller in Munich in 1908 by the Library of Congress.[5]

Franklin's original manuscript remained out of sight for many years until John Bigelow, American minister to France in 1865–66, began a search for it. Just as he was about to leave Paris for home, his inquiries were rewarded by its discovery in the possession of a collateral descendant of the unfortunate Le Veillard. Bigelow bought

---

me to have recourse to opium, that between the effects of both, I have but little time in which I can write anything." He added that his grandson had begun "copying what is done."

5. Most of what we have called Part Two was printed from this translation, though with a few changes, in *La Décade Philosophique, Littéraire et Politique,* No. 15 (Feb. 18, 1798), pp. 345–58. In 1828 a French publisher, Jules Renouard, brought out an edition of Franklin's writings, *Mémoires sur la vie de Benjamin Franklin, écrits par lui-même,* 2 vols., consisting chiefly of fresh translations from William Temple Franklin's *Memoirs,* but adding (II, 1–9) Le Veillard's translation of Part Four of the autobiography. This was the first publication in any form of this final installment; it seems to have remained unnoticed by subsequent nineteenth-century publishers of the work.

it in 1867, together with what is almost certainly the copy of Franklin's original outline, which Abel James had sent him in 1782 and which bears additional notes in Franklin's hand. In 1868, ninety-seven long years after Franklin began to write his memoirs, Bigelow triumphantly published the first edition of the work to be based directly on the original manuscript.[6] Later he gave the manuscript outline to Pierpont Morgan for his library; the original of the autobiography, after passing through two other hands, came at last to rest at the Henry E. Huntington Library and Art Gallery.

Bigelow's printed text is not as accurate as he thought it was; only in 1949 did a highly reliable printing of the original become available. Max Farrand, director of research at the Huntington Library, prepared and the University of California Press published after his death an edition which has become the standard recourse for all scholars interested in the precise textual form of the autobiography. This is *Benjamin Franklin's Memoirs Parallel Text Edition.* It prints in parallel columns the four versions of the work that are most important for the actual text. These are: 1. the original manuscript (all four parts); 2. the William Temple Franklin version (lacking the final installment); 3. the Le Veillard French translation (all four parts); 4. the Buisson French translation (Part One only). The arrangement permits ready comparison of the phraseology of any sentence or paragraph in all versions, but, useful as it is to scholars, it is inevitably too clumsy and forbidding to be attractive to the majority of potential readers.

At the time of his death in 1945 Farrand was also working on a restoration of the text as he believed Franklin intended to leave it. In most passages where the Temple Franklin version differs from the original manuscript he followed Temple; in others he followed the

6. John Bigelow, ed., *Autobiography of Benjamin Franklin. Edited from His Manuscript, with Notes and an Introduction* (Phila., 1868).

manuscript; sometimes a consideration of the Buisson or Le Veillard translations influenced his choice. Other members of the Huntington Library Research Group completed the work after Farrand's death and it was published, also in 1949, with a jacket designation of "The First Authoritative Text."[7] The word "Authoritative" was unfortunately chosen. The version contains demonstrable errors (the evangelist George Keith, for example, is still called governor) and the choice of versions to follow, when these differ, is often highly subjective. In any case, at this late date there is simply not enough evidence as to Franklin's "final intentions," if indeed during those last months of his life he can be said to have had any such, to warrant making a composite or "restored" text. One must choose either to reproduce faithfully the original manuscript or to follow the Temple Franklin edition with all its "improvements." There can be no third choice.[8]

THE PRESENT EDITION

The reasons the editors have chosen to use the original manuscript here are perhaps implicit in what has been said above. They can be briefly summarized as follows: 1. The informal, easy style and the use of vivid, colloquial expressions usually found in the original

7. *The Autobiography of Benjamin Franklin A Restoration of a "Fair Copy"* (Berkeley and Los Angeles, University of California Press, 1949).

8. Two major review articles on the Parallel Text Edition and Farrand's Donald H. Mugridge in *William and Mary Quarterly*, 3d series, VI (Oct. 1949), 649–59, and by Verner W. Crane in *Modern Philology*, XLVII (Nov. 1949), 127–34. The senior editor of the present edition deeply regrets the necessity of the adverse comments made above on the restored text edition—the last work of a man in whose graduate courses he sat and whom he remembers with warm regard. But that intellectual honesty that Max Farrand endeavored to inculcate in all his students leaves one with no choice but to state fairly one's best judgment on any matter of historical scholarship.

manuscript, but too often transformed into heavy and "dignified" phraseology in the Temple edition, are characteristic of Franklin's writing at its best and are an important part of the charm of the autobiography. It would be a pity to abandon any part of this style or any of these happily chosen words unnecessarily. 2. We know that the text of the original manuscript—every word of it—was written by Benjamin Franklin himself; it is all in his own handwriting. But in the many places where the Temple Franklin edition differs from the manuscript, we do not know, and almost certainly will never know, whether Franklin authorized the changes or one of his grandsons was responsible. We prefer to stand by the demonstrably genuine text.

In preparing this text for the printer we have used in the first instance the highly reliable version as printed in Farrand's *Parallel Text Edition.* But, knowing from our own experience in preparing the volumes of *The Papers of Benjamin Franklin* how easy it is to let little errors creep into any transcription from an eighteenth-century manuscript, we have carefully proofread the printer's copy from a photostat of the manuscript. One person has held the copy and followed closely while another has read aloud from the photostat, indicating every capital letter and mark of punctuation and spelling out every word that differs from modern standard usage. In case of a dubious rendering or of unclear handwriting a consultation has followed. It is highly gratifying to report that we have found only a very few places in which to revise what appears in the *Parallel Text Edition.*

In converting Franklin's handwritten words into type we have followed the same general rules we adopted for our edition of *The Papers of Benjamin Franklin.* We have retained his capitalization, spelling, and punctuation, except that we have reduced all superior letters to the line and spelled out abbreviations and contractions not easily recognizable today; we have expanded the ampersand (&) to "and," except in the form "&c"; we have made every separate sentence begin with a capital letter and end with a period; we have placed a period after every abbreviated title such as "Mr." and "Dr." In some instances when Franklin made a change he failed to complete the correction, usually in the matter of punctuation or of a capital letter; we have carried out what we believed was his intention.[9] Many of Franklin's paragraphs are extremely long; for the convenience of readers we have taken the liberty of dividing some of them where natural breaks appear.

The annotation is divided into two parts: explanatory notes on matters discussed in the text are placed on the appropriate pages; brief biographical notes on persons Franklin mentions (sometimes repeatedly, sometimes only once or twice) are assembled in alphabetical order at the back of the book. If Franklin misspells a surname or fails to identify the individual adequately, a footnote on the page supplies the information necessary to locate the name among the biographical notes; if virtually nothing is known about a person beyond what Franklin tells us, a footnote to that effect is inserted to save a vain search among the biographical notes. Persons mentioned merely incidentally, such as authors whose books Franklin read without ever coming into direct contact with the men themselves, are not included. There is no biographical note, for example, on Daniel Defoe, whose *Essay on Projects* influenced Franklin as a boy, or on any of the Earls of Pembroke responsible for creating Wilton House, the show place that he visited in 1757.

The footnotes are intended for readers of varied tastes and interests. They are largely based on the editors' studies in preparing the first seven volumes of *The Papers of Benjamin Franklin*, which cover virtually the same part of his life with which the autobiography

9. For a more extended description of the rules followed, see *The Papers of Benjamin Franklin*, I (New Haven, 1959), xl–xliv.

deals. Some of those in Parts Three and Four, where Franklin is describing his public career and political activities rather than his private affairs, are designed especially for readers interested in the historical events discussed; other readers may safely ignore them. The alterations and corrections which appear in the original manuscript are only noted when they seem to be of special interest. With rare exceptions no attempt is made here to cite authorities, but reference to the appropriate volume and page of the general edition (cited simply as *Papers*) frequently informs the reader where he may find, if interested, the full text of a document Franklin mentions or more extended treatment of the matter in hand. In the biographical notes citation of authorities and sources of information are similarly omitted, except that if a sketch of an individual appears in either the *Dictionary of American Biography* or the *Dictionary of National Biography* the fact is indicated by appending to the note the abbreviation *DAB* or *DNB*. Useful full-length biographies are occasionally indicated. A chronology of the main events in Franklin's career and a selective bibliography are also included.

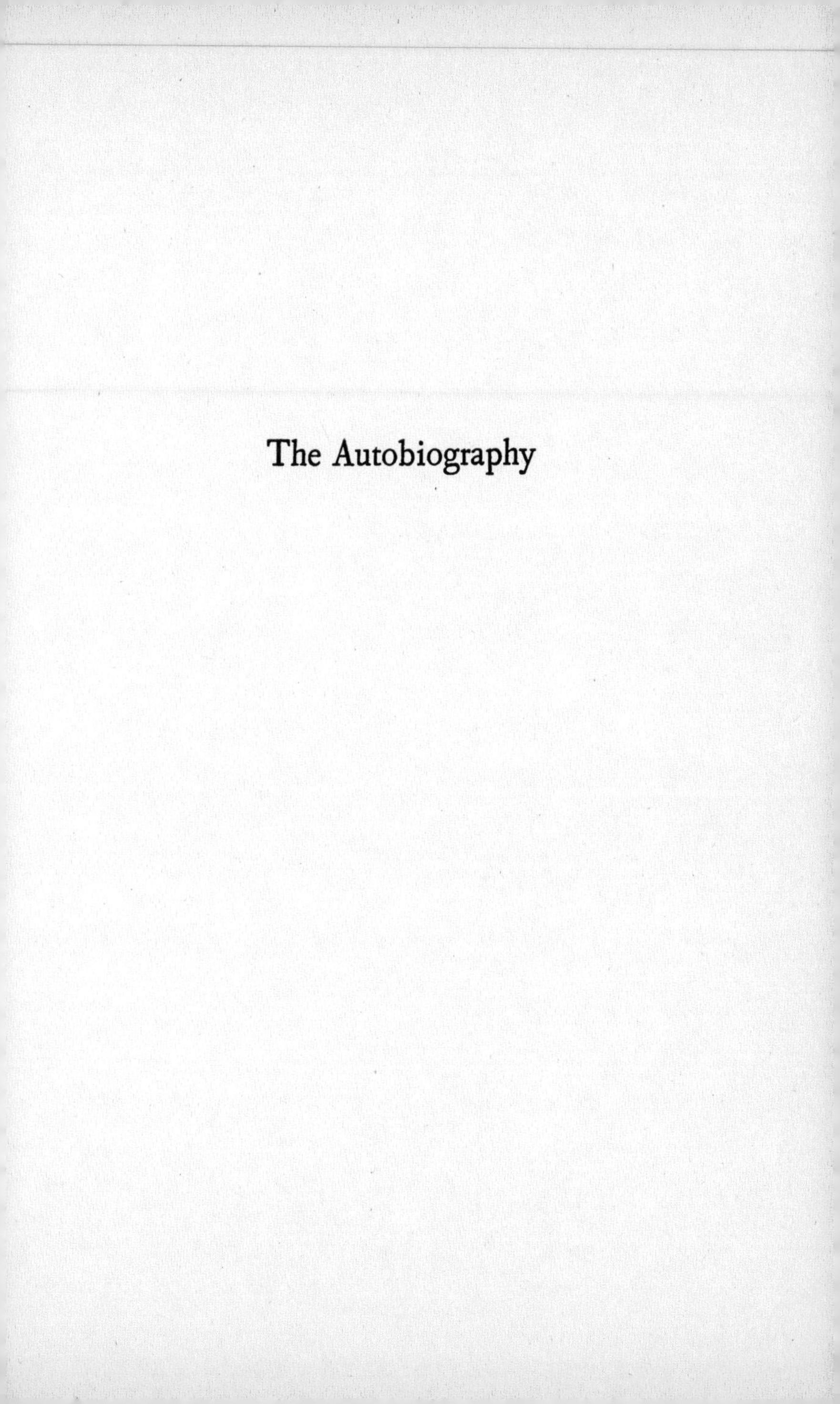

The Autobiography

Part One

Twyford, at the Bishop of St. Asaph's 1771.

Dear Son,

I have ever had a Pleasure in obtaining any little Anecdotes of my Ancestors. You may remember the Enquiries I made among the Remains of my Relations when you were with me in England; and the Journey I took for that purpose.[1] Now imagining it may be equally agreeable to you to know the Circumstances of *my* Life, many of which you are yet unacquainted with; and expecting a Weeks uninterrupted Leisure in my present Country Retirement, I sit down to write them for you. To which I have besides some other Inducements. Having emerg'd from the Poverty and Obscurity in which I was born and bred, to a State of Affluence and some Degree of Reputation in the World, and having gone so far thro' Life with a considerable Share of Felicity, the conducing Means I made use of, which, with the Blessing of God, so well succeeded, my Posterity may like to know, as they may find some of them suitable to their own Situations, and therefore fit to be imitated. That Felicity, when I reflected on it, has induc'd me sometimes to say, that were it offer'd to my Choice, I should have no Objection to a Repetition of the same Life from its Beginning, only asking the Advantage Authors have in a second Edition to correct some Faults of the first.[2] So would I if I might, besides corr[ectin]g the Faults, change some sinister Accidents and Events of it for others more favourable, but tho' this were deny'd, I should

1. On the visits of the Franklins, father and son, to Ecton and Banbury in 1758, see below, p. 46 n.

2. A natural figure of speech for the former printer, which becomes an underlying theme of this part of the memoirs; repeatedly he describes one of his own faulty actions as an *erratum*—the technical term for a writer's or printer's error. His epitaph, composed about 1728 (but not used on his gravestone), also compares his life to a book:

still accept the Offer. However, since such a Repetition is not to be expected, the next Thing most like living one's Life over again, seems to be a *Recollection* of that Life; and to make that Recollection as durable as possible, the putting it down in Writing. Hereby, too, I shall indulge the Inclination so natural in old Men, to be talking of themselves and their own past Actions, and I shall indulge it, without being troublesome to others who thro' respect to Age might think themselves oblig'd to give me a Hearing, since this may be read or not as any one pleases. And lastly, (I may as well confess it, since my Denial of it will be believ'd by no body) perhaps I shall a good deal gratify my own *Vanity*. Indeed I scarce ever heard or saw the introductory Words, *Without Vanity I may say*, &c. but some vain thing immediately follow'd. Most People dislike Vanity in others whatever Share they have of it themselves, but I give it fair Quarter wherever I meet with it, being persuaded that it is often productive of Good to the Possessor and to others that are within his Sphere of Action: And therefore in many Cases it would not be quite absurd if a Man were to thank God for his Vanity among the other Comforts of Life.

The Body of
B. Franklin,
Printer;
Like the Cover of an old Book,
Its contents torn out,
And stript of its Lettering and Gilding,
Lies here, Food for Worms,
But the Work shall not be wholly lost:
For it will, as he believ'd, appear once more,
In a new & more perfect Edition,
Corrected and amended
By the Author.
He was born Jan. 6. 1706.
Died 17

And now I speak of thanking God, I desire with all Humility to acknowledge, that I owe the mention'd Happiness of my past Life to his kind Providence, which led me to the Means I us'd and gave them Success. My Belief of this, induces me to *hope,* tho' I must not *presume,* that the same Goodness will still be exercis'd towards me in continuing that Happiness, or in enabling me to bear a fatal Reverse, which I may experience as others have done, the Complexion of my future Fortune being known to him only: and in whose Power it is to bless to us even our Afflictions.

The Notes one of my Uncles (who had the same kind of Curiosity in collecting Family Anecdotes) once put into my Hands, furnish'd me with several Particulars relating to our Ancestors.[3] From these Notes I learnt that the Family had liv'd in the same Village, Ecton in Northamptonshire, for 300 Years, and how much longer he knew not (perhaps from the Time when the Name *Franklin* that before was the Name of an Order of People, was assum'd by them for a Surname, when others took Surnames all over the Kingdom). (Here a Note)[4] on a Freehold[5] of about 30

3. Benjamin Franklin the Elder ("Uncle Benjamin"). These manuscript "notes," dated "21 June 1717," are now in the Yale University Library. Extended genealogies of the Franklin and Folger families appear in *Papers,* I, xlix-lxxvii.

4. Franklin did not insert in his manuscript the note he intended here, but Temple Franklin's edition includes at this point a long one, perhaps written by his grandfather, quoting on this subject a fifteenth-century English legal authority, Sir John Fortescue. Benjamin's father had written him, May 26, 1739, discussing the origin of the name and giving some account of the English Franklins. *Papers,* II, 229–32. Franklin evidently believed that the name meant "free man" (in Middle English "frank" means "free"), next in the social order below a "gentleman." One of the characters in Chaucer's *Canterbury Tales* is a franklin.

5. A piece of land which in feudal times was held in the freest possible tenure.

Acres, aided by the Smith's Business which had continued in the Family till his Time, the eldest Son being always bred to that Business. A Custom which he and my Father both followed as to their eldest Sons. When I search'd the Register at Ecton, I found an Account of their Births, Marriages and Burials, from the Year 1555 only, there being no Register kept in that Parish at any time preceding.[6] By that Register I perceiv'd that I was the youngest Son of the youngest Son for 5 Generations back.

My Grandfather Thomas, who was born in 1598, lived at Ecton till he grew too old to follow Business longer, when he went to live with his Son John, a Dyer at Banbury in Oxfordshire, with whom my Father serv'd an Apprenticeship. There my Grandfather died and lies buried. We saw his Gravestone in 1758. His eldest Son Thomas liv'd in the House at Ecton, and left it with the Land to his only Child, a Daughter, who with her Husband, one Fisher of Wellingborough sold it to Mr. Isted, now Lord of the Manor there.[7] My Grandfather had 4 Sons that grew up, viz. Thomas, John,

6. In July 1758 the Franklins visited Ecton in Northamptonshire and saw the house in which Benjamin's father had been born (1657) and where his ancestors had lived for generations. "It is a decayed old stone building," he wrote his wife, Sept. 6, 1758, "but still known by the name of Franklin House." The local rector showed them the church registers, and his wife, "a goodnatured chatty old lady," took them to the churchyard, where Billy copied the inscriptions on the family gravestones. The two Franklins went on to Birmingham, where they looked up some of Deborah Franklin's relatives. On the way back to London they visited Banbury, another family home. This trip helped Franklin to prepare an elaborate genealogical chart, reproduced in *Pennsylvania Magazine of History and Biography*, XXIII (1899), facing p. 2.

7. Mary Fisher, Franklin's first cousin, died soon after he had visited her in 1758, leaving her estate in equal shares to her seven surviving cousins. Franklin divided his share between two English relatives, "they being ancient Women and poor."

Benjamin and Josiah. I will give you what Account I can of them at this distance from my Papers, and if they are not lost in my Absence, you will among them find many more Particulars. Thomas was bred a Smith under his Father, but being ingenious, and encourag'd in Learning (as all his Brothers like wise were) by an Esquire Palmer[8] then the principal Gentleman in that Parish, he qualify'd for the Business of Scrivener,[9] became a considerable Man in the County Affairs, was a chief Mover of all publick Spirited Undertakings, for the County, or Town of Northampton and his own Village, of which many Instances were told us at Ecton and he was much taken Notice of and patroniz'd by the then Lord Halifax. He died in 1702, Jan. 6, old Stile, just 4 Years to a Day before I was born.[1] The Account we receiv'd of his Life and Character from some old People at Ecton, I remember struck you, as something extraordinary from its Similarity to what you knew of

8. John Palmer.

9. A professional writer, skilled in the drawing of contracts and other legal documents.

1. Until 1752 England and her colonies followed the "Old Style" or Julian calendar. Because it inaccurately measured the length of the solar year, this calendar gradually fell behind the true course of the earth around the sun. In 1582 the "New Style" or Gregorian calendar was adopted in many countries, dropping out ten days in the first year to correct the accumulated error and changing the rule which governed future leap years. England and some other countries were slow to make the change and by the eighteenth century they were eleven days behind the rest of western Europe. January 6 in England and her colonies, for example, was January 17 in France. The British world caught up in 1752 under an act of Parliament by dropping out eleven days: Wednesday, September 2, was immediately followed by Thursday, September 14. At the same time the beginning of the official year was changed from March 25 to January 1. In subsequent years anniversaries, such as birthdays, had to be changed to correspond. Franklin had to celebrate his birthday on January 17 instead of January 6, and Washington his on February 22 instead of February 11.

mine. Had he died on the same Day, you said one might have suppos'd a Transmigration.

John was bred a Dyer, I believe of Woollens. Benjamin, was bred a Silk Dyer, serving an Apprenticeship at London. He was an ingenious Man, I remember him well, for when I was a Boy he came over to my Father in Boston, and lived in the House with us some Years. He lived to a great Age. His Grandson Samuel Franklin now lives in Boston. He left behind him two Quarto Volumes, M.S. of his own Poetry, consisting of little occasional Pieces address'd to his Friends and Relations, of which the following sent to me, is a Specimen. (Here insert it.)[2] He had form'd a Shorthand of his own, which he taught me, but never practising it I have

2. The original manuscript contains no such verses now, but the Le Veillard translation included two of the three pieces the elder Benjamin Franklin is known to have written to his namesake. They may have been in the copy of the autobiography made by Benny Bache and sent to Le Veillard in 1789 or, more probably, on a loose sheet laid into the original manuscript which Le Veillard later acquired from Temple Franklin. They are reprinted here from Uncle Benjamin's commonplace book now in the American Antiquarian Society:

Sent to My Name upon a Report
of his Inclineation to Martial affaires
7 July 1710

Beleeve me Ben. It is a Dangerous Trade—
The Sword has Many Marr'd as well as Made.
By it doe many fall, Not Many Rise;
Makes Many poor, few Rich and fewer Wise;
Fills Towns with Ruin, fields with blood beside;
Tis Sloth's Maintainer, And the Shield of pride;
Fair Citties Rich to Day, in plenty flow,
War fills with want, Tomorrow, and with woe.
Ruin'd Estates, The Nurse of Vice, broke limbs and scarts
Are the Effects of Desolating Warrs.

now forgot it. I was nam'd after this Uncle, there being a particular Affection between him and my Father. He was very pious, a great Attender of Sermons of the best Preachers, which he took down in his Shorthand and had with him many Volumes of them. He was also much of a Politician, too much perhaps for his Station. There fell lately into my Hands in London a Collection he had made of all the principal Pamphlets relating to Publick Affairs from 1641 to 1717. Many of the Volumes are wanting, as appears by the Numbering, but there still remains 8 Vols. Folio, and 24 in 4to and 8vo. A Dealer in old Books met with them, and knowing me by my sometimes buying of him, he brought them to me. It seems my Uncle must have left them here when he went to America, which was

---

[Acrostic]

Sent to B.F. in N.E. 15 July 1710

Be to thy parents an Obedient son;
Each Day let Duty constantly be Done;
Never give Way to sloth or lust or pride
If free you'd be from Thousand Ills beside.
Above all Ills be sure Avoide the shelfe:
Mans Danger lyes in Satan, sin and selfe.
In vertue, Learning, Wisdome progress make.
Nere shrink at suffering for thy saviours sake;
Fraud and all Falshood in thy Dealings Flee;
Religious Always in thy station be;
Adore the Maker of thy Inward part:
Now's the Accepted time, Give him thy Heart.
Keep a Good Conscience, 'tis a constant Frind;
Like Judge and Witness This Thy Acts Attend.
In Heart with bended knee Alone Adore
None but the Three in One Forevermore.

The third of these pieces, entitled "To My Name 1713," is printed in *Papers*, I, 5.

above 50 Years since. There are many of his Notes in the Margins.[3]

This obscure Family of ours was early in the Reformation, and continu'd Protestants thro' the Reign of Queen Mary, when they were sometimes in Danger of Trouble on Account of their Zeal against Popery.[4] They had got an English Bible, and to conceal and secure it, it was fastned open with Tapes under and within the Frame of a Joint Stool. When my Great Great Grandfather read in it to his Family, he turn'd up the Joint Stool upon his Knees, turning over the Leaves then under the Tapes. One of the Children stood at the Door to give Notice if he saw the Apparitor coming, who was an Officer of the Spiritual Court. In that Case the Stool was turn'd down again upon its feet, when the Bible remain'd conceal'd under it as before. This Anecdote I had from my Uncle Benjamin.[5] The Family continu'd all of the Church of England till about the End of Charles the 2ds Reign, when some of the Ministers that had been outed for Nonconformity, holding Conventicles in Northamptonshire, Benjamin and Josiah adher'd to them, and so continu'd all their Lives. The rest of the Family remain'd with the Episcopal Church.

3. In July 1771, less than a month before Franklin wrote this, an old-book dealer had shown him this collection of pamphlets. He identified their original owner chiefly by the handwriting of the marginal notes. "The oddity is that the Bookseller who could suspect nothing of any Relation between me and the Collector should happen to make me the Offer of them." Of course Franklin bought the collection at once.

4. Queen Mary, Henry VIII's elder daughter and a Roman Catholic, succeeded her half-brother Edward VI, a Protestant, in 1553. She and her ministers undertook to restore the former state religion by measures which earned for her the nickname of "Bloody Mary." Upon her death in 1558 her half-sister Elizabeth became queen and supported a reversion to a form of Protestantism somewhat less extreme than had been advanced under Edward.

5. Franklin's father also related this anecdote to his son in a letter of May 26, 1739, *Papers*, II, 230–1.

Josiah, my Father, married young, and carried his Wife with three Children unto New England, about 1682.[6] The Conventicles having been forbidden by Law, and frequently disturbed, induced some considerable Men of his Acquaintance to remove to that Country, and he was prevail'd with to accompany them thither, where they expected to enjoy their Mode of Religion with Freedom. By the same Wife he had 4 Children more born there, and by a second Wife ten more, in all 17, of which I remember 13 sitting at one time at his Table, who all grew up to be Men and Women, and married.[7] I was the youngest Son and the youngest Child but two, and was born in Boston, N. England.

My Mother the 2d Wife was Abiah Folger, a Daughter of Peter Folger, one of the first Settlers of New England,[8] of whom honourable mention is made by Cotton Mather, in his Church History of that Country, (entitled Magnalia Christi Americana) as a *godly learned Englishman,* if I remember the words rightly. I have heard that he wrote sundry small occasional Pieces, but only one of them was printed which I saw now many Years since.[9] It was written in

6. Actually 1683. Josiah's first wife was Ann Child.

7. Franklin recalled this occasion in a letter to his youngest sister Jane Mecom, Jan. 9, 1760. It took place, probably about 1714 or 1715, when his half-brother Josiah, "who had been absent in the East-Indies, and unheard of for nine Years," returned briefly to Boston. He was lost at sea soon afterwards. At the time Franklin began writing his autobiography only Jane and he were still living.

8. The Folgers were among the most prominent families that settled Nantucket Island, which was for many years the leading whaling center in America. A memorial now stands on the site of the house where Abiah was born in 1667.

9. *A Looking Glass for the Times, or the Former Spirit of New England Revived in This Generation* (Boston, 1676). It has been described as being "without one sparkle of poetry, [but] . . . great in frankness and force." Moses C. Tyler, *A History of American Literature* (London, 1879), II, 20.

1675, in the homespun Verse of that Time and People, and address'd to those then concern'd in the Government there. It was in favour of Liberty of Conscience, and in behalf of the Baptists, Quakers, and other Sectaries, that had been under Persecution; ascribing the Indian Wars and other Distresses, that had befallen the Country to that Persecution, as so many Judgments of God, to punish so heinous an Offence; and exhorting a Repeal of those uncharitable Laws. The whole appear'd to me as written with a good deal of Decent Plainness and manly Freedom. The six last concluding Lines I remember, tho' I have forgotten the two first of the Stanza, but the Purport of them was that his Censures proceeded from *Goodwill,* and therefore he would be known as the Author,

> because to be a Libeller, (says he)
> I hate it with my Heart.
> From Sherburne Town* where now I dwell,
> My Name I do put here,
> Without Offence, your real Friend,
> It is Peter Folgier.[1]

My elder Brothers were all put Apprentices to different Trades. I was put to the Grammar School at Eight Years of Age, my Father intending to devote me as the Tithe of his Sons to the Service of the Church. My early Readiness in learning to read (which must have

---

*In the Island of Nantucket.

1. The six lines preceding this quotation are:

> I am for Peace, and not for War,
> and that's the Reason why,
> I write more plain than some Men do,
> that use to daub and lie;
> But I shall cease and set my Name
> to what I here insert,

been very early, as I do not remember when I could not read) and the Opinion of all his Friends that I should certainly make a good Scholar, encourag'd him in this Purpose of his. My Uncle Benjamin too approv'd of it, and propos'd to give me all his Shorthand Volumes of Sermons I suppose as a Stock to set up with, if I would learn his Character. I continu'd however at the Grammar School not quite one Year, tho' in that time I had risen gradually from the Middle of the Class of that Year to be the Head of it, and farther was remov'd into the next Class above it, in order to go with that into the third at the End of the Year. But my Father in the mean time, from a View of the Expence of a College Education which, having so large a Family, he could not well afford, and the mean Living many so educated were afterwards able to obtain, Reasons that he gave to his Friends in my Hearing, altered his first Intention, took me from the Grammar School, and sent me to a School for Writing and Arithmetic kept by a then famous Man, Mr. Geo. Brownell, very successful in his Profession generally, and that by mild encouraging Methods. Under him I acquired fair Writing pretty soon, but I fail'd in the Arithmetic, and made no Progress in it.

At Ten Years old, I was taken home to assist my Father in his Business, which was that of a Tallow Chandler and Sope-Boiler. A Business he was not bred to, but had assumed on his Arrival in New England and on finding his Dying Trade would not maintain his Family, being in little Request. Accordingly I was employed in cutting Wick for the Candles, filling the Dipping Mold, and the Molds for cast Candles, attending the Shop, going of Errands, &c. I dislik'd the Trade and had a strong Inclination for the Sea; but my Father declar'd against it; however, living near the Water, I was much in and about it, learnt early to swim well,[2] and to manage

2. There are several references in the autobiography and in Franklin's other writings to his skill as a swimmer and his fondness of the sport.

Boats, and when in a Boat or Canoe with other Boys I was commonly allow'd to govern, especially in any case of Difficulty; and upon other Occasions I was generally a Leader among the Boys, and sometimes led them into Scrapes, of which I will mention one Instance, as it shows an early projecting public Spirit, tho' not then justly conducted. There was a Salt Marsh that bounded part of the Mill Pond, on the Edge of which at Highwater, we us'd to stand to fish for Minews. By much Trampling, we had made it a mere Quagmire. My Proposal was to build a Wharf there fit for us to stand upon, and I show'd my Comrades a large Heap of Stones which were intended for a new House near the Marsh, and which would very well suit our Purpose. Accordingly in the Evening when the Workmen were gone, I assembled a Number of my Playfellows, and working with them diligently like so many Emmets,[3] sometimes two or three to a Stone, we brought them all away and built our little Wharff. The next Morning the Workmen were surpriz'd at Missing the Stones; which were found in our Wharff; Enquiry was made after the Removers; we were discovered and complain'd of; several of us were corrected by our Fathers; and tho' I pleaded the Usefulness of the Work, mine convinc'd me that nothing was useful which was not honest.

I think you may like to know Something of his Person and Character. He had an excellent Constitution of Body, was of middle Stature, but well set and very strong. He was ingenious, could draw prettily, was skill'd a little in Music and had a clear pleasing Voice, so that when he play'd Psalm Tunes on his Violin and sung withal as he sometimes did in an Evening after the Business of the Day was over, it was extreamly agreable to hear. He had a mechanical Genius too, and on occasion was very handy in the Use of other Tradesmen's Tools. But his great Excellence lay in a sound Understanding, and solid Judgment in prudential Matters, both in private

3. Ants.

and publick Affairs. In the latter indeed he was never employed, the numerous Family he had to educate and the straitness of his Circumstances, keeping him close to his Trade, but I remember well his being frequently visited by leading People, who consulted him for his Opinion in Affairs of the Town or of the Church he belong'd to and show'd a good deal of Respect for his Judgment and Advice. He was also much consulted by private Persons about their Affairs when any Difficulty occur'd, and frequently chosen an Arbitrator between contending Parties. At his Table he lik'd to have as often as he could, some sensible Friend or Neighbour, to converse with, and always took care to start some ingenious or useful Topic for Discourse, which might tend to improve the Minds of his Children. By this means he turn'd our Attention to what was good, just, and prudent in the Conduct of Life; and little or no Notice was ever taken of what related to the Victuals on the Table, whether it was well or ill drest, in or out of season, of good or bad flavour, preferable or inferior to this or that other thing of the kind; so that I was bro't up in such a perfect Inattention to those Matters as to be quite Indifferent what kind of Food was set before me; and so unobservant of it, that to this Day, if I am ask'd I can scarce tell, a few Hours after Dinner, what I din'd upon. This has been a Convenience to me in travelling, where my Companions have been sometimes very unhappy for want of a suitable Gratification of their more delicate because better instructed Tastes and Appetites.[4]

4. Though Franklin's tastes may have been relatively simple, he thoroughly enjoyed good food, and his wife Deborah knew it. He wrote her appreciatively of the roast beef and mince pies she sent him in the winter of 1756 when he was building forts in the Pennsylvania mountains and of the dried apples and other "goodys for my Pappy" she shipped to him in England later. And among his papers are several recipes, some in English, some in French, for various dishes that he appears particularly to have enjoyed.

My Mother had likewise an excellent Constitution. She suckled all her 10 Children. I never knew either my Father or Mother to have any Sickness but that of which they dy'd, he at 89 and she at 85 Years of age. They lie buried together at Boston, where I some Years since plac'd a Marble stone over their Grave with this Inscription

Josiah Franklin
And Abiah his Wife
Lie here interred.
They lived lovingly together in Wedlock
Fifty-five Years.
Without an Estate or any gainful Employment,
By constant labour and Industry,
With God's Blessing,
They maintained a large Family
Comfortably;
And brought up thirteen Children,
And seven Grand Children
Reputably.
From this Instance, Reader,
Be encouraged to Diligence in thy Calling,
And distrust not Providence.
He was a pious & prudent Man,
She a discreet and virtuous Woman.
Their youngest Son,
In filial Regard to their Memory,
Places this Stone.
J.F. born 1655—Died 1744. Ætat 89
A.F. born 1667—died 1752——85[5]

By my rambling Digressions I perceive my self to be grown old. I us'd to write more methodically. But one does not dress for

5. The original stone in the Granary Burying Ground was replaced in 1827, by public subscription, with a 20-foot granite monument on which a bronze tablet repeats the epitaph, slightly modified. *Papers*, VII, 229–30.

private Company as for a publick Ball. 'Tis perhaps only Negligence.

To return. I continu'd thus employ'd in my Father's Business for two Years, that is till I was 12 Years old; and my Brother John, who was bred to that Business having left my Father, married and set up for himself at Rhodeisland, there was all Appearance that I was destin'd to supply his Place and be a Tallow Chandler. But my Dislike to the Trade continuing, my Father was under Apprehensions that if he did not find one for me more agreable, I should break away and get to Sea, as his Son Josiah had done to his great Vexation. He therefore sometimes took me to walk with him, and see Joiners, Bricklayers, Turners, Braziers, &c. at their Work, that he might observe my Inclination, and endeavour to fix it on some Trade or other on Land. It has ever since been a Pleasure to me to see good Workmen handle their Tools; and it has been useful to me, having learnt so much by it, as to be able to do little Jobs my self in my House, when a Workman could not readily be got; and to construct little Machines for my Experiments while the Intention of making the Experiment was fresh and warm in my Mind. My Father at last fix'd upon the Cutler's Trade, and my Uncle Benjamin's Son Samuel who was bred to that Business in London being about that time establish'd in Boston, I was sent to be with him some time on liking. But his Expectations of a Fee with me displeasing my Father, I was taken home again.

From a Child I was fond of Reading, and all the little Money that came into my Hands was ever laid out in Books. Pleas'd with the Pilgrim's Progress, my first Collection was of John Bunyan's Works, in separate little Volumes.[6] I afterwards sold them to enable me to buy R. Burton's Historical Collections; they were small

6. *The Pilgrim's Progress* (1678) is the best known of the many religious books and tracts written by the English Puritan preacher John Bunyan.

Chapmen's Books and cheap, 40 or 50 in all.[7] My Father's little Library consisted chiefly of Books in polemic Divinity, most of which I read, and have since often regretted, that at a time when I had such a Thirst for Knowledge, more proper Books had not fallen in my Way, since it was now resolv'd I should not be a Clergyman. Plutarch's Lives there was, in which I read abundantly, and I still think that time spent to great Advantage.[8] There was also a Book of Defoe's, called an Essay on Projects, and another of Dr. Mather's, call'd Essays to do Good which perhaps gave me a Turn of Thinking that had an Influence on some of the principal future Events of my Life.[9]

This Bookish Inclination at length determin'd my Father to make me a Printer, tho' he had already one Son, (James) of that Profession. In 1717 my Brother James return'd from England with a Press and Letters to set up his Business in Boston. I lik'd it much better than that of my Father, but still had a Hankering for the Sea. To prevent the apprehended Effect of such an Inclination, my Father was impatient to have me bound to my Brother. I stood out some time, but at last was persuaded and signed the Indentures,

7. Nathaniel Crouch, who wrote as either Robert or Richard Burton, "melted down the best of our English histories into twelve penny books, which are filled with wonders, rareties, and curiosities." *DNB*.

8. The very widely read *Parallel Lives* of the Greek writer Plutarch (46–120 A.D.) is a series of forty-six biographies, mostly in pairs coupling a noted Greek and a Roman comparable in activity or personal quality.

9. Daniel Defoe's *Essay upon Projects* (1697) proposing numerous schemes for civic and economic improvement, and Cotton Mather's *Bonifacius. An Essay Upon the Good, that is to be Devised and Designed, by those Who Desire . . . to Do Good While they Live* (1710). The Mather essay was an important inspiration to Franklin in forming the Junto, and to some extent he modeled his club on the neighborhood benefit societies Mather had organized in Boston.

when I was yet but 12 Years old.[1] I was to serve as an Apprentice till I was 21 Years of Age, only I was to be allow'd Journeyman's Wages during the last Year. In a little time I made great Proficiency in the Business, and became a useful Hand to my Brother. I now had Access to better Books. An Acquaintance with the Apprentices of Booksellers, enabled me sometimes to borrow a small one, which I was careful to return soon and clean. Often I sat up in my Room reading the greatest Part of the Night, when the Book was borrow'd in the Evening and to be return'd early in the Morning lest it should be miss'd or wanted. And after some time an ingenious Tradesman Mr. Matthew Adams who had a pretty Collection of Books, and who frequented our Printing House, took Notice of me, invited me to his Library, and very kindly lent me such Books as I chose to read. I now took a Fancy to Poetry, and made some little Pieces. My Brother, thinking it might turn to account encourag'd me, and put me on composing two occasional Ballads. One was called the *Light House Tragedy*, and contain'd an Account of the drowning of Capt. Worthilake with his Two Daughters; the other was a Sailor Song on the Taking of *Teach* or Blackbeard the Pirate.[2] They were wretched Stuff, in the Grubstreet Ballad Stile, and when they were printed he sent me about the Town to sell them. The first sold wonderfully, the Event being recent, having made a great

1. James Franklin was nine years older than Benjamin. This difference probably helps to account for the friction that developed between the two: it was too much for them to have had the bond of a shared childhood, but too little to permit the relation of master and apprentice to be entirely comfortable for either brother.

2. The full texts of these two ballads are not certainly known. Some verses of what may have been Franklin's compositions, however, are printed in *Papers*, 1, 6–7. George Worthylake, keeper of the light on Beacon Island, Boston Harbor, his wife, and one daughter were drowned Nov. 3, 1718. The famous pirate Edward Teach, known as "Blackbeard," was attacked in North Carolina waters by forces from Virginia and killed Nov. 22, 1718.

Noise. This flatter'd my Vanity. But my Father discourag'd me, by ridiculing my Performances, and telling me Verse-makers were generally Beggars; so I escap'd being a Poet, most probably a very bad one. But as Prose Writing has been of great Use to me in the Course of my Life, and was a principal Means of my Advancement, I shall tell you how in such a Situation I acquir'd what little Ability I have in that Way.

There was another Bookish Lad in the Town, John Collins by Name, with whom I was intimately acquainted.[3] We sometimes disputed, and very fond we were of Argument, and very desirous of confuting one another. Which disputacious Turn, by the way, is apt to become a very bad Habit, making People often extreamly disagreable in Company, by the Contradiction that is necessary to bring it into Practice, and thence, besides souring and spoiling the Conversation, is productive of Disgusts and perhaps Enmities where you may have occasion for Friendship. I had caught it by reading my Father's Books of Dispute about Religion. Persons of good Sense, I have since observ'd, seldom fall into it, except Lawyers, University Men, and Men of all Sorts that have been bred at Edinborough. A Question was once some how or other started between Collins and me, of the Propriety of educating the Female Sex in Learning, and their Abilities for Study. He was of Opinion that it was improper; and that they were naturally unequal to it. I took the contrary Side, perhaps a little for Dispute sake.[4] He was

3. Nothing more is known of John Collins than what Franklin relates in these pages.

4. In one of his Silence Dogood letters, written about this time, Franklin quoted Defoe's *Essay on Projects* in favor of education for women. *Papers,* I, 20. Later on he saw to it that his daughter Sally learned French and music as well as such "useful" subjects as arithmetic and bookkeeping, and in England he helped his landlady's daughter, Polly Stevenson, to acquire some understanding of science.

naturally more eloquent, had a ready Plenty of Words, and sometimes as I thought bore me down more by his Fluency than by the Strength of his Reasons. As we parted without settling the Point, and were not to see one another again for some time, I sat down to put my Arguments in Writing, which I copied fair and sent to him. He answer'd and I reply'd. Three or four Letters of a Side had pass'd, when my Father happen'd to find my Papers, and read them.[5] Without entring into the Discussion, he took occasion to talk to me about the Manner of my Writing, observ'd that tho' I had the Advantage of my Antagonist in correct Spelling and pointing (which I ow'd to the Printing House)[6] I fell far short in elegance of Expression, in Method and in Perspicuity, of which he convinc'd me by several Instances. I saw the Justice of his Remarks, and thence grew more attentive to the *Manner* in Writing, and determin'd to endeavour at Improvement.

About this time I met with an odd Volume of the Spectator.[7] It

5. Crossed out: "I lodged then at his House."

6. Even among well educated men, spelling and punctuation ("pointing") were slow to become standardized; but by the eighteenth century "correct" forms were more and more becoming recognized, especially in printed works. Yet even important people still felt no shame in spelling many words as they pronounced them, rather than as compilers of dictionaries and other authorities agreed was proper. As the text of Franklin's autobiography shows, he was generally, but not entirely, consistent in his spelling, though several of the forms he used have undergone change since his time, especially in American usage as compared to British.

7. *The Spectator* was a paper issued daily between March 1, 1711, and Dec. 6, 1712, containing essays of which Joseph Addison wrote nearly half and Richard Steele most of the rest. They dealt with many topics, including literary criticism, aesthetics, and the satirical treatment of society and manners. The style, which Samuel Johnson called "familiar, but not coarse and elegant but not ostentatious," greatly influenced English prose writing. A set of bound volumes of the papers was kept in James Franklin's printing office.

was the third. I had never before seen any of them. I bought it, read it over and over, and was much delighted with it. I thought the Writing excellent, and wish'd if possible to imitate it. With that View, I took some of the Papers, and making short Hints of the Sentiment in each Sentence, laid them by a few Days, and then without looking at the Book, try'd to compleat the Papers again, by expressing each hinted Sentiment at length and as fully as it had been express'd before, in any suitable Words, that should come to hand.

Then I compar'd my Spectator with the Original, discover'd some of my Faults and corrected them. But I found I wanted a Stock of Words or a Readiness in recollecting and using them, which I thought I should have acquir'd before that time, if I had gone on making Verses, since the continual Occasion for Words of the same Import but of different Length, to suit the Measure, or of different Sound for the Rhyme, would have laid me under a constant Necessity of searching for Variety, and also have tended to fix that Variety in my Mind, and make me Master of it. Therefore I took some of the Tales and turn'd them into Verse: And after a time, when I had pretty well forgotten the Prose, turn'd them back again. I also sometimes jumbled my Collections of Hints into Confusion, and after some Weeks, endeavour'd to reduce them into the best Order, before I began to form the full Sentences, and compleat the Paper. This was to teach me Method in the Arrangement of Thoughts. By comparing my work afterwards with the original, I discover'd many faults and amended them; but I sometimes had the Pleasure of Fancying that in certain Particulars of small Import, I had been lucky enough to improve the Method or the Language and this encourag'd me to think I might possibly in time come to be a tolerable English Writer, of which I was extreamly ambitious.

My Time for these Exercises and for Reading, was at Night, after Work or before Work began in the Morning; or on Sundays, when I contrived to be in the Printing House alone, evading as much as I could the common Attendance on publick Worship, which my Father used to exact of me when I was under his Care: And which indeed I still thought a Duty; tho' I could not, as it seemed to me, afford the Time to practise it.

When about 16 Years of Age, I happen'd to meet with a Book, written by one Tryon, recommending a Vegetable Diet.[8] I determined to go into it. My Brother being yet unmarried, did not keep House, but boarded himself and his Apprentices in another Family. My refusing to eat Flesh occasioned an Inconveniency, and I was frequently chid for my singularity. I made my self acquainted with Tryon's Manner of preparing some of his Dishes, such as Boiling Potatoes or Rice, making Hasty Pudding, and a few others, and then propos'd to my Brother, that if he would give me Weekly half the Money he paid for my Board I would board my self. He instantly agreed to it, and I presently found that I could save half what he paid me. This was an additional Fund for buying Books: But I had another Advantage in it. My Brother and the rest going from the Printing House to their Meals, I remain'd there alone, and dispatching presently my light Repast, (which often was no more than a Bisket or a Slice of Bread, a Handful of Raisins or a Tart from the Pastry Cook's, and a Glass of Water) had the rest of the Time till their Return, for Study, in which I made the greater Progress from that greater Clearness of Head and quicker Apprehension which usually attend Temperance in Eating and Drinking. And now it was that being on some Occasion made asham'd of my Ignorance in Figures, which I had twice failed in learning when at School, I took Cocker's Book of Arithmetick,[9] and went thro'

8. Thomas Tryon, *The Way to Health, long Life and Happiness, or a Discourse of Temperance* (2d edit., London, 1691).

9. Edward Cocker (1631–1675) was the author of several arithmetical works; which one Franklin used is not known.

the whole by my self with great Ease. I also read Seller's and Sturmy's Books of Navigation,[1] and became acquainted with the little Geometry they contain, but never proceeded far in that Science. And I read about this Time Locke on Human Understanding, and the Art of Thinking by Messrs. du Port Royal.[2]

While I was intent on improving my Language, I met with an English Grammar (I think it was Greenwood's)[3] at the End of which there were two little Sketches of the Arts of Rhetoric and Logic, the latter finishing with a Specimen of a Dispute in the Socratic Method. And soon after I procur'd Xenophon's Memorable Things of Socrates, wherein there are many Instances of the same Method.[4] I was charm'd with it, adopted it, dropt my abrupt Contradiction, and positive Argumentation, and put on the humble Enquirer and Doubter. And being then, from reading Shaftsbury and Collins,[5] become a real Doubter in many Points of our Religious Doctrine, I found this Method safest for my self and very embarassing to those against whom I used it, therefore I took a Delight in it,

1. John Seller, *An Epitome of the Art of Navigation* (London, 1681), and Samuel Sturmy, *The Mariner's Magazine; or, Sturmy's Mathematical and Practical Arts* (London, 1669).

2. John Locke's *Essay Concerning Human Understanding* (1690). Franklin paid tribute to this enormously influential work in *Poor Richard* for 1748. *Papers*, III, 259. Antoine Arnauld and Pierre Nicole, of Port Royal, *Logic: or the Art of Thinking*, English translation (London, 1687) of the Latin work of 1662. This was one of the long-lasting textbooks on logic; James Franklin's printing office owned a copy.

3. James Greenwood, *An Essay towards a Practical English Grammar* (London, 1711). Franklin recommended this book in 1749 for the academy he proposed in Pennsylvania. *Papers*, III, 410.

4. Xenophon, *The Memorable Things of Socrates*, translated by Edward Bysshe (London, 1712).

5. Anthony Ashley Cooper, third Earl of Shaftesbury (1671–1713), moralist and religious skeptic, and Anthony Collins (1676–1729), deist.

practis'd it continually and grew very artful and expert in drawing People even of superior Knowledge into Concessions the Consequences of which they did not foresee, entangling them in Difficulties out of which they could not extricate themselves, and so obtaining Victories that neither my self nor my Cause always deserved.

I continu'd this Method some few Years, but gradually left it, retaining only the Habit of expressing my self in Terms of modest Diffidence, never using when I advance any thing that may possibly be disputed, the Words, *Certainly, undoubtedly,* or any others that give the Air of Positiveness to an Opinion; but rather say, I conceive, or I apprehend a Thing to be so or so, It appears to me, or I should think it so or so for such and such Reasons, or I imagine it to be so, or it is so if I am not mistaken. This Habit I believe has been of great Advantage to me, when I have had occasion to inculcate my Opinions and persuade Men into Measures that I have been from time to time engag'd in promoting. And as the chief Ends of Conversation are to *inform,* or to be *informed,* to *please* or to *persuade,* I wish wellmeaning sensible Men would not lessen their Power of doing Good by a Positive assuming Manner that seldom fails to disgust, tends to create Opposition, and to defeat every one of those Purposes for which Speech was given us, to wit, giving or receiving Information, or Pleasure: For if you would *inform,* a positive dogmatical Manner in advancing your Sentiments, may provoke Contradiction and prevent a candid Attention. If you wish Information and Improvement from the Knowledge of others and yet at the same time express your self as firmly fix'd in your present Opinions, modest sensible Men, who do not love Disputation, will probably leave you undisturb'd in the Possession of your Error; and by such a Manner you can seldom hope to recommend your self in *pleasing* your Hearers, or to persuade those whose Concurrence you desire. Pope says, judiciously,

Men should be taught as if you taught them not,
And things unknown propos'd as things forgot,

farther recommending it to us,

To speak tho' sure, with seeming Diffidence.[6]

And he might have coupled with this Line that which he has coupled with another, I think less properly,

For Want of Modesty is Want of Sense.

If you ask why, *less properly,* I must repeat the Lines;

Immodest Words admit of *no* Defence;
For Want of Modesty is Want of Sense.[7]

Now is not *Want of Sense* (where a Man is so unfortunate as to want it) some Apology for his *Want of Modesty?* and would not the Lines stand more justly thus?

Immodest Words admit *but this* Defence,
That Want of Modesty is Want of Sense.

This however I should submit to better Judgments.[8]

My Brother had in 1720 or 21, begun to print a Newspaper. It was the second that appear'd in America, and was called *The New England Courant.* The only one before it, was *the Boston News*

6. Alexander Pope, *Essay on Criticism* (1711), lines 574–5, 567.

7. Wentworth Dillon, Earl of Roscommon, *Essay on Translated Verse* (1684), lines 113–14, where the second line actually reads "For want of decency is want of sense." These lines have often been incorrectly attributed to Pope.

8. Modesty in conversation was a favorite theme of Franklin's; comments and quotations similar to these occur often in his newspaper and almanacs.

Letter.[9] I remember his being dissuaded by some of his Friends from the Undertaking, as not likely to succeed, one Newspaper being in their Judgment enough for America. At this time 1771 there are not less than five and twenty. He went on however with the Undertaking, and after having work'd in composing the Types and printing off the Sheets I was employ'd to carry the Papers thro' the Streets to the Customers. He had some ingenious Men among his Friends who amus'd themselves by writing little Pieces for this Paper, which gain'd it Credit, and made it more in Demand; and these Gentlemen often visited us.[1] Hearing their Conversations, and their Accounts of the Approbation their Papers were receiv'd with, I was excited to try my Hand among them. But being still a Boy, and suspecting that my Brother would object to printing any Thing of mine in his Paper if he knew it to be mine, I contriv'd to disguise my Hand, and writing an anonymous Paper I put it in at Night under the Door of the Printing House. It was found in the Morning and communicated to his Writing Friends when they

9. Franklin was in error here. Except for a single issue of *Public Occurrences,* Sept. 25, 1690, *The Boston News-Letter,* established April 24, 1704, was the first newspaper in the English colonies; *The Boston Gazette,* Dec. 21, 1719, was the second; *The American Weekly Mercury,* Philadelphia, Dec. 22, 1719, was the third; and James's *New England Courant,* Aug. 7, 1721, was the fourth. But because James had for a short time been the printer (though never the publisher) of *The Boston Gazette,* Benjamin's confusion of memory is understandable.

1. This group of "ingenious Men" included about a dozen individuals, among whom Dr. William Douglass, John Checkley, and Thomas Fleet appear in *Dictionary of American Biography.* There is in the British Museum a file of the first 111 issues of the *Courant* (lacking only two) which probably belonged to Benjamin Franklin. He had written the names or initials of the authors at the heads of many of the articles. Most of these pieces were written in a lighter vein than was customary in Boston papers; some were critical of the government or clergy; a number took violent issue with the movement for smallpox inoculation then being agitated in Boston.

call'd in as usual. They read it, commented on it in my Hearing, and I had the exquisite Pleasure, of finding it met with their Approbation, and that in their different Guesses at the Author none were named but Men of some Character among us for Learning and Ingenuity.

I suppose now that I was rather lucky in my Judges: And that perhaps they were not really so very good ones as I then esteem'd them. Encourag'd however by this, I wrote and convey'd in the same Way to the Press several more Papers, which were equally approv'd, and I kept my Secret till my small Fund of Sense for such Performances was pretty well exhausted, and then I discovered it; when I began to be considered a little more by my Brother's Acquaintance, and in a manner that did not quite please him, as he thought, probably with reason, that it tended to make me too vain.[2] And perhaps this might be one Occasion of the Differences that we frequently had about this Time. Tho' a Brother, he considered himself as my Master, and me as his Apprentice; and accordingly expected the same Services from me as he would from another; while I thought he demean'd me too much in some he requir'd of me, who from a Brother expected more Indulgence. Our Disputes were often brought before our Father, and I fancy I was either generally in the right, or else a better Pleader, because the Judgment was generally in my favour: But my Brother was passionate and had often beaten me, which I took extreamly amiss; and thinking my Apprenticeship very tedious, I was continually wishing

2. These were the fourteen letters of Silence Dogood, printed in the *Courant* between April 12 and Oct. 8, 1722, Franklin's earliest surviving writings. In the guise of the widow of a country minister writing to the publisher, he commented on manners and morals, satirized the students of Harvard College, scoffed at fashions in women's clothes and their pride of dress, and attacked hypocrisy in religion. Though highly imitative in style, the essays were remarkable compositions for a boy of sixteen. *Papers*, I, 8–45.

for some Opportunity of shortening it, which at length offered in a manner unexpected.*

One of the Pieces in our News-Paper, on some political Point which I have now forgotten, gave Offence to the Assembly. He was taken up, censur'd and imprison'd for a Month by the Speaker's Warrant, I suppose because he would not discover his Author. I too was taken up and examin'd before the Council; but tho' I did not give them any Satisfaction, they contented themselves with admonishing me, and dismiss'd me; considering me perhaps as an Apprentice who was bound to keep his Master's Secrets. During my Brother's Confinement, which I resented a good deal, notwithstanding our private Differences, I had the Management of the Paper, and I made bold to give our Rulers some Rubs in it, which my Brother took very kindly, while others began to consider me in an unfavourable Light, as a young Genius that had a Turn for Libelling and Satyr. My Brother's Discharge was accompany'd with an Order of the House, (a very odd one) *that James Franklin should no longer print the Paper called the New England Courant.* There was a Consultation held in our Printing House among his Friends what he should do in this Case. Some propos'd to evade the Order by changing the Name of the Paper; but my Brother seeing Inconveniences in that, it was finally concluded on as a better Way, to let it be printed for the future under the Name of *Benjamin Franklin.* And to avoid the Censure of the Assembly that might fall on him, as still printing it by his Apprentice, the Contrivance was, that my old Indenture should be return'd to me with a full Discharge on the Back of it, to be shown on Occasion; but to secure to him the Benefit of my Service I was to sign new In-

---

**Note.* I fancy his harsh and tyrannical Treatment of me, might be a means of impressing me with that Aversion to arbitrary Power that has stuck to me thro' my whole Life.

dentures for the Remainder of the Term, which were to be kept private. A very flimsy Scheme it was, but however it was immediately executed, and the Paper went on accordingly under my Name for several Months.[3] At length a fresh Difference arising between my Brother and me, I took upon me to assert my Freedom, presuming that he would not venture to produce the new Indentures. It was not fair in me to take this Advantage, and this I therefore reckon one of the first Errata of my Life: But the Unfairness of it weigh'd little with me, when under the Impressions of Resentment, for the Blows his Passion too often urg'd him to bestow upon me. Tho' he was otherwise not an ill-natur'd Man: Perhaps I was too saucy and provoking.

When he found I would leave him, he took care to prevent my getting Employment in any other Printing-House of the Town, by going round and speaking to every Master, who accordingly refus'd to give me Work. I then thought of going to New York as

3. Franklin somewhat telescopes these events. On June 11, 1722, the *Courant* insinuated that the authorities had been lax in looking for a pirate, and the General Court (the legislative body) committed James to jail for a month because of this criticism of governmental officers. On July 5 the Council voted that he be allowed to print the *Courant* only after clearing the contents of each issue with the provincial secretary and that he should post a £100 bond. The House of Representatives did not concur, but when James offended the authorities again, Jan. 14, 1723, the General Court appointed a joint investigating committee and then forbade him to publish the paper without submitting it to prior censorship. He disobediently brought out one more issue and went into hiding when he was ordered arrested and held for trial. Since the stipulation about censorship applied only to James, the issue of February 11 appeared over Benjamin's name. James reappeared and gave bond the next day; the grand jury did not indict, and he was discharged May 7. This was the last attempt at such political censorship in Massachusetts. *Papers*, I, 27, 47–50. The *Courant* continued to appear over Benjamin's name until at least June 25, 1726 (the last issue located), nearly three years after he had left Boston. It had ceased publication by the beginning of 1727.

the nearest Place where there was a Printer: and I was the rather inclin'd to leave Boston, when I reflected that I had already made myself a little obnoxious to the governing Party; and from the arbitrary Proceedings of the Assembly in my Brother's Case it was likely I might if I stay'd soon bring myself into Scrapes; and farther that my indiscrete Disputations about Religion began to make me pointed at with Horror by good People, as an Infidel or Atheist. I determin'd on the Point: but my Father now siding with my Brother, I was sensible that if I attempted to go openly, Means would be used to prevent me. My Friend Collins therefore undertook to manage a little for me. He agreed with the Captain of a New York Sloop for my Passage, under the Notion of my being a young Acquaintance of his that had got a naughty Girl with Child, whose Friends would compel me to marry her, and therefore I could not appear or come away publickly. So I sold some of my Books to raise a little Money, Was taken on board privately, and as we had a fair Wind in three Days I found my self in New York near 300 Miles from home, a Boy of but 17, without the least Recommendation to or Knowledge of any Person in the Place, and with very little Money in my Pocket.

My Inclinations for the Sea, were by this time worne out, or I might now have gratify'd them. But having a Trade, and supposing my self a pretty good Workman, I offer'd my Service to the Printer of the Place, old Mr. Wm. Bradford, (who had been the first Printer in Pensilvania, but remov'd from thence upon the Quarrel of Geo. Keith). He could give me no Employment, having little to do, and Help enough already: But, says he, my Son[4] at Philadelphia has lately lost his principal Hand, Aquila Rose, by Death. If you go thither I believe he may employ you. Philadelphia was 100 Miles farther. I set out, however, in a Boat for Amboy, leaving my Chest and Things to follow me round by Sea. In cross-

4. Andrew Bradford.

ing the Bay we met with a Squall that tore our rotten Sails to pieces, prevented our getting into the Kill, and drove us upon Long Island.[5] In our Way a drunken Dutchman, who was a Passenger too, fell over board; when he was sinking I reach'd thro' the Water to his shock Pate and drew him up so that we got him in again. His Ducking sober'd him a little, and he went to sleep, taking first out of his Pocket a Book which he desir'd I would dry for him. It prov'd to be my old favourite Author Bunyan's Pilgrim's Progress in Dutch, finely printed on good Paper with copper Cuts, a Dress better than I had ever seen it wear in its own Language. I have since found that it has been translated into most of the Languages of Europe, and suppose it has been more generally read than any other Book except perhaps the Bible. Honest John was the first that I know of who mix'd Narration and Dialogue, a Method of Writing very engaging to the Reader, who in the most interesting Parts finds himself as it were brought into the Company, and present at the Discourse. Defoe in his Cruso, his Moll Flanders, Religious Courtship, Family Instructor, and other Pieces, has imitated it with Success. And Richardson has done the same in his Pamela, &c.[6]

When we drew near the Island we found it was at a Place where there could be no Landing, there being a great Surff on the stony Beach. So we dropt Anchor and swung round towards the Shore. Some People came down to the Water Edge and hallow'd to us, as we did to them. But the Wind was so high and the Surff so loud,

5. The Kill van Kull and Arthur Kill are narrow channels separating Staten Island from New Jersey. Perth Amboy is at the southern end of the Arthur Kill on the New Jersey side. Long Island is on the eastern side of New York Bay, not the western, for which the boat was headed.

6. Daniel Defoe, *Robinson Crusoe* (1719), *Moll Flanders* (1722), *Religious Courtship* (1722), *The Family Instructor* (1715–18); Samuel Richardson, *Pamela, or Virtue Rewarded* (1740). Franklin's reprint of *Pamela* in 1744 was the first novel published in America. In his own writing Franklin often "mix'd Narration and Dialogue" with great success.

that we could not hear so as to understand each other. There were Canoes on the Shore, and we made Signs and hallow'd that they should fetch us, but they either did not understand us, or thought it impracticable. So they went away, and Night coming on, we had no Remedy but to wait till the Wind should abate, and in the mean time the Boatman and I concluded to sleep if we could, and so crouded into the Scuttle with the Dutchman who was still wet, and the Spray beating over the Head of our Boat, leak'd thro' to us, so that we were soon almost as wet as he. In this Manner we lay all Night with very little Rest. But the Wind abating the next Day, we made a Shift to reach Amboy before Night, having been 30 Hours on the Water without Victuals, or any Drink but a Bottle of filthy Rum: The Water we sail'd on being salt.

In the Evening I found my self very feverish, and went in to Bed. But having read somewhere that cold Water drank plentifully was good for a Fever, I follow'd the Prescription, sweat plentifully most of the Night, my Fever left me, and in the Morning crossing the Ferry, I proceeded on my Journey, on foot, having 50 Miles to Burlington,[7] where I was told I should find Boats that would carry me the rest of the Way to Philadelphia.

It rain'd very hard all the Day, I was thoroughly soak'd and by Noon a good deal tir'd, so I stopt at a poor Inn, where I staid all Night, beginning now to wish I had never left home. I cut so miserable a Figure too, that I found by the Questions ask'd me I was suspected to be some runaway Servant, and in danger of being taken up on that Suspicion. However I proceeded the next Day, and got in the Evening to an Inn within 8 or 10 Miles of Burlington, kept by one Dr. Brown.[8]

He entred into Conversation with me while I took some Refreshment, and finding I had read a little, became very sociable and

7. In western New Jersey, approximately 18 miles up the Delaware River from Philadelphia.

8. Dr. John Browne.

friendly. Our Acquaintance continu'd as long as he liv'd. He had been, I imagine, an itinerant Doctor, for there was no Town in England, or Country in Europe, of which he could not give a very particular Account. He had some Letters, and was ingenious, but much of an Unbeliever, and wickedly undertook some Years after to travesty the Bible in doggrel Verse as Cotton had done Virgil.[9] By this means he set many of the Facts in a very ridiculous Light, and might have hurt weak minds if his Work had been publish'd: but it never was. At his House I lay that Night, and the next Morning reach'd Burlington. But had the Mortification to find that the regular Boats were gone, a little before my coming, and no other expected to go till Tuesday, this being Saturday. Wherefore I return'd to an old Woman in the Town of whom I had bought Gingerbread to eat on the Water, and ask'd her Advice; she invited me to lodge at her House till a Passage by Water should offer: and being tired with my foot Travelling, I accepted the Invitation. She understanding I was a Printer, would have had me stay at that Town and follow my Business, being ignorant of the Stock necessary to begin with. She was very hospitable, gave me a Dinner of Ox Cheek with great Goodwill, accepting only of a Pot of Ale in return. And I tho't my self fix'd till Tuesday should come. However walking in the Evening by the Side of the River a Boat came by, which I found was going towards Philadelphia, with several People in her. They took me in, and as there was no Wind, we row'd all the Way; and about Midnight not having yet seen the City, some of the Company were confident we must have pass'd it, and would row no farther, the others knew not where we were, so we put towards the Shore, got into a Creek, landed near an old Fence with the Rails of which we made a Fire, the Night being cold, in October, and there we remain'd till Daylight. Then one of the

9. Charles Cotton, *Scarronides, or the First Book of Virgil Travestie* (London, 1664).

Company knew the Place to be Cooper's Creek a little above Philadelphia, which we saw as soon as we got out of the Creek, and arriv'd there about 8 or 9 a Clock, on the Sunday morning, and landed at the Market street Wharff.[1]

I have been the more particular in this Description of my Journey, and shall be so of my first Entry into that City, that you may in your Mind compare such unlikely Beginnings with the Figure I have since made there. I was in my Working Dress, my best Cloaths being to come round by Sea. I was dirty from my Journey; my Pockets were stuff'd out with Shirts and Stockings; I knew no Soul, nor where to look for Lodging. I was fatigu'd with Travelling, Rowing and Want of Rest. I was very hungry, and my whole Stock of Cash consisted of a Dutch Dollar and about a Shilling in Copper. The latter I gave the People of the Boat for my Passage, who at first refus'd it on Account of my Rowing; but I insisted on their taking it, a Man being sometimes more generous when he has but a little Money than when he has plenty, perhaps thro' Fear of being thought to have but little.

Then I walk'd up the Street, gazing about, till near the Market House I met a Boy with Bread.[2] I had made many a Meal on Bread, and inquiring where he got it, I went immediately to the Baker's

1. Franklin arrived in Philadelphia in October 1723, but the exact date is not known.

2. Market (or High) Street was the widest street in early Philadelphia. Several public markets were erected at different times in the middle of the way; the so-called "Jersey Market" was nearest to the wharf. As young Franklin trudged along he would have passed the prison erected in 1695 and, at the Second Street intersection, the Court House built about 1709, before passing John Read's house on his left, between Third and Fourth Streets. In 1764–65, after he had acquired title to several adjoining plots at that location, he built the large house in which he spent the last years of his life. A map of the city showing many of the places associated with Franklin is in *Papers*, II, following p. 456.

he directed me to in second Street; and ask'd for Bisket, intending such as we had in Boston, but they it seems were not made in Philadelphia, then I ask'd for a threepenny Loaf, and was told they had none such: so not considering or knowing the Difference of Money and the greater Cheapness nor the Names of his Bread, I bad him give me three penny worth of any sort. He gave me accordingly three great Puffy Rolls. I was surpriz'd at the Quantity, but took it, and having no room in my Pockets, walk'd off, with a Roll under each Arm, and eating the other. Thus I went up Market Street as far as fourth Street, passing by the Door of Mr. Read, my future Wife's Father, when she standing at the Door saw me, and thought I made as I certainly did a most awkward ridiculous Appearance. Then I turn'd and went down Chestnut Street and part of Walnut Street, eating my Roll all the Way, and coming round found my self again at Market Street Wharff, near the Boat I came in, to which I went for a Draught of the River Water, and being fill'd with one of my Rolls, gave the other two to a Woman and her Child that came down the River in the Boat with us and were waiting to go farther. Thus refresh'd I walk'd again up the Street, which by this time had many clean dress'd People in it who were all walking the same Way; I join'd them, and thereby was led into the great Meeting House of the Quakers near the Market. I sat down among them, and after looking round a while and hearing nothing said, being very drowzy thro' Labour and want of Rest the preceding Night, I fell fast asleep, and continu'd so till the Meeting broke up, when one was kind enough to rouse me. This was therefore the first House I was in or slept in, in Philadelphia.[3]

Walking again down towards the River, and looking in the Faces of People, I met a young Quaker Man whose Countenance I

3. The Quaker Great Meeting House stood on Second Street, a few feet south of Market Street.

lik'd, and accosting him requested he would tell me where a Stranger could get Lodging. We were then near the Sign of the Three Mariners. Here, says he, is one Place that entertains Strangers, but it is not a reputable House; if thee wilt walk with me, I'll show thee a better. He brought me to the Crooked Billet in Water-Street.[4] Here I got a Dinner. And while I was eating it, several sly Questions were ask'd me, as it seem'd to be suspected from my youth and Appearance, that I might be some Runaway. After Dinner my Sleepiness return'd: and being shown to a Bed, I lay down without undressing, and slept till Six in the Evening; was call'd to Supper; went to Bed again very early and slept soundly till the next Morning. Then I made my self as tidy as I could, and went to Andrew Bradford the Printer's. I found in the Shop the old Man his Father, whom I had seen at New York, and who travelling on horse back had got to Philadelphia before me. He introduc'd me to his Son, who receiv'd me civilly, gave me a Breakfast, but told me he did not at present want a Hand, being lately supply'd with one. But there was another Printer in town lately set up, one Keimer, who perhaps might employ me; if not, I should be welcome to lodge at his House, and he would give me a little Work to do now and then till fuller Business should offer.

The old Gentleman said, he would go with me to the new Printer: And when we found him, Neighbour, says Bradford, I have brought to see you a young Man of your Business, perhaps you may want such a One. He ask'd me a few Questions, put a Composing Stick in my Hand to see how I work'd, and then said he would employ me soon, tho' he had just then nothing for me to do. And taking old Bradford whom he had never seen before, to be one of the Towns People that had a Good Will for him, enter'd into a Conversation on his present Undertaking and Prospects;

4. The Crooked Billet Tavern stood on Water Street, near the river, between Market and Chestnut Streets.

while Bradford not discovering[5] that he was the other Printer's Father, on Keimer's saying he expected soon to get the greatest Part of the Business into his own Hands, drew him on by artful Questions and starting little Doubts, to explain all his Views, what Interest he rely'd on, and in what manner he intended to proceed. I who stood by and heard all, saw immediately that one of them was a crafty old Sophister, and the other a mere Novice. Bradford left me with Keimer, who was greatly surpriz'd when I told him who the old Man was.

Keimer's Printing House I found, consisted of an old shatter'd Press, and one small worn-out Fount of English, which he was then using himself, composing in it an Elegy on Aquila Rose beforementioned, an ingenious young Man of excellent Character much respected in the Town, Clerk of the Assembly, and a pretty Poet. Keimer made Verses, too, but very indifferently. He could not be said to write them, for his Manner was to compose them in the Types directly out of his Head; so there being no Copy, but one Pair of Cases, and the Elegy likely to require all the Letter, no one could help him. I endeavour'd to put his Press (which he had not yet us'd, and of which he understood nothing) into Order fit to be work'd with; and promising to come and print off his Elegy as soon as he should have got it ready, I return'd to Bradford's who gave me a little Job to do for the present, and there I lodged and dieted. A few Days after Keimer sent for me to print off the Elegy.[6] And now he had got another Pair of Cases, and a Pamphlet to reprint, on which he set me to work.

These two Printers I found poorly qualified for their Business. Bradford had not been bred to it, and was very illiterate; and

5. Disclosing.

6. This was a single leaf, entitled *An Elegy On the much Lamented Death of the Ingenious and Well-Beloved Aquila Rose, Clerk to the Honourable Assembly at Philadelphia, who died the 24th of the 4th month, 1723. Aged 28.* Keimer offered it for sale for twopence.

Keimer tho' something of a Scholar, was a mere Compositor, knowing nothing of Presswork. He had been one of the French Prophets[7] and could act their enthusiastic Agitations. At this time he did not profess any particular Religion, but something of all on occasion; was very ignorant of the World, and had, as I afterwards found, a good deal of the Knave in his Composition. He did not like my Lodging at Bradford's while I work'd with him. He had a House indeed, but without Furniture, so he could not lodge me: But he got me a Lodging at Mr. Read's before-mentioned, who was the Owner of his House. And my Chest and Clothes being come by this time, I made rather a more respectable Appearance in the Eyes of Miss Read, than I had done when she first happen'd to see me eating my Roll in the Street.

I began now to have some Acquaintance among the young People of the Town, that were Lovers of Reading with whom I spent my Evenings very pleasantly and gaining Money by my Industry and Frugality, I lived very agreably, forgetting Boston as much as I could, and not desiring that any there should know where I resided, except my Friend Collins who was in my Secret, and kept it when I wrote to him. At length an Incident happened that sent me back again much sooner than I had intended.

I had a Brother-in-law, Robert Holmes,[8] Master of a Sloop, that traded between Boston and Delaware. He being at New Castle 40 Miles below Philadelphia, heard there of me, and wrote me a Letter, mentioning the Concern of my Friends in Boston at my abrupt Departure, assuring me of their Goodwill to me, and that every thing would be accommodated to my Mind if I would return, to which he exhorted me very earnestly. I wrote an Answer to his Letter, thank'd him for his Advice, but stated my Reasons for quitting Boston

7. A group of French Protestant refugees in England in 1706, given to trances and revelations, proclaiming a Messianic kingdom soon to come.

8. Robert Homes.

fully, and in such a Light as to convince him I was not so wrong as he had apprehended.

Sir William Keith Governor of the Province, was then at New Castle, and Capt. Holmes happening to be in Company with him when my Letter came to hand, spoke to him of me, and show'd him the Letter. The Governor read it, and seem'd surpriz'd when he was told my Age. He said I appear'd a young Man of promising Parts, and therefore should be encouraged: The Printers at Philadelphia were wretched ones, and if I would set up there, he made no doubt I should succeed; for his Part, he would procure me the publick Business, and do me every other Service in his Power. This my Brother-in-Law afterwards told me in Boston. But I knew as yet nothing of it; when one Day Keimer and I being at Work together near the Window, we saw the Governor and another Gentleman (which prov'd to be Col. French,[9] of New Castle) finely dress'd, come directly across the Street to our House, and heard them at the Door. Keimer ran down immediately, thinking it a Visit to him. But the Governor enquir'd for me, came up, and with a Condescension and Politeness I had been quite unus'd to, made me many Compliments, desired to be acquainted with me, blam'd me kindly for not having made my self known to him when I first came to the Place, and would have me away with him to the Tavern where he was going with Col. French to taste as he said some excellent Madeira. I was not a little surpriz'd, and Keimer star'd like a Pig poison'd. I went however with the Governor and Col. French, to a Tavern the Corner of Third Street, and over the Madeira he propos'd my Setting up my Business, laid before me the Probabilities of Success, and both he and Col. French assur'd me I should have their Interest and Influence in procuring the Publick Business of both Governments. On my doubting whether my Father would

9. John French; crossed out after the name: "a principal Man."

assist me in it, Sir William said he would give me a Letter to him, in which he would state the Advantages, and he did not doubt of prevailing with him. So it was concluded I should return to Boston in the first Vessel with the Governor's Letter recommending me to my Father. In the mean time the Intention was to be kept secret, and I went on working with Keimer as usual, the Governor sending for me now and then to dine with him, a very great Honour I thought it, and conversing with me in the most affable, familiar, and friendly manner imaginable.

About the End of April 1724. a little Vessel offer'd for Boston. I took Leave of Keimer as going to see my Friends. The Governor gave me an ample Letter, saying many flattering things of me to my Father,[1] and strongly recommending the Project of my setting up at Philadelphia, as a Thing that must make my Fortune. We struck on a Shoal in going down the Bay and sprung a Leak, we had a blustring time at Sea, and were oblig'd to pump almost continually, at which I took my Turn. We arriv'd safe however at Boston in about a Fortnight. I had been absent Seven Months and my Friends had heard nothing of me; for my Br. Holmes was not yet return'd; and had not written about me. My unexpected Appearance surpriz'd the Family; all were however very glad to see me and made me Welcome, except my Brother. I went to see him at his Printing-House: I was better dress'd than ever while in his Service, having a genteel new Suit from Head to foot, a Watch, and my Pockets lin'd with near Five Pounds Sterling in Silver. He receiv'd me not very frankly, look'd me all over, and turn'd to his Work again. The Journey-Men were inquisitive where I had been, what sort of a Country it was, and how I lik'd it? I prais'd it much, and the happy Life I led in it; expressing strongly my Intention of returning to it; and one of them asking what kind of Money we had there, I pro-

1. Crossed out: "and which I read before it was seal."

duc'd a handful of Silver and spread it before them, which was a kind of Raree-Show[2] they had not been us'd to, Paper being the Money of Boston. Then I took an Opportunity of letting them see my Watch: and lastly, (my Brother still grum and sullen) I gave them a Piece of Eight to drink and took my Leave. This Visit of mine offended him extreamly. For when my Mother some time after spoke to him of a Reconciliation, and of her Wishes to see us on good Terms together, and that we might live for the future as Brothers, he said, I had insulted him in such a Manner before his People that he could never forget or forgive it. In this however he was mistaken.

My Father receiv'd the Governor's Letter with some apparent Surprize; but said little of it to me for some Days; when Capt. Homes returning, he show'd it to him, ask'd if he knew Keith, and what kind of a Man he was: Adding his Opinion that he must be of small Discretion, to think of setting a Boy up in Business who wanted yet 3 Years of being at Man's Estate. Homes said what he could in favour of the Project; but my Father was clear in the Impropriety of it;[3] and at last gave a flat Denial to it. Then he wrote a civil Letter to Sir William thanking him for the Patronage he had so kindly offered me, but declining to assist me as yet in Setting up, I being in his Opinion too young to be trusted with the Management of a Business so important, and for which the Preparation must be so expensive.

My Friend and Companion Collins, who was a Clerk at the Post-Office, pleas'd with the Account I gave him of my new Country, determin'd to go thither also: And while I waited for my Fathers Determination, he set out before me by Land to Rhode-island, leaving his Books which were a pretty Collection of Mathe-

2. Raree-show: a small street show, usually carried around in a box.

3. Crossed out: "said he had advanc'd too much already to my Brother James."

maticks and Natural Philosophy, to come with mine and me to New York where he propos'd to wait for me. My Father, tho' he did not approve Sir William's Proposition was yet pleas'd that I had been able to obtain so advantageous a Character from a Person of such Note where I had resided, and that I had been so industrious and careful as to equip my self so handsomely in so short a time: therefore seeing no Prospect of an Accommodation between my Brother and me, he gave his Consent to my Returning again to Philadelphia, advis'd me to behave respectfully to the People there, endeavour to obtain the general Esteem, and avoid lampooning and libelling to which he thought I had too much Inclination; telling me, that by steady Industry and a prudent Parsimony, I might save enough by the time I was One and Twenty to set me up, and that if I came near the Matter he would help me out with the rest. This was all I could obtain, except some small Gifts as Tokens of his and my Mother's Love, when I embark'd again for New-York, now with their Approbation and their Blessing.

The Sloop putting in at Newport, Rhodeisland, I visited my Brother John, who had been married and settled there some Years. He received me very affectionately, for he always lov'd me. A Friend of his, one Vernon, having some Money due to him in Pensilvania, about 35 Pounds Currency, desired I would receive it for him, and keep it till I had his Directions what to remit it in. Accordingly he gave me an Order. This afterwards occasion'd me a good deal of Uneasiness. At Newport we took in a Number of Passengers for New York: Among which were two young Women, Companions, and a grave, sensible Matron-like Quaker-Woman with her Attendants. I had shown an obliging readiness to do her some little Services which impress'd her I suppose with a degree of Good-will towards me. Therefore when she saw a daily growing Familiarity between me and the two Young Women, which they appear'd to encourage, she took me aside and said, Young Man, I am concern'd for thee, as thou has no Friend with thee, and seems not to know much of the World, or of the Snares Youth is expos'd to; depend upon it those are very bad Women, I can see it in all their Actions, and if thee art not upon thy Guard, they will draw thee into some Danger: they are Strangers to thee, and I advise thee in a friendly Concern for thy Welfare, to have no Acquaintance with them. As I seem'd at first not to think so ill of them as she did, she mention'd some Things she had observ'd and heard that had escap'd my Notice; but now convinc'd me she was right. I thank'd her for her kind Advice, and promis'd to follow it. When we arriv'd at New York, they told me where they liv'd, and invited me to come and see them: but I avoided it. And it was well I did: For the next Day, the Captain miss'd a Silver Spoon and some other Things that had been taken out of his Cabbin, and knowing that these were a Couple of Strumpets, he got a Warrant to search their Lodgings, found the stolen Goods, and had the Thieves punish'd. So tho' we had escap'd a sunken Rock which we scrap'd upon in the Passage, I thought this Escape of rather more Importance to me.

At New York I found my Friend Collins, who had arriv'd there some Time before me. We had been intimate from Children, and had read the same Books together. But he had the Advantage of more time for reading, and Studying and a wonderful Genius for Mathematical Learning in which he far outstript me. While I liv'd in Boston most of my Hours of Leisure for Conversation were spent with him, and he continu'd a sober as well as an industrious Lad; was much respected for his Learning by several of the Clergy and other Gentlemen, and seem'd to promise making a good Figure in Life: but during my Absence he had acquir'd a Habit of Sotting with Brandy; and I found by his own Account and what I heard from others, that he had been drunk every day since his Arrival at New York, and behav'd very oddly. He had gam'd too and lost his Money, so that I was oblig'd to discharge his Lodgings, and defray his Expences to and at Philadelphia: Which prov'd extreamly inconvenient to me. The then Governor of N York, Burnet, Son of Bishop Burnet hearing from the Captain that a young Man, one of his Passengers, had a great many Books, desired he would bring me to see him. I waited upon him accordingly, and should have taken Collins with me but that he was not sober. The Governor treated me with great Civility, show'd me his Library, which was a very large one, and we had a good deal of Conversation about Books and Authors. This was the second Governor who had done me the Honour to take Notice of me, which to a poor Boy like me was very pleasing.[4]

We proceeded to Philadelphia. I received on the Way Vernon's Money, without which we could hardly have finish'd our Journey. Collins wish'd to be employ'd in some Counting House; but whether they discover'd his Dramming by his Breath, or by his Behaviour, tho' he had some Recommendations, he met with no Success in any Application, and continu'd Lodging and Boarding at the same House with me and at my Expence. Knowing I had that Money of Vernon's he was continually borrowing of me, still promising Repayment as soon as he should be in Business. At length he had got so much of it, that I was distress'd to think what I should do, in case of being call'd on to remit it. His Drinking continu'd about which we sometimes quarrel'd, for when a little intoxicated he was very fractious. Once in a Boat on the Delaware with some other young Men, he refused to row in his Turn: I will be row'd home, says he. We will not row you, says I. You must or stay all Night on the Water, says he, just as you please. The others said, Let us row; what signifies it? But my Mind being soured with his other Conduct, I continu'd to refuse. So he swore he would make me row, or throw me overboard; and coming along stepping on the

4. Crossed out in the manuscript: "Collins was too drunk to go with me on this Visit."

Thwarts towards me, when he came up and struck at me I clapt my Hand under his Crutch, and rising pitch'd him head-foremost into the River. I knew he was a good Swimmer, and so was under little Concern about him; but before he could get round to lay hold of the Boat, we had with a few Strokes pull'd her out of his Reach. And ever when he drew near the Boat, we ask'd if he would row, striking a few Strokes to slide her away from him. He was ready to die with Vexation, and obstinately would not promise to row; however seeing him at last beginning to tire, we lifted him in; and brought him home dripping wet in the Evening. We hardly exchang'd a civil Word afterwards; and a West India Captain who had a Commission to procure a Tutor for the Sons of a Gentleman at Barbadoes, happening to meet with him, agreed to carry him thither. He left me then, promising to remit me the first Money he should receive in order to discharge the Debt. But I never heard of him after.

The Breaking into this Money of Vernon's was one of the first great Errata of my Life. And this Affair show'd that my Father was not much out in his Judgment when he suppos'd me too young to manage Business of Importance. But Sir William, on reading his Letter, said he was too prudent. There was great Difference in Persons, and Discretion did not always accompany Years, nor was Youth always without it. And since he will not set you up, says he, I will do it my self. Give me an Inventory of the Things necessary to be had from England, and I will send for them. You shall repay me when you are able; I am resolv'd to have a good Printer here, and I am sure you must succeed. This was spoken with such an Appearance of Cordiality, that I had not the least doubt of his meaning what he said. I had hitherto kept the Proposition of my Setting up a Secret in Philadelphia, and I still kept it. Had it been known that I depended on the Governor, probably some Friend that knew him better would have advis'd me not to rely on him, as I afterwards heard it as his known Character to be liberal of Promises which he never meant to keep. Yet unsolicited as he was by me, how could I think his generous Offers insincere? I believ'd him one of the best Men in the World.

I presented him an Inventory of a little Printing House, amounting by my Computation to about £100 Sterling.[5] He lik'd it, but ask'd me if my being on the Spot in England to chuse the Types and see that every thing was good of the kind, might not be of some Advantage. Then, says he, when there, you may make Acquaintances and establish Correspondencies in the Bookselling and Stationary Way. I agreed that this might be advantageous. Then says he, get yourself ready to go with Annis;[6] which was the annual Ship, and the only one at that Time usually passing between London and Philadelphia. But it would be some Months before Annis sail'd, so I continu'd working with Keimer, fretting about the Money Collins had got from me, and in daily Apprehensions of being call'd upon by Vernon, which however did not happen for some Years after.

I believe I have omitted mentioning that in my first Voyage from Boston, being becalm'd off Block Island, our People set about catching Cod and hawl'd up a great many. Hitherto I had stuck to my Resolution of not eating animal Food; and on this Occasion, I consider'd with my Master Tryon, the taking every Fish as a kind of unprovok'd Murder, since none of them had or ever could do us any Injury that might justify the Slaughter. All this seem'd very reasonable. But I had formerly been a great Lover of Fish, and when this came hot out of the Frying Pan, it smelt admirably well. I balanc'd some time between Principle and Inclination: till I recollected, that when the Fish were opened, I saw smaller Fish taken

5. For a detailed inventory of equipment that by 1753 Franklin considered suitable for a "small Printing Office," see *Papers*, v, 82–3.

6. Capt. Thomas Annis, master of the "annual Ship."

out of their Stomachs: Then thought I, if you eat one another, I don't see why we mayn't eat you. So I din'd upon Cod very heartily and continu'd to eat with other People, returning only now and than occasionally to a vegetable Diet. So convenient a thing it is to be a *reasonable Creature*, since it enables one to find or make a Reason for every thing one has a mind to do.

Keimer and I liv'd on a pretty good familiar Footing and agreed tolerably well: for he suspected nothing of my Setting up. He retain'd a great deal of his old Enthusiasms, and lov'd Argumentation. We therefore had many Disputations. I us'd to work him so with my Socratic Method, and had trapann'd him so often by Questions apparently so distant from any Point we had in hand, and yet by degrees led to the Point, and brought him into Difficulties and Contradictions that at last he grew ridiculously cautious, and would hardly answer me the most common Question, without asking first, *What do you intend to infer from that?* However it gave him so high an Opinion of my Abilities in the Confuting Way, that he seriously propos'd my being his Colleague in a Project he had of setting up a new Sect. He was to preach the Doctrines, and I was to confound all Opponents. When he came to explain with me upon the Doctrines, I found several Conundrums which I objected to unless I might have my Way a little too, and introduce some of mine. Keimer wore his Beard at full Length, because somewhere in the Mosaic Law it is said, *thou shalt not mar the Corners of thy Beard.*[7] He likewise kept the seventh day Sabbath; and these two Points were Essentials with him. I dislik'd both, but agreed to admit them upon Condition of his adopting the Doctrine of using no animal Food. I doubt, says he, my Constitution will not bear that. I assur'd him it would, and that he would be the better for it. He was usually a great Glutton, and I promis'd my self some Diversion

7. "Ye shall not round the corners of your heads, neither shalt thou mar the corners of thy beard." Leviticus 19:27.

in half-starving him. He agreed to try the Practice if I would keep him Company. I did so and we held it for three Months. We had our Victuals dress'd and brought to us regularly by a Woman in the Neighbourhood, who had from me a List of 40 Dishes to be prepar'd for us at different times, in all which there was neither Fish Flesh nor Fowl, and the whim suited me the better at this time from the Cheapness of it, not costing us above 18*d.* Sterling each, per Week. I have since kept several Lents most strictly, Leaving the common Diet for that, and that for the common, abruptly, without the least Inconvenience: So that I think there is little in the Advice of making those Changes by easy Gradations. I went on pleasantly, but poor Keimer suffer'd grievously, tir'd of the Project, long'd for the Flesh Pots of Egypt, and order'd a roast Pig. He invited me and two Women Friends to dine with him, but it being brought too soon upon table, he could not resist the Temptation, and ate it all up before we came.

I had made some Courtship during this time to Miss Read. I had a great Respect and Affection for her, and had some Reason to believe she had the same for me: but as I was about to take a long Voyage, and we were both very young, only a little above 18. it was thought most prudent by her Mother to prevent our going too far at present, as a Marriage if it was to take place would be more convenient after my Return, when I should be as I expected set up in my Business. Perhaps too she thought my Expectations not so wellfounded as I imagined them to be.

My chief Acquaintances at this time were, Charles Osborne, Joseph Watson, and James Ralph; All Lovers of Reading. The two first were Clerks to an eminent Scrivener or Conveyancer in the Town, Charles Brogden;[8] the other was Clerk to a Merchant. Watson was a pious sensible young Man, of great Integrity. The others rather more lax in their Principles of Religion, particularly Ralph,

8. Charles Brockden.

who as well as Collins had been unsettled by me, for which they both made me suffer. Osborne was sensible, candid, frank, sincere, and affectionate to his Friends; but in litterary Matters too fond of Criticising. Ralph, was ingenious, genteel in his Manners, and extreamly eloquent; I think I never knew a prettier Talker. Both of them great Admirers of Poetry, and began to try their Hands in little Pieces. Many pleasant Walks we four had together on Sundays into the Woods near Skuylkill, where we read to one another and conferr'd on what we read.

Ralph was inclin'd to pursue the Study of Poetry, not doubting but he might become eminent in it and make his Fortune by it, alledging that the best Poets must when they first began to write, make as many Faults as he did. Osborne dissuaded him, assur'd him he had no Genius for Poetry, and advis'd him to think of nothing beyond the Business he was bred to; that in the mercantile way tho' he had no Stock, he might by his Diligence and Punctuality recommend himself to Employment as a Factor, and in time acquire wherewith to trade on his own Account. I approv'd the amusing one's self with Poetry now and then, so far as to improve one's Language, but no farther. On this it was propos'd that we should each of us at our next Meeting produce a Piece of our own Composing, in order to improve by our mutual Observations, Criticisms and Corrections. As Language and Expression was what we had in View, we excluded all Considerations of Invention, by agreeing that the Task should be a Version of the 18th Psalm, which describes the Descent of a Deity. When the Time of our Meeting drew nigh, Ralph call'd on me first, and let me know his Piece was ready. I told him I had been busy, and having little Inclination had done nothing. He then show'd me his Piece for my Opinion; and I much approv'd it, as it appear'd to me to have great Merit. Now, says he, Osborne never will allow the least Merit in any thing of mine, but makes 1000 Criticisms out of mere Envy. He is not so jealous of you. I wish therefore you would take this Piece, and produce it as yours. I will pretend not to have had time, and so produce nothing: We shall then see what he will say to it. It was agreed, and I immediately transcrib'd it that it might appear in my own hand. We met. Watson's Performance was read: there were some Beauties in it: but many Defects. Osborne's was read: It was much better. Ralph did it Justice, remark'd some Faults, but applauded the Beauties. He himself had nothing to produce. I was backward, seem'd desirous of being excus'd, had not had sufficient Time to correct; &c. but no Excuse could be admitted, produce I must. It was read and repeated; Watson and Osborne gave up the Contest; and join'd in applauding it immoderately. Ralph only made some Criticisms and propos'd some Amendments, but I defended my Text. Osborne was against Ralph, and told him he was no better a Critic than Poet; so he dropt the Argument. As they two went home together, Osborne express'd himself still more strongly in favour of what he thought my Production, having restrain'd himself before as he said, lest I should think it Flattery. But who would have imagin'd, says he, that Franklin had been capable of such a Performance; such Painting, such Force! such Fire! he has even improv'd the Original! In his common Conversation, he seems to have no Choice of Words; he hesitates and blunders; and yet, good God, how he writes! When we next met, Ralph discover'd the Trick, we had plaid him, and Osborne was a little laught at. This Transaction fix'd Ralph in his Resolution of becoming a Poet. I did all I could to dissuade him from it, but He continued scribbling Verses, till Pope cur'd him.[9] He became however a pretty good Prose Writer. More of him hereafter.

But as I may not have occasion again to mention the other two, I shall just remark here, that Watson died in my Arms a few Years after, much lamented, being the best of our Set. Osborne went to

9. See also below, p. 248 n.

the West Indies, where he became an eminent Lawyer and made Money, but died young. He and I had made a serious Agreement, that the one who happen'd first to die, should if possible make a friendly Visit to the other, and acquaint him how he found things in that Separate State. But he never fulfill'd his Promise.

The Governor, seeming to like my Company, had me frequently to his House; and his Setting me up was always mention'd as a fix'd thing. I was to take with me Letters recommendatory to a Number of his Friends, besides the Letter of Credit to furnish me with the necessary Money for purchasing the Press and Types, Paper, &c. For these Letters I was appointed to call at different times, when they were to be ready, but a future time was still named. Thus we went on till the Ship whose Departure too had been several times postponed was on the Point of sailing. Then when I call'd to take my Leave and Receive the Letters, his Secretary, Dr. Bard,[1] came out to me and said the Governor was extreamly busy, in writing, but would be down at Newcastle before the Ship, and there the Letters would be delivered to me.

Ralph, tho' married and having one Child, had determined to accompany me in this Voyage. It was thought he intended to establish a Correspondence, and obtain Goods to sell on Commission. But I found afterwards, that thro' some Discontent with his Wifes Relations, he purposed to leave her on their Hands, and never return again. Having taken leave of my Friends, and interchang'd some Promises with Miss Read, I left Philadelphia in the Ship, which anchor'd at Newcastle. The Governor was there. But when I went to his Lodging, the Secretary came to me from him with the civillest Message in the World, that he could not then see me being engag'd in Business of the utmost Importance; but should send the Letters to me on board, wish'd me heartily a good Voyage and a speedy Return, &c. I return'd on board, a little puzzled, but still not doubting.

1. Dr. Patrick Baird.

Mr. Andrew Hamilton, a famous Lawyer of Philadelphia, had taken Passage in the same Ship for himself and Son: and with Mr. Denham a Quaker Merchant, and Messrs. Onion and Russel Masters of an Iron Work in Maryland, had engag'd the Great Cabin; so that Ralph and I were forc'd to take up with a Birth in the Steerage: And none on board knowing us, were considered as ordinary Persons. But Mr. Hamilton and his Son (it was James, since Governor) return'd from New Castle to Philadelphia, the Father being recall'd by a great Fee to plead for a seized Ship. And just before we sail'd Col. French coming on board, and showing me great Respect, I was more taken Notice of, and with my Friend Ralph invited by the other Gentlemen to come into the Cabin, there being now Room. Accordingly we remov'd thither.

Understanding that Col. French had brought on board the Governor's Dispatches, I ask'd the Captain for those Letters that were to be under my Care. He said all were put into the Bag together; and he could not then come at them; but before we landed in England, I should have an Opportunity of picking them out. So I was satisfy'd for the present, and we proceeded on our Voyage. We had a sociable Company in the Cabin, and lived uncommonly well, having the Addition of all Mr. Hamilton's Stores, who had laid in plentifully. In this Passage Mr. Denham contracted a Friendship for me that continued during his Life. The Voyage was otherwise not a pleasant one, as we had a great deal of bad Weather.

When we came into the Channel, the Captain kept his Word with me, and gave me an Opportunity of examining the Bag for the Governor's Letters. I found none upon which my Name was put, as under my Care; I pick'd out 6 or 7 that by the Hand writing I thought might be the promis'd Letters, especially as one of them was directed to Basket the King's Printer, and another to some Stationer. We arriv'd in London the 24th of December, 1724. I waited upon the Stationer who came first in my Way, delivering the Letter as from Gov. Keith. I don't know such a Person, says he: but opening the Letter, O, this is from Riddlesden; I have lately found him to be a compleat Rascal, and I will have nothing to do with him, nor receive any Letters from him. So putting the Letter into my Hand, he turn'd on his Heel and left me to serve some Customer. I was surprized to find these were not the Governor's Letters. And after recollecting and comparing Circumstances, I began to doubt his Sincerity. I found my Friend Denham, and opened the whole Affair to him. He let me into Keith's Character, told me there was not the least Probability that he had written any Letters for me, that no one who knew him had the smallest Dependance on him, and he laught at the Notion of the Governor's giving me a Letter of Credit, having as he said no Credit to give. On my expressing some Concern about what I should do: He advis'd me to endeavour getting some Employment in the Way of my Business. Among the Printers here, says he, you will improve yourself; and when you return to America, you will set up to greater Advantage.

We both of us happen'd to know, as well as the Stationer, that Riddlesden the Attorney, was a very Knave. He had half ruin'd Miss Read's Father by drawing him in to be bound for him. By his Letter it appear'd, there was a secret Scheme on foot to the Prejudice of Hamilton, (Suppos'd to be then coming over with us,) and that Keith was concern'd in it with Riddlesden. Denham, who was a Friend of Hamilton's, thought he ought to be acquainted with it. So when he arriv'd in England, which was soon after, partly from Resentment and Ill-Will to Keith and Riddlesden, and partly from Good Will to him: I waited on him, and gave him the Letter. He thank'd me cordially, the Information being of Importance to him. And from that time he became my Friend, greatly to my Advantage afterwards on many Occasions.

But what shall we think of a Governor's playing such pitiful Tricks, and imposing so grossly on a poor ignorant Boy! It was a Habit he had acquired. He wish'd to please every body; and having little to give, he gave Expectations. He was otherwise an ingenious sensible Man, a pretty good Writer, and a good Governor for the People, tho' not for his Constituents the Proprietaries, whose Instructions he sometimes disregarded. Several of our best Laws were of his Planning, and pass'd during his Administration.

Ralph and I were inseparable Companions.[2] We took Lodgings together in Little Britain[3] at 3*s.* 6*d.* per Week, as much as we could then afford. He found some Relations, but they were poor and unable to assist him. He now let me know his Intentions of remaining in London, and that he never meant to return to Philadelphia. He had brought no Money with him, the whole he could muster having been expended in paying his Passage. I had 15 Pistoles: So he borrowed occasionally of me, to subsist while he was looking out for Business. He first endeavoured to get into the Playhouse, believing himself qualify'd for an Actor; but Wilkes, to whom he apply'd, advis'd him candidly not to think of that, Employment, as it was impossible he should succeed in it. Then he propos'd to Roberts, a Publisher in Paternoster Row, to write for him a Weekly Paper like the Spectator, on certain Conditions, which Roberts did not approve. Then he endeavour'd to get Employment as a Hackney Writer to copy for the Stationers and Lawyers about the Temple: but could find no Vacancy.

2. Crossed out: "He led me about and show'd me the City, with which he had been."

3. A short street between Aldersgate Street and Duck Lane (later called Duke Street), near St. Bartholomew's Hospital and north of St. Paul's Cathedral. It was destroyed during the Second World War. For an illustration, see *Papers,* I, 70. After "together" in this sentence "at a Fan Shop" was first written, then crossed out.

I immediately got into Work at Palmer's then a famous Printing House in Bartholomew Close;[4] and here I continu'd near a Year. I was pretty diligent; but spent with Ralph a good deal of my Earnings in going to Plays and other Places of Amusement. We had together consum'd all my Pistoles, and now just rubb'd on from hand to mouth. He seem'd quite to forget his Wife and Child, and I by degrees my Engagements with Miss Read, to whom I never wrote more than one Letter, and that was to let her know I was not likely soon to return. This was another of the great Errata of my Life, which I should wish to correct[5] if I were to live it over again. In fact, by our Expences, I was constantly kept unable to pay my Passage.

At Palmer's I was employ'd in composing for the second Edition of Woollaston's Religion of Nature.[6] Some of his Reasonings not appearing to me well-founded, I wrote a little metaphysical Piece, in which I made Remarks on them. It was entitled, *A Dissertation on Liberty and Necessity, Pleasure and pain.* I inscrib'd it to my Friend Ralph. I printed a small Number. It occasion'd my being more consider'd by Mr. Palmer, as a young Man of some Ingenuity, tho' he seriously expostulated with me upon the Principles of my Pamphlet which to him appear'd abominable. My printing this Pamphlet was another Erratum.[7]

4. An irregular open space or square, long a center for the printing business; one entrance opened from Little Britain.

5. Crossed out after "correct": "in Living a second Edition."

6. Actually the third edition of *The Religion of Nature Delineated* (first privately printed, 1722), a treatise on rational morality by William Wollaston, Anglican clergyman and schoolmaster.

7. Franklin recalled in 1779 that after giving a few copies to friends he came to dislike what he had written and burned all the rest but one. Four copies are known to survive: in the British Museum, Library of Congress, John Carter Brown Library, and Yale University Library. It is reprinted in *Papers,* I, 57–71. Franklin's youthful exercise in logic left so little to an omnipotent God that he has been described, inaccurately, as being at this time an atheist.

While I lodg'd in Little Britain I made an Acquaintance with one Wilcox a Bookseller, whose Shop was at the next Door. He had an immense Collection of second-hand Books. Circulating Libraries were not then in Use; but we agreed that on certain reasonable Terms which I have now forgotten, I might take, read and return any of his Books. This I esteem'd a great Advantage, and I made as much use of it as I could.

My Pamphlet by some means falling into the Hands of one Lyons, a Surgeon, Author of a Book intituled *The Infallibility of Human Judgment*, it occasioned an Acquaintance between us; he took great Notice of me, call'd on me often, to converse on those Subjects, carried me to the Horns a pale Ale-House in [blank] Lane, Cheapside, and introduc'd me to Dr. Mandevile, Author of the Fable of the Bees[8] who had a Club there, of which he was the Soul, being a most facetious entertaining Companion. Lyons too introduc'd me, to Dr. Pemberton, at Batson's Coffee House,[9] who promis'd to give me an Opportunity some time or other of seeing Sir Isaac Newton, of which I was extreamly desirous; but this never happened.

I had brought over a few Curiosities among which the principal was a Purse made of the Asbestos, which purifies by Fire. Sir Hans Sloane heard of it, came to see me, and invited me to his House in Bloomsbury Square, where he show'd me all his Curi-

8. First published, 1705, as *The Grumbling Hive, or Knaves Turned Honest,* Bernard Mandeville's doggerel poem was republished, 1714, as *The Fable of the Bees, or Private Vices Public Benefits.* Moralists denounced its cynicism, but it went through many editions.

9. Batson's, in Cornhill near the Royal Exchange, was a favorite meeting place of physicians, often used for consultations, but disdained by literary men, who found there "a gloomy class of mortals, not less intent on gain than the stock-jobbers: I mean the dispensers of life and death, who flock together like birds of prey watching for carcasses."

osities, and persuaded me to let him add that to the Number, for which he paid me handsomely.[1]

In our House there lodg'd[2] a young Woman; a Millener, who I think had a Shop in the Cloisters. She had been genteelly bred, was sensible and lively, and of most pleasing Conversation. Ralph read Plays to her in the Evenings, they grew intimate, she took another Lodging, and he follow'd her. They liv'd together some time, but he being still out of Business, and her Income not sufficient to maintain them with her Child, he took a Resolution of going from London, to try for a Country School, which he thought himself well qualify'd to undertake, as he wrote an excellent Hand, and was a Master of Arithmetic and Accounts. This however he deem'd a Business below him, and confident of future better Fortune when he should be unwilling to have it known that he once was so meanly employ'd, he chang'd his Name, and did me the Honour to assume mine. For I soon after had a Letter from him, acquainting me, that he was settled in a small Village in Berkshire, I think it was, where he taught reading and writing to 10 or a dozen Boys at 6 pence each per Week, recommending Mrs. T. to my Care, and desiring me to write to him directing for Mr. Franklin Schoolmaster at such a Place. He continu'd to write frequently, sending me large Specimens of an Epic Poem, which he was then composing, and desiring my Remarks and Corrections. These I gave him from time to time, but endeavour'd rather to discourage his Proceeding. One of Young's Satires was then just publish'd. I copy'd and sent him a great Part of it, which set in a strong

1. Franklin implies here that Sloane took the initiative in the matter; actually Franklin wrote him an unsolicited letter, June 2, 1725, offering to show and sell him the purse and other "Curiosities." *Papers,* I, 54. The purse is now in the British Museum (Natural History).

2. Crossed out: "two single Women that had some" and "one a Mantuamaker who one of them."

Light the Folly of pursuing the Muses with any Hope of Advancement by them.[3] All was in vain. Sheets of the Poem continu'd to come by every Post.[4] In the mean time Mrs. T. having on his Account lost her Friends and Business, was often in Distresses, and us'd to send for me, and borrow what I could spare to help her out of them. I grew fond of her Company, and being at this time under no Religious Restraints, and presuming on my Importance to her, I attempted Familiarities, (another Erratum) which she repuls'd with a proper Resentment, and acquainted him with my Behaviour. This made a Breach between us, and when he return'd again to London, he let me know he thought I had cancel'd all the Obligations he had been under to me. So I found I was never to expect his Repaying me what I lent to him or advanc'd for him. This was however not then of much Consequence, as he was totally unable. And in the Loss of his Friendship I found my self reliev'd from a Burthen. I now began to think of getting a little Money beforehand; and expecting better Work, I left Palmer's to work at Watts's near Lincoln's Inn Fields, a still greater Printing House. Here I continu'd all the rest of my Stay in London.

At my first Admission into this Printing House, I took to working at Press, imagining I felt a Want of the Bodily Exercise I had been us'd to in America, where Presswork is mix'd with Composing. I drank only Water; the other Workmen, near 50 in Number, were great Guzzlers of Beer. On occasion I carried up and down Stairs a large Form of Types in each hand, when others carried but one in both Hands. They wonder'd to see from this and several Instances that the Water-American as they call'd me

3. Probably Satire IV (first published in 1725), beginning at line 159, of Edward Young, *Love of Fame, The Universal Passion.*

4. Crossed out: "so that the Postage was a Burthen." At this time postage was almost always paid by the recipient.

was *stronger* than themselves who drank *strong* Beer. We had an Alehouse Boy who attended always in the House to supply the Workmen. My Companion at the Press, drank every day a Pint before Breakfast, a Pint at Breakfast with his Bread and Cheese; a Pint between Breakfast and Dinner; a Pint at Dinner; a Pint in the Afternoon about Six o'Clock, and another when he had done his Day's-Work. I thought it a detestable Custom. But it was necessary, he suppos'd, to drink *strong* Beer that he might be *strong* to labour. I endeavour'd to convince him that the Bodily Strength afforded by Beer could only be in proportion to the Grain or Flour of the Barley dissolved in the Water of which it was made; that there was more Flour in a Penny-worth of Bread, and therefore if he would eat that with a Pint of Water, it would give him more Strength than a Quart of Beer. He drank on however, and had 4 or 5 Shillings to pay out of his Wages every Saturday Night for that muddling Liquor; an Expence I was free from. And thus these poor Devils keep themselves always under.

Watts after some Weeks desiring to have me in the Composing Room, I left the Pressmen. A new *Bienvenu* or Sum for Drink, being 5 *s.*, was demanded of me by the Compositors. I thought it an Imposition, as I had paid below. The Master thought so too, and forbad my Paying it. I stood out two or three Weeks, was accordingly considered as an Excommunicate, and had so many little Pieces of private Mischief done me, by mixing my Sorts, transposing my Pages, breaking my Matter, &c. &c. if I were ever so little out of the Room, and all ascrib'd to the Chapel Ghost, which they said ever haunted those not regularly admitted, that notwithstanding the Master's Protection, I found myself oblig'd to comply and pay the Money; convinc'd of the Folly of being on ill Terms with those one is to live with continually. I was now on a fair Footing with them, and soon acquir'd considerable Influence.

I propos'd some reasonable Alterations in their Chapel* Laws, and carried them against all Opposition. From my Example a great Part of them, left their muddling Breakfast of Beer and Bread and Cheese, finding they could with me be supply'd from a neighbouring House with a large Porringer of hot Water-gruel, sprinkled with Pepper, crumb'd with Bread, and a Bit of Butter in it, for the Price of a Pint of Beer, viz, three halfpence. This was a more comfortable as well as cheaper Breakfast, and kept their Heads clearer. Those who continu'd sotting with Beer all day, were often, by not paying, out of Credit at the Alehouse, and us'd to make Interest with me to get Beer, *their Light,* as they phras'd it, *being out.* I watch'd the Pay table on Saturday Night, and collected what I stood engag'd for them, having to pay some times near Thirty Shillings a Week on their Accounts. This, and my being esteem'd a pretty good Riggite, that is a jocular verbal Satyrist, supported my Consequence in the Society. My constant Attendance, (I never making a St. Monday),[6] recommended me to the Master; and my uncommon Quickness at Composing, occasion'd my being put upon all Work of Dispatch which was generally better paid. So I went on now very agreably.

My Lodging in Little Britain being too remote, I found another in Duke-street opposite to the Romish Chapel.[7] It was two pair

---

*A Note A Printing House is always called a Chappel by the Workmen.[5]

5. By extension the term "chapel" also applied to the collective body of journeymen printers in one establishment. Each such group was commonly organized for mutual benefit under the senior member, called the "father of the chapel," and had its own rules or by-laws.

6. That is, to be absent from work on Monday because of week-end dissipation.

7. This Duke Street (one of several by that name in London; now called Sardinia Street) is two blocks south of Wild Court, where Watts's printing

of Stairs backwards at an Italian Warehouse. A Widow Lady kept the House; she had a Daughter and a Maid Servant, and a Journeyman who attended the Warehouse, but lodg'd abroad. After sending to enquire my Character at the House where I last lodg'd, she agreed to take me in at the same Rate, 3*s.* 6*d.* per Week, cheaper as she said from the Protection she expected in having a Man lodge in the House. She was a Widow, an elderly Woman, had been bred a Protestant, being a Clergyman's Daughter, but was converted to the Catholic Religion by her Husband, whose Memory she much revered, had lived much among People of Distinction, and knew a 1000 Anecdotes of them as far back as the Times of Charles the Second. She was lame in her Knees with the Gout, and therefore seldom stirr'd out of her Room, so sometimes wanted Company; and hers was so highly amusing to me; that I was sure to spend an Evening with her whenever she desired it. Our Supper was only half an Anchovy each, on a very little Strip of Bread and Butter, and half a Pint of Ale between us. But the Entertainment was in her Conversation. My always keeping good Hours, and giving little Trouble in the Family, made her unwilling to part with me; so that when I talk'd of a Lodging I had heard of, nearer my Business, for 2*s.* a Week, which, intent as I now was on saving Money, made some Difference; she bid me not think of it, for she would abate me two Shillings a Week for the future, so I remain'd with her at 1*s.* 6*d.* as long as I staid in London.

In a Garret of her House there lived a Maiden Lady of 70 in the most retired Manner, of whom my Landlady gave me this Account, that she was a Roman Catholic, had been sent abroad when young and lodg'd in a Nunnery with an Intent of becoming

---

office was located. The Roman Catholic Chapel of Saints Anselm and Cecilia, located there, was destroyed in 1780 in the anti-Catholic Gordon riots, but was later rebuilt.

a Nun: but the Country not agreeing with her, she return'd to England, where there being no Nunnery, she had vow'd to lead the Life of a Nun as near as might be done in those Circumstances: Accordingly she had given all her Estate to charitable Uses, reserving only Twelve Pounds a Year to live on, and out of this Sum she still gave a great deal in Charity, living her self on Water-gruel only, and using no Fire but to boil it. She had lived many Years in that Garret, being permitted to remain there gratis by successive Catholic Tenants of the House below, as they deem'd it a Blessing to have her there. A Priest visited her, to confess her every Day. I have ask'd her, says my Landlady, how she, as she liv'd, could possibly find so much Employment for a Confessor? O, says she, it is impossible to avoid *vain Thoughts*. I was permitted once to visit her: She was chearful and polite, and convers'd pleasantly. The Room was clean, but had no other Furniture than a Matras, a Table with a Crucifix and Book, a Stool, which she gave me to sit on, and a Picture over the Chimney of St. Veronica, displaying her Handkerchief with the miraculous Figure of Christ's bleeding Face on it, which she explain'd to me with great Seriousness. She look'd pale, but was never sick, and I give it as another Instance on how small an Income Life and Health may be supported.

At Watts's Printinghouse I contracted an Acquaintance with an ingenious young Man, one Wygate, who having wealthy Relations, had been better educated than most Printers, was a tolerable Latinist, spoke French, and lov'd Reading. I taught him, and a Friend of his, to swim, at twice going into the River, and they soon became good Swimmers. They introduc'd me to some Gentlemen from the Country who went to Chelsea by Water to see the College and Don Saltero's Curiosities.[8] In our Return, at the

8. Chelsea College: presumably Chelsea Hospital for disabled soldiers, designed by Christopher Wren and erected in 1682 on the site of the former

Request of the Company, whose Curiosity Wygate had excited, I stript and leapt into the River, and swam from near Chelsea to Blackfryars,[9] performing on the Way many Feats of Activity both upon and under Water, that surpriz'd and pleas'd those to whom they were Novelties. I had from a Child been ever delighted with this Exercise, had studied and practis'd all Thevenot's Motions and Positions,[1] added some of my own, aiming at the graceful and easy, as well as the Useful. All these I took this Occasion of exhibiting to the Company, and was much flatter'd by their Admiration. And Wygate, who was desirous of becoming a Master, grew more and more attach'd to me, on that account, as well as from the Similarity of our Studies. He at length propos'd to me travelling all over Europe together, supporting ourselves everywhere by working at our Business. I was once inclin'd to it. But mentioning it to my good Friend Mr. Denham, with whom I often spent an Hour, when I had Leisure. He dissuaded me from it, advising me to think only of returning to Pensilvania, which he was now about to do.

I must record one Trait of this good Man's Character. He had formerly been in Business at Bristol, but fail'd in Debt to a Number of People, compounded and went to America. There, by a close Application to Business as a Merchant, he acquir'd a plentiful Fortune in a few Years. Returning to England in the Ship with me, He invited his old Creditors to an Entertainment, at which

---

Chelsea College founded in 1610 by James I. Don Saltero's Curiosities: James Salter, a former servant of Sir Hans Sloane, opened in 1695 in Cheyne Walk, Chelsea, a coffee house and museum in which he exhibited such strange and often foolish objects as a petrified crab, William the Conqueror's sword, and Job's tears.

9. About three and a half miles.

1. Melchisédeck de Thévenot, *The Art of Swimming. Illustrated by Proper Figures . . . Done out of French* (London, 1699).

he thank'd them for the easy Composition they had favour'd him with, and when they expected nothing but the Treat, every Man at the first Remove, found under his Plate an Order on a Banker for the full Amount of the unpaid Remainder with Interest.

He now told me he was about to return to Philadelphia, and should carry over a great Quantity of Goods in order to open a Store there: He propos'd to take me over as his Clerk, to keep his Books (in which he would instruct me) copy his Letters, and attend the Store. He added, that as soon as I should be acquainted with mercantile Business he would promote me by sending me with a Cargo of Flour and Bread &c. to the West Indies, and procure me Commissions from others; which would be profitable, and if I manag'd well, would establish me handsomely. The Thing pleas'd me, for I was grown tired of London, remember'd with Pleasure the happy Months I had spent in Pennsylvania, and wish'd again to see it. Therefore I immediately agreed, on the Terms of Fifty Pounds a Year, Pensylvania Money; less indeed than my present Gettings as a Compostor, but affording a better Prospect.

I now took Leave of Printing, as I thought for ever, and was daily employ'd in my new Business; going about with Mr. Denham among the Tradesmen, to purchase various Articles, and seeing them pack'd up, doing Errands, calling upon Workmen to dispatch, &c. and when all was on board, I had a few Days Leisure. On one of these Days I was to my Surprize sent for by a great Man I knew only by Name, a Sir William Wyndham and I waited upon him. He had heard by some means or other of my Swimming from Chelsey to Blackfryars, and of my teaching Wygate and another young Man to swim in a few Hours. He had two Sons about to set out on their Travels; he wish'd to have them first taught Swimming; and propos'd to gratify me handsomely if I would teach them. They were not yet come to Town and my Stay was uncertain, so I could not undertake it. But from this Incident I thought it likely, that if I were to remain in England and open a Swimming School, I might get a good deal of Money. And it struck me so strongly, that had the Overture been sooner made me, probably I should not so soon have returned to America. After many Years, you and I had something of more Importance to do with one of these Sons of Sir William Wyndham, become Earl of Egremont, which I shall mention in its Place.

Thus I spent about 18 Months in London. Most Part of the Time, I work'd hard at my Business, and spent but little upon my self except in seeing Plays and in Books. My Friend Ralph had kept me poor. He owed me about 27 Pounds; which I was now never likely to receive; a great Sum out of my small Earnings. I lov'd him notwithstanding, for he had many amiable Qualities.[2] Tho' I had by no means improv'd my Fortune. But I had pick'd up some very ingenious Acquaintance whose Conversation was of great Advantage to me, and I had read considerably.

We sail'd from Gravesend on the 23d of July 1726. For the Incidents of the Voyage, I refer you to my Journal, where you will find them all minutely related.[3] Perhaps the most important Part of that Journal is the *Plan* to be found in it which I formed at Sea, for regulating my future Conduct in Life.[4] It is the more remarkable, as being form'd when I was so young, and yet being pretty faithfully adhered to quite thro' to old Age. We landed in Philadelphia the 11th of October, where I found sundry Alterations. Keith was no longer Governor, being superceded by Major Gordon: I met him walking the Streets as a common Citizen. He seem'd a little asham'd at seeing me, but pass'd without saying any thing. I should

2. Crossed out before "Tho' ": "I had improv'd my Knowledge, however, by Reading and Conversation,"

3. *Papers*, I, 72–99.

4. Only "the preamble and heads of it" survive. *Papers*, I, 99–100. The "*Plan*" itself is lost.

have been as much asham'd at seeing Miss Read, had not her Friends, despairing with Reason of my Return, after the Receipt of my Letter, persuaded her to marry another, one Rogers, a Potter, which was done in my Absence. With him however she was never happy, and soon parted from him, refusing to cohabit with him, or bear his Name It being now said that he had another Wife. He was a worthless Fellow tho' an excellent Workman which was the Temptation to her Friends. He[5] got into Debt, and ran away in 1727 or 28. Went to the West Indies, and died there. Keimer had got a better House, a Shop well supply'd with Stationary, plenty of new Types, a number of Hands tho' none good, and seem'd to have a great deal of Business.

Mr. Denham took a Store in Water Street, where we open'd our Goods. I attended the Business diligently, studied Accounts, and grew in a little Time expert at selling. We lodg'd and boarded together, he counsell'd me as a Father, having a sincere Regard for me: I respected and lov'd him: and we might have gone on together very happily: But in the Beginning of Feby. 1726/7 when I had just pass'd my 21st Year, we both were taken ill. My Distemper was a Pleurisy, which very nearly carried me off: I suffered a good deal, gave up the Point in my own mind, and was rather disappointed when I found my Self recovering; regretting in some degree that I must now some time or other have all that disagreable Work to do over again. I forget what his Distemper was. It held him a long time, and at length carried him off. He left me a small Legacy in a nuncupative Will,[6] as a Token of his Kindness for me, and he left me once more to the wide World. For the Store was taken into the Care of his Executors, and my Employment under him ended: My Brother-in-law Homes, being now at Philadelphia, advis'd my

5. Crossed out: "soon spent what he receiv'd with her." That is, as dowry.

6. An oral, not a written, will.

Return to my Business. And Keimer tempted me with an Offer of large Wages by the Year to come and take the Management of his Printing-House, that he might better attend his Stationer's Shop. I had heard a bad Character of him in London, from his Wife and her Friends, and was not fond of having any more to do with him. I try'd for farther Employment as a Merchant's Clerk; but not readily meeting with any, I clos'd again with Keimer.

I found in *his* House these Hands; Hugh Meredith a Welsh-Pensilvanian, 30 Years of Age, bred to Country Work: honest, sensible, had a great deal of solid Observation, was something of a Reader, but given to drink: Stephen Potts, a young Country Man of full Age, bred to the Same: of uncommon natural Parts, and great Wit and Humour, but a little idle. These he had agreed with at extream low Wages, per Week, to be rais'd a Shilling every 3 Months, as they would deserve by improving in their Business, and the Expectation of these high Wages to come on hereafter was what he had drawn them in with. Meredith was to work at Press, Potts at Bookbinding, which he by Agreement, was to teach them, tho' he knew neither one nor t'other. John——a wild Irishman brought up to no Business, whose Service for 4 Years Keimer had purchas'd from the Captain of a Ship. He too was to be made a Pressman. George Webb, an Oxford Scholar, whose Time for 4 Years he had likewise bought, intending him for a Compositor: of whom more presently. And David Harry, a Country Boy, whom he had taken Apprentice. I soon perceiv'd that the Intention of engaging me at Wages so much higher than he had been us'd to give, was to have these raw cheap Hands form'd thro' me, and as soon as I had instructed them, then, they being all articled to him, he should be able to do without me. I went on however, very chearfully; put his Printing House in Order, which had been in great Confusion, and brought his Hands by degrees to mind their Business and to do it better.

It was an odd Thing to find an Oxford Scholar in the Situation of a bought Servant. He was not more than 18 Years of Age, and gave me this Account of himself; that he was born in Gloucester, educated at a Grammar School there, had been distinguish'd among the Scholars for some apparent Superiority in performing his Part when they exhibited Plays; belong'd to the Witty Club there, and had written some Pieces in Prose and Verse which were printed in the Gloucester Newspapers. Thence he was sent to Oxford; there he continu'd about a Year, but not well-satisfy'd, wishing of all things to see London and become a Player. At length receiving his Quarterly Allowance of 15 Guineas, instead of discharging his Debts, he walk'd out of Town, hid his Gown in a Furz Bush, and footed it to London, where having no Friend to advise him, he fell into bad Company, soon spent his Guineas, found no means of being introduc'd among the Players, grew necessitous, pawn'd his Cloaths and wanted Bread. Walking the Street very hungry, and not knowing what to do with himself, a Crimp's Bill[7] was put into his Hand, offering immediate Entertainment and Encouragement to such as would bind themselves to serve in America. He went directly, sign'd the Indentures, was put into the Ship and came over; never writing a Line to acquaint his Friends what was become of him. He was lively, witty, good-natur'd, and a pleasant Companion, but idle, thoughtless and imprudent to the last Degree.

John the Irishman soon ran away. With the rest I began to live very agreably; for they all respected me, the more as they found Keimer incapable of instructing them, and that from me they learnt something daily. We never work'd on a Saturday, that being Keimer's Sabbath. So I had two Days for Reading. My Acquaintance with Ingenious People in the Town, increased. Keimer himself

7. Crimp: one whose business it was to lure or entrap men into military or sea service, or to persuade them to become indentured servants in return for transportation to the colonies.

treated me with great Civility, and apparent Regard; and nothing now made me uneasy but my Debt to Vernon, which I was yet unable to pay being hitherto but a poor Oeconomist. He however kindly made no Demand of it.

Our Printing-House often wanted Sorts,[8] and there was no Letter Founder in America. I had seen Types cast at James's in London,[9] but without much Attention to the Manner: However I now contriv'd a Mould, made use of the Letters we had, as Puncheons, struck the Matrices in Lead, and thus supply'd in a pretty tolerable way all Deficiencies. I also engrav'd several Things on occasion. I made the Ink, I was Warehouse-man and every thing, in short quite a Factotum.

But however serviceable I might be, I found that my Services became every Day of less Importance, as the other Hands improv'd in the Business. And when Keimer paid my second Quarter's Wages, he let me know that he felt them too heavy, and thought I should make an Abatement. He grew by degrees less civil, put on more of the Master, frequently found Fault, was captious and seem'd ready for an Out-breaking. I went on nevertheless with a good deal of Patience, thinking that his incumber'd Circumstances were partly the Cause. At length[1] a Trifle snapt our Connexion. For a great Noise happening near the Courthouse, I put my Head out of the Window to see what was the Matter. Keimer being in the Street look'd up and saw me, call'd out to me in a loud Voice and angry Tone to mind my Business, adding some reproachful Words,

8. Sort: a letter or character in a font of type, a term normally used, as here, in the plural with reference to a lack of necessary type. A printer who is "out of sorts" tends to become angry; hence the familiar expression.

9. The type foundry of Thomas James, the largest in London at the time, was near Palmer's printing house in Bartholomew Close, where Franklin had worked.

1. Crossed out: "on the Day of the County Election."

that nettled me the more for their Publicity, all the Neighbours who were looking out on the same Occasion being Witnesses how I was treated. He came up immediately into the Printing-House, continu'd the Quarrel, high Words pass'd on both Sides, he gave me the Quarter's Warning we had stipulated, expressing a Wish that he had not been oblig'd to so long a Warning: I told him his Wish was unnecessary for I would leave him that Instant; and so taking my Hat walk'd out of Doors; desiring Meredith whom I saw below to take care of some Things I left, and bring them to my Lodging.

Meredith came accordingly in the Evening, when we talk'd my Affair over. He had conceiv'd a great Regard for me, and was very unwilling that I should leave the House while he remain'd in it. He dissuaded me from returning to my native Country which I began to think of. He reminded me that Keimer was in debt for all he possess'd, that his Creditors began to be uneasy, that he kept his Shop miserably, sold often without Profit for ready Money, and often trusted without keeping Accounts. That he must therefore fail; which would make a Vacancy I might profit of. I objected my Want of Money. He then let me know, that his Father[2] had a high Opinion of me, and from some Discourse that had pass'd between them, he was sure would advance Money to set us up, if I would enter into Partnership with him. My Time, says he, will be out with Keimer in the Spring. By that time we may have our Press and Types in from London: I am sensible I am no Workman. If you like it, Your Skill in the Business shall be set against the Stock I furnish; and we will share the Profits equally. The Proposal was agreable, and I consented. His Father was in Town, and approv'd of it, the more as he saw I had great Influence with his Son, had prevail'd on him to abstain long from Dramdrinking, and he hop'd might break him of that wretched Habit entirely, when we came to be so closely connected. I gave an Inventory to the Father, who

2. Simon Meredith.

carry'd it to a Merchant; the Things were sent for; the Secret was to be kept till they should arrive, and in the mean time I was to get work if I could at the other Printing House. But I found no Vacancy there, and so remain'd idle a few Days, when Keimer, on a Prospect of being employ'd to print some Paper-money, in New Jersey, which would require Cuts and various Types that I only could supply, and apprehending Bradford might engage me and get the Jobb from him, sent me a very civil Message, that old Friends should not part for a few Words, the Effect of sudden Passion, and wishing me to return. Meredith persuaded me to comply, as it would give more Opportunity for his Improvement under my daily Instructions. So I return'd, and we went on more smoothly than for some time before. The New Jersey Jobb was obtain'd. I contriv'd a Copper-Plate Press for it, the first that had been seen in the Country. I cut several Ornaments and Checks for the Bills. We went together to Burlington, where I executed the Whole to Satisfaction, and he received so large a Sum for the Work, as to be enabled thereby to keep his Head much longer above Water.[3]

At Burlington I made an Acquaintance with many principal People of the Province. Several of them had been appointed by the Assembly a Committee to attend the Press, and take Care that no more Bills were printed than the Law directed. They were therefore by Turns constantly with us, and generally he who attended brought with him a Friend or two for Company. My Mind having been much more improv'd by Reading than Keimer's, I suppose it was for that Reason my Conversation seem'd to be more valu'd. They had me to their Houses, introduc'd me to their Friends and show'd me much Civility, while he, tho' the Master, was a little neglected. In truth he was an odd Fish, ignorant of common Life, fond of rudely opposing receiv'd Opinions, slovenly to extream dirtiness,

3. This paper money, printed in Burlington during the spring and summer of 1728, replaced an earlier issue which had proved easy to counterfeit.

enthusiastic in some Points of Religion, and a little Knavish withal. We continu'd there near 3 Months, and by that time I could reckon among my acquired Friends, Judge Allen, Samuel Bustill, the Secretary of the Province, Isaac Pearson, Joseph Cooper and several of the Smiths,[4] Members of Assembly, and Isaac Decow the Surveyor General. The latter was a shrewd sagacious old Man, who told me that he began for himself when young by wheeling Clay for the Brickmakers, learnt to write after he was of Age, carry'd the Chain for Surveyors, who taught him Surveying, and he had now by his Industry acquir'd a good Estate; and says he, I foresee, that you will soon work this Man out of his Business and make a Fortune in it at Philadelphia. He had not then the least Intimation of my Intention to set up there or any where. These Friends were afterwards of great Use to me, as I occasionally was to some of them. They all continued their Regard for me as long as they lived.

Before I enter upon my public Appearance in Business it may be well to let you know the then State of my Mind, with regard to my Principles and Morals, that you may see how far those influenc'd the future Events of my Life. My Parents had early given me religious Impressions, and brought me through my Childhood piously in the Dissenting Way. But I was scarce 15 when, after doubting by turns of several Points as I found them disputed in the different Books I read, I began to doubt of Revelation it self. Some Books against Deism fell into my Hands; they were said to be the Substance of Sermons preached at Boyle's Lectures.[5] It happened

4. It is not known which members of this numerous and prominent family Franklin referred to.

5. Established 1692 by the bequest of the chemist Robert Boyle (1627–1691) to defend Christianity against unbelievers. The lectures of Samuel Clarke for 1704 and 1705, which Franklin may have read, also had an unintended influence on David Hume, who told James Boswell that "he never had entertained any belief in Religion since he began to read Locke and Clarke."

that they wrought an Effect on me quite contrary to what was intended by them: For the Arguments of the Deists which were quoted to be refuted, appeared to me much stronger than the Refutations. In short I soon became a thorough Deist. My Arguments perverted some others, particularly Collins and Ralph: but each of them having afterwards wrong'd me greatly without the least Compunction and recollecting Keith's Conduct towards me, (who was another Freethinker) and my own towards Vernon and Miss Read which at Times gave me great Trouble, I began to suspect that this Doctrine tho' it might be true, was not very useful. My London Pamphlet, which had for its Motto those Lines of Dryden

> ——*Whatever is, is right.*——
> *Tho' purblind Man*
> *Sees but a Part of the Chain, the nearest Link,*
> *His Eyes not carrying to the equal Beam,*
> *That poizes all, above.*[6]

And from the Attributes of God, his infinite Wisdom, Goodness and Power concluded that nothing could possibly be wrong in the World, and that Vice and Virtue were empty Distinctions, no such Things existing: appear'd now not so clever a Performance as I once thought it; and I doubted whether some Error had not insinuated itself unperceiv'd into my Argument, so as to infect all that follow'd, as is common in metaphysical Reasonings. I grew convinc'd that *Truth, Sincerity and Integrity* in Dealings between Man and Man, were of the utmost Importance to the Felicity of Life, and I form'd written Resolutions, (which still remain in my Journal Book) to practice them ever while I lived. Revelation had indeed no

6. The first line as given here is not from Dryden but from Pope, *Essay on Man* (1733), Epistle I, line 284. In *Liberty and Necessity* Franklin quoted John Dryden (*Oedipus,* III, i, 244–8) correctly:

> Whatever is, is in its Causes just
> Since all Things are by Fate, but purblind Man *etc.*

weight with me as such; but I entertain'd an Opinion, that tho' certain Actions might not be bad *because* they were forbidden by it, or good *because* it commanded them; yet probably those Actions might be forbidden *because* they were bad for us, or commanded *because* they were beneficial to us, in their own Natures, all the Circumstances of things considered. And this Persuasion, with the kind hand of Providence, or some guardian Angel, or accidental favourable Circumstances and Situations, or all together, preserved me (thro' this dangerous Time of Youth and the hazardous Situations I was sometimes in among Strangers, remote from the Eye and Advice of my Father) without any *wilful* gross Immorality or Injustice that might have been expected from my Want of Religion.[7] I say *wilful*, because the Instances I have mentioned, had something of *Necessity* in them, from my Youth, Inexperience, and the Knavery of others. I had therefore a tolerable Character to begin the World with, I valued it properly, and determin'd to preserve it.

We had not been long return'd to Philadelphia, before the New Types arriv'd from London. We settled with Keimer, and left him by his Consent before he heard of it. We found a House to hire near the Market, and took it.[8] To lessen the Rent, (which was then but £24 a Year tho' I have since known it let for 70) We took in Tho' Godfrey a Glazier and his Family, who were to pay a considerable Part of it to us, and we to board with them. We had scarce opened our Letters and put our Press in Order, before George House, an Acquaintance of Mine, brought a Country-man to us; whom he had met in the Street enquiring for a Printer. All

7. Crossed out: "some foolish Intrigues with low Women excepted, which from the Expence were rather more prejudicial to me than to them."

8. The present 139 Market Street, a few doors below Second Street. Here Franklin lived and maintained "The New Printing-Office," 1728–39. He moved both his residence and place of business to what is now No. 131, four doors nearer the river, in 1739.

our Cash was now expended in the Variety of Particulars we had been obliged to procure and this Countryman's Five Shillings being our first Fruits, and coming so seasonably, gave me more Pleasure than any Crown[9] I have since earn'd; and from the Gratitude I felt towards House, has made me often more ready than perhaps I should otherwise have been to assist young Beginners.

There are Croakers in every Country always boding its Ruin. Such a one then lived in Philadelphia, a Person of Note, an elderly Man, with a wise Look, and very grave Manner of speaking. His Name was Samuel Mickle. This Gentleman, a Stranger to me, stopt one Day at my Door, and asked me if I was the young Man who had lately opened a new Printing House: Being answer'd in the Affirmative; he said he was sorry for me, because it was an expensive Undertaking and the Expence would be lost; for Philadelphia was a sinking Place, the People already half Bankrupts or near being so; all Appearances of the contrary, such as new Buildings and the Rise of Rents being to his certain Knowledge fallacious, for they were in fact among the Things that would soon ruin us. And he gave me such a Detail of Misfortunes, now existing or that were soon to exist, that he left me half-melancholy. Had I known him before I engag'd in this Business, probably I never should have done it. This Man continu'd to live in this decaying Place; and to declaim in the same Strain, refusing for many Years to buy a House there, because all was going to Destruction, and at last I had the Pleasure of seeing him give five times as much for one as he might have bought it for when he first began his Croaking.

I should have mention'd before, that in the Autumn of the preceding Year I had form'd most of my ingenious Acquaintance into a Club for mutual Improvement, which we call'd the Junto. We met on Friday Evenings. The Rules I drew up requir'd that every Member in his Turn should produce one or more Queries on any

9. A five-shilling coin.

Point of Morals, Politics or Natural Philosophy, to be discuss'd by the Company, and once in three Months produce and read an Essay of his own Writing on any Subject he pleased. Our Debates were to be under the Direction of a President, and to be conducted in the sincere Spirit of Enquiry after Truth, without Fondness for Dispute, or Desire of Victory; and to prevent Warmth all Expressions of Positiveness in Opinion, or of direct Contradiction, were after some time made contraband and prohibited under small pecuniary Penalties.[1] The first Members were Joseph Brientnal, a Copyer of Deeds for the Scriveners; a good-natur'd friendly middle-ag'd Man, a great Lover of Poetry, reading all he could meet with, and writing some that was tolerable; very ingenious in many little Nicknackeries, and of sensible Conversation. Thomas Godfrey, a self-taught Mathematician, great in his Way, and afterwards Inventor of what is now call'd Hadley's Quadrant. But he knew little out of his way, and was not a pleasing Companion, as like most Great Mathematicians I have met with, he expected unusual Precision in every thing said, or was forever denying or distinguishing upon Trifles, to the Disturbance of all Conversation. He soon left us. Nicholas Scull, a Surveyor, afterwards Surveyor-General, Who lov'd Books, and sometimes made a few Verses. William Parsons, bred a Shoemaker, but loving Reading, had acquir'd a considerable Share of Mathematics, which he first studied with a View to Astrology that he afterwards laught at. He also became Surveyor General. William Maugridge, a Joiner, a most exquisite Mechanic and a solid sensible Man. Hugh Meredith, Stephen Potts, and George Webb, I have Characteris'd before. Robert Grace, a young Gentleman of

1. The full original rules do not survive, but twenty-four "Standing Queries" to be read and answered at each meeting, the four qualifications every candidate for membership was required to meet, and a series of Proposals and Queries for discussions at meetings, all apparently dating from about 1732, are printed in *Papers*, I, 255–64.

some Fortune, generous, lively and witty, a Lover of Punning and of his Friends. And William Coleman, then a Merchant's Clerk, about my Age, who had the coolest clearest Head, the best Heart, and the exactest Morals, of almost any Man I ever met with. He became afterwards a Merchant of great Note, and one of our Provincial Judges: Our Friendship continued without Interruption to his Death upwards of 40 Years.[2]

And the club continu'd almost as long and was the best School of Philosophy, Morals and Politics that then existed in the Province; for our Queries which were read the Week preceding their Discussion, put us on Reading with Attention upon the several Subjects, that we might speak more to the purpose: and here too we acquired better Habits of Conversation, every thing being studied in our Rules which might prevent our disgusting each other. From hence the long Continuance of the Club, which I shall have frequent Occasion to speak farther of hereafter; But my giving this Account of it here, is to show something of the Interest I had, every one of these exerting themselves in recommending Business to us. Brientnal particularly procur'd us from the Quakers, the Printing 40 Sheets of their History, the rest being to be done by Keimer: and upon this we work'd exceeding hard, for the Price was low.[3] It was a Folio, Pro Patria Size, in Pica with Long Primer Notes. I compos'd of it a Sheet a Day, and Meredith work'd it off at Press. It was often 11 at Night and sometimes later, before I had finish'd my

2. Among other early members of the Junto were Philip Syng and Hugh Roberts, who with Franklin, were the last survivors. Several of these young men later attained considerable prominence.

3. William Sewel, *The History of the Rise, Increase, and Progress Of the Christian People called Quakers: Intermixed with Several Remarkable Occurrences* (Phila., 1728). Differences in type show that Franklin and Meredith printed pp. 533–694 and the 16-page index. Each sheet made four pages, measuring 7 by 11½ inches, trimmed size.

Distribution for the next days Work: For the little Jobbs sent in by our other Friends now and then put us back. But so determin'd I was to continue doing a Sheet a Day of the Folio, that one Night when having impos'd my Forms, I thought my Days Work over, one of them by accident was broken and two Pages reduc'd to Pie, I immediately distributed and compos'd it over again before I went to bed. And this Industry visible to our Neighbours began to give us Character and Credit; particularly I was told, that mention being made of the new Printing Office at the Merchants every-night-Club, the general Opinion was that it must fail, there being already two Printers in the Place, Keimer and Bradford; but Doctor Baird (whom you and I saw many Years after at his native Place, St. Andrews in Scotland) gave a contrary Opinion; for the Industry of that Franklin, says he, is superior to any thing I ever saw of the kind: I see him still at work when I go home from Club; and he is at Work again before his Neighbours are out of bed. This struck the rest, and we soon after had Offers from one of them to Supply us with Stationary. But as yet we did not chuse to engage in Shop Business.

I mention this Industry the more particularly and the more freely, tho' it seems to be talking in my own Praise, that those of my Posterity who shall read it, may know the Use of that Virtue, when they see its Effects in my Favour throughout this Relation.

George Webb, who had found a Female Friend that lent him wherewith to purchase his Time of Keimer, now came to offer himself as a Journeyman to us. We could not then imploy him, but I foolishly let him know, as a Secret, that I soon intended to begin a Newspaper, and might then have Work for him. My Hopes of Success as I told him were founded on this, that the then only Newspaper, printed by Bradford was a paltry thing, wretchedly manag'd, and no way entertaining; and yet was profitable to him.[4] I therefore

4. *The American Weekly Mercury*, established Dec. 22, 1719.

thought a good Paper could scarcely fail of good Encouragement. I requested Webb not to mention it, but he told it to Keimer, who immediately, to be beforehand with me, published Proposals for Printing one himself, on which Webb was to be employ'd. I resented this, and to counteract them, as I could not yet begin our Paper, I wrote several Pieces of Entertainment for Bradford's Paper, under the Title of the Busy Body which Brientnal continu'd some Months.[5] By this means the Attention of the Publick was fix'd on that Paper, and Keimers Proposals which we burlesqu'd and ridicul'd, were disregarded. He began his Paper however, and after carrying it on three Quarters of a Year, with at most only 90 Subscribers, he offer'd it to me for a Trifle, and I having been ready some time to go on with it, took it in hand directly, and it prov'd in a few Years extreamly profitable to me.[6]

I perceive that I am apt to speak in the singular Number, though our Partnership still continu'd. The Reason may be, that in fact the whole Management of the Business lay upon me. Meredith was no Compositor, a poor Pressman, and seldom sober. My Friends lamented my Connection with him, but I was to make the best of it.

5. Franklin wrote the first four numbers and parts of two others; they appeared in *The American Weekly Mercury* in February and March 1729. In January the *Mercury* had printed letters ridiculing Keimer, signed "Martha Careful" and "Caelia Shortface" but probably also written by Franklin. *Papers*, I, 111–39.

6. Keimer began his dull and unimaginative paper Dec. 24, 1728, calling it *The Universal Instructor in all Arts and Sciences: and Pennsylvania Gazette.* When Franklin and Meredith took it over, Oct. 2, 1729, they shortened the title to *The Pennsylvania Gazette*, and it soon became perhaps the liveliest and most readable newspaper in all the colonies. Franklin's connection with it ceased entirely in 1766, though it continued until 1815. Its relationship to the modern *Saturday Evening Post* is extremely remote; certainly the assertion formerly made that Franklin founded the *Post* in 1728 is historically incorrect.

Our first Papers made a quite different Appearance from any before in the Province, a better Type and better printed: but some spirited Remarks[7] of my Writing on the Dispute then going on between Govr. Burnet and the Massachusetts Assembly, struck the principal People, occasion'd the Paper and the Manager of it to be much talk'd of, and in a few Weeks brought them all to be our Subscribers. Their Example was follow'd by many, and our Number went on growing continually. This was one of the first good Effects of my having learnt a little to scribble. Another was, that the leading Men, seeing a News Paper now in the hands of one who could also handle a Pen, thought it convenient to oblige and encourage me. Bradford still printed the Votes and Laws and other Publick Business. He had printed an Address of the House to the Governor in a coarse blundering manner; We reprinted it elegantly and correctly, and sent one to every Member. They were sensible of the Difference, it strengthen'd the Hands of our Friends in the House, and they voted us their Printers for the Year ensuing.

Among my Friends in the House I must not forget Mr. Hamilton before mentioned, who was now returned from England and had a Seat in it.[8] He interested himself* for me strongly in that Instance, as he did in many others afterwards, continuing his Patronage till his Death. Mr. Vernon about this time put me in mind

*I got his Son once £500.[9]

7. In old age Franklin wrote on the margin of the manuscript at this point: "Insert these Remarks in a Note." They are printed in *Papers*, I, 159–61, from the *Gazette* of Oct. 9, 1729, but are not reproduced here. William Burnet, whom Franklin had met in New York in 1724, had since become governor of Massachusetts and engaged in a dispute with the Assembly over his salary, a controversy cut short by his death. Franklin's remarks supported the Assembly's "ardent Spirit of Liberty."

8. Andrew Hamilton was speaker of the Assembly in 1729–30 and succeeding sessions.

9. The occasion has not been established.

of the Debt I ow'd him: but did not press me. I wrote him an ingenuous Letter of Acknowledgments, crav'd his Forbearance a little longer which he allow'd me, and as soon as I was able I paid the Principal with Interest and many Thanks. So that *Erratum* was in some degree corrected.

But now another Difficulty came upon me, which I had never the least Reason to expect. Mr. Meredith's Father, who was to have paid for our Printing House according to the Expectations given me, was able to advance only one Hundred Pounds, Currency, which had been paid, and a Hundred more was due to the Merchant; who grew impatient and su'd us all. We gave Bail, but saw that if the Money could not be rais'd in time, the Suit must come to a Judgment and Execution, and our hopeful Prospects must with us be ruined, as the Press and Letters must be sold for Payment, perhaps at half Price. In this Distress two true Friends whose Kindness I have never forgotten nor ever shall forget while I can remember any thing, came to me separately unknown to each other, and without any Application from me, offering each of them to advance me all the Money that should be necessary to enable me to take the whole Business upon my self if that should be practicable, but they did not like my continuing the Partnership with Meredith, who as they said was often seen drunk in the Streets, and playing at low Games in Alehouses, much to our Discredit. These two Friends were William Coleman and Robert Grace. I told them I could not propose a Separation while any Prospect remain'd of the Merediths fulfilling their Part of our Agreement. Because I thought myself under great Obligations to them for what they had done and would do if they could. But if they finally fail'd in their Performance, and our Partnership must be dissolv'd, I should then think myself at Liberty to accept the Assistance of my Friends.

Thus the matter rested for some time. When I said to my Partner, perhaps your Father is dissatisfied at the Part you have undertaken in this Affair of ours, and is unwilling to advance for you and me what he would for you alone: If that is the Case, tell me, and I will resign the whole to you and go about my Business. No says he, my Father has really been disappointed and is really unable; and I am unwilling to distress him farther. I see this is a Business I am not fit for. I was bred a Farmer, and it was a Folly in me to come to Town and put my Self at 30 Years of Age an Apprentice to learn a new Trade. Many of our Welsh People are going to settle in North Carolina where Land is cheap: I am inclin'd to go with them, and follow my old Employment. You may find Friends to assist you. If you will take the Debts of the Company upon you, return to my Father the hundred Pound he has advanc'd, pay my little personal Debts, and give me Thirty Pounds and a new Saddle, I will relinquish the Partnership and leave the whole in your Hands. I agreed to this Proposal. It was drawn up in Writing, sign'd and seal'd immediately. I gave him what he demanded and he went soon after to Carolina; from whence he sent me next Year two long Letters, containing the best Account that had been given of that Country, the Climate, Soil, Husbandry, &c. for in those Matters he was very judicious. I printed them in the Papers,[1] and they gave grate Satisfaction to the Publick.

As soon as he was gone, I recurr'd to my two Friends; and because I would not give an unkind Preference to either, I took half what each had offered and I wanted, of one, and half of the other; paid off the Company Debts, and went on with the Business in my own Name, advertising that the Partnership was dissolved. I think this was in or about the Year 1729.[2]

About this Time there was a Cry among the People for more Paper-Money, only £15,000, being extant in the Province and that

1. *Pennsylvania Gazette,* May 6, 13, 1731.

2. Actually July 14, 1730 (*Papers,* 1, 175), but Meredith's name remained on the *Gazette* until May 11, 1732.

soon to be sunk. The wealthy Inhabitants oppos'd any Addition, being against all Paper Currency, from an Apprehension that it would depreciate as it had done in New England to the Prejudice of all Creditors. We had discuss'd this Point in our Junto, where I was on the Side of an Addition, being persuaded that the first small Sum struck in 1723 had done much good, by increasing the Trade Employment, and Number of Inhabitants in the Province, since I now saw all the old Houses inhabited, and many new ones building, where as I remember'd well, that when I first walk'd about the Streets of Philadelphia, eating my Roll, I saw most of the Houses in Walnut street between Second and Front streets with Bills on their Doors, to be let; and many likewise in Chesnut Street, and other Streets; which made me then think the Inhabitants of the City were one after another deserting it. Our Debates possess'd me so fully of the Subject, that I wrote and printed an anonymous Pamphlet on it, entituled, *The Nature and Necessity of a Paper Currency.*[3] It was well receiv'd by the common People in general; but the Rich Men dislik'd it; for it increas'd and strengthen'd the Clamour for more Money; and they happening to have no Writers among them that were able to answer it, their Opposition slacken'd, and the Point was carried by a Majority in the House. My Friends there, who conceiv'd I had been of some Service, thought fit to reward me, by employing me in printing the Money, a very profitable Jobb, and a great Help to me.[4] This was another Advantage gain'd by my being able to write. The Utility of this Currency be-

3. A *Modest Enquiry into the Nature and Necessity of a Paper-Currency.* Franklin signed with the initials "B.B." and dated the pamphlet April 3, 1729; *Papers,* I, 139–57. At some points Franklin leaned heavily on Sir William Petty, *Treatise of Taxes and Contributions* (London, 1662).

4. Franklin's memory was in error here. Actually Andrew Bradford printed the £20,000 voted in 1729, but Franklin got the next contract, one for £40,000 in 1731. He was paid £100 plus the cost of the paper.

came by Time and Experience so evident, as never afterwards to be much disputed, so that it grew soon to £55000, and in 1739 to £80,000 since which it arose during War to upwards of £350,000. Trade, Building and Inhabitants all the while increasing. Tho' I now think there are Limits beyond which the Quantity may be hurtful.

I soon after obtain'd, thro' my Friend Hamilton, the Printing of the New Castle Paper Money, another profitable Jobb, as I then thought it; small Things appearing great to those in small Circumstances.[5] And these to me were really great Advantages, as they were great Encouragements. He procured me also the Printing of the Laws and Votes of that Government which continu'd in my Hands as long as I follow'd the Business.[6]

I now open'd a little Stationer's Shop. I had in it Blanks of all Sorts the correctest that ever appear'd among us, being assisted in that by my Friend Brientnal; I had also Paper, Parchment, Chapmen's Books, &c.[7] One Whitemash a Compositor I had known in London, an excellent Workman now came to me and work'd with me constantly and diligently, and I took an Apprentice the Son of Aquila Rose. I began now gradually to pay off the Debt I was under for the Printing-House. In order to secure my Credit and Character as a Tradesman, I took care not only to be in *Reality* Industrious and frugal, but to avoid all *Appearances* of the Contrary. I drest plainly; I was seen at no Places of idle Diversion; I

5. "The Counties of New-Castle, Kent, and Sussex on Delaware" (now the State of Delaware) had the same proprietary governor as Pennsylvania but a separate legislature. Andrew Hamilton was speaker of both Assemblies.

6. Franklin began printing the annual acts of the Delaware Assembly in 1734 and published the collected laws in 1741. The earliest entry found in his accounts for the printing of "New Castle Paper Money" appears to be that for the issue of 1739, though he may also have printed the issues of 1729 and 1734.

7. Franklin's earliest surviving account books suggest that he opened this shop about July 1730.

never went out a-fishing or shooting; a Book, indeed, sometimes debauch'd me from my Work; but that was seldom, snug, and gave no Scandal: and to show that I was not above my Business, I sometimes brought home the Paper I purchas'd at the Stores, thro' the Streets on a Wheelbarrow. Thus being esteem'd an industrious thriving young Man, and paying duly for what I bought, the Merchants who imported Stationary solicited my Custom, others propos'd supplying me with Books, and I went on swimmingly. In the mean time Keimer's Credit and Business declining daily, he was at last forc'd to sell his Printing-house to satisfy his Creditors. He went to Barbadoes, and there lived some Years, in very poor Circumstances.

His Apprentice David Harry, whom I had instructed while I work'd with him, set up in his Place at Philadelphia, having bought his Materials. I was at first apprehensive of a powerful Rival in Harry, as his Friends were very able, and had a good deal of Interest. I therefore propos'd a Partnership to him; which he, fortunately for me, rejected with Scorn. He was very proud, dress'd like a Gentleman, liv'd expensively, took much Diversion and Pleasure abroad, ran in debt, and neglected his Business, upon which all Business left him; and finding nothing to do, he follow'd Keimer to Barbadoes; taking the Printinghouse with him. There this Apprentice employ'd his former Master as a Journeyman. They quarrel'd often. Harry went continually behindhand, and at length was forc'd to sell his Types, and return to his Country Work in Pensilvania. The Person that bought them, employ'd Keimer to use them, but in a few years he died. There remain'd now no Competitor with me at Philadelphia, but the old one, Bradford, who was rich and easy, did a little Printing now and then by straggling Hands, but was not very anxious about the Business. However, as he kept the Post Office, it was imagined he had better Opportunities of obtaining News, his Paper was thought a better Distributer of Advertisements than mine, and therefore had many more, which was a profitable thing to him and a Disadvantage to me. For tho' I did indeed receive and send Papers by Post, yet the publick Opinion was otherwise; for what I did send was by Bribing the Riders who took them privately: Bradford being unkind enough to forbid it: which occasion'd some Resentment on my Part; and I thought so meanly of him for it, that when I afterwards came into his Situation, I took care never to imitate it.

I had hitherto continu'd to board with Godfrey who lived in Part of my House with his Wife and Children, and had one Side of the Shop for his Glazier's Business, tho' he work'd little, being always absorb'd in his Mathematics.[8] Mrs. Godfrey projected a Match for me with a Relation's Daughter, took Opportunities of bringing us often together, till a serious Courtship on my Part ensu'd, the Girl being in herself very deserving.[9] The old Folks encourag'd me by continual Invitations to Supper, and by leaving us together, till at length it was time to explain. Mrs. Godfrey manag'd our little Treaty. I let her know that I expected as much Money with their Daughter as would pay off my Remaining Debt for the Printinghouse, which I believe was not then above a Hundred Pounds. She brought me Word they had no such Sum to spare. I said they might mortgage their House in the Loan Office. The Answer to this after some Days was, that they did not approve the Match; that on Enquiry of Bradford they had been inform'd the Printing Business was not a profitable one, the Types would soon be worn out and more wanted, that S. Keimer and D. Harry had fail'd one after the other, and I should probably soon follow them; and therefore I was forbidden the House, and the Daughter shut up. Whether this was a real Change of Sentiment, or only Artifice,

8. At this time Godfrey was developing his quadrant.
9. The girl's name is unknown.

on a Supposition of our being too far engag'd in Affection to retract, and therefore that we should steal a Marriage, which would leave them at Liberty to give or withold what they pleas'd, I know not: But I suspected the latter, resented it, and went no more. Mrs. Godfrey brought me afterwards some more favourable Accounts of their Disposition, and would have drawn me on again: but I declared absolutely my Resolution to have nothing more to do with that Family.[1] This was resented by the Godfreys, we differ'd, and they removed, leaving me the whole House, and I resolved to take no more Inmates.

But this Affair having turn'd my Thoughts to Marriage, I look'd round me, and made Overtures of Acquaintance in other Places; but soon found that the Business of a Printer being generally thought a poor one, I was not to expect Money with a Wife unless with such a one, as I should not otherwise think agreable. In the mean time, that hard-to-be-govern'd Passion of Youth, had hurried me frequently into Intrigues with low Women that fell in my Way, which were attended with some Expence and great Inconvenience, besides a continual Risque to my Health by a Distemper which of all Things I dreaded, tho' by great good Luck I escaped it.

A friendly Correspondence as Neighbours and old Acquaintances, had continued between me and Mrs. Read's Family,[2] who all

1. According to the customs of the day, marriages were often arranged in which financial considerations were more important than romantic affection, if the parties seemed to each other and their families adequately "deserving." Franklin's expectation of a monetary settlement as part of the proposed "Treaty" was by no means unusual.

2. Crossed out: "Her youngest Daughter had married my Friend Watson (early mentioned in this Relation) and had some Regard for me on his Account." This was probably Frances Read, who, following Watson's death, married John Croker about 1729.

had a Regard for me from the time of my first Lodging in their House. I was often invited there and consulted in their Affairs, wherein I sometimes was of service. I pity'd poor Miss Read's unfortunate Situation, who was generally dejected, seldom chearful, and avoided Company. I consider'd my Giddiness and Inconstancy when in London as in a great degree the Cause of her Unhappiness; tho' the Mother was good enough to think the Fault more her own than mine, as she had prevented our Marrying before I went thither, and persuaded the other Match in my Absence. Our mutual Affection was revived, but there were now great Objections to our Union. That Match was indeed look'd upon as invalid, a preceding Wife being said to be living in England; but this could not easily be prov'd, because of the Distance. And tho' there was a Report of his Death, it was not certain. Then tho' it should be true, he had left many Debts which his Successor might be call'd on to pay. We ventured however, over all these Difficulties, and I [took] her to Wife Sept. 1. 1730. None of the Inconveniencies happened that we had apprehended, she prov'd a good and faithful Helpmate, assisted me much by attending the Shop, we throve together, and have ever mutually endeavour'd to make each other happy. Thus I corrected that great *Erratum* as well as I could.[3]

3. In the absence of full proof that John Rogers had a "preceding Wife" in England, Deborah could not get her marriage to him legally annulled, and Pennsylvania had no law under which she could have divorced him. On the other hand, quite apart from the matter of Rogers' debts, if she and Franklin had gone through the marriage ceremony prescribed by Pennsylvania law and Rogers had later reappeared, both Deborah and Benjamin could have been convicted of bigamy and punished by whipping with thirty-nine lashes on the bare back and imprisonment at hard labor for life. The difficulties in their situation were fully recognized; Deborah's family and all friends and acquaintances thereafter accepted this informal "common-law" marriage as adequate, and the two children she is known to have borne him were regarded as legitimate.

About this Time our Club meeting, not at a Tavern, but in a little Room of Mr. Grace's set apart for that Purpose;[4] a Proposition was made by me that since our Books were often referr'd to in our Disquisitions upon the Queries, it might be convenient to us to have them all together where we met, that upon Occasion they might be consulted; and by thus clubbing our Books to a common Library, we should, while we lik'd to keep them together, have each of us the Advantage of using the Books of all the other Members, which would be nearly as beneficial as if each owned the whole. It was lik'd and agreed to, and we fill'd one End of the Room with such Books as we could best spare. The Number was not so great as we expected; and tho' they had been of great Use, yet some Inconveniencies occurring for want of due Care of them, the Collection after about a Year was separated, and each took his Books home again.

And now I set on foot my first Project of a public Nature, that for a Subscription Library. I drew up the Proposals, got them put into Form by our great Scrivener Brockden, and by the help of my Friends in the Junto, procur'd Fifty Subscribers of 40*s*. each to begin with and 10*s*. a Year for 50 Years, the Term our Company was to continue. We afterwards obtain'd a Charter, the Company being increas'd to 100. This was the Mother of all the N American Subscription Libraries now so numerous.[5] It is become a great thing itself, and continually increasing. These Libraries have im-

4. Grace's house (to which Franklin moved in 1739) stood on the lot that is now 131 Market Street. The Junto room was probably in a small building at the rear of the property reached from Pewter Platter Alley.

5. The Library Company of Philadelphia—still an active and distinguished institution—was indeed the first *subscription* library in North America, though there were a good many public or semi-public collections of books long before 1731, most of them very small and usually established under religious auspices.

prov'd the general Conversation of the Americans, made the common Tradesmen and Farmers as intelligent as most Gentlemen from other Countries, and perhaps have contributed in some degree to the Stand so generally made throughout the Colonies in Defence of their Privileges.[6]

6. At this point Franklin added a memorandum: "My Manner of acting to engage People in this and future Undertakings." Apparently he intended to take up this topic next. When he resumed writing in 1784 he wrote a paragraph on it at the end of his enlarged account of the founding of the Library Company.

Two Letters

Memo.

Thus far was written with the Intention express'd in the Beginning and therefore contains several little family Anecdotes of no Importance to others. What follows was written many Years after in compliance with the Advice contain'd in these Letters, and accordingly intended for the Publick. The Affairs of the Revolution occasion'd the Interruption.

Letter from Mr. Abel James with Notes of my Life, to be here inserted. Also

Letter from Mr. Vaughan to the same purpose[1]

My dear and honored Friend.[2]

I have often been desirous of writing to thee, but could not be reconciled to the Thoughts that the Letter might fall into the Hands of the British, lest some Printer or busy Body should publish some Part of the Contents and give our Friends Pain and myself Censure.

1. Neither of these letters is in the manuscript, but part of the one from James and apparently all of that from Vaughan are in both the Temple Franklin edition and the Le Veillard translation and indicate thereby what Franklin intended to include. Before leaving France Franklin seems to have given Le Veillard copies of the whole James letter and of the outline of the autobiography James had sent him; Le Veillard apparently lent these to Thomas Jefferson in 1786; and William Short, his secretary, made copies which are now in the Jefferson Papers at the Library of Congress. Julian P. Boyd et al., eds., *The Papers of Thomas Jefferson,* IX (Princeton, 1954), 483–95. For several reasons Short's copy of the James letter appears more accurate than Temple Franklin's text, so it is used here, but omitting, as Temple and Le Veillard had done, the last half referring chiefly to James's business interests. The Vaughan letter is reprinted from the Temple Franklin edition.

2. The surviving copies of this letter are undated, but it was almost certainly written in 1782.

Some Time since there fell into my Hands to my great Joy about 23 Sheets in thy own hand-writing containing an Account of the Parentage and Life of thyself, directed to thy Son ending in the Year 1730 with which there were Notes likewise in thy writing,[3] a Copy of which I inclose in Hopes it may be a means if thou continuedst it up to a later period, that the first and latter part may be put together, and if it is not yet continued, I hope thou wilt not delay it, Life is uncertain as the Preacher tells us, and what will the World say if kind, humane and benevolent Ben Franklin should leave his Friends and the World deprived of so pleasing and profitable a Work, a Work which would be useful and entertaining not only to a few, but to millions.

The Influence Writings under that Class have on the Minds of Youth is very great, and has no where appeared so plain as in our public Friend's Journal. It almost insensibly leads the Youth into the Resolution of endeavouring to become as good and as eminent as the Journalist. Should thine for Instance when published, and I think it could not fail of it, lead the Youth to equal the Industry and Temperance of thy early Youth, what a Blessing with that Class would such a Work be. I know of no Character living nor many of them put together, who has so much in his Power as Thyself to promote a greater Spirit of Industry and early Attention to Business, Frugality and Temperance with the American Youth. Not that I think the Work would have no other Merit and Use in the World, far from it, but the first is of such vast Importance, that I know nothing that can equal it. . . . ABEL JAMES

The foregoing letter and the minutes accompanying it being shewn to a friend, I received from him the following:[4]

3. Franklin's outline of the autobiography, printed below, pp. 267–72.

4. This sentence is taken from the Temple Franklin edition; Le Veillard's manuscript also includes a translation.

Benjamin Franklin

Paris, January 31, 1783.

My dearest sir,

When I had read over your sheets of minutes of the principal incidents of your life, recovered for you by your Quaker acquaintance; I told you I would send you a letter expressing my reasons why I thought it would be useful to complete and publish it as he desired. Various concerns have for some time past prevented this letter being written, and I do not know whether it was worth any expectation: happening to be at leisure however at present, I shall by writing at least interest and instruct myself; but as the terms I am inclined to use may tend to offend a person of your manners, I shall only tell you how I would address any other person, who was as good and as great as yourself, but less diffident. I would say to him, Sir, I *solicit* the history of your life from the following motives.

Your history is so remarkable, that if you do not give it, somebody else will certainly give it; and perhaps so as nearly to do as much harm, as your own management of the thing might do good.

It will moreover present a table of the internal circumstances of your country, which will very much tend to invite to it settlers of virtuous and manly minds. And considering the eagerness with which such information is sought by them, and the extent of your reputation, I do not know of a more efficacious advertisement than your Biography would give.

All that has happened to you is also connected with the detail of the manners and situation of *a rising* people; and in this respect I do not think that the writings of Caesar and Tacitus can be more interesting to a true judge of human nature and society.

But these, Sir, are small reasons in my opinion, compared with the chance which your life will give for the forming of future great men; and in conjunction with your Art of Virtue, (which you design to publish) of improving the features of private character, and consequently of aiding all happiness both public and domestic.

The two works I allude to, Sir, will in particular give a noble rule and example of *self-education.* School and other education constantly proceed upon false principles, and shew a clumsy apparatus pointed at a false mark; but your apparatus is simple, and the mark a true one; and while parents and young persons are left destitute of other just means of estimating and becoming prepared for a reasonable course in life, your discovery that the thing is in many a man's private power, will be invaluable!

Influence upon the private character late in life, is not only an influence late in life, but a weak influence. It is in *youth* that we plant our chief habits and prejudices; it is in youth that we take our party as to profession, pursuits, and matrimony. In youth therefore the turn is given; in youth the education even of the next generation is given; in youth the private and public character is determined; and the term of life extending but from youth to age, life ought to begin well from youth; and more especially *before* we take our party as to our principal objects.

But your Biography will not merely teach self-education, but the education of *a wise man;* and the wisest man will receive lights and improve his progress, by seeing detailed the conduct of another wise man. And why are weaker men to be deprived of such helps, when we see our race has been blundering on in the dark, almost without a guide in this particular, from the farthest trace of time? Shew then, Sir, how much is to be done, *both to sons and fathers;* and invite all wise men to become like yourself; and other men to become wise.

When we see how cruel statesmen and warriors can be to the humble race, and how absurd distinguished men can be to their acquaintance, it will be instructive to observe the instances multiply of pacific acquiescing manners; and to find how compatible it is to be great and *domestic;* enviable and yet *good-humored.*

The little private incidents which you will also have to relate, will have considerable use, as we want above all things, *rules of pru-*

dence in ordinary affairs; and it will be curious to see how you have acted in these. It will be so far a sort of key to life, and explain many things that all men ought to have once explained to them, to give them a chance of becoming wise by foresight.

The nearest thing to having experience of one's own, is to have other people's affairs brought before us in a shape that is interesting; this is sure to happen from your pen. Your affairs and management will have an air of simplicity or importance that will not fail to strike; and I am convinced you have conducted them with as much originality as if you had been conducting discussions in politics or philosophy; and what more worthy of experiments and system, (its importance and its errors considered) than human life!

Some men have been virtuous blindly, others have speculated fantastically, and others have been shrewd to bad purposes; but you, Sir, I am sure, will give under your hand, nothing but what is at the same moment, wise, practical, and good.

Your account of yourself (for I suppose the parallel I am drawing for Dr. Franklin, will hold not only in point of character but of private history), will shew that you are ashamed of no origin; a thing the more important, as you prove how little necessary all origin is to happiness, virtue, or greatness.

As no end likewise happens without a means, so we shall find, Sir, that even you yourself framed a plan by which you became considerable; but at the same time we may see that though the event is flattering, the means are as simple as wisdom could make them; that is, depending upon nature, virtue, thought, and habit.

Another thing demonstrated will be the propriety of every man's waiting for his time for appearing upon the stage of the world. Our sensations being very much fixed to the moment, we are apt to forget that more moments are to follow the first, and consequently that man should arrange his conduct so as to suit the *whole* of a life. Your attribution appears to have been applied to your *life*, and the passing moments of it have been enlivened with content and enjoyment, instead of being tormented with foolish impatience or regrets. Such a conduct is easy for those who make virtue and themselves their standard, and who try to keep themselves in countenance by examples of other truly great men, of whom patience is so often the characteristic.

Your Quaker correspondent, Sir, (for here again I will suppose the subject of my letter resembling Dr. Franklin,) praised your frugality, diligence, and temperance, which he considered as a pattern for all youth: but it is singular that he should have forgotten your modesty, and your disinterestedness, without which you never could have waited for your advancement, or found your situation in the mean time comfortable; which is a strong lesson to shew the poverty of glory, and the importance of regulating our minds.

If this correspondent had known the nature of your reputation as well as I do, he would have said; your former writings and measures would secure attention to your Biography and Art of Virtue; and your Biography and Art of Virtue, in return, would secure attention to them. This is an advantage attendant upon a various character, and which brings all that belongs to it into greater play; and it is the more useful, as perhaps more persons are at a loss for the *means* of improving their minds and characters, than they are for the time or the inclination to do it.

But there is one concluding reflection, Sir, that will shew the use of your life as a mere piece of biography. This style of writing seems a little gone out of vogue, and yet it is a very useful one; and your specimen of it may be particularly serviceable, as it will make a subject of comparison with the lives of various public cutthroats and intriguers, and with absurd monastic self-tormentors, or vain literary triflers. If it encourages more writings of the same kind with your own, and induces more men to spend lives fit to be written; it will be worth all Plutarch's Lives put together.

But being tired of figuring to myself a character of which every feature suits only one man in the world, without giving him the praise of it; I shall end my letter, my dear Dr. Franklin, with a personal application to your proper self.

I am earnestly desirous then, my dear Sir, that you should let the world into the traits of your genuine character, as civil broils may otherwise tend to disguise or traduce it. Considering your great age, the caution of your character, and your peculiar style of thinking, it is not likely that any one besides yourself can be sufficiently master of the facts of your life, or the intentions of your mind.

Besides all this, the immense revolution of the present period, will necessarily turn our attention towards the author of it; and when virtuous principles have been pretended in it, it will be highly important to shew that such have really influenced; and, as your own character will be the principal one to receive a scrutiny, it is proper (even for its effects upon your vast and rising country, as well as upon England and upon Europe), that it should stand respectable and eternal. For the furtherance of human happiness, I have always maintained that it is necessary to prove that man is not even at present a vicious and detestable animal; and still more to prove that good management may greatly amend him; and it is for much the same reason, that I am anxious to see the opinion established, that there are fair characters existing among the individuals of the race; for the moment that all men, without exception, shall be conceived abandoned, good people will cease efforts deemed to be hopeless, and perhaps think of taking their share in the scramble of life, or at least of making it comfortable principally for themselves.

Take then, my dear Sir, this work most speedily into hand: shew yourself good as you are good, temperate as you are temperate; and above all things, prove yourself as one who from your infancy have loved justice, liberty, and concord, in a way that has made it natural and consistent for you to have acted, as we have seen you act in the last seventeen years of your life. Let Englishmen be made not only to respect, but even to love you. When they think well of individuals in your native country, they will go nearer to thinking well of your country; and when your countrymen see themselves well thought of by Englishmen, they will go nearer to thinking well of England. Extend your views even further; do not stop at those who speak the English tongue, but after having settled so many points in nature and politics, think of bettering the whole race of men.

As I have not read any part of the life in question, but know only the character that lived it, I write somewhat at hazard. I am sure however, that the life, and the treatise I allude to (on the Art of Virtue), will necessarily fulfil the chief of my expectations; and still more so if you take up the measure of suiting these performances to the several views above stated. Should they even prove unsuccessful in all that a sanguine admirer of yours hopes from them, you will at least have framed pieces to interest the human mind; and whoever gives a feeling of pleasure that is innocent to man, has added so much to the fair side of a life otherwise too much darkened by anxiety, and too much injured by pain.

In the hope therefore that you will listen to the prayer addressed to you in this letter, I beg to subscribe myself, my dearest Sir, &c. &c. BENJ. VAUGHAN.

Part Two

Continuation of the Account of my Life. Begun at Passy 1784

It is some time since I receiv'd the above Letters, but I have been too busy till now to think of complying with the Request they contain. It might too be much better done if I were at home among my Papers, which would aid my Memory and help to ascertain Dates. But my Return being uncertain, and having just now a little Leisure,[1] I will endeavour to recollect and write what I can; if I live to get home, it may there be corrected and improv'd.

Not having any Copy here of what is already written, I know not whether an Account is given of the means I used to establish the Philadelphia publick Library, which from a small Beginning is now become so considerable, though I remember to have come down to near the Time of that Transaction, 1730. I will therefore begin here, with an Account of it, which may be struck out if found to have been already given.

At the time I establish'd my self in Pensylvania, there was not a good Bookseller's Shop in any of the Colonies to the Southward of Boston. In New-York and Philadelphia the Printers were indeed Stationers, they sold only Paper, &c., Almanacks, Ballads, and a few common School Books. Those who lov'd Reading were oblig'd to send for their Books from England. The Members of the Junto had each a few. We had left the Alehouse where we first met, and hired a Room to hold our Club in. I propos'd that we should all of us bring our Books to that Room, where they would not only be

1. The definitive Treaty of Peace with Great Britain was signed in Paris, Sept. 3, 1783. Franklin asked Congress for permission to come home, but he remained as minister until Thomas Jefferson succeeded him in May 1785. He left Paris for America that July. At the time he wrote this part of his autobiography he was seventy-eight years old.

ready to consult in our Conferences, but become a common Benefit, each of us being at Liberty to borrow such as he wish'd to read at home. This was accordingly done, and for some time contented us. Finding the Advantage of this little Collection, I propos'd to render the Benefit from Books more common by commencing a Public Subscription Library. I drew a Sketch of the Plan and Rules that would be necessary, and got a skilful Conveyancer, Mr. Charles Brockden to put the whole in Form of Articles of Agreement to be subscribed; by which each Subscriber engag'd to pay a certain Sum down for the first Purchase of Books and an annual Contribution for encreasing them. So few were the Readers at that time in Philadelphia, and the Majority of us so poor, that I was not able with great Industry to find more than Fifty Persons, mostly young Tradesmen, willing to pay down for this purpose Forty shillings each, and Ten Shillings per Annum. On this little Fund we began. The Books were imported.[2] The Library was open one Day in the Week for lending them to the Subscribers, on their Promisory Notes to pay Double the Value if not duly returned. The Institution soon manifested its Utility, was imitated by other Towns and in other Provinces, the Librarys were augmented by Donations, Reading became fashionable, and our People having no publick Amusements to divert their Attention from Study became better acquainted with Books, and in a few Years were observ'd by Strangers to be better instructed and more intelligent than People of the same Rank generally are in other Countries.

When we were about to sign the above-mentioned Articles, which were to be binding on us, our Heirs, &c. for fifty Years, Mr Brockden, the Scrivener, said to us, "You are young Men, but

2. The list of books in the first order sent to England, March 31, 1732, comprising some forty-five titles, is printed in *Pennsylvania Magazine of History* and *Biography*, XXX (1906), 300–1.

it is scarce probable that any of you will live to see the Expiration of the Term fix'd in this Instrument." A Number of us, however, are yet living: But the Instrument was after a few Years rendered null by a Charter that incorporated and gave Perpetuity to the Company.[3]

The Objections, and Reluctances I met with in Soliciting the Subscriptions, made me soon feel the Impropriety of presenting one's self as the Proposer of any useful Project that might be suppos'd to raise one's Reputation in the smallest degree above that of one's Neighbours, when one has need of their Assistance to accomplish that Project. I therefore put my self as much as I could out of sight, and stated it as a Scheme of a *Number of Friends,* who had requested me to go about and propose it to such as they thought Lovers of Reading. In this way my Affair went on more smoothly, and I ever after practis'd it on such Occasions; and from my frequent Successes, can heartily recommend it. The present little Sacrifice of your Vanity will afterwards be amply repaid. If it remains a while uncertain to whom the Merit belongs, some one more vain than yourself will be encourag'd to claim it, and then even Envy will be dispos'd to do you Justice, by plucking those assum'd Feathers, and restoring them to their right Owner.

This Library afforded me the means of Improvement by constant Study, for which I set apart an Hour or two each Day; and thus repair'd in some Degree the Loss of the Learned Education my Father once intended for me. Reading was the only Amusement I allow'd my self. I spent no time in Taverns, Games, or Frolicks of any kind. And my Industry in my Business continu'd as indefatigable as it was necessary. I was in debt for my Printing-

3. Gov. George Thomas signed the charter on behalf of the Proprietors, March 25, 1742. Fifty-three members signed the formal acceptance on the following May 3. *Papers,* II, 345–8.

house, I had a young Family coming on to be educated,[4] and I had to contend with for Business two Printers who were establish'd in the Place before me. My Circumstances however grew daily easier: my original Habits of Frugality continuing. And my Father having among his Instructions to me when a Boy, frequently repeated a Proverb of Solomon, "*Seest thou a Man diligent in his Calling, he shall stand before Kings, he shall not stand before mean Men.*"[5] I from thence consider'd Industry as a Means of obtaining Wealth and Distinction, which encourag'd me, tho' I did not think that I should ever literally stand before Kings, which however has since happened.—for I have stood before five, and even had the honour of sitting down with one, the King of Denmark, to Dinner.[6]

We have an English Proverb that says,

He that would thrive
Must ask his Wife;

4. Franklin's children were: William, called by his family and close friends "Billy," born about 1731; Francis Folger, called "Frankie," born 1732, died 1736; and Sarah, called "Sally," born 1743. There are no direct descendants with the surname Franklin today. There are many in the United States with other surnames, descended through Sarah, who married Richard Bache in 1767. Direct descendants in England trace through William's granddaughter Ellen Franklin, who married Capel Hanbury in 1818.

5. Proverbs 22:29.

6. When King Christian VI of Denmark was in England in 1768, he invited Franklin and others to dine with him on October 1. Franklin's account of the dinner and diagram of the seating arrangements are in Carl Van Doren, ed., *The Letters of Benjamin Franklin and Jane Mecom* (Princeton, 1950), pp. 104–6, and facing p. 317. During a trip to France in 1767 he was presented to Louis XV and watched the royal family at a formal dinner. Louis XVI received him and the other American commissioners, March 20, 1778, soon after the signing of the Treaty of Alliance, and Franklin was present at court on several later occasions. The other two kings before whom he stood were probably George II and George III of Great Britain, but the occasions are not certain.

it was lucky for me that I had one as much dispos'd to Industry and Frugality as my self. She assisted me chearfully in my Business, folding and stitching Pamphlets, tending Shop, purchasing old Linen Rags for the Paper-makers, &c. &c.[7] We kept no idle Servants, our Table was plain and simple, our Furniture of the cheapest. For instance my Breakfast was a long time Bread and Milk, (no Tea) and I ate it out of a twopenny earthen Porringer with a Pewter Spoon. But mark how Luxury will enter Families, and make a Progress, in Spite of Principle. Being call'd one Morning to Breakfast, I found it in a China Bowl with a Spoon of Silver. They had been bought for me without my Knowledge by my Wife, and had cost her the enormous Sum of three and twenty Shillings, for which she had no other Excuse or Apology to make, but that she thought *her* Husband deserv'd a Silver Spoon and China Bowl as well as any of his Neighbours. This was the first Appearance of Plate and China in our House, which afterwards in a Course of Years as our Wealth encreas'd augmented gradually to several Hundred Pounds in Value.

I had been religiously educated as a Presbyterian;[8] and tho' some of the Dogmas of that Persuasion, such as the Eternal Decrees of God, Election, Reprobation, &c. appear'd to me unintelligible, others doubtful, and I early absented myself from the Public As-

7. Deborah Franklin carried efficiently a good deal of responsibility for tending her husband's stationery and bookshop and for handling other business when he was away from Philadelphia. The shop book in which she recorded many of the sales she made, usually on credit, 1735–39, is described in *Papers,* II, 127–8.

8. Strictly speaking, Franklin had been baptized and educated in what was coming to be called the Congregational Church, not the Presbyterian. Both had a common origin in the doctrines of John Calvin and by the beginning of the eighteenth century differed primarily only in their systems of church organization and government. Their similarities made it easy for a

semblies of the Sect, Sunday being my Studying-Day, I never was without some religious Principles; I never doubted, for instance, the Existance of the Deity, that he made the World, and govern'd it by his Providence; that the most acceptable Service of God was the doing Good to Man; that our Souls are immortal; and that all Crime will be punished and Virtue rewarded either here or hereafter;[9] these I esteem'd the Essentials of every Religion, and being to be found in all the Religions we had in our Country I respected them all, tho' with different degrees of Respect as I found them more or less mix'd with other Articles which without any Tendency to inspire, promote or confirm Morality, serv'd principally to divide us and make us unfriendly to one another. This Respect to all, with an Opinion that the worst had some good Effects, induc'd me to avoid all Discourse that might tend to lessen the good Opinion another might have of his own Religion; and as our Province increas'd in People and new Places of worship were continually wanted, and generally erected by voluntary Contribution, my Mite for such purpose, whatever might be the Sect, was never refused.[1]

---

person to change from one denomination to the other when, as was the case when Franklin went from Boston to Philadelphia, he moved to a new community which had no church of his original affiliation. Deborah Franklin was raised in the Church of England (the Episcopal Church in America today) and retained a life-long association with Christ Church, Philadelphia.

9. For a somewhat more formal statement of these beliefs, generally deistic in nature, which he wrote at about this time, see below, p. 162.

1. Franklin's respect for and tolerance of all religious groups was an important characteristic of the man, and the records bear out his statement of financial aid to all sects that asked him for it. The charge, made in 1934 by American Fascist sympathizers, renewed in the New York political campaign of 1938, and still occasionally repeated, that he was anti-Semitic and had delivered a speech against the Jews in the Federal Constitutional Convention of 1787, is based on a forgery and is utterly without historical founda-

Tho' I seldom attended any Public Worship, I had still an Opinion of its Propriety, and of its Utility when rightly conducted, and I regularly paid my annual Subscription for the Support of the only Presbyterian Minister or Meeting we had in Philadelphia.[2] He us'd to visit me sometimes as a Friend, and admonish me to attend his Administrations, and I was now and then prevail'd on to do so, once for five Sundays successively. Had he been, *in my Opinion,* a good Preacher perhaps I might have continued, notwithstanding the occasion I had for the Sunday's Leisure in my Course of Study: But his Discourses were chiefly either polemic Arguments, or Explications of the peculiar Doctrines of our Sect, and were all to me very dry, uninteresting and unedifying, since not a single moral Principle was inculcated or enforc'd, their Aim seeming to be rather to make us Presbyterians than good Citizens. At length he took for his Text that Verse of the 4th Chapter of Philippians, *Finally, Brethren, Whatsoever Things are true, honest, just, pure, lovely, or of good report, if there be any virtue, or any praise, think on these Things;*[3] and I imagin'd in a Sermon on such a Text, we could not miss of having some Morality: But he confin'd himself to five Points only as meant by the Apostle, viz. 1. Keeping holy the Sabbath Day. 2. Being diligent in Reading the Holy Scriptures. 3. Attending duly the Publick Worship. 4. Partaking of the Sacrament. 5. Paying a due Respect to God's Ministers. These might be all good Things, but as they were not the

tion. On the other hand, the archives of Congregation Mikveh Israel in Philadelphia contain a subscription paper dated April 30, 1788, in which Franklin, together with forty-four other citizens of all faiths, contributed towards relieving the Congregation's debt incurred in building a synagogue. Franklin's donation and those of two others are the largest on the list.

2. The Rev. Jedediah Andrews.

3. Phil. 4:8. Franklin apparently quoted from memory. The King James Version of the Bible, with which he was most familiar, differs slightly in this verse.

kind of good Things that I expected from that Text, I despaired of ever meeting with them from any other, was disgusted, and attended his Preaching no more. I had some Years before compos'd a little Liturgy or Form of Prayer for my own private Use, viz, in 1728. entitled, *Articles of Belief and Acts of Religion.*[4] I return'd to the Use of this, and went no more to the public Assemblies. My Conduct might be blameable, but I leave it without attempting farther to excuse it, my present purpose being to relate Facts, and not to make Apologies for them.

It was about this time that I conceiv'd the bold and arduous Project of arriving at moral Perfection.[5] I wish'd to live without committing any Fault at any time; I would conquer all that either Natural Inclination, Custom, or Company might lead me into. As I knew, or thought I knew, what was right and wrong, I did not see why I might not *always* do the one and avoid the other. But I soon found I had undertaken a Task of more Difficulty than I had imagined. While my *Attention was taken up* in guarding against one Fault, I was often surpriz'd by another. Habit took the Advantage of Inattention. Inclination was sometimes too strong for Reason. I concluded at length, that the mere speculative Conviction that it was our Interest to be compleatly virtuous, was not sufficient to prevent our Slipping, and that the contrary Habits must be broken and good ones acquired and established, before we can have any Dependance on a steady uniform Rectitude of Conduct. For this purpose I therefore contriv'd the following Method.

4. In two parts, of which only the first, in Franklin's own copy, survives. *Papers*, I, 101–8.

5. At this point Franklin begins to discuss the scheme for moral improvement which for many years he had planned to develop into a small book. By 1784 he probably realized he would never write such a separate work, so he compromised by introducing the main outlines of his plan into the autobiography here.

In the various Enumerations of the moral Virtues I had met with in my Reading, I found the Catalogue more or less numerous, as different Writers included more or fewer Ideas under the same Name. Temperance, for Example, was by some confin'd to Eating and Drinking, while by others it was extended to mean the moderating every other Pleasure, Appetite, Inclination or Passion, bodily or mental, even to our Avarice and Ambition. I propos'd to myself, for the sake of Clearness, to use rather more Names with fewer Ideas annex'd to each, than a few Names with more Ideas; and I included under Thirteen Names of Virtues all that at that time occurr'd to me as necessary or desirable, and annex'd to each a short Precept, which fully express'd the Extent I gave to its Meaning.

These Names of Virtues with their Precepts were

1. TEMPERANCE.

Eat not to Dulness.
Drink not to Elevation.

2. SILENCE.

Speak not but what may benefit others or yourself. Avoid trifling Conversation.

3. ORDER.

Let all your Things have their Places. Let each Part of your Business have its Time.

4. RESOLUTION.

Resolve to perform what you ought. Perform without fail what you resolve.

5. FRUGALITY.

Make no Expence but to do good to others or yourself: i.e. Waste nothing.

6. INDUSTRY.

Lose no Time. Be always employ'd in something useful. Cut off all unnecessary Actions.

7. Sincerity.

Use no hurtful Deceit.
Think innocently and justly; and, if you speak, speak accordingly.

8. Justice.

Wrong none, by doing Injuries or omitting the Benefits that are your Duty.

9. Moderation.

Avoid Extreams. Forbear resenting Injuries so much as you think they deserve.

10. Cleanliness

Tolerate no Uncleanness in Body, Cloaths or Habitation.

11. Tranquility

Be not disturbed at Trifles, or at Accidents common or unavoidable.

12. Chastity.

Rarely use Venery but for Health or Offspring; Never to Dulness, Weakness, or the Injury of your own or another's Peace or Reputation.

13. Humility.

Imitate Jesus and Socrates.

My Intention being to acquire the *Habitude* of all these Virtues, I judg'd it would be well not to distract my Attention by attempting the whole at once, but to fix it on one of them at a time, and when I should be Master of that, then to proceed to another, and so on till I should have gone thro' the thirteen. And as the previous Acquisition of some might facilitate the Acquisition of certain others, I arrang'd them with that View as they stand above. *Temperance* first, as it tends to procure that Coolness and Clearness of Head, which is so necessary where constant Vigilance was to be kept up, and Guard maintained, against the unremitting Attraction of ancient Habits, and the Force of perpetual Temptations. This being acquir'd and establish'd, *Silence* would be more easy, and my

Desire being to gain Knowledge at the same time that I improv'd in Virtue, and considering that in Conversation it was obtain'd rather by the use of the Ears than of the Tongue, and therefore wishing to break a Habit I was getting into of Prattling, Punning and Joking, which only made me acceptable to trifling Company, I gave *Silence* the second Place. This, and the next, *Order*, I expected would allow me more Time for attending to my Project and my Studies; RESOLUTION, once become habitual, would keep me firm in my Endeavours to obtain all the subsequent Virtues; *Frugality* and *Industry*, by freeing me from my remaining Debt, and producing Affluence and Independance, would make more easy the Practice of *Sincerity* and *Justice*, &c. &c. Conceiving then that agreable to the Advice of Pythagoras in his Golden Verses[6] daily Examination would be necessary, I contriv'd the following Method for conducting that Examination.

I made a little Book in which I allotted a Page for each of the Virtues. I rul'd each Page with red Ink, so as to have seven Columns, one for each Day of the Week, marking each Column with a Letter for the Day. I cross'd these Columns with thirteen red Lines, marking the Beginning of each Line with the first Letter of one of the Virtues, on which Line and in its proper Column I might mark by a little black Spot every Fault I found upon Examination to have been committed respecting that Virtue upon that Day.

I determined to give a Week's strict Attention to each of the Virtues successively. Thus in the first Week my great Guard was

6. A marginal note in the manuscript directed the insertion of the appropriate verses, which may be translated: "Let sleep not close your eyes till you have thrice examined the transactions of the day: where have I strayed, what have I done, what good have I omitted?" Available to Franklin were longer, poetic translations such as those of Nicholas Rowe or Isaac Watts.

to avoid every the least Offence against Temperance, leaving the other Virtues to their ordinary Chance, only marking every Evening the Faults of the Day. Thus if in the first Week I could keep my first Line marked T clear of Spots, I suppos'd the Habit of that Virtue so much strengthen'd and its opposite weaken'd, that I might venture extending my Attention to include the next, and for the following Week keep both Lines clear of Spots. Proceeding thus to the last, I could go thro' a Course compleat in Thirteen Weeks, and four Courses in a Year. And like him who having a Garden to weed, does not attempt to eradicate all the bad Herbs at once, which would exceed his Reach and his Strength, but works on one of the Beds at a time, and having accomplish'd the first proceeds to a Second; so I should have, (I hoped) the encouraging Pleasure of seeing on my Pages the Progress I made in Virtue, by clearing successively my Lines of their Spots, till in the End by a Number of Courses, I should be happy in viewing a clean Book after a thirteen Weeks daily Examination.

Form of the Pages

TEMPERANCE.

Eat not to Dulness.
Drink not to Elevation.

	S	M	T	W	T	F	S
T							
S	••	•		•		•	
O	•	•	•		•	•	•
R			•			•	
F		•			•		
I			•				
S							
J							
M							
Cl.							
T							
Ch.							
H							

This my little Book had for its Motto these Lines from Addison's *Cato;*

Here will I hold: If there is a Pow'r above us,
(And that there is, all Nature cries aloud
Thro' all her Works) he must delight in Virtue,
And that which he delights in must be happy.[7]

Another from Cicero.

O Vitæ Philosophia Dux! O Virtutum indagatrix, expultrixque vitiorum! Unus dies bene, et ex preceptis tuis actus, peccanti immortalitati est anteponendus.[8]

Another from the Proverbs of Solomon speaking of Wisdom or Virtue;

Length of Days is in her right hand, and in her Left Hand Riches and Honours; Her Ways are Ways of Pleasantness, and all her Paths are Peace. III, 16, 17.

And conceiving God to be the Fountain of Wisdom, I thought it right and necessary to solicit his Assistance for obtaining it; to this End I form'd the following little Prayer, which was prefix'd to my Tables of Examination; for daily Use.

O Powerful Goodness! bountiful Father! merciful Guide! Increase in me that Wisdom which discovers my truest Interests; Strengthen my Resolutions to perform what that Wisdom dictates. Accept my kind Offices to thy other Children, as the only Return in my Power for thy continual Favours to me.

7. Joseph Addison, *Cato, A Tragedy* (1713), V, i, 15–18.

8. *Tusculan Disputations*, V, ii, 5. Several lines of the original are omitted after *vitiorum*. "Oh philosophy, guide of life! Oh searcher out of virtues and expeller of vices! . . . One day lived well and according to thy precepts is to be preferred to an eternity of sin."

I us'd also sometimes a little Prayer which I took from Thomson's Poems. viz

Father of Light and Life, thou Good supreme,
O teach me what is good, teach me thy self!
Save me from Folly, Vanity and Vice,
From every low Pursuit, and fill my Soul
With Knowledge, conscious Peace, and Virtue pure,
Sacred, substantial, neverfading Bliss![9]

The Precept of *Order* requiring that *every Part of my Business should have its allotted Time,* one Page in my little Book contain'd the following Scheme of Employment for the Twenty-four Hours of a natural Day,

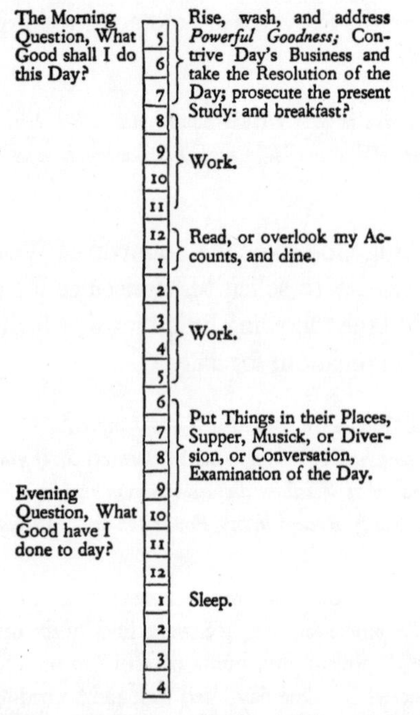

9. James Thomson, *The Seasons,* "Winter," lines 218–23.

I enter'd upon the Execution of this Plan for Self Examination, and continu'd it with occasional Intermissions for some time. I was surpriz'd to find myself so much fuller of Faults than I had imagined, but I had the Satisfaction of seeing them diminish. To avoid the Trouble of renewing now and then my little Book, which by scraping out the Marks on the Paper of old Faults to make room for new Ones in a new Course, became full of Holes: I transferr'd my Tables and Precepts to the Ivory Leaves of a Memorandum Book, on which the Lines were drawn with red Ink that made a durable Stain, and on those Lines I mark'd my Faults with a black Lead Pencil, which Marks I could easily wipe out with a wet Sponge. After a while I went thro' one Course only in a Year, and afterwards only one in several Years, till at length I omitted them entirely, being employ'd in Voyages and Business abroad with a Multiplicity of Affairs, that interfered, but I always carried my little Book with me.

My Scheme of ORDER, gave me the most Trouble, and I found, that tho' it might be practicable where a Man's Business was such as to leave him the Disposition of his Time, that of a Journey-man Printer for instance, it was not possible to be exactly observ'd by a Master, who must mix with the World, and often receive People of Business at their own Hours. *Order* too, with regard to Places for Things, Papers, &c. I found extreamly difficult to acquire. I had not been early accustomed to *Method*, and having an exceeding good Memory, I was not so sensible of the Inconvenience attending Want of Method. This Article therefore cost me so much painful Attention and my Faults in it vex'd me so much, and I made so little Progress in Amendment, and had such frequent Relapses, that I was almost ready to give up the Attempt, and content my self with a faulty Character in that respect. Like the Man who in buying an Ax of a Smith my neighbour, desired to have the whole of its Surface as bright as the Edge; the Smith consented to grind it bright for him if he would turn the Wheel. He turn'd while the Smith press'd the broad Face of the Ax hard and heavily on the Stone, which made the Turning of it very fatiguing. The Man came every now and then from the Wheel to see how the Work went on; and at length would take his Ax as it was without farther Grinding. No, says the Smith, Turn on, turn on; we shall have it bright by and by; as yet 'tis only speckled. Yes, says the Man; but—*I think I like a speckled Ax best.* And I believe this may have been the Case with many who having for want of some such Means as I employ'd found the Difficulty of obtaining good, and breaking bad Habits, in other Points of Vice and Virtue, have given up the Struggle, and concluded that *a speckled Ax was best.* For something that pretended to be Reason was every now and then suggesting to me, that such extream Nicety as I exacted of my self might be a kind of Foppery in Morals, which if it were known would make me ridiculous; that a perfect Character might be attended with the Inconvenience of being envied and hated; and that a benevolent Man should allow a few Faults in himself, to keep his Friends in Countenance.

In Truth I found myself incorrigible with respect to *Order;* and now I am grown old, and my Memory bad, I feel very sensibly the want of it.[1] But on the whole, tho' I never arrived at the Perfection I had been so ambitious of obtaining, but fell far short of it, yet I was by the Endeavour a better and a happier Man than I otherwise should have been, if I had not attempted it; As those who aim at perfect Writing by imitating the engraved Copies, tho' they never reach the wish'd for Excellence of those Copies, their Hand is mended by the Endeavour, and is tolerable while it continues fair and legible.

1. When John Adams joined Franklin in the diplomatic mission to France, 1778, he complained repeatedly of the disorderly way the older man had been keeping his official records. Lyman H. Butterfield et al., eds., *Diary and Autobiography of John Adams,* IV, 77, 88, 111.

And it may be well my Posterity should be informed, that to this little Artifice, with the Blessing of God, their Ancestor ow'd the constant Felicity of his Life down to his 79th Year in which this is written. What Reverses may attend the Remainder is in the Hand of Providence: But if they arrive the Reflection on past Happiness enjoy'd ought to help his Bearing them with more Resignation. To *Temperance* he ascribes his long-continu'd Health, and what is still left to him of a good Constitution. To *Industry* and *Frugality* the early Easiness of his Circumstances, and Acquisition of his Fortune, with all that Knowledge which enabled him to be an useful Citizen, and obtain'd for him some Degree of Reputation among the Learned. To *Sincerity* and *Justice* the Confidence of his Country, and the honourable Employs it conferr'd upon him. And to the joint Influence of the whole Mass of the Virtues, even in the imperfect State he was able to acquire them, all that Evenness of Temper, and that Chearfulness in Conversation which makes his Company still sought for, and agreable even to his younger Acquaintance. I hope therefore that some of my Descendants may follow the Example and reap the Benefit.

It will be remark'd that, tho' my Scheme was not wholly without Religion there was in it no Mark of any of the distinguishing Tenets of any particular Sect. I had purposely avoided them; for being fully persuaded of the Utility and Excellency of my Method, and that it might be serviceable to People in all Religions, and intending some time or other to publish it, I would not have any thing in it that should prejudice any one of any Sect against it. I purposed writing a little Comment on each Virtue, in which I would have shown the Advantages of possessing it, and the Mischiefs attending its opposite Vice; and I should have called my Book the ART *of Virtue*, because it would have shown the *Means* and *Manner* of obtaining Virtue, which would have distinguish'd it from the mere Exhortation to be good, that does not instruct and indicate the Means; but is like the Apostle's Man of verbal Charity, who only, without showing to the Naked and the Hungry *how* or where they might get Cloaths or Victuals, exhorted them to be fed and clothed. *James* II, 15, 16.[2]

But it so happened that my Intention of writing and publishing this Comment was never fulfilled. I did indeed, from time to time put down short Hints of the Sentiments, Reasonings, &c. to be made use of in it; some of which I have still by me: But the necessary close Attention to private Business in the earlier part of Life, and public Business since, have occasioned my postponing it. For it being connected in my Mind with a *great and extensive Project* that required the whole Man to execute, and which an unforeseen Succession of Employs prevented my attending to, it has hitherto remain'd unfinish'd.

In this Piece it was my Design to explain and enforce this Doctrine, that vicious Actions are not hurtful because they are forbidden, but forbidden because they are hurtful, the Nature of Man alone consider'd: That it was therefore every one's Interest to be virtuous, who wish'd to be happy even in this World. And I should from this Circumstance, there being always in the World a Number of rich Merchants, Nobility, States and Princes, who have need of honest Instruments for the Management of their Affairs, and such being so rare have endeavoured to convince young Persons, that no Qualities were so likely to make a poor Man's Fortune as those of Probity and Integrity.

My List of Virtues contain'd at first but twelve: But a Quaker Friend having kindly inform'd me that I was generally thought proud; that my Pride show'd itself frequently in Conversation;

2. "15. If a brother or sister be naked, and destitute of daily food, 16. And one of you say unto them, Depart in peace, be ye warmed and filled; notwithstanding ye give them not those things which are needful to the body; what doth it profit?"

that I was not content with being in the right when discussing any Point, but was overbearing and rather insolent; of which he convinc'd me by mentioning several Instances; I determined endeavouring to cure myself if I could of this Vice or Folly among the rest, and I added *Humility* to my List, giving an extensive Meaning to the Word. I cannot boast of much Success in acquiring the *Reality* of this Virtue; but I had a good deal with regard to the *Appearance* of it. I made it a Rule to forbear all direct Contradiction to the Sentiments of others, and all positive Assertion of my own. I even forbid myself agreable to the old Laws of our Junto, the Use of every Word or Expression in the Language that imported a fix'd Opinion; such as *certainly, undoubtedly,* &c. and I adopted instead of them, *I conceive, I apprehend,* or *I imagine* a thing to be so or so, or it so appears to me at present.[3] When another asserted something, that I thought an Error, I deny'd my self the Pleasure of contradicting him abruptly, and of showing immediately some Absurdity in his Proposition; and in answering I began by observing that in certain Cases or Circumstances his Opinion would be right, but that in the present case there *appear'd* or *seem'd* to me some Difference, &c. I soon found the Advantage of this Change in my Manners. The Conversations I engag'd in went on more pleasantly. The modest way in which I propos'd my Opinions, procur'd them a readier Reception and less Contradiction; I had less Mortification when I was found to be in the wrong, and I more easily prevail'd with others to give up their Mistakes and join with me when I happen'd to be in the right. And this Mode, which I at first put on, with some violence to natural Inclination, became at length so easy and so habitual to me, that perhaps for these Fifty Years past no one has ever heard a dogmatical Expression escape

3. Here Franklin repeats and underscores the point he had made earlier about the desirability of expressing one's views "in Terms of Modest Diffidence." See above, pp. 65–6.

me. And to this Habit (after my Character of Integrity) I think it principally owing, that I had early so much Weight with my Fellow Citizens, when I proposed new Institutions, or Alterations in the old; and so much Influence in public Councils when I became a Member. For I was but a bad Speaker, never eloquent, subject to much Hesitation in my choice of Words, hardly correct in Language, and yet I generally carried my Points.[4]

In reality there is perhaps no one of our natural Passions so hard to subdue as *Pride*. Disguise it, struggle with it, beat it down, stifle it, mortify it as much as one pleases, it is still alive, and will every now and then peep out and show itself. You will see it perhaps often in this History. For even if I could conceive that I had compleatly overcome it, I should probably by [be] proud of my Humility.

Thus far written at Passy 1784

4. Thomas Jefferson observed of Franklin and Washington as legislators that "I never heard either of them speak ten minutes at a time, nor to any but the main point which was to decide a question. They laid their shoulders to the great points, knowing that the little ones would follow of themselves." On the other hand, Jefferson found an evening's conversation with Franklin "more valued . . . than the whole week at Paris." Paul L. Ford, ed., *The Works of Thomas Jefferson,* I (N.Y., 1904), 90; Julian P. Boyd et al., eds., *The Papers of Thomas Jefferson,* x (Princeton, 1954), 250.

Part Three

I am now about to write at home, August 1788. but cannot have the help expected from my Papers, many of them being lost in the War: I have however found the following.

Having mentioned *a great and extensive Project* which I had conceiv'd, it seems proper that some Account should be here given of that Project and its Object. Its first Rise in my Mind appears in the following little Paper, accidentally preserved, viz

OBSERVATIONS on my Reading History in Library, May 9. 1731.

"That the great Affairs of the World, the Wars, Revolutions, &c. are carried on and effected by Parties.

"That the View of these Parties is their present general Interest, or what they take to be such.

"That the different Views of these different Parties, occasion all Confusion.

"That while a Party is carrying on a general Design, each Man has his particular private Interest in View.

"That as soon as a Party has gain'd its general Point, each Member becomes Intent upon his particular Interest, which thwarting others, breaks that Party into Divisions, and occasions more Confusion.

"That few in Public Affairs act from a meer View of the Good of their Country, whatever they may pretend; and tho' their Actings bring real Good to their Country, yet Men primarily consider'd that their own and their Country's Interest was united, and did not act from a Principle of Benevolence.

"That fewer still in public Affairs act with a View to the Good of Mankind.

"There seems to me at present to be great Occasion for raising an united Party for Virtue, by forming the Virtuous and good

Men of all Nations into a regular Body, to be govern'd by suitable good and wise Rules, which good and wise Men may probably be more unanimous in their Obedience to, than common People are to common Laws.

"I at present think, that whoever attempts this aright, and is well qualified, cannot fail of pleasing God, and of meeting with Success. B.F."

Revolving this Project in my Mind, as to be undertaken hereafter when my Circumstances should afford me the necessary Leisure, I put down from time to time on Pieces of Paper such Thoughts as occur'd to me respecting it. Most of these are lost; but I find one purporting to be the Substance of an intended Creed, containing as I thought the Essentials of every known Religion, and being free of every thing that might shock the Professors of any Religion. It is express'd in these Words. viz

"That there is one God who made all things.

"That he governs the World by his Providence.

"That he ought to be worshipped by Adoration, Prayer and Thanksgiving.

"But that the most acceptable Service of God is doing Good to Man.

"That the Soul is immortal.

"And that God will certainly reward Virtue and punish Vice either here or hereafter."

My Ideas at that time were, that the Sect should be begun and spread at first among young and single Men only; that each Person to be initiated should not only declare his Assent to such Creed, but should have exercis'd himself with the Thirteen Weeks Examination and Practice of the Virtues as in the before-mention'd Model; that the Existence of such a Society should be kept a Secret till it was become considerable, to prevent Solicitations for the Admission of improper Persons; but that the Members should each of them search among his Acquaintance for ingenuous well-disposed

Youths, to whom with prudent Caution the Scheme should be gradually communicated: That the Members should engage to afford their Advice Assistance and Support to each other in promoting one another's Interest, Business and Advancement in Life: That for Distinction, we should be call'd the Society of the ***Free and Easy;*** Free, as being by the general Practice and Habit of the Virtues, free from the Dominion of Vice, and particularly by the Practice of Industry and Frugality, free from Debt, which exposes a Man to Confinement and a Species of Slavery to his Creditors. This is as much as I can now recollect of the Project, except that I communicated it in part to two young Men, who adopted it with some Enthusiasm. But my then narrow Circumstances, and the Necessity I was under of sticking close to my Business, occasion'd my Postponing the farther Prosecution of it at that time, and my multifarious Occupations public and private induc'd me to continue postponing, so that it has been omitted till I have no longer Strength or Activity left sufficient for such an Enterprize: Tho' I am still of Opinion that it was a practicable Scheme, and might have been very useful, by forming a great Number of good Citizens: And I was not discourag'd by the seeming Magnitude of the Undertaking, as I have always thought that one Man of tolerable Abilities may work great Changes, and accomplish great Affairs among Mankind, if he first forms a good Plan, and, cutting off all Amusements or other Employments that would divert his Attention, makes the Execution of that same Plan his sole Study and Business.

In 1732 I first published my Almanack, under the Name of *Richard Saunders;* it was continu'd by me about 25 Years, commonly call'd *Poor Richard's* Almanack.[1] I endeavour'd to make it

1. The first issue, for the year 1733, was advertised as "just published" Dec. 19, 1732. *Papers,* I, 280–318, includes a complete facsimile. Prefaces, poems, sayings, and other material from Franklin's twenty-five later almanacs are printed in *Papers* at the beginning of each year.

both entertaining and useful, and it accordingly came to be in such Demand that I reap'd considerable Profit from it, vending annually near ten Thousand. And observing that it was generally read, scarce any Neighbourhood in the Province being without it, I consider'd it as a proper Vehicle for conveying Instruction among the common People, who bought scarce any other Books. I therefore filled all the little Spaces that occurr'd between the Remarkable Days in the Calendar, with Proverbial Sentences, chiefly such as inculcated Industry and Frugality, as the Means of procuring Wealth and thereby securing Virtue, it being more difficult for a Man in Want to act always honestly, as (to use here one of those Proverbs) *it is hard for an empty Sack to stand upright.* These Proverbs, which contained the Wisdom of many Ages and Nations, I assembled and form'd into a connected Discourse prefix'd to the Almanack of 1757, as the Harangue of a wise old Man to the People attending an Auction.[2] The bringing all these scatter'd Counsels thus into a Focus, enabled them to make greater Impression. The Piece being universally approved was copied in all the Newspapers of the Continent, reprinted in Britain on a Broadside to be stuck up in Houses, two Translations were made of it in French, and great Numbers bought by the Clergy and Gentry to distribute gratis among their poor Parishioners and Tenants. In Pennsylvania, as it discouraged useless Expence in foreign Superfluities, some thought it had its share of Influence in producing that growing Plenty of Money which was observable for several Years after its Publication.

2. Written in the summer of 1757 during Franklin's voyage to England, but printed in the almanac for 1758. *Papers,* VII, 340–50. This famous preface, known in different versions as "Father Abraham's Speech" and "The Way to Wealth" (in French, "La Science du Bonhomme Richard") was reprinted at least 145 times in seven different languages before the end of the eighteenth century and countless times since.

I consider'd my Newspaper also as another Means of Communicating Instruction, and in that View frequently reprinted in it Extracts from the Spectator and other moral Writers, and sometimes publish'd little Pieces of my own which had been first compos'd for Reading in our Junto. Of these are a Socratic Dialogue tending to prove, that, whatever might be his Parts and Abilities, a vicious Man could not properly be called a Man of Sense. And a Discourse on Self denial, showing that Virtue was not secure, till its Practice became a Habitude, and was free from the Opposition of contrary Inclinations. These may be found in the Papers about the beginning of 1735.[3] In the Conduct of my Newspaper I carefully excluded all Libelling and Personal Abuse, which is of late Years become so disgraceful to our Country. Whenever I was solicited to insert any thing of that kind, and the Writers pleaded as they generally did, the Liberty of the Press, and that a Newspaper was like a Stage Coach in which any one who would pay had a Right to a Place, my Answer was, that I would print the Piece separately if desired, and the Author might have as many Copies as he pleased to distribute himself, but that I would not take upon me to spread his Detraction, and that having contracted with my Subscribers to furnish them with what might be either useful or entertaining, I could not fill their Papers with private Altercation in which they had no Concern without doing them manifest Injustice. Now many of our Printers make no scruple of gratifying the Malice of Individuals by false Accusations of the fairest Characters among ourselves, augmenting Animosity even to the producing of Duels, and are moreover so indiscreet as to print scurrilous Reflections on the Government of neighbouring States, and even on the Conduct of our best national Allies, which may be attended with the most pernicious Consequences. These Things I mention as a Caution to young Printers, and that they may be

3. *Pa. Gazette*, Feb. 11 and 18, 1735; reprinted in *Papers*, II, 15–21.

encouraged not to pollute their Presses and disgrace their Profession by such infamous Practices, but refuse steadily; as they may see by my Example, that such a Course of Conduct will not on the whole be injurious to their Interests.

In 1733, I sent one of my Journeymen to Charleston South Carolina where a Printer was wanting.[4] I furnish'd him with a Press and Letters, on an Agreement of Partnership, by which I was to receive One Third of the Profits of the Business, paying One Third of the Expence. He was a Man of Learning and honest, but ignorant in Matters of Account; and tho' he sometimes made me Remittances, I could get no Account from him, nor any satisfactory State of our Partnership while he lived. On his Decease, the Business was continued by his Widow, who being born and bred in Holland, where as I have been inform'd the Knowledge of Accompts makes a Part of Female Education, she not only sent me as clear a State as she could find of the Transactions past, but continu'd to account with the greatest Regularity and Exactitude every Quarter afterwards; and manag'd the Business with such Success that she not only brought up reputably a Family of Children, but at the Expiration of the Term was able to purchase of me the Printing House and establish her Son in it. I mention this Affair chiefly for the Sake of recommending that Branch of Education for our young Females, as likely to be of more Use to them and their children in Case of Widowhood than either Music or Dancing, by preserving them from Losses by Imposition of crafty Men, and enabling them to continue perhaps a profitable mercantile House with establish'd Correspondence till a Son is grown up fit to

4. Louis Timothée; he succeeded Thomas Whitmarsh, another former journeyman with whom Franklin had made a similar contract in 1731 but who had since died. The contracts with both these men are in *Papers*, I, 205–8, 339–42. Timothée's wife Elizabeth and son Peter later conducted the business.

undertake and go on with it, to the lasting Advantage and enriching of the Family.

About the Year 1734. there arrived among us from Ireland, a young Presbyterian Preacher named Hemphill, who delivered with a good Voice, and apparently extempore, most excellent Discourses, which drew together considerable Numbers of different Persuasions, who join'd in admiring them. Among the rest I became one of his constant Hearers, his Sermons pleasing me, as they had little of the dogmatical kind, but inculcated strongly the Practice of Virtue, or what in the religious Stile are called Good Works. Those however, of our Congregation, who considered themselves as orthodox Presbyterians, disapprov'd his Doctrine, and were join'd by most of the old Clergy, who arraign'd him of Heterodoxy before the Synod, in order to have him silenc'd. I became his zealous Partisan, and contributed all I could to raise a Party in his Favour; and we combated for him a while with some Hopes of Success. There was much Scribbling pro and con upon the Occasion; and finding that tho' an elegant Preacher he was but a poor Writer, I lent him my Pen and wrote for him two or three Pamphlets, and one Piece in the Gazette of April 1735.[5] Those Pamphlets, as is generally the Case with controversial Writings, tho' eagerly read at the time, were soon out of Vogue, and I question whether a single Copy of them now exists.

During the Contest an unlucky Occurrence hurt his Cause exceedingly. One of our Adversaries having heard him preach a Sermon that was much admired, thought he had somewhere read that Sermon before, or at least a part of it. On Search he found that Part quoted at length in one of the British Reviews, from a Discourse of Dr. Forster's.[6] This Detection gave many of our Party Disgust, who accordingly abandoned his Cause, and oc-

5. Reprinted in *Papers,* II, 27–33, 37–126.

6. James Foster.

casion'd our more speedy Discomfiture in the Synod. I stuck by him however, as I rather approv'd his giving us good Sermons compos'd by others, than bad ones of his own Manufacture; tho' the latter was the Practice of our common Teachers. He afterwards acknowledg'd to me that none of those he preach'd were his own; adding that his Memory was such as enabled him to retain and repeat any Sermon after one Reading only. On our Defeat he left us, in search elsewhere of better Fortune, and I quitted the Congregation, never joining it after, tho' I continu'd many Years my Subscription for the Support of its Ministers.

I had begun in 1733 to study Languages. I soon made myself so much a Master of the French as to be able to read the Books with Ease. I then undertook the Italian. An Acquaintance[7] who was also learning it, us'd often to tempt me to play Chess with him. Finding this took up too much of the Time I had to spare for Study, I at length refus'd to play any more, unless on this Condition, that the Victor in every Game, should have a Right to impose a Task, either in Parts of the Grammar to be got by heart, or in Translation, &c. which Tasks the Vanquish'd was to perform upon Honour before our next Meeting. As we play'd pretty equally we thus beat one another into that Language. I afterwards with a little Painstaking acquir'd as much of the Spanish as to read their Books also.

I have already mention'd that I had only one Years Instruction in a Latin School, and that when very young, after which I neglected that Language entirely. But when I had attained an Acquaintance with the French, Italian and Spanish, I was surpriz'd to find, on looking over a Latin Testament, that I understood so much more of that Language than I had imagined; which encouraged me to apply my self again to the Study of it, and I met with the more Success, as those preceding Languages had greatly smooth'd my Way. From these Circumstances I have thought that there is some Incon-

7. Probably David Martin.

sistency in our common Mode of Teaching Languages. We are told that it is proper to begin first with the Latin, and having acquir'd that it will be more easy to attain those modern Languages which are deriv'd from it; and yet we do not begin with the Greek in order more easily to acquire the Latin. It is true, that if you can clamber and get to the Top of a Stair-Case without using the Steps, you will more easily gain them in descending: but certainly if you begin with the lowest you will with more Ease ascend to the Top. And I would therefore offer it to the Consideration of those who superintend the Educating of our Youth, whether, since many of those who begin with the Latin, quit the same after spending some Years, without having made any great Proficiency, and what they have learnt becomes almost useless, so that their time has been lost, it would not have been better to have begun them with the French, proceeding to the Italian &c. for tho' after spending the same time they should quit the Study of Languages, and never arrive at the Latin, they would however have acquir'd another Tongue or two that being in modern Use might be serviceable to them in common Life.

After ten Years Absence from Boston, and having become more easy in my Circumstances, I made a Journey thither to visit my Relations, which I could not sooner well afford. In returning I call'd at Newport, to see my Brother then settled there with his Printing-House. Our former Differences were forgotten, and our Meeting was very cordial and affectionate. He was fast declining in his Health, and requested of me that in case of his Death which he apprehended not far distant, I would take home his Son, then but 10 Years of Age, and bring him up to the Printing Business. This I accordingly perform'd, sending him a few Years to School before I took him into the Office.[8] His Mother carry'd on the Business till

8. Young James Franklin's indenture to his uncle and a bill for his education are in *Papers*, II, 261–3, 388.

he was grown up, when I assisted him with an Assortment of new Types, those of his Father being in a Manner worn out. Thus it was that I made my Brother ample Amends for the Service I had depriv'd him of by leaving him so early.

In 1736 I lost one of my Sons,[9] a fine Boy of 4 Years old, by the Small Pox taken in the common way. I long regretted bitterly and still regret that I had not given it to him by Inoculation; This I mention for the Sake of Parents, who omit that Operation on the Supposition that they should never forgive themselves if a Child died under it; my Example showing that the Regret may be the same either way, and that therefore the safer should be chosen.

Our Club, the Junto, was found so useful, and afforded such Satisfaction to the Members, that several were desirous of introducing their Friends, which could not well be done without exceeding what we had settled as a convenient Number, viz. Twelve. We had from the Beginning made it a Rule to keep our Institution a Secret, which was pretty well observ'd. The Intention was, to avoid Applications of improper Persons for Admittance, some of whom perhaps we might find it difficult to refuse. I was one of those who were against any Addition to our Number, but instead of it made in Writing a Proposal, that every Member separately should endeavour to form a subordinate Club, with the same Rules respecting Queries, &c. and without informing them of the Connexion with the Junto. The Advantages propos'd were the Improvement of so many more young Citizens by the Use of our Institutions; Our better Acquaintance with the general Sentiments of the Inhabitants on any Occasion, as the Junto-Member might propose what Queries we should desire, and was to report to Junto what

9. Francis Folger Franklin. To stop rumors Franklin printed a newspaper announcement that the boy had not died following inoculation, but had not been inoculated because he had not yet recovered from a protracted intestinal disorder. *Papers,* II, 154.

pass'd in his separate Club; the Promotion of our particular Interests in Business by more extensive Recommendations; and the Increase of our Influence in public Affairs and our Power of doing Good by spreading thro' the several Clubs the Sentiments of the Junto. The Project was approv'd, and every Member undertook to form his Club: but they did not all succeed. Five or six only were compleated, which were call'd by different Names, as the Vine, the Union, the Band, &c. They were useful to themselves, and afforded us a good deal of Amusement, Information and Instruction, besides answering in some considerable Degree our Views of influencing the public Opinion on particular Occasions, of which I shall give some Instances in course of time as they happened.

My first Promotion was my being chosen in 1736 Clerk of the General Assembly. The Choice was made that Year without Opposition; but the Year following when I was again propos'd (the Choice, like that of the Members being annual) a new Member[1] made a long Speech against me, in order to favour some other Candidate. I was however chosen; which was the more agreable to me, as besides the Pay for immediate Service as Clerk, the Place gave me a better Opportunity of keeping up an Interest among the Members, which secur'd to me the Business of Printing the Votes, Laws, Paper Money, and other occasional Jobbs for the Public, that on the whole were very profitable. I therefore did not like the Opposition of this new Member, who was a Gentleman of Fortune, and Education, with Talents that were likely to give him in time great Influence in the House, which indeed afterwards happened. I did not however aim at gaining his Favour by paying any servile Respect to him, but after some time took this other Method. Having heard that he had in his Library a certain very scarce and curious Book, I wrote a Note to him expressing my Desire of per-

1. Probably Isaac Norris, later Franklin's close associate in the Assembly and in the leadership of the anti-proprietary party.

using that Book, and requesting he would do me the Favour of lending it to me for a few Days. He sent it immediately; and I return'd it in about a Week, with another Note expressing strongly my Sense of the Favour. When we next met in the House he spoke to me, (which he had never done before) and with great Civility. And he ever afterwards manifested a Readiness to serve me on all Occasions, so that we became great Friends, and our Friendship continu'd to his Death. This is another Instance of the Truth of an old Maxim I had learnt, which says, *He that has once done you a Kindness will be more ready to do you another, than he whom you yourself have obliged.* And it shows how much more profitable it is prudently to remove, than to resent, return and continue inimical Proceedings.

In 1737, Col. Spotswood, late Governor of Virginia, and then Post-master, General, being dissatisfied with the Conduct of his Deputy at Philadelphia, respecting some Negligence in rendering, and Inexactitude of his Accounts, took from him the Commission and offered it to me.[2] I accepted it readily, and found it of great Advantage; for tho' the Salary was small, it facilitated the Corespondence that improv'd my Newspaper, encreas'd the Number demanded, as well as the Advertisements to be inserted, so that it came to afford me a very considerable Income. My old Competitor's Newspaper declin'd proportionably, and I was satisfy'd without retaliating his Refusal, while Postmaster, to permit my Papers being carried by the Riders.[3] Thus he suffer'd greatly from his Neglect in due Accounting; and I mention it as a Lesson to those

2. Franklin succeeded Andrew Bradford early in October 1737. On his conduct of the Philadelphia post office, 1737–53, see *Papers,* II, 178–83.

3. Actually, in 1739 Spotswood ordered Franklin to deny Bradford's paper free carriage because of the former postmaster's continued "neglect in due Accounting." A newspaper controversy followed. *Papers,* II, 235–6, 274–81.

young Men who may be employ'd in managing Affairs for others that they should always render Accounts and make Remittances with Great Clearness and Punctuality. The Character of observing such a Conduct is the most powerful of all Recommendations to new Employments and Increase of Business.

I began now to turn my Thoughts a little to public Affairs, beginning however with small Matters. The City Watch was one of the first Things that I conceiv'd to want Regulation. It was managed by the Constables of the respective Wards in Turn. The Constable warn'd a Number of Housekeepers to attend him for the Night. Those who chose never to attend paid him Six Shillings a Year to be excus'd, which was suppos'd to be for hiring Substitutes; but was in reality much more than was necessary for that purpose, and made the Constableship a Place of Profit. And the Constable for a little Drink often got such Ragamuffins about him as a Watch, that reputable Housekeepers did not chuse to mix with. Walking the rounds too was often neglected, and most of the Night spent in Tippling. I thereupon wrote a Paper to be read in Junto, representing these Irregularities, but insisting more particularly on the Inequality of this Six Shilling Tax of the Constables, respecting the Circumstances of those who paid it, since a poor Widow Housekeeper, all whose Property to be guarded by the Watch did not perhaps exceed the Value of Fifty Pounds, paid as much as the wealthiest Merchant who had Thousands of Poundsworth of Goods in his Stores. On the whole I proposed as a more effectual Watch, the Hiring of proper Men to serve constantly in that Business; and as a more equitable Way of supporting the Charge, the levying a Tax that should be proportion'd to Property. This Idea being approv'd by the Junto, was communicated to the other Clubs, but as arising in each of them. And tho' the Plan was not immediately carried into Execution, yet by preparing the Minds of People for the Change, it paved the Way for the Law obtain'd a few Years after, when the Members of our Clubs were grown into more Influence.[4]

About this time I wrote a Paper, (first to be read in Junto but it was afterwards publish'd) on the different Accidents and Carelessnesses by which Houses were set on fire, with Cautions against them, and Means proposed of avoiding them.[5] This was much spoken of as a useful Piece, and gave rise to a Project, which soon followed it, of forming a Company for the more ready Extinguishing of Fires, and mutual Assistance in Removing and Securing of Goods when in Danger. Associates in this Scheme were presently found amounting to Thirty. Our Articles of Agreement oblig'd every Member to keep always in good Order and fit for Use, a certain Number of Leather Buckets, with strong Bags and Baskets (for packing and transporting of Goods) which were to be brought to every Fire; and we agreed to meet once a Month and spend a social Evening together, in discoursing and communicating such Ideas as occur'd to us upon the Subject of Fires as might be useful in our Conduct on such Occasions.[6]

The Utility of this Institution soon appear'd, and many more desiring to be admitted than we thought convenient for one Company, they were advised to form another, which was accordingly done. And this went on, one new Company being formed after another, till they became so numerous as to include most of the

4. Franklin's "few Years" actually were seventeen; he wrote the Junto paper about 1735, a Philadelphia Grand Jury echoed his complaints about the watch in 1743, the Pennsylvania governor and Assembly passed enabling legislation in 1751, and the Philadelphia City Council (of which Franklin was a member) finally issued orders regulating the watch, as he proposed, on July 7, 1752. *Papers*, IV, 327–32.

5. First printed in *Pa. Gazette*, Feb. 4, 1735. *Papers*, II, 12–15.

6. The articles of the Union Fire Co., signed by Franklin and nineteen other charter members, Dec. 7, 1736, are in *Papers*, II, 150–3.

Inhabitants who were Men of Property; and now at the time of my Writing this, tho' upwards of Fifty Years since its Establishment, that which I first formed, called the Union Fire Company, still subsists and flourishes, tho' the first Members are all deceas'd but myself and one who is older by a Year than I am.[7] The small Fines that have been paid by Members for Absence at the Monthly Meetings, have been apply'd to the Purchase of Fire Engines, Ladders, Firehooks, and other useful Implements for each Company, so that I question whether there is a City in the World better provided with the Means of putting a Stop to beginning Conflagrations; and in fact since those Institutions, the City has never lost by Fire more than one or two Houses at a time, and the Flames have often been extinguish'd before the House in which they began has been half consumed.

In 1739 arriv'd among us from England the Rev. Mr. Whitefiel,[8] who had made himself remarkable there as an itinerant Preacher. He was at first permitted to preach in some of our Churches; but the Clergy taking a Dislike to him, soon refus'd him their Pulpits and he was oblig'd to preach in the Fields. The Multitudes of all Sects and Denominations that attended his Sermons were enormous, and it was matter of Speculation to me who was one of the Number, to observe the extraordinary Influence of his Oratory on his Hearers, and how much they admir'd and respected him, notwithstanding his common Abuse of them, by assuring them they were naturally *half Beasts and half Devils*. It was wonderful to see the Change soon made in the Manners of our Inhabitants; from being thoughtless or indifferent about Religion, it seem'd as if all the World were growing Religious; so that one could not walk thro' the Town in an Evening without Hearing Psalms sung in

7. Philip Syng.
8. George Whitefield.

different Families of every Street.[9] And it being found inconvenient to assemble in the open Air, subject to its Inclemencies, the Building of a House to meet in was no sooner propos'd and Persons appointed to receive Contributions, but sufficient Sums were soon receiv'd to procure the Ground and erect the Building which was 100 feet long and 70 broad, about the Size of Westminster-hall; and the Work was carried on with such Spirit as to be finished in a much shorter time than could have been expected. Both House and Ground were vested in Trustees, expressly for the Use of any Preacher of any religious Persuasion who might desire to say something to the People of Philadelphia, the Design in building not being to accommodate any particular Sect, but the Inhabitants in general, so that even if the Mufti of Constantinople were to send a Missionary to preach Mahometanism to us, he would find a Pulpit at his Service.[1] (The Contributions being made by People of different Sects promiscuously, Care was taken in the Nomination of Trustees to avoid giving a Predominancy to any Sect, so that one of each was appointed, viz. one Church of England-man, one Presbyterian, one Baptist, one Moravian, &c.).

Mr. Whitfield, in leaving us, went preaching all the Way thro' the Colonies to Georgia. The Settlement of that Province had lately been begun; but instead of being made with hardy industrious Husbandmen accustomed to Labour, the only People fit for such

9. *Pa. Gazette,* June 12, 1740, reported that "The Alteration in the Face of Religion here is altogether surprizing.... All which, under God, is owing to the successful Labours of the Reverend Mr. Whitefield." *Papers,* II, 287–8.

1. This was the "New Building," erected near the corner of Fourth and Arch (Mulberry) Streets, later occupied by the Academy and College of Philadelphia. Whitefield first preached in the still unfinished structure, Nov. 9, 1740. It was designed for nonsectarian use as a charity school and for Protestant worship; Franklin exaggerated when he wrote that it would have been made available to a Moslem missionary.

an Enterprise, it was with Families of broken Shopkeepers and other insolvent Debtors, many of indolent and idle habits, taken out of the Goals, who being set down in the Woods, unqualified for clearing Land, and unable to endure the Hardships of a new Settlement, perished in Numbers, leaving many helpless Children unprovided for. The Sight of their miserable Situation inspired the benevolent Heart of Mr. Whitefield with the Idea of building an Orphan House there, in which they might be supported and educated. Returning northward he preach'd up this Charity, and made large Collections; for his Eloquence had a wonderful Power over the Hearts and Purses of his Hearers, of which I myself was an Instance. I did not disapprove of the Design, but as Georgia was then destitute of Materials and Workmen, and it was propos'd to send them from Philadelphia at a great Expence, I thought it would have been better to have built the House here and brought the Children to it. This I advis'd, but he was resolute in his first Project, and rejected my Counsel, and I thereupon refus'd to contribute. I happened soon after to attend one of his Sermons, in the Course of which I perceived he intended to finish with a Collection, and I silently resolved he should get nothing from me. I had in my Pocket a Handful of Copper Money, three or four silver Dollars, and five Pistoles in Gold. As he proceeded I began to soften, and concluded to give the Coppers. Another Stroke of his Oratory made me asham'd of that, and determin'd me to give the Silver; and he finish'd so admirably, that I empty'd my Pocket wholly into the Collector's Dish, Gold and all. At this Sermon there was also one of our Club,[2] who being of my Sentiments respecting the Building in Georgia, and suspecting a Collection might be intended, had by Precaution emptied his Pockets before he came from home; towards the Conclusion of the Discourse however, he felt a strong Desire to give, and apply'd to a Neigh-

2. Thomas Hopkinson.

bour who stood near him to borrow some Money for the Purpose. The Application was unfortunately to perhaps the only Man in the Company who had the firmness not to be affected by the Preacher. His Answer was, *At any other time, Friend Hopkinson, I would lend to thee freely; but not now; for thee seems to be out of thy right Senses.*

Some of Mr. Whitfield's Enemies affected to suppose that he would apply these Collections to his own private Emolument; but I, who was intimately acquainted with him, (being employ'd in printing his Sermons and Journals, &c.[3]) never had the least Suspicion of his Integrity, but am to this day decidedly of Opinion that he was in all his Conduct, a perfectly *honest Man.* And methinks my Testimony in his Favour ought to have the more Weight, as we had no religious Connection. He us'd indeed sometimes to pray for my Conversion, but never had the Satisfaction of believing that his Prayers were heard. Ours was a mere civil Friendship, sincere on both Sides, and lasted to his Death.

The following Instance will show something of the Terms on which we stood. Upon one of his Arrivals from England at Boston, he wrote to me that he should come soon to Philadelphia, but knew not where he could lodge when there, as he understood his old kind Host Mr. Benezet[4] was remov'd to Germantown. My Answer was; You know my House, if you can make shift with its scanty Accommodations you will be most heartily welcome. He reply'd, that if I made that kind Offer for Christ's sake, I should not miss of a Reward. And I return'd, *Don't let me be mistaken; it was not for Christ's sake, but for your sake.* One of our common

3. Franklin printed eight different installments of Whitefield's journals of travels in Europe and America (listed in *Papers,* II, 243 n) and nine books or pamphlets containing his sermons or other writings, nearly all issued between 1739 and 1741.

4. John Stephen Benezet. The exchange of letters (now lost) probably took place in 1745.

Acquaintance jocosely remark'd, that knowing it to be the Custom of the Saints, when they receiv'd any favour, to shift the Burthen of the Obligation from off their own Shoulders, and place it in Heaven, I had contriv'd to fix it on Earth.

The last time I saw Mr. Whitefield was in London, when he consulted me about his Orphan House Concern, and his Purpose of appropriating it to the Establishment of a College.

He had a loud and clear Voice, and articulated his Words and Sentences so perfectly that he might be heard and understood at a great Distance, especially as his Auditories, however numerous, observ'd the most exact Silence. He preach'd one Evening from the Top of the Court House Steps, which are in the Middle of Market Street, and on the West Side of Second Street which crosses it at right angles. Both Streets were fill'd with his Hearers to a considerable Distance. Being among the hindmost in Market Street, I had the Curiosity to learn how far he could be heard, by retiring backwards down the Street towards the River, and I found his Voice distinct till I came near Front-Street,[5] when some Noise in that Street, obscur'd it. Imagining then a Semi-Circle, of which my Distance should be the Radius, and that it were fill'd with Auditors, to each of whom I allow'd two square feet, I computed that he might well be heard by more than Thirty-Thousand. This reconcil'd me to the Newspaper Accounts of his having preach'd to 25000 People in the Fields, and to the antient Histories of Generals haranguing whole Armies, of which I had sometimes doubted.[6]

5. About 500 feet from the Court House steps. On the basis of this distance Franklin's calculation is faulty; but in *Poor Richard*, 1749, in discussing the same matter he pointed out more accurately that 45,000 persons might stand in a space 100 yards square or 21,780 on an acre of ground.

6. Whitefield attracted crowds estimated at 6,000 to 8,000, remarkable in a city of about 10,000 people.

By hearing him often I came to distinguish easily between Sermons newly compos'd, and those which he had often preach'd in the Course of his Travels. His Delivery of the latter was so improv'd by frequent Repetitions, that every Accent, every Emphasis, every Modulation of Voice, was so perfectly well turn'd and well plac'd, that without being interested in the Subject, one could not help being pleas'd with the Discourse, a Pleasure of much the same kind with that receiv'd from an excellent Piece of Musick. This is an Advantage itinerant Preachers have over those who are stationary: as the latter cannot well improve their Delivery of a Sermon by so many Rehearsals.

His Writing and Printing from time to time gave great Advantage to his Enemies. Unguarded Expressions and even erroneous Opinions del[ivere]d in Preaching might have been afterwards explain'd, or qualify'd by supposing others that might have accompany'd them; or they might have been deny'd; But *litera scripta manet.*[7] Critics attack'd his Writings violently, and with so much Appearance of Reason as to diminish the Number of his Votaries, and prevent their Encrease. So that I am of Opinion, if he had never written any thing he would have left behind him a much more numerous and important Sect. And his Reputation might in that case have been still growing, even after his Death; as there being nothing of his Writing on which to found a censure; and give him a lower Character, his Proselites would be left at liberty to feign for him as great a Variety of Excellencies, as their enthusiastic Admiration might wish him to have possessed.

My Business was now continually augmenting, and my Circumstances growing daily easier, my Newspaper having become very profitable, as being for a time almost the only one in this and the neighbouring Provinces. I experienc'd too the

7. "The written letter remains."

Truth of the Observation, that *after getting the first hundred Pound, it is more easy to get the second:* Money itself being of a prolific Nature.

The Partnership at Carolina having succeeded, I was encourag'd to engage in others, and to promote several of my Workmen who had behaved well, by establishing them with Printing-Houses in different Colonies, on the same Terms with that in Carolina.[8] Most of them did well, being enabled at the End of our Term, Six Years, to purchase the Types of me; and go on working for themselves, by which means several Families were raised. Partnerships often finish in Quarrels, but I was happy in this, that mine were all carry'd on and ended amicably; owing I think a good deal to the Precaution of having very explicitly settled in our Articles every thing to be done by or expected from each Partner, so that there was nothing to dispute, which Precaution I would therefore recommend to all who enter into Partnerships, for whatever Esteem Partners may have for and Confidence in each other at the time of the Contract, little Jealousies and Disgusts may arise, with Ideas of Inequality in the Care and Burthen of the Business, &c. which are attended often with Breach of Friendship and of the Connection, perhaps with Lawsuits and other disagreable Consequences.

I had on the whole abundant Reason to be satisfied with my being established in Pennsylvania. There were however two things that I regretted: There being no Provision for Defence, nor for a compleat Education of Youth; No Militia nor any College. I there-

8. With Louis Timothée, 1733 (see above, p. 166). In addition, Franklin established working arrangements, not all actual partnerships, with James Parker (1742) in New York, Thomas Smith (1748) and Benjamin Mecom (1752) in Antigua, Samuel Holland (1753) in Lancaster, Pa., and several German printers in Philadelphia. He also helped found presses in New Haven and Dominica.

fore in 1743, drew up a Proposal for establishing an Academy; and at that time thinking the Revd. Mr. Peters,[9] who was out of Employ, a fit Person to superintend such an Institution, I communicated the Project to him. But he having more profitable Views in the Service of the Proprietors, which succeeded, declin'd the Undertaking. And not knowing another at that time suitable for such a Trust, I let the Scheme lie a while dormant. I succeeded better the next Year, 1744, in proposing and establishing a Philosophical Society.[1] The Paper I wrote for that purpose will be found among my Writings when collected.

With respect to Defence, Spain having been several Years at War against Britain, and being at length join'd by France, which brought us into greater Danger;[2] and the laboured and long-continued Endeavours of our Governor Thomas to prevail with our Quaker Assembly to pass a Militia Law, and make other Provisions for the Security of the Province having proved abortive, I determined to try what might be done by a voluntary Association of the People. To promote this I first wrote and published a Pamphlet, intitled, PLAIN TRUTH, in which I stated our defenceless Situation in strong Lights, with the Necessity of Union and Discipline for our Defence, and promis'd to propose

9. Richard Peters. Nothing more is known of the "Proposal" Franklin made at this time.

1. Dated May 14, 1743; *Papers*, II, 378–83. The idea, however, was not Franklin's, but probably originated with the botanist John Bartram. The society was organized but did not prosper until years later.

2. Great Britain declared war on Spain in 1739 (the War of Jenkins' Ear), and on France in 1744 (the War of the Austrian Succession, or, in America, King George's War). French and Spanish privateers in Delaware Bay during the spring and summer of 1747 caused the immediate alarm, which ended when news of the Peace of Aix-la-Chapelle reached Philadelphia in August 1748.

in a few Days an Association to be generally signed for that purpose.[3] The Pamphlet had a sudden and surprizing Effect. I was call'd upon for the Instrument of Association: And having settled the Draft of it with a few Friends, I appointed a Meeting of the Citizens in the large Building before mentioned. The House was pretty full. I had prepared a Number of printed Copies, and provided Pens and Ink dispers'd all over the Room. I harangu'd them a little on the Subject, read the Paper and explain'd it, and then distributed the Copies, which were eagerly signed, not the least Objection being made. When the Company separated, and the Papers were collected we found above Twelve hundred Hands; and other Copies being dispers'd in the Country the Subscribers amounted at length to upwards of Ten Thousand. These all furnish'd themselves as soon as they could with Arms; form'd themselves into Companies, and Regiments, chose their own Officers, and met every Week to be instructed in the manual Exercise, and other Parts of military Discipline. The Women, by Subscriptions among themselves, provided Silk Colours, which they presented to the Companies, painted with different Devices and Mottos which I supplied. The Officers of the Companies composing the Philadelphia Regiment, being met, chose me for their Colonel; but conceiving myself unfit, I declin'd that Station, and recommended Mr. Lawrence,[4] a fine Person and Man of Influence, who was accordingly appointed.

I then propos'd a Lottery to defray the Expence of Building a Battery below the Town, and furnishing it with Cannon. It filled expeditiously and the Battery was soon erected, the Merlons being

3. *Plain Truth: or, Serious Considerations On the Present State of the City of Philadelphia, and Province of Pennsylvania.* By a Tradesman of Philadelphia (Phila., 1747). Reprinted in *Papers,* III, 188–204.

4. Thomas Lawrence. He was, in fact, lieutenant colonel of the regiment; Abraham Taylor was colonel.

fram'd of Logs and fill'd with Earth.[5] We bought some old Cannon from Boston, but these not being sufficient, we wrote to England for more, soliciting at the same Time our Proprietaries for some Assistance, tho' without much Expectation of obtaining it. Mean while Colonel Lawrence, William Allen, Abraham Taylor, Esquires, and myself were sent to New York by the Associators, commission'd to borrow some Cannon of Governor Clinton. He at first refus'd us peremptorily: but at a Dinner with his Council where there was great Drinking of Madeira Wine, as the Custom at that Place then was, he soften'd by degrees, and said he would lend us Six. After a few more Bumpers he advanc'd to Ten. And at length he very good-naturedly conceded Eighteen. They were fine Cannon, 18 pounders, with their Carriages, which we soon transported and mounted on our Battery, where the Associators kept a nightly Guard while the War lasted: And among the rest I regularly took my Turn of Duty there as a common Soldier.[6]

My Activity in these Operations was agreable to the Governor and Council; they took me into Confidence, and I was consulted by them in every Measure wherein their Concurrence was thought useful to the Association. Calling in the Aid of Religion, I propos'd to them the Proclaiming a Fast, to promote Reformation, and implore the Blessing of Heaven on our Undertaking. They embrac'd the Motion, but as it was the first Fast ever thought of in the Province, the Secretary had no Precedent from which to draw the Proclamation. My Education in New England, where a Fast is proclaim'd every Year, was here of some Advantage. I drew

5. The main battery was erected at Wicaco below Old Swedes (Gloria Dei) Church, and a smaller one on Atwood's Wharf, a little below the foot of Pine Street.

6. Documents relating to this episode, including the Form of Association, the schemes for two lotteries, and the proclamation for a fast, are printed in *Papers,* III, 205–316 *passim.*

it in the accustomed Stile, it was translated into German, printed in both Languages and divulg'd thro' the Province. This gave the Clergy of the different Sects an Opportunity of Influencing their Congregations to join in the Association; and it would probably have been general among all but Quakers if the Peace had not soon interven'd.

It was thought by some of my Friends that by my Activity in these Affairs, I should offend that Sect, and thereby lose my Interest in the Assembly where they were a great Majority. A young Gentleman[7] who had likewise some Friends in the House, and wished to succeed me as their Clerk, acquainted me that it was decided to displace me at the next Election, and he therefore in good Will advis'd me to resign, as more consistent with my Honour than being turn'd out. My Answer to him was, that I had read or heard of some Public Man, who made it a Rule never to ask for an Office, and never to refuse one when offer'd to him. I approve, says I, of his Rule, and will practise it with a small Addition; I shall never *ask*, never *refuse*, nor ever *resign* an Office.[8] If they will have my Office of Clerk to dispose of to another, they shall take it from me. I will not by giving it up, lose my right of some time or other making Reprisals on my Adversaries. I heard however no more of this. I was chosen again, unanimously as usual, at the next Election. Possibly as they dislik'd my late Intimacy with the Members of Council, who had join'd the Governors in all the Disputes about military Preparations with which the House had long been harass'd, they might have been pleas'd if I would voluntarily have left them; but they did not care to displace me on Ac-

7. James Read. Franklin wrote after the dispute that he and Read "were not on Speaking Terms." *Papers*, III, 377.

8. In spite of this and other disclaimers of ever asking for a public office, Franklin actually did apply for the Assembly clerkship in 1736 and the deputy postmaster generalship in 1751.

count merely of my Zeal for the Association; and they could not well give another Reason. Indeed I had some Cause to believe, that the Defence of the Country was not disagreeable to any of them, provided they were not requir'd to assist in it. And I found that a much greater Number of them than I could have imagined, tho' against offensive war, were clearly for the defensive. Many Pamphlets *pro* and *con.* were publish'd on the Subject, and some by good Quakers in favour of Defence, which I believe convinc'd most of their younger People.

A Transaction in our Fire Company gave me some Insight into their prevailing Sentiments. It had been propos'd that we should encourage the Scheme for building a Battery by laying out the present Stock, then about Sixty Pounds, in Tickets of the Lottery. By our Rules no Money could be dispos'd of but at the next Meeting after the Proposal. The Company consisted of Thirty Members, of which Twenty-two were Quakers, and Eight only of other Persuasions.[9] We eight punctually attended the Meeting; but tho' we thought that some of the Quakers would join us, we were by no means sure of a Majority. Only one Quaker, Mr. James Morris, appear'd to oppose the Measure. He express'd much Sorrow that it had ever been propos'd, as he said *Friends* were all against it, and it would create such Discord as might break up the Company. We told him, that we saw no reason for that; we were the Minority, and if *Friends* were against the Measure and outvoted us, we must and should, agreable to the Usage of all Societies, submit. When the Hour for Business arriv'd, it was mov'd to put the Vote. He allow'd we might then do it by the Rules, but as he could assure us that a Number of Members intended to be present for the purpose of opposing it, it would be but candid to allow a little time for their appearing. While we were disputing this, a Waiter came to tell me two Gentlemen below desir'd to speak with me. I went

9. *Papers*, II, 376, lists the members of the Union Fire Company in 1743.

down, and found they were two of our Quaker Members. They told me there were eight of them assembled at a Tavern just by; that they were determin'd to come and vote with us if there should be occasion, which they hop'd would not be the Case; and desir'd we would not call for their Assistance if we could do without it, as their Voting for such a Measure might embroil them with their Elders and Friends. Being thus secure of a Majority, I went up, and after a little seeming Hesitation, agreed to a Delay of another Hour. This Mr. Morris allow'd to be extreamly fair. Not one of his opposing Friends appear'd, at which he express'd great Surprize; and at the Expiration of the Hour, we carry'd the Resolution Eight to one; And as of the 22 Quakers, Eight were ready to vote with us and Thirteen by their Absence manifested that they were not inclin'd to oppose the Measure, I afterwards estimated the Proportion of Quakers sincerely against Defence as one to twenty one only. For these were all regular Members, of that Society, and in good Reputation among them, and had due Notice of what was propos'd at that Meeting.[1]

The honourable and learned Mr. Logan, who had always been of that Sect, was one who wrote an Address to them, declaring his Approbation of defensive War, and supporting his Opinion by many strong Arguments:[2] He put into my Hands Sixty Pounds to be laid out in Lottery Tickets for the Battery,[3] with Directions to apply what Prizes might be drawn wholly to that Service. He told

1. One other fire company besides Franklin's bought lottery tickets, but a third, dominated by Quakers, voted 19 to 3 not to buy any. *Papers*, III, 220–1.

2. Logan's address, written in 1741 and printed by Franklin, is reprinted in *Pennsylvania Magazine of History and Biography*, VI (1882), 402–11. He also wrote approvingly of the lottery to Franklin before the details were publicly announced. *Papers*, III, 220.

3. Actually £250; *Papers*, III, 274.

me the following Anecdote of his old Master Wm. Penn, respecting Defence. He came over from England, when a young Man, with that Proprietary, and as his Secretary. It was War Time, and their Ship was chas'd by an armed Vessel suppos'd to be an Enemy. Their Captain prepar'd for Defence, but told Wm. Penn and his Company of Quakers, that he did not expect their Assistance, and they might retire into the Cabin; which they did, except James Logan, who chose to stay upon Deck, and was quarter'd to a Gun. The suppos'd Enemy prov'd a Friend; so there was no Fighting. But when the Secretary went down to communicate the Intelligence, Wm. Penn rebuk'd him severely for staying upon Deck and undertaking to assist in defending the Vessel, contrary to the Principles of *Friends,* especially as it had not been required by the Captain. This Reproof being before all the Company, piqu'd the Secretary, who answer'd, *I being thy Servant, why did thee not order me to come down: but thee was willing enough that I should stay and help to fight the Ship when thee thought there was Danger.*[4]

My being many Years in the Assembly, the Majority of which were constantly Quakers, gave me frequent Opportunities of seeing the Embarassment given them by their Principle against War,

4. Frederick B. Tolles repeats this anecdote and acutely comments: "There was a basic temperamental difference between the two men and the difference could not but be reflected in their attitudes toward the Quaker faith and its cardinal tenet of nonresistance. William Penn was by nature an enthusiast, an idealist; to him nonresistance was an integral part of the New Testament vision of life to which he was committed. In practice, as Proprietor of a great province in the British Empire, he might sometimes have to compromise his absolute testimony, but he would always cling tenaciously to the principle. Logan, on the other hand, was a practical, earth-bound man, whose religious faith could never carry him beyond the limits of reason and experience. To him nonresistance was a noble ideal for which the world was not ready, and he felt no inner compulsion to lead the way." *James Logan and the Culture of Provincial America* (Boston, 1957), pp. 13–14.

whenever Application was made to them by Order of the Crown to grant Aids for military Purposes. They were unwilling to offend Government on the one hand, by a direct Refusal, and their Friends the Body of Quakers on the other, by a Compliance contrary to their Principles. Hence a Variety of Evasions to avoid Complying, and Modes of disguising the Compliance when it became unavoidable. The common Mode at last was to grant Money under the Phrase of its being *for the King's Use*, and never to enquire how it was applied. But if the Demand was not directly from the Crown, that Phrase was found not so proper, and some other was to be invented. As when Powder was wanting, (I think it was for the Garrison at Louisburg,) and the Government of New England solicited a Grant of some from Pensilvania, which was much urg'd on the House by Governor Thomas, they could not grant Money to buy Powder, because that was an Ingredient of War, but they voted an Aid to New England, of Three Thousand Pounds, to be put into the hands of the Governor, and appropriated it for the Purchasing of Bread, Flour, Wheat, *or other Grain.* Some of the Council desirous of giving the House still farther Embarassment, advis'd the Governor not to accept Provision, as not being the Thing he had demanded. But he reply'd, "I shall take the Money, for I understand very well their Meaning; *Other Grain,* is Gunpowder;" which he accordingly bought; and they never objected to it.[5] It was in Allusion to this Fact, that when in our Fire Company we feared the Success of our Proposal in favour of the Lottery, and I had said to my Friend Mr. Syng, one of our Members, if we fail, let us move the Purchase of a Fire Engine with the Money; the Quakers can have no Objection to that: and then if you nominate me, and I you, as a Committee for that purpose, we will

5. Thomas approved the appropriation, for £4000, in July 1745; *Papers,* III, 195 n. In the margin Franklin wrote "See the Votes," a reference to the minutes of the Pa. Assembly where the transaction is duly recorded.

buy a great Gun, which is certainly a *Fire-Engine:* I see, says he, you have improv'd by being so long in the Assembly; your equivocal Project would be just a Match for their Wheat *or other Grain.*

These Embarassments that the Quakers suffer'd from having establish'd and published it as one of their Principles, that no kind of War was lawful, and which being once published, they could not afterwards, however they might change their Minds, easily get rid of, reminds me of what I think a more prudent Conduct in another Sect among us; that of the Dunkers. I was acquainted with one of its Founders, Michael Welfare,[6] soon after it appear'd. He complain'd to me that they were grievously calumniated by the Zealots of other Persuasions, and charg'd with abominable Principles and Practices to which they were utter Strangers. I told him this had always been the case with new Sects; and that to put a Stop to such Abuse, I imagin'd it might be well to publish the Articles of their Belief and the Rules of their Discipline. He said that it had been propos'd among them, but not agreed to, for this Reason; "When we were first drawn together as a Society, says he, it had pleased God to inlighten our Minds so far, as to see that some Doctrines which we once esteemed Truths were Errors, and that others which we had esteemed Errors were real Truths. From time to time he has been pleased to afford us farther Light, and our Principles have been improving, and our Errors diminishing. Now we are not sure that we are arriv'd at the End of this Progression, and at the Perfection of Spiritual or Theological Knowledge; and we fear that if we should once print our Confession of Faith, we should feel ourselves as if bound and confin'd by it, and perhaps be unwilling to receive farther Improvement; and our Successors still more so, as conceiving what we their Elders and Founders had

6. Michael Wohlfahrt. The Dunkers (Dunkards, or Church of the Brethren) were members of a German Baptist denomination who began to migrate to Pennsylvania in 1719.

done, to be something sacred, never to be departed from." This Modesty in a Sect is perhaps a singular Instance in the History of Mankind, every other Sect supposing itself in Possession of all Truth, and that those who differ are so far in the Wrong: Like a Man travelling in foggy Weather: Those at some Distance before him on the Road he sees wrapt up in the Fog, as well as those behind him, and also the People in the Fields on each side; but near him all appears clear. Tho' in truth he is as much in the Fog as any of them. To avoid this kind of Embarrassment the Quakers have of late Years been gradually declining the public Service in the Assembly and in the Magistracy. Chusing rather to quit their Power than their Principle.[7]

In Order of Time I should have mentioned before, that having in 1742 invented an open Stove, for the better warming of Rooms and at the same time saving Fuel, as the fresh Air admitted was warmed in Entring, I made a Present of the Model to Mr. Robert Grace, one of my early Friends, who having an Iron Furnace, found the Casting of the Plates for these Stoves a profitable Thing, as they were growing in Demand. To promote that Demand I wrote and published a Pamphlet Intitled, *An Account of the New-Invented* PENNSYLVANIA FIRE PLACES: *Wherein their Construction and manner of Operation is particularly explained; their Advantages above every other Method of warming Rooms demonstrated; and all Objections that have been raised against the Use of them answered and obviated.* &c.[8] This Pamphlet had a good Effect, Govr.

7. In 1756 ten Quaker pacifists resigned Assembly seats and three others refused to run for re-election.

8. Though Franklin used his invention as early as the winter of 1739–40, he first advertised this pamphlet for sale Nov. 14, 1744 (printed with the original illustrations, *Papers*, II, 419–46). The stove sharply reduced the heat wasted up the fireplace chimney and distributed warmth by convection as well as by radiation and conduction. With it, he asserted, the common room

Thomas was so pleas'd with the Construction of this Stove, as describ'd in it that he offer'd to give me a Patent for the sole Vending of them for a Term of Years; but I declin'd it from a Principle which has ever weigh'd with me on such Occasions, viz. *That as we enjoy great Advantages from the Inventions of others, we should be glad of an Opportunity to serve others by any Invention of ours, and this we should do freely and generously.* An Ironmonger in London, however, after assuming a good deal of my Pamphlet, and working it up into his own, and making some small Changes in the Machine, which rather hurt its Operation, got a Patent for it there, and made as I was told a little Fortune by it.[9] And this is not the only Instance of Patents taken out for my Inventions by others, tho' not always with the same Success: which I never contested, as having no Desire of profiting by Patents my self, and hating Disputes. The Use of these Fireplaces in very many Houses both of this and the neighbouring Colonies, has been and is a great Saving of Wood to the Inhabitants.

Peace being concluded, and the Association Business therefore at an End, I turn'd my Thoughts again to the Affair of establishing an Academy. The first Step I took was to associate in the Design a Number of active Friends, of whom the Junto furnished a good

---

was "twice as warm as it used to be, with a quarter of the Wood I formerly consum'd there." None of his original stoves is known to have survived; the "Franklin stove" as now known is a great modification, since it does not use convection—the drawing in of a current of air to be heated and then circulated.

9. Possibly J. Durno, who published in London in 1753 *A Description of a New-Invented Stove-Grate.* He described and commended Franklin's fireplace, but criticized it as being intended only for wood, not well adapted to coàl, and therefore difficult to clean. Or Franklin may have been referring to James Sharp, who published in London in 1781 *An Account of the Principle and Effects of American Stoves; . . . together with a Description of the late Additions and Improvements made to them.*

Part: the next was to write and publish a Pamphlet intitled, *Proposals relating to the Education of Youth in Pennsylvania.*[1] This I distributed among the principal Inhabitants gratis; and as soon as I could suppose their Minds a little prepared by the Perusal of it, I set on foot a Subscription for Opening and Supporting an Academy; it was to be paid in Quotas yearly for Five Years; by so dividing it I judg'd the Subscription might be larger, and I believe it was so, amounting to no less (if I remember right) than Five thousand Pounds.[2] In the Introduction to these Proposals, I stated their Publication not as an Act of mine, but of some *publick-spirited Gentlemen;* avoiding as much as I could, according to my usual Rule, the presenting myself to the Publick as the Author of any Scheme for their Benefit.

The Subscribers, to carry the Project into immediate Execution chose out of their Number Twenty-four Trustees, and appointed Mr. Francis, then Attorney General, and myself, to draw up Constitutions for the Government of the Academy, which being done and signed, a House was hired, Masters engag'd and the Schools opened I think in the same Year 1749.[3] The Scholars Encreasing fast, the House was soon found too small, and we were looking out for a Piece of Ground properly situated, with Intention to build, when Providence[4] threw into our way a large House ready built, which with a few Alterations might well serve our pur-

1. Published in the fall of 1749; reprinted in *Papers,* III, 397–421.

2. Twenty-four trustees and Governor Hamilton signed the initial subscription paper, Nov. 14, 1749; their pledges, ranging from £6 to £75 per year, totaled nearly £2000 for the five-year period. Franklin promised £10 per year. *Papers,* III, 428–9.

3. Franklin's chronology is somewhat faulty here. While negotiations for the "New Building" began in November 1749, the school was not opened until Jan. 7, 1751, and even then had to be conducted in temporary quarters until remodeling of the "New Building" was completed a few weeks later. *Papers,* III, 435–6; IV, 34–7, 194.

4. Franklin at first wrote and then crossed out "Fortune."

pose, this was the building before mentioned erected by the Hearers of Mr. Whitefield, and was obtain'd for us in the following Manner.

It is to be noted, that the Contributions to this Building being made by People of different Sects, Care was taken in the Nomination of Trustees, in whom the Building and Ground was to be vested, that a Predominancy should not be given to any Sect, lest in time that Predominancy might be a means of appropriating the whole to the Use of such Sect, contrary to the original Intention; it was therefore that one of each Sect was appointed, viz. one Church-of-England-man, one Presbyterian, one Baptist, one Moravian, &c. those in case of Vacancy by Death were to fill it by Election from among the Contributors. The Moravian[5] happen'd not to please his Colleagues, and on his Death, they resolved to have no other of that Sect. The Difficulty then was, how to avoid having two of some other Sect, by means of the new Choice. Several Persons were named and for that reason not agreed to. At length one mention'd me, with the Observation that I was merely an honest Man, and of no Sect at all; which prevail'd with them to chuse me. The Enthusiasm which existed when the House was built, had long since abated, and its Trustees had not been able to procure fresh Contributions for paying the Ground Rent, and discharging some other Debts the Building had occasion'd, which embarrass'd them greatly. Being now a Member of both Sets of Trustees, that for the Building and that for the Academy, I had good Opportunity of negociating with both, and brought them finally to an Agreement, by which the Trustees for the Building were to cede it to those of the Academy, the latter undertaking to discharge the Debt,

5. Probably Thomas Noble. The original nine "Trustees for Use" of the building were not assigned by denomination but were all Whitefield's zealous supporters, included five Moravians. After he broke with the Moravians in the early 1740s, they were denied a voice in the management.

to keep forever open in the Building a large Hall for occasional Preachers according to the original Intention, and maintain a Free School for the Instruction of poor Children. Writings were accordingly drawn, and on paying the Debts the Trustees of the Academy were put in Possession of the Premises, and by dividing the great and lofty Hall into Stories, and different Rooms above and below for the several Schools, and purchasing some additional Ground, the whole was soon made fit for our purpose, and the Scholars remov'd into the Building. The Care and Trouble of agreeing with the Workmen, purchasing Materials, and superintending the Work fell upon me, and I went thro' it the more chearfully, as it did not then interfere with my private Business, having the Year before taken a very able, industrious and honest Partner, Mr. David Hall, with whose Character I was well acquainted, as he had work'd for me four Years. He took off my Hands all Care of the Printing-Office, paying me punctually my Share of the Profits. This Partnership continued Eighteen Years, successfully for us both.[6]

The Trustees of the Academy after a while were incorporated by a Charter from the Governor; their Funds were increas'd by Contributions in Britain, and Grants of Land from the Proprietaries, to which the Assembly has since made considerable Addition, and thus was established the present University of Philadelphia. I have been continued one of its Trustees from the Beginning, now near forty Years, and have had the very great Pleasure of seeing a Number of the Youth who have receiv'd their Education in it,

6. The partnership agreement, dated Jan. 1, 1748, was to begin on January 21 following. Franklin supplied the presses and equipment and Hall was to manage the business; all operating expenses and all profits and losses were to be shared equally between them. At the end of the partnership Hall was to have the option of buying the equipment at a fair valuation or of returning it to Franklin. *Papers,* III, 263–7.

distinguish'd by their improv'd Abilities, serviceable in public Stations, and Ornaments to their Country.[7]

When I disengag'd myself as above mentioned from private Business,[8] I flatter'd myself that by the sufficient tho' moderate Fortune I had acquir'd, I had secur'd Leisure during the rest of my Life, for Philosophical Studies[9] and Amusements; I purchas'd all Dr. Spence's[1] Apparatus, who had come from England to lecture here; and I proceeded in my Electrical Experiments with great Alacrity; but the Publick now considering me as a Man of Leisure, laid hold of me for their Purposes; every Part of our Civil Government, and almost at the same time, imposing some Duty upon me. The Governor put me into the Commission of the Peace; the Corporation of the City chose me of the Common Council, and soon after an Alderman; and the Citizens at large chose me a Burgess to represent them in Assembly.[2] This latter Station was the more agre-

7. The Academy, now the University of Pennsylvania, received its first charter on July 13, 1753, and an additional one as an Academy and College on May 14, 1755; *Papers*, v, 7–11; vi, 28–37. Political differences with a majority of the trustees caused Franklin's displacement as president of the board by Richard Peters, May 11, 1756. Deeply hurt, Franklin wrote a friend, July 28, 1759, that "The Trustees had reap'd the full Advantage of my Head, Hands, Heart and Purse, in getting through the first Difficulties of the Design, and when they thought they could do without me, they laid me aside." He continued as one of the trustees, however, until his death.

8. Upon forming the partnership with David Hall, 1748, Franklin moved his residence from Market Street to a house at the northwest corner of Race (Sassafras) and Second Streets, "a more quiet Part of the Town."

9. In the eighteenth century the word "philosophy" in such a context as this meant "natural philosophy" or what we call "science," and often specifically "physics."

1. Archibald Spencer.

2. Franklin became justice of the peace on June 3, 1749; a member of the Philadelphia City Council on Oct. 4, 1748; an alderman on Oct. 1, 1751; and

able to me, as I was at length tired with sitting there to hear Debates in which as Clerk I could take no part, and which were often so unentertaining, that I was induc'd to amuse myself with making magic Squares, or Circles, or any thing to avoid Weariness.[3] And I conceiv'd my becoming a Member would enlarge my Power of doing Good. I would not however insinuate that my Ambition was not flatter'd by all these Promotions. It certainly was. For considering my low Beginning they were great Things to me. And they were still more pleasing, as being so many spontaneous Testimonies of the public's good Opinion, and by me entirely unsolicited.

The Office of Justice of the Peace I try'd a little, by attending a few Courts, and sitting on the Bench to hear Causes. But finding that more Knowledge of the Common Law than I possess'd, was necessary to act in that Station with Credit, I gradually withdrew from it, excusing myself by my being oblig'd to attend the higher Dutys of a Legislator in the Assembly. My Election to this Trust was repeated every Year for Ten Years, without my ever asking any Elector for his Vote, or signifying either directly or indirectly any Desire of being chosen.[4] On taking my Seat in the House, my Son was appointed their Clerk.

The Year following, a Treaty being to be held with the Indians at Carlisle, the Governor sent a Message to the House, proposing

---

an assemblyman on Aug. 13, 1751. In 1750 he was a candidate for recorder of the Common Council, but was defeated, 19 to 24, by Tench Francis.

3. He began to make his magic squares and circles in 1736–37. Some of them, including the most complicated ones, were published and republished in England and France, 1767–73. *Papers*, IV, 392–403, 435, reproduce several with his accompanying explanations.

4. Franklin was re-elected annually until 1764 when he and Joseph Galloway lost a close, hard-fought contest. In this election as in earlier ones, Franklin may not have solicited votes directly, but he certainly had lieutenants working very hard on his behalf, and was himself fully engaged politically.

that they should nominate some of their Members to be join'd with some Members of Council as Commissioners for that purpose. The House nam'd the Speaker (Mr. Norris) and myself; and being commission'd we went to Carlisle, and met the Indians accordingly.[5] As those People are extreamly apt to get drunk, and when so are very quarrelsome and disorderly, we strictly forbad the selling any Liquor to them; and when they complain'd of this Restriction, we told them that if they would continue sober during the Treaty, we would give them Plenty of Rum when Business was over. They promis'd this; and they kept their Promise—because they could get no Liquor—and the Treaty was conducted very orderly, and concluded to mutual Satisfaction. They then claim'd and receiv'd the Rum. This was in the Afternoon. They were near 100 Men, Women and Children, and were lodg'd in temporary Cabins built in the Form of a Square just without the Town. In the Evening, hearing a great Noise among them, the Commissioners walk'd out to see what was the Matter. We found they had made a great Bonfire in the Middle of the Square. They were all drunk Men and Women, quarrelling and fighting. Their dark-colour'd Bodies, half naked, seen only by the gloomy Light of the Bonfire, running after and beating one another with Firebrands, accompanied by their horrid Yellings, form'd a Scene the most resembling our Ideas of Hell that could well be imagin'd. There was no appeasing the Tumult, and we retired to our Lodging. At Midnight a Number of them came thundering at our Door, demanding more Rum; of which we took no Notice. The next Day, sensible they had misbehav'd in giving us that Disturbance, they sent three of their old Counsellors

5. Gov. James Hamilton named Richard Peters of the Council and Isaac Norris and Franklin of the Assembly as commissioners, Sept. 22, 1753, while the House was not in session but after conferring with such members as were in town. Preliminary documents and the text of the treaty, in the colorful language customary in Indian negotiations, are in *Papers*, v, 62–6, 84–107.

to make their Apology. The Orator acknowledg'd the Fault, but laid it upon the Rum; and then endeavour'd to excuse the Rum, by saying, "*The great Spirit who made all things made every thing for some Use, and whatever Use he design'd any thing for, that Use it should always be put to; Now, when he made Rum, he said,* LET THIS BE FOR INDIANS TO GET DRUNK WITH. *And it must be so.*" And indeed if it be the Design of Providence to extirpate these Savages in order to make room for Cultivators of the Earth, it seems not improbable that Rum may be the appointed Means. It has already annihilated all the Tribes who formerly inhabited the Sea-coast.[6]

In 1751. Dr. Thomas Bond, a particular Friend of mine, conceiv'd the Idea of establishing a Hospital in Philadelphia, for the Reception and Cure of poor sick Persons, whether Inhabitants of the Province or Strangers. A very beneficent Design, which has been ascrib'd to me, but was originally his. He was zealous and active in endeavouring to procure subscriptions for it; but the Proposal being a Novelty in America, and at first not well understood, he met with small Success. At length he came to me, with the Compliment that he found there was no such thing as carrying a public Spirited Project through, without my being concern'd in it; "for, says he, I am often ask'd by those to whom I propose Subscribing, Have you consulted Franklin upon this Business? and what does he think of it? And when I tell them that I have not, (supposing it rather out of your Line) they do not subscribe, but say they will consider of it." I enquir'd into the Nature, and probable Utility of his Scheme, and receiving from him a very satisfactory Explanation,

6. In their report of this conference the three commissioners had placed the blame where it really belonged: on the Indian traders who supplied the Indians with liquor and who "by their own Intemperence, unfair Dealings, and Irregularities, will, it is to be feared, entirely estrange the Affections of the Indians from the English." *Papers*, v, 107.

I not only subscrib'd to it myself, but engag'd heartily in the Design of Procuring Subscriptions from others. Previous however to the Solicitation, I endeavoured to prepare the Minds of the People by writing on the Subject in the Newspapers, which was my usual Custom in such Cases, but which he had omitted.[7]

The Subscriptions afterwards were more free and generous, but beginning to flag, I saw they would be insufficient without some Assistance from the Assembly, and therefore propos'd to petition for it, which was done. The Country Members did not at first relish the Project. They objected that it could only be serviceable to the City, and therefore the Citizens should alone be at the Expence of it; and they doubted whether the Citizens themselves generally approv'd of it: My Allegation on the contrary, that it met with such Approbation as to leave no doubt of our being able to raise £2000 by voluntary Donations, they considered as a most extravagant Supposition, and utterly impossible. On this I form'd my Plan; and asking Leave to bring in a Bill, for incorporating the Contributors according to the Prayer (of their) Petition, and granting them a blank Sum of Money, which Leave was obtain'd chiefly on the Consideration that the House could throw the Bill out if they did not like it, I drew it so as to make the important Clause a conditional One, viz. "And be it enacted by the Authority aforesaid That when the said Contributors shall have met and chosen their Managers and Treasurer, *and shall have raised by their Contributions a Capital Stock of £2000 Value,* (the yearly Interest of which is to be applied to the Accommodating of the Sick Poor in the said Hos-

7. Franklin's appeal for public support of the hospital, printed in *Pa. Gazette,* Aug. 8 and 15, 1751 (*Papers,* IV, 147–54), came after, not before, the petition to the Assembly, January 23 (mentioned below), and the passage of the act of incorporation, May 11. Franklin included the texts of these and other relevant documents in a pamphlet, *Some Account of the Pennsylvania Hospital,* published in 1754. *Papers,* IV, 108–11; V, 283–330.

pital, free of Charge for Diet, Attendance, Advice and Medicines) and *shall make the same appear to the Satisfaction of the Speaker of the Assembly* for the time being; that *then* it shall and may be lawful for the said Speaker, and he is hereby required to sign an Order on the Provincial Treasurer for the Payment of Two Thousand Pounds in two yearly Payments, to the Treasurer of the said Hospital, to be applied to the Founding, Building and Finishing of the same." This Condition carried the Bill through; for the Members who had oppos'd the Grant, and now conceiv'd they might have the Credit of being charitable without the Expence, agreed to its Passage; And then in soliciting Subscriptions among the People we urg'd the conditional Promise of the Law as an additional Motive to give, since every Man's Donation would be doubled. Thus the Clause work'd both ways. The Subscriptions accordingly soon exceeded the requisite sum, and we claim'd and receiv'd the Public Gift, which enabled us to carry the Design into Execution. A convenient and handsome Building was soon erected, the Institution has by constant Experience been found useful, and flourishes to this Day. And I do not remember any of my political Manoeuvres, the Success of which gave me at the time more Pleasure. Or that in after-thinking of it, I more easily excus'd my-self for having made some Use of Cunning.[8]

It was about this time that another Projector, the Revd. Gilbert Tennent, came to me, with a Request that I would assist him in procuring a Subscription for erecting a new Meeting-house. It was to be for the Use of a Congregation he had gathered among the Presbyterians who were originally Disciples of Mr. Whitefield. Unwilling to make myself disagreable to my fellow Citizens, by too frequently soliciting their Contributions, I absolutely refus'd. He then desir'd I would furnish him with a List of the Names of Per-

8. Franklin's eloquent inscription on the cornerstone of the building erected in 1755 is printed in *Papers*, VI, 61–2.

sons I knew by Experience to be generous and public-spirited. I thought it would be unbecoming in me, after their kind Compliance with my Solicitations, to mark them out to be worried by other Beggars, and therefore refus'd also to give such a List. He then desir'd I would at least give him my Advice. That I will readily do, said I; and, in the first Place, I advise you to apply to all those whom you know will give something; next to those whom you are uncertain whether they will give any thing or not; and show them the List of those who have given: and lastly, do not neglect those who you are sure will give nothing; for in some of them you may be mistaken. He laugh'd, thank'd me, and said he would take my Advice. He did so, for he ask'd of *every body;* and he obtain'd a much larger Sum than he expected, with which he erected the capacious and very elegant Meeting-house that stands in Arch Street.[9]

Our City, tho' laid out with a beautifull Regularity, the Streets large, strait, and crossing each other at right Angles, had the Disgrace of suffering those Streets to remain long unpav'd, and in wet Weather the Wheels of heavy Carriages plough'd them into a Quagmire, so that it was difficult to cross them. And in dry Weather the Dust was offensive. I had liv'd near the Jersey Market, and saw with Pain the Inhabitants wading in Mud while purchasing their Provisions. A Strip of Ground down the middle of that Market was at length pav'd with Brick, so that being once in the Market they had firm Footing, but were often over Shoes in Dirt to get there. By talking and writing on the Subject, I was at length instrumental in getting the Street pav'd with Stone between the Market and the brick'd Foot-Pavement that was on each Side next the Houses. This for some time gave an easy Access to the Market, dry-shod. But the rest of the Street not being pav'd, whenever a Carriage came out of the Mud upon this Pavement, it shook off and left its Dirt

9. The Second Presbyterian Church, organized in 1743, opened its new building at Arch (Mulberry) and Third Streets in 1752.

upon it, and it was soon cover'd with Mire, which was not remov'd, the City as yet having no Scavengers. After some Enquiry I found a poor industrious Man, who was willing to undertake keeping the Pavement clean, by sweeping it twice a week and carrying off the Dirt from before all the Neighbours Doors, for the Sum of Sixpence per Month, to be paid by each House. I then wrote and printed a Paper, setting forth the Advantages to the Neighbourhood that might be obtain'd by this small Expence; the greater Ease in keeping our Houses clean, so much Dirt not being brought in by People's Feet; the Benefit to the Shops by more Custom, as Buyers could more easily get at them, and by not having in windy Weather the Dust blown in upon their Goods, &c. &c. I sent one of these Papers to each House, and in a Day or two went round to see who would subscribe an Agreement to pay these Sixpences. It was unanimously sign'd, and for a time well executed. All the Inhabitants of the City were delighted with the Cleanliness of the Pavement that surrounded the Market, it being a Convenience to all; and this rais'd a general Desire to have all the Streets paved; and made the People more willing to submit to a Tax for that purpose.

After some time I drew a Bill for Paving the City, and brought it into the Assembly. It was just before I went to England in 1757. and did not pass till I was gone, and then with an Alteration in the Mode of Assessment, which I thought not for the better, but with an additional Provision for lighting as well as Paving the Streets, which was a great Improvement.[1] It was by a private Person, the late Mr. John Clifton, his giving a Sample of the Utility of Lamps by placing one at his Door, that the People were first impress'd

1. The *Votes and Proceedings* of the Pa. Assembly, 1757, do not record that Franklin brought in a street paving bill. One, perhaps based on his bill, passed the Assembly on March 26, 1762. An act of 1751 had provided for street lights in Philadelphia; it was renewed in 1756. Perhaps Franklin's memory confused these several measures.

with the Idea of enlightning all the City. The Honour of this public Benefit has also been ascrib'd to me, but it belongs truly to that Gentleman. I did but follow his Example; and have only some Merit to claim respecting the Form of our Lamps as differing from the Globe Lamps we at first were supply'd with from London. Those we found inconvenient in these respects; they admitted no Air below, the Smoke therefore did not readily go out above, but circulated in the Globe, lodg'd on its Inside, and soon obstructed the Light they were intended to afford; giving, besides, the daily Trouble of wiping them clean; and an accidental Stroke on one of them would demolish it, and render it totally useless. I therefore suggested the composing them of four flat Panes, with a long Funnel above to draw up the Smoke, and Crevices admitting Air below, to facilitate the Ascent of the Smoke. By this means they were kept clean, and did not grow dark in a few Hours as the London Lamps do, but continu'd bright till Morning; and an accidental Stroke would generally break but a single Pane, easily repair'd.[2] I have sometimes wonder'd that the Londoners did not, from the Effect Holes in the Bottom of the Globe Lamps us'd at Vauxhall, have in keeping them clean, learn to have such Holes in their Street Lamps. But those Holes being made for another purpose, viz. to communicate Flame more suddenly to the Wick, by a little Flax hanging down thro' them, the other Use of letting in Air seems not to have been thought of. And therefore, after the Lamps have been lit a few Hours, the Streets of London are very poorly illuminated.

The Mention of these Improvements puts me in mind of one I propos'd when in London, to Dr. Fothergill, who was among the best Men I have known, and a great Promoter of useful Projects. I had observ'd that the Streets when dry were never swept and the

2. Post lamps which follow in general Franklin's design now stand in Independence Square, Philadelphia.

light Dust carried away, but it was suffer'd to accumulate till wet Weather reduc'd it to Mud, and then after lying some Days so deep on the Pavement that there was no Crossing but in Paths kept clean by poor People with Brooms, it was with great Labour rak'd together and thrown up into Carts open above, the Sides of which suffer'd some of the Slush at every jolt on the Pavement to shake out and fall, some times to the Annoyance of Foot-Passengers. The Reason given for not sweeping the dusty Streets was, that the Dust would fly into the Windows of Shops and Houses. An accidental Occurrence had instructed me how much Sweeping might be done in a little Time. I found at my Door in Craven Street[3] one Morning a poor Woman sweeping my Pavement with a birch Broom. She appeared very pale and feeble as just come out of a Fit of Sickness. I ask'd who employ'd her to sweep there. She said, "Nobody; but I am very poor and in Distress, and I sweeps before Gentlefolkeses Doors, and hopes they will give me something." I bid her sweep the whole Street clean and I would give her a Shilling. This was at 9 a Clock. At 12 she came for the Shilling. From the slowness I saw at first in her Working, I could scarce believe that the Work was done so soon, and sent my Servant to examine it, who reported that the whole Street was swept perfectly clean, and all the Dust plac'd in the Gutter which was in the Middle. And the next Rain wash'd it quite away, so that the Pavement and even the Kennel were perfectly clean. I then judg'd that if that feeble Woman could sweep such a Street in 3 Hours, a strong active Man might have done it in half the time. And here let me remark the Convenience of having but one Gutter in such a narrow Street, running down its Middle instead of two, one on each Side near the Footway. For where all the Rain that falls on a Street runs from the

3. In London, off the Strand near Charing Cross, where Franklin lived for fifteen years (1757–62, 1764–75), lodging in the house of Mrs. Margaret Stevenson.

Sides and meets in the middle, it forms there a Current strong enough to wash away all the Mud it meets with: But when divided into two Channels, it is often too weak to cleanse either, and only makes the Mud it finds more fluid, so that the Wheels of Carriages and Feet of Horses throw and dash it up on the Foot Pavement which is thereby rendred foul and slippery, and sometimes splash it upon those who are walking. My Proposal communicated to the good Doctor, was as follows.

"For the more effectual cleaning and keeping clean the Streets of London and Westminister, it is proposed,

"That the several Watchmen be contracted with to have the Dust swept up in dry Seasons, and the Mud rak'd up at other Times, each in the several Streets and Lanes of his Round.

"That they be furnish'd with Brooms and other proper Instruments for these purposes, to be kept at their respective Stands, ready to furnish the poor People they may employ in the Service.

"That in the dry Summer Months the Dust be all swept up into Heaps at proper Distances, before the Shops and Windows of Houses are usually opened: when the Scavengers with close-covered Carts shall also carry it all away.

"That the Mud when rak'd up be not left in Heaps to be spread abroad again by the Wheels of Carriages and Trampling of Horses; but that the Scavengers be provided with Bodies of Carts, not plac'd high upon Wheels, but low upon Sliders; with Lattice Bottoms, which being cover'd with Straw, will retain the Mud thrown into them, and permit the Water to drain from it, whereby it will become much lighter, Water making the greatest Part of its Weight. These Bodies of Carts to be plac'd at convenient Distances, and the Mud brought to them in Wheelbarrows, they remaining where plac'd till the Mud is drain'd, and then Horses brought to draw them away."

I have since had Doubts of the Practicability of the latter Part of this Proposal, on Account of the Narrowness of some Streets, and the Difficulty of placing the Draining Sleds so as not to encumber too much the Passage: But I am still of Opinion that the former, requiring the Dust, to be swept up and carry'd away before the Shops are open, is very practicable in the Summer, when the Days are long: For in Walking thro' the Strand and Fleetstreet one Morning at 7 a Clock I observ'd there was not one shop open tho' it had been Day-light and the Sun up above three Hours. The Inhabitants of London chusing voluntarily to live much by Candle Light, and sleep by Sunshine; and yet often complain a little absurdly, of the Duty on Candles and the high Price of Tallow.[4]

Some may think these trifling Matters not worth minding or relating. But when they consider, that tho' Dust blown into the Eyes of a single Person or into a single Shop on a windy Day, is but of small Importance, yet the great Number of the Instances in a populous City, and its frequent Repetitions give it Weight and Consequence; perhaps they will not censure very severely those who bestow some of Attention to Affairs of this seemingly low Nature. Human Felicity is produc'd not so much by great Pieces of good Fortune that seldom happen, as by little Advantages that occur every Day. Thus if you teach a poor young Man to shave himself and keep his Razor in order, you may contribute more to the Happiness of his Life than in giving him a 1000 Guineas. The Money may be soon spent, the Regret only remaining of having foolishly consum'd it. But in the other Case he escapes the frequent Vexation of waiting for Barbers, and of their some times, dirty Fingers, offensive Breaths and dull Razors. He shaves when most convenient to him, and enjoys daily the Pleasure of its being done with a good Instrument. With these Sentiments I have hazarded

4. This passage echoes a paper that Franklin published in the *Journal de Paris*, April 26, 1784, suggesting a scheme, commonly called his "Economical Project," which anticipated in principle, though not in method, our present system of Daylight Saving Time.

the few preceding Pages, hoping they may afford Hints which some time or other may be useful to a City I love, having lived many Years in it very happily; and perhaps to some of our Towns in America.

Having been for some time employed by the Postmaster General of America,[5] as his Comptroller, in regulating the several Offices, and bringing the Officers to account, I was upon his Death in 1753 appointed jointly with Mr. William Hunter to succeed him, by a Commission from the Postmaster General in England. The American Office had never hitherto paid any thing to that of Britain. We were to have £600 a Year between us if we could make that Sum out of the Profits of the Office. To do this, a Variety of Improvements were necessary; some of these were inevitably at first expensive; so that in the first four Years the Office became above £900 in debt to us. But it soon after began to repay us, and before I was displac'd, by a Freak of the Minister's, of which I shall speak hereafter, we had brought it to yield *three times* as much clear Revenue to the Crown as the Post-Office of Ireland. Since that imprudent Transaction, they have receiv'd from it,—Not one Farthing.[6]

The Business of the Post-Office occasion'd my taking a Journey this Year to New England, where the College of Cambridge of

5. Elliott Benger.

6. Franklin solicited the deputy postmaster generalship in May 1751; he and Hunter were commissioned on Aug. 10, 1753, and before the end of that year issued detailed instructions to postmasters in North America. The secrets of their success were improved service and insistence on prompt and careful accounting by local postmasters. *Papers,* IV, 134–6; V, 18, 161–77. The American post office yielded a profit of nearly £3000 per year to the Crown at the time of Franklin's removal from office, Jan. 30, 1774, the day after Solicitor General Alexander Wedderburn abused and humiliated him before a committee of the Privy Council for his part in the publication of the Hutchinson letters.

their own Motion, presented me with the Degree of Master of Arts. Yale College in Connecticut, had before made me a similar Compliment.[7] Thus without Studying in any College I came to partake of their Honours. They were confer'd in Consideration of my Improvements and Discoveries in the electric Branch of Natural Philosophy.

In 1754, War with France being again apprehended, a Congress of Commissioners from the different Colonies, was by an Order of the Lords of Trade, to be assembled at Albany, there to confer with the Chiefs of the Six Nations, concerning the Means of defending both their Country and ours.[8] Governor Hamilton, having receiv'd this Order, acquainted the House with it, requesting they would furnish proper Presents for the Indians to be given on this Occasion; and naming the Speaker (Mr. Norris) and my self, to join Mr. Thomas Penn[9] and Mr. Secretary Peters, as Commissioners to act for Pennsylvania. The House approv'd the Nomination, and provided the Goods for the Present, tho' they did not much like treating out of the Province, and we met the other Commissioners and met at Albany about the Middle of June. In our Way thither, I projected and drew up a Plan for the Union of all the Colonies, under one Government so far as might be necessary for

7. Franklin's memory erred on the sequence of these events; Harvard honored him on July 25, 1753, Yale seven weeks later, on September 12. *Papers,* v, 16–17, 58.

8. British officials were concerned about the possible defection to the French of the Iroquois (Six Nations), whose grievances over exploitation, especially by New York traders, were making them more and more restive. Some of the most far-sighted colonial leaders also hoped to use this congress to work out a plan of organized colonial union of the colonies. As early as 1751 Franklin had offered the broad outlines of such a plan. *Papers,* IV, 117–21.

9. John, not Thomas Penn. Governor Hamilton signed the commissions on May 13, 1754. *Papers,* v, 275–80.

Defence, and other important general Purposes. As we pass'd thro' New York, I had there shown my Project to Mr. James Alexander and Mr. Kennedy,[1] two Gentlemen of great Knowledge in public Affairs, and being fortified by their Approbation I ventur'd to lay it before the Congress. It then appear'd that several of the Commissioners had form'd Plans of the same kind. A previous Question was first taken whether a Union should be established, which pass'd in the Affirmative unanimously.

A Committee was then appointed one Member from each Colony, to consider the several Plans and report. Mine happen'd to be prefer'd, and with a few Amendments was accordingly reported. By this Plan, the general Government was to be administred by a President General appointed and supported by the Crown, and a Grand Council to be chosen by the Representatives of the People of the several Colonies met in their respective Assemblies. The Debates upon it in Congress went on daily hand in hand with the Indian Business. Many Objections and Difficulties were started, but at length they were all overcome, and the Plan was unanimously agreed to, and Copies ordered to be transmitted to the Board of Trade and to the Assemblies of the several Provinces.[2] Its Fate was singular. The Assemblies did not adopt it as they all thought there was too much *Prerogative* in it; and in England it was judg'd to have too much of the *Democratic*:[3] The Board of Trade therefore

1. Archibald Kennedy. Franklin's preliminary plan is in *Papers,* v, 335–41.

2. Full records of the Albany Congress, including substantiation of Franklin's leading role in drafting the Plan of Union proposed there, are in *Papers,* v, 344–92. His "Reasons and Motives" for the scheme as voted, written shortly after the Congress, is in *Papers,* v, 397–417.

3. This statement greatly oversimplifies the reasons for the failure of the Albany Plan. The colonial assemblies and most of the people were narrowly provincial in outlook, mutually jealous, and suspicious of any central taxing

did not approve of it; nor recommend it for the Approbation of his Majesty; but another Scheme was form'd (suppos'd better to answer the same Purpose) whereby the Governors of the Provinces with some Members of their respective Councils were to meet and order the raising of Troops, building of Forts, &c. &c. to draw on the Treasury of Great Britain for the Expence, which was afterwards to be refunded by an Act of Parliament laying a Tax on America. My Plan, with my Reasons in support of it, is to be found among my political Papers that are printed.

Being the Winter following in Boston, I had much Conversation with Govr. Shirley upon both the Plans. Part of what pass'd between us on the Occasion may also be seen among those Papers.[4] The different and contrary Reasons of dislike to my Plan, makes me suspect that it was really the true Medium; and I am still of Opinion it would have been happy for both Sides the Water if it had been adopted. The Colonies so united would have been sufficiently strong to have defended themselves; there would then have been no need of Troops from England; of course the subsequent Pretence for Taxing America, and the bloody Contest it occasioned, would have been avoided. But such Mistakes are not new; History is full of the Errors of States and Princes.

"*Look round the habitable World, how few*
Know their own Good, or knowing it pursue."[5]

---

authority. British officials, already troubled by the actions of some of the strong-willed colonial assemblies, disliked the idea of any super-legislature in America, in the election of which the assemblies would have a part, and soon became preoccupied with plans for a military expedition under General Braddock, from which they did not wish to divert colonial energies.

4. Franklin's letters to Gov. William Shirley, December 1754, remarkably foreshadowing some of the causes of the American Revolution and often reprinted following 1765, are in *Papers,* V, 441–51.

5. John Dryden's translation, lines 1–2, of Juvenal's tenth *Satire,* lines 1–3.

Those who govern, having much Business on their hands, do not generally like to take the Trouble of considering and carrying into Execution new Projects. The best public Measures are therefore seldom *adopted from previous Wisdom,* but *forc'd by the Occasion.*

The Governor of Pennsylvania in sending it down to the Assembly, express'd his Approbation of the Plan "as appearing to him to be drawn up with great Clearness and Strength of Judgment, and therefore recommended it as well worthy their closest and most serious Attention." The House however, by the Management of a certain Member,[6] took it up when I happen'd to be absent, which I thought not very fair, and reprobated it without paying any Attention to it at all, to my no small Mortification.

In my Journey to Boston this Year I met at New York with our new Governor, Mr. Morris,[7] just arriv'd there from England, with whom I had been before intimately acquainted. He brought a Commission to supersede Mr. Hamilton, who, tir'd with the Disputes his Proprietary Instructions subjected him to, had resigned. Mr. Morris ask'd me, if I thought he must expect as uncomfortable an Administration. I said, No; you may on the contrary have a very comfortable one, if you will only take care not to enter into any Dispute with the Assembly. "My dear Friend, says he, pleasantly, how can you advise my avoiding Disputes. You know I love Disputing; it is one of my greatest Pleasures: However, to show the Regard I have for your Counsel, I promise you I will if possible avoid them." He had some Reason for loving to dispute, being eloquent, an acute Sophister, and therefore generally successful in

6. Probably Isaac Norris; in deference to Quaker colleagues in the Assembly, he opposed parts of the Albany Plan of Union. On Aug. 17, 1754, the House voted against referring the Plan to the next Assembly. *Papers,* V, 375, 427 n.

7. Robert Hunter Morris.

argumentative Conversation. He had been brought up to it from a Boy, his Father (as I have heard) accustoming his Children to dispute with one another for his Diversion while sitting at Table after Dinner. But I think the Practice was not wise, for in the Course of my Observation, these disputing, contradicting and confuting People are generally unfortunate in their Affairs. They get Victory sometimes, but they never get Good Will, which would be of more use to them. We parted, he going to Philadelphia, and I to Boston. In returning, I met at New York with the Votes of the Assembly, by which it appear'd that notwithstanding his Promise to me, he and the House were already in high Contention, and it was a continual Battle between them, as long as he retain'd the Government. I had my Share of it; for as soon as I got back to my Seat in the Assembly, I was put on every Committee for answering his Speeches and Messages, and by the Committees always desired to make the Drafts. Our Answers as well as his Messages were often tart, and sometimes indecently abusive. And as he knew I wrote for the Assembly, one might have imagined that when we met we could hardly avoid cutting Throats. But he was so good-natur'd a Man, that no personal Difference between him and me was occasion'd by the Contest, and we often din'd together.[8]

One Afternoon in the height of this public Quarrel, we met in the Street. "Franklin, says he, you must go home with me and spend the Evening. I am to have some Company that you will like;" and taking me by the Arm he led me to his House. In gay Conversation over our Wine after Supper he told us Jokingly that he much admir'd the Idea of Sancho Panza, who when it was propos'd to give him a Government, requested it might be a Government of *Blacks*, as then, if he could not agree with his People he

8. Franklin's mild, even-tempered recollection of Pennsylvania politics and of the negotiations with the Penns in London belies the bitterness of these events revealed in contemporary documents.

might sell them. One of his Friends who sat next me, says, "Franklin, why do you continue to side with these damn'd Quakers? had not you better sell them? the Proprietor would give you a good Price." The Governor, says I, has not yet *black'd* them enough. He had indeed labour'd hard to blacken the Assembly in all his Messages, but they wip'd off his Colouring as fast as he laid it on, and plac'd it in return thick upon his own Face; so that finding he was likely to be negrify'd himself, he as well as Mr. Hamilton, grew tir'd of the Contest, and quitted the Government.

These public Quarrels were all at bottom owing to the Proprietaries, our hereditary Governors; who when any Expence was to be incurr'd for the Defence of their Province, with incredible Meanness instructed their Deputies to pass no Act for levying the necessary Taxes, unless their vast Estates were in the same Act expresly excused; and they had even taken Bonds of these Deputies to observe such Instructions. The Assemblies for three Years held out against this Injustice, tho' constrain'd to bend at last. At length Capt. Denny, who was Governor Morris's Successor, ventur'd to disobey those Instructions; how that was brought about I shall show hereafter.[9]

But I am got forward too fast with my Story; there are still some Transactions to be mentioned that happened during the Administration of Governor Morris.

War being, in a manner, commenced with France, the Government of Massachusets Bay projected an Attack upon Crown Point, and sent Mr. Quincy to Pennsylvania, and Mr. Pownall, afterwards Govr. Pownall, to N. York to sollicit Assistance. As I was in the

9. The Assembly had been trying since 1751 to get the Proprietors to share some of the expenses of government but did not attempt to tax their estates directly until 1755. All efforts failed until 1759, when partly under pressure from the military and partly by what amounted to a bribe, Governor Denny agreed to sign such a bill. By then Franklin was in England.

Assembly, knew its Temper, and was Mr. Quincy's Countryman, he apply'd to me for my Influence and Assistance. I dictated his Address to them which was well receiv'd. They voted an Aid of Ten Thousand Pounds, to be laid out in Provisions. But the Governor refusing his Assent to their Bill, (which included this with other Sums granted for the Use of the Crown) unless a Clause were inserted exempting the Proprietary Estate from bearing any Part of the Tax that would be necessary, the Assembly, tho' very desirous of making their Grant to New England effectual, were at a Loss how to accomplish it. Mr. Quincy laboured hard with the Governor to obtain his Assent, but he was obstinate.[1] I then suggested a Method of doing the Business without the Governor, by Orders on the Trustees of the Loan-Office, which by Law the Assembly had the Right of Drawing.[2] There was indeed little or no Money at that time in the Office, and therefor I propos'd that the Orders should be payable in a Year and to bear an Interest of Five per Cent. With these Orders I suppos'd the Provisions might easily be purchas'd. The Assembly with very little Hesitation adopted the Proposal. The Orders were immediately printed, and I was one of the Committee directed to sign and dispose of them. The Fund for Paying them was the Interest of all the Paper Currency then extant in the Province upon Loan, together with the Revenue arising from the Excise which being known to be more than suffi-

1. The memorial to the Pa. Assembly Franklin wrote for Josiah Quincy, April 1, 1755, is in *Papers*, VI, 3–5. Governor Morris rejected the £25,000 supply bill because he believed it violated royal orders forbidding emission of paper money; the Assembly did not pass a tax on the proprietary estates until August 1755.

2. The original chief function of the Loan Office was to lend out the paper money authorized by legislative act, usually secured by mortgages on real estate, and to receive the interest on the loans. The Assembly had power to direct the expenditure of these receipts.

cient, they obtain'd instant Credit, and were not only receiv'd in Payment for the Provisions, but many money'd People who had Cash lying by them, vested it in those Orders, which they found advantageous, as they bore Interest while upon hand, and might on any Occasion be used as Money: So that they were eagerly all bought up, and in a few Weeks none of them were to be seen. Thus this important Affair was by my means compleated, Mr. Quincy return'd Thanks to the Assembly in a handsome Memorial, went home highly pleas'd with the Success of his Embassy, and ever after bore for me the most cordial and affectionate Friendship.

The British Government not chusing to permit the Union of the Colonies, as propos'd at Albany, and to trust that Union with their Defence, lest they should thereby grow too military, and feel their own Strength, Suspicions and Jealousies at this time being entertain'd of them;[3] sent over General Braddock with two Regiments of Regular English Troops for that purpose. He landed at Alexandria in Virginia, and thence march'd to Frederic Town in Maryland,[4] where he halted for Carriages. Our Assembly apprehending, from some Information, that he had conceived violent Prejudices against them, as averse to the Service, wish'd me to wait upon him, not as from them, but as Postmaster General, under the guise of proposing to settle with him the Mode of conducting with most Celerity and Certainty the Dispatches between him and the Governors of the several Provinces, with whom he must necessarily have continual Correspondence, and of which they propos'd to pay the Expence. My Son accompanied me on this Journey. We

3. This comment reflects Franklin's post-1776 hostility toward Great Britain; in fact, it is doubtful that any British action in 1755 could have sufficiently united the colonies to make them capable of defending themselves without British help against the large-scale French and Indian assaults of 1755–57.

4. Now Frederick, fifty miles northwest of Annapolis.

found the General at Frederic Town, waiting impatiently for the Return of those he had sent thro' the back Parts of Maryland and Virginia to collect Waggons. I staid with him several Days, Din'd with him daily, and had full Opportunity of removing all his Prejudices, by the Information of what the Assembly had before his Arrival actually done and were still willing to do to facilitate his Operations.

When I was about to depart, the Returns of Waggons to be obtain'd were brought in, by which it appear'd that they amounted only to twenty-five, and not all of those were in serviceable Condition. The General and all the Officers were surpriz'd, declar'd the Expedition was then at an End, being impossible, and exclaim'd against the Ministers for ignorantly landing them in a Country destitute of the Means of conveying their Stores, Baggage, &c. not less than 150 Waggons being necessary. I happen'd to say, I thought it was pity they had not been landed rather in Pennsylvania, as in that Country almost every Farmer had his Waggon. The General eagerly laid hold of my Words, and said, "Then you, Sir, who are a Man of Interest there, can probably procure them for us; and I beg you will undertake it." I ask'd what Terms were to be offer'd the Owners of the Waggons; and I was desir'd to put on Paper the Terms that appear'd to me necessary. This I did, and they were agreed to, and a Commission and Instructions accordingly prepar'd immediately. What those Terms were will appear in the Advertisement I publish'd as soon as I arriv'd at Lancaster; which being, from the great and sudden Effect it produc'd, a Piece of some Curiosity, I shall insert at length, as follows.

(Here insert it, from the Quire Book of Letters written during this Transaction).[5]

5. The "Advertisement" is not in the manuscript autobiography but is reprinted here from the original printed broadside. Franklin's "Quire Book of Letters" has disappeared, but other documents on his assistance to Braddock are printed in *Papers*, VI, 13–68 *passim*, and 207–9.

Advertisement

Lancaster, April 26, 1755.

Whereas 150 Waggons, with 4 Horses to each Waggon, and 1500 Saddle or Pack-Horses are wanted for the Service of his Majesty's Forces now about to rendezvous at Wills's Creek;[6] and his Excellency General Braddock hath been pleased to impower me to contract for the Hire of the same; I hereby give Notice, that I shall attend for that Purpose at Lancaster from this Time till next Wednesday Evening; and at York from next Thursday Morning 'till Friday Evening; where I shall be ready to agree for Waggons and Teams, or single Horses, on the following Terms, viz.

1st. That these shall be paid for each Waggon with 4 good Horses and a Driver, Fifteen Shillings per *Diem:* And for each able Horse with a Pack-Saddle or other Saddle and Furniture, Two Shillings per *Diem.* And for each able Horse without a Saddle, Eighteen Pence per *Diem.*

2dly, That the Pay commence from the Time of their joining the Forces at Wills's Creek (which must be on or before the twentieth of May ensuing) and that a reasonable Allowance be made over and above for the Time necessary for their travelling to Wills's Creek and home again after their Discharge.

3dly, Each Waggon and Team, and every Saddle or Pack Horse is to be valued by indifferent Persons, chosen between me and the Owner, and in Case of the Loss of any Waggon, Team or other Horse in the Service, the Price according to such Valuation, is to be allowed and paid.

4thly, Seven Days Pay is to be advanced and paid in hand by me to the Owner of each Waggon and Team, or Horse, at the Time of contracting, if required; and the Remainder to be paid by Gen-

6. Fort Cumberland in western Maryland, at the confluence of Wills Creek and the Potomac River.

eral Braddock, or by the Paymaster of the Army, at the Time of their Discharge, or from time to time as it shall be demanded.

5thly, No Drivers of Waggons, or Persons taking care of the hired Horses, are on any Account to be called upon to do the Duty of Soldiers, or be otherwise employ'd than in conducting or taking Care of their Carriages and Horses.

6thly, All Oats, Indian Corn or other Forage, that Waggons or Horses bring to the Camp more than is necessary for the Subsistence of the Horses, is to be taken for the Use of the Army, and a reasonable Price paid for it.

Note. My Son William Franklin, is impowered to enter into like Contracts with any Person in Cumberland County.

B. FRANKLIN.

To the Inhabitants of the Counties of Lancaster, York, and Cumberland.

Friends and Countrymen,

Being occasionally at the Camp at Frederic a few Days since, I found the General and Officers of the Army extreamly exasperated, on Account of their not being supply'd with Horses and Carriages, which had been expected from this Province as most able to furnish them; but thro' the Dissensions between our Governor and Assembly, Money had not been provided nor any Steps taken for that Purpose.

It was proposed to send an armed Force immediately into these Counties, to seize as many of the best Carriages and Horses as should be wanted, and compel as many Persons into the Service as would be necessary to drive and take care of them.

I apprehended that the Progress of a Body of Soldiers thro' these Counties on such an Occasion, especially considering the Temper they are in, and their Resentment against us, would be attended with many and great Inconveniencies to the Inhabitants; and therefore more willingly undertook the Trouble of trying first what might be done by fair and equitable Means.

The People of these back Counties have lately complained to the Assembly that a sufficient Currency was wanting; you have now an Opportunity of receiving and dividing among you a very considerable Sum; for if the Service of this Expedition should continue (as it's more than probable it will) for 120 Days, the Hire of these Waggons and Horses will amount to upwards of Thirty thousand Pounds, which will be paid you in Silver and Gold of the King's Money.

The Service will be light and easy, for the Army will scarce march above 12 Miles per Day, and the Waggons and Baggage Horses, as they carry those Things that are absolutely necessary to the Welfare of the Army, must march with the Army and no faster, and are, for the Army's sake, always plac'd where they can be most secure, whether on a March or in Camp.

If you are really, as I believe you are, good and loyal Subjects to His Majesty, you may now do a most acceptable Service, and make it easy to yourselves; for three or four of such as cannot separately spare from the Business of their Plantations a Waggon and four Horses and a Driver, may do it together, one furnishing the Waggon, another one or two Horses, and another the Driver, and divide the Pay proportionably between you. But if you do not this Service to your King and Country voluntarily, when such good Pay and reasonable Terms are offered you, your Loyalty will be strongly suspected; the King's Business must be done; so many brave Troops, come so far for your Defence, must not stand idle, thro' your backwardness to do what may be reasonably expected from you; Waggons and Horses must be had; violent Measures will probably be used; and you will be to seek for a Recompence where you can find it, and your Case perhaps be little pitied or regarded.

I have no particular Interest in this Affair; as (except the Satisfaction of endeavouring to do Good and prevent Mischief) I shall have only my Labour for my Pains. If this Method of obtaining the Waggons and Horses is not like to succeed, I am oblig'd to send Word to the General in fourteen Days; and I suppose Sir John St. Clair the Hussar, with a Body of Soldiers, will immediately enter the Province, for the Purpose aforesaid, of which I shall be sorry to hear, because I am, very sincerely and truly your Friend and Well-wisher, B. FRANKLIN.

I receiv'd of the General about £800 to be disburs'd in Advance-money to the Waggon-Owners &c: but that Sum being insufficient, I advanc'd upwards of £200 more, and in two Weeks, the 150 Waggons with 259 carrying Horses were on their March for the Camp. The Advertisement promised Payment according to the Valuation, in case any Waggon or Horse should be lost. The Owners however, alledging they did not know General Braddock, or what dependance might be had on his Promise, insisted on my Bond for the Performance, which I accordingly gave them.

While I was at the Camp, supping one Evening with the Officers of Col. Dunbar's Regiment, he represented to me his Concern for the Subalterns, who he said were generally not in Affluence, and could ill afford in this dear Country to lay in the Stores that might be necessary in so long a March thro' a Wilderness where nothing was to be purchas'd. I commiserated their case, and resolved to endeavor procuring them some relief. I said nothing, however, to him of my Intention, but wrote the next Morning to the Committee of Assembly, who had the Disposition of some public Money, warmly recommending the Case of these Officers to their Consideration, and proposing that a Present should be sent them of Necessaries and Refreshments. My Son, who had had some Experience of a Camp Life, and of its Wants, drew up a List for me, which I inclos'd in my Letter.[7] The Committee approv'd, and used such Diligence, that conducted by my Son, the Stores arrived at the Camp as soon as the Waggons. They consisted of 20 Parcels, each containing

6 lb Loaf Sugar
6 lb good Muscovado Do.
1 lb good Green Tea
1 lb good Bohea Do.
6 lb good ground Coffee
6 lb Chocolate
½ cwt. best white Biscuit
½ lb Pepper
1 Quart best white Wine Vinegar
1 Gloucester Cheese
1 Kegg containing 20 lb good Butter
2 Doz. old Madeira Wine
2 Gallons Jamaica Spirits
1 Bottle Flour of Mustard
2 well-cur'd Hams
½ Doz. dry'd Tongues
6 lb Rice
6 lb Raisins.

These 20 Parcels well pack'd were plac'd on as many Horses, each Parcel with the Horse, being intended as a Present for one Officer. They were very thankfully receiv'd, and the Kindness acknowledg'd by Letters to me from the Colonels of both Regiments[8] in the most grateful Terms. The General too was highly satisfied with my Conduct in procuring him the Waggons, &c. and readily paid my Account of Disbursements; thanking me repeatedly and requesting my farther Assistance in sending Provisions after him.

7. William had been an ensign in a Pennsylvania company encamped at Albany during the winter of 1746–47 as part of the colonial army raised for what proved to be an abortive expedition against Canada.

8. Thomas Dunbar and Sir Peter Halkett.

I undertook this also, and was busily employ'd in it till we heard of his Defeat, advancing, for the Service, of my own Money, upwards of £1000 Sterling, of which I sent him an Account. It came to his Hands luckily for me a few Days before the Battle, and he return'd me immediately an Order on the Paymaster for the round Sum of £1000 leaving the Remainder to the next Account. I consider this Payment as good Luck; having never been able to obtain that Remainder of which more hereafter.

This General was I think a brave Man, and might probably have made a Figure as a good Officer in some European War. But he had too much self-confidence, too high an Opinion of the Validity of Regular Troops, and too mean a One of both Americans and Indians. George Croghan, our Indian Interpreter, join'd him on his March with 100 of those People, who might have been of great Use to his Army as Guides, Scouts, &c. if he had treated them kindly; but he slighted and neglected them, and they gradually left him.

In Conversation with him one day, he was giving me some Account of his intended Progress. "After taking Fort DuQuesne, says he, I am to proceed to Niagara; and having taken that, to Frontenac, if the Season will allow time; and I suppose it will; for Duquesne can hardly detain me above three or four Days; and then I see nothing that can obstruct my March to Niagara." Having before revolv'd in my Mind the long Line his Army must make in their March, by a very narrow Road to be cut for them thro' the Woods and Bushes; and also what I had read of a former Defeat of 1500 French who invaded the Iroquois Country,[9] I had conceiv'd some Doubts and some Fears for the Event of the Campaign. But

9. Perhaps the campaign of the Marquis de Denonville against the Senecas in 1687. Denonville's army was ambushed, rallied to drive off the Indians, and then proceeded to burn their villages, but he was forced to retire with his sick and decimated ranks, leaving the Senecas in possession of their country and nearly as strong as ever.

I ventur'd only to say, To be sure, Sir, if you arrive well before Duquesne, with these fine Troops so well provided with Artillery, that Place, not yet compleatly fortified, and as we hear with no very strong Garrison, can probably make but a short Resistance. The only Danger I apprehend of Obstruction to your March, is from Ambuscades of Indians, who by constant Practice are dextrous in laying and executing them. And the slender Line near four Miles long, which your Army must make, may expose it to be attack'd by Surprize in its Flanks, and to be cut like a Thread into several Pieces, which from their Distance cannot come up in time to support each other. He smil'd at my Ignorance, and reply'd, "These Savages may indeed be a formidable Enemy to your raw American Militia; but upon the King's regular and disciplin'd Troops, Sir, it is impossible they should make any Impression." I was conscious of an Impropriety in my Disputing with a military Man in Matters of his Profession, and said no more.

The Enemy however did not take the Advantage of his Army which I apprehended its long Line of March expos'd it to, but let it advance without Interruption till within 9 Miles of the Place; and then when more in a Body, (for it had just pass'd a River where the Front had halted till all were come over) and in a more open Part of the Woods than any it had pass'd, attack'd its advanc'd Guard, by a heavy Fire from behind Trees and Bushes; which was the first Intelligence the General had of an Enemy's being near him.[1] This Guard being disordered, the General hurried the Troops up to their Assistance, which was done in great Confusion thro'

1. Braddock failed to provide adequate reconnaissance for his advance, yet the battle was not the result of an ambush but one in which the two forces came together to the surprise of both. The French and their Indian allies, however, rallied more quickly and took advantage of the terrain to pour a destructive fire into the head and flanks of the British until Braddock's troops broke and ran.

Waggons, Baggage and Cattle; and presently the Fire came upon their Flank; the Officers being on Horseback were more easily distinguish'd, pick'd out as Marks, and fell very fast; and the Soldiers were crowded together in a Huddle, having or hearing no Orders, and standing to be shot at till two thirds of them were killed, and then being seiz'd with a Pannick the whole fled with Precipitation. The Waggoners took each a Horse out of his Team, and scamper'd; their Example was immediately follow'd by others, so that all the Waggons, Provisions, Artillery and Stores were left to the Enemy. The General being wounded was brought off with Difficulty, his Secretary Mr. Shirley[2] was killed by his Side, and out of 86 Officers 63 were killed or wounded, and 714 Men killed out of 1100.[3] These 1100 had been picked Men, from the whole Army, the Rest had been left behind with Col. Dunbar, who was to follow with the heavier Part of the Stores, Provisions and Baggage.

The Flyers, not being pursu'd, arriv'd at Dunbar's Camp, and the Pannick they brought with them instantly seiz'd him and all his People. And tho' he had now above 1000 Men, and the Enemy who had beaten Braddock did not at most exceed 400,[4] Indians and French together; instead of Proceeding and endeavouring to recover some of the lost Honour, he order'd all the Stores Ammunition, &c. to be destroy'd, that he might have more Horses to assist his Flight towards the Settlements, and less Lumber to remove. He was there met with Requests from the Governor's of Virginia, Maryland and Pennsylvania,[5] that he would post his Troops

2. William Shirley, Jr.

3. More accurate reports indicate that of 1469 men of all ranks engaged 456 were killed and 520 wounded.

4. More probably about 800; they lost about 25 killed and an equal number wounded.

5. Robert Dinwiddie, Horatio Sharpe, and Robert Hunter Morris, respectively.

on the Frontiers so as to afford some Protection to the Inhabitants; but he continu'd his hasty March thro' all the Country, not thinking himself safe till he arriv'd at Philadelphia, where the Inhabitants could protect him. This whole Transaction gave us Americans the first Suspicion that our exalted Ideas of the Prowess of British Regulars had not been well founded.

In their first March too, from their Landing till they got beyond the Settlements, they had plundered and stript the Inhabitants, totally ruining some poor Families, besides insulting, abusing and confining the People if they remonstrated. This was enough to put us out of Conceit of such Defenders if we had really wanted any. How different was the Conduct of our French Friends in 1781, who during a March thro' the most inhabited Part of our Country, from Rhodeisland to Virginia, near 700 Miles, occasion'd not the smallest Complaint, for the Loss of a Pig, a Chicken, or even an Apple![6]

Capt. Orme, who was one of the General's Aid de Camps, and being grievously wounded was brought off with him, and continu'd with him to his Death, which happen'd in a few Days, told me, that he was totally silent, all the first Day, and at Night only said, *Who'd have thought it?* that he was silent again the following Days, only saying at last, *We shall better know how to deal with them another time;* and dy'd a few Minutes after.

The Secretary's Papers with all the General's Orders, Instructions and Correspondence falling into the Enemy's Hands, they selected and translated into French a Number of the Articles, which

6. This paragraph, inserted in the margin of the manuscript, reflects Franklin's post-1776 attitudes. Braddock and his army were welcomed enthusiastically in the colonies. True, he impressed wagons, horses, and indentured servants, his officers were arrogant, and his soldiers probably committed a fair share of depredations, but the inhabitants seem to have made only the usual complaints.

they printed to prove the hostile Intentions of the British Court before the Declaration of War.[7] Among these I saw some Letters of the General to the Ministry speaking highly of the great Service I had rendred the Army, and recommending me to their Notice. David Hume too, who was some Years after Secretary to Lord Harcourt[8] when Minister in France, and afterwards to Genl. Conway when Secretary of State, told me he had seen among the Papers in that Office Letters from Braddock highly recommending me. But the Expedition having been unfortunate, my Service it seems was not thought of much Value, for those Recommendations were never of any Use to me.

As to Rewards from himself, I ask'd only one, which was, that he would give Orders to his Officers not to enlist any more of our bought Servants, and that he would discharge such as had been already enlisted. This he readily granted, and several were accordingly return'd to their Masters on my Application. Dunbar, when the Command devolv'd on him, was not so generous. He Being at Philadelphia on his Retreat, or rather Flight, I apply'd to him for the Discharge of the Servants of three poor Farmers of Lancaster County that he had inlisted, reminding him of the late General's Orders on that head. He promis'd me, that if the Masters would come to him at Trenton, where he should be in a few Days on his March to New York, he would there deliver their Men to them. They accordingly were at the Expence and Trouble of going to Trenton, and there he refus'd to perform his Promise, to their great Loss and Disappointment.[9]

7. *Mémoire contenant le précis des faits, avec leur pièces justificatives* (Paris, 1756), was translated and printed in Philadelphia and New York in 1757. A letter from Braddock in it, dated June 5, 1755, refers warmly to Franklin.

8. The Earl of Hertford, not Harcourt.

9. Enlistment of indentured servants, for whom masters had paid large sums and might have received little service yet in return, continued after

As soon as the Loss of the Waggons and Horses was generally known, all the Owners came upon me for the Valuation which I had given Bond to pay. Their Demands gave me a great deal of Trouble, my acquainting them that the Money was ready in the Paymaster's Hands, but that Orders for paying it must first be obtained from General Shirley,[1] and my assuring them that I had apply'd to that General by Letter, but he being at a Distance an Answer could not soon be receiv'd, and they must have Patience; all this was not sufficient to satisfy, and some began to sue me. General Shirley at length reliev'd me from this terrible Situation, by appointing Commissioners to examine the Claims and ordering Payment. They amounted to near twenty Thousand Pound, which to pay would have ruined me.

Before we had the News of this Defeat, the two Doctors Bond[2] came to me with a Subscription Paper, for raising Money to defray the Expence of a grand Fire Work, which it was intended to exhibit at a Rejoicing on receipt of the News of our Taking Fort Duquesne. I looked grave and said "it would, I thought, be time enough to prepare for the Rejoicing when we knew we should have occasion to rejoice." They seem'd surpriz'd that I did not immediately comply with their Proposal. "Why, the D——l," says one of them, "you surely don't suppose that the Fort will not be taken?" "I don't know that it will not be taken; but I know that the Events of War are subject to great Uncertainty." I gave them the reasons of my doubting. The Subscription was dropt, and the Projectors

Braddock's time and caused great hard feeling between the colonists and British officers. Franklin advocated the masters' case many times. *Papers*, VI, 190, 207, 396–400, 474–5; VIII, 224–8.

1. The governor of Massachusetts, who held an army commission as major general, succeeded to the command of British forces on Braddock's death.

2. Thomas and Phineas Bond.

thereby miss'd the Mortification they would have undergone if the Firework had been prepared. Dr. Bond on some other Occasions afterwards said, that he did not like Franklin's forebodings.

Governor Morris who had continually worried the Assembly with Message after Message before the Defeat of Braddock, to beat them into the making of Acts to raise Money for the Defence of the Province without Taxing among others the Proprietary Estates, and had rejected all their Bills for not having such an exempting Clause, now redoubled his Attacks, with more hope of Success, the Danger and Necessity being greater. The Assembly however continu'd firm, believing they had Justice on their side, and that it would be giving up an essential Right, if they suffered the Governor to amend their Money-Bills. In one of the last, indeed, which was for granting £50,000 his propos'd Amendment was only of a single Word; the Bill express'd that all Estates real and personal were to be taxed, those of the Proprietaries *not* excepted. His Amendment was; for *not* read *only*. A small but very material Alteration![3]

However, when the News of this Disaster reach'd England, our Friends there whom we had taken care to furnish with all the Assembly's Answers to the Governor's Messages, rais'd a Clamour against the Proprietaries for their Meanness and Injustice in giving their Governor such Instructions, some going so far as to say that by obstructing the Defence of their Province, they forfeited their Right to it. They were intimidated by this, and sent Orders to their Receiver General to add £5000 of their Money to whatever Sum might be given by the Assembly, for such Purpose.[4] This being notified to the House, was accepted in Lieu of their Share of a general Tax, and a new Bill was form'd with an exempting Clause

3. This dispute occurred in August 1755. *Papers,* VI, 129–66.

4. *Papers,* VI, 257 n, 279–81, 529-30, provide a full account of the Proprietors' £5000 gift and its crucial effect on passage of the £60,000 supply bill of Nov. 27, 1755.

which pass'd accordingly. By this Act I was appointed one of the Commissioners for disposing of the Money, £60,000.[5] I had been active in modelling it, and procuring its Passage: and had at the same time drawn a Bill for establishing and disciplining a voluntary Militia, which I carried thro' the House without much Difficulty, as Care was taken in it, to leave the Quakers at their Liberty. To promote the Association necessary to form the Militia, I wrote a Dialogue,* stating and answering all the Objections I could think of to such a Militia, which was printed and had as I thought great Effect.[6]

While the several Companies in the City and Country were forming and learning their Exercise, the Governor prevail'd with me to take Charge of our Northwestern Frontier, which was infested by the Enemy, and provide for the Defence of the Inhabitants by raising Troops, and building a Line of Forts.[7] I undertook this

*This Dialogue and the Militia Act are in the Gent. Magazine for February and March 1756.

5. Two of the seven commissioners were supporters of the Proprietors, but the others were political associates of Franklin. The commissioners assisted in vigorous defense measures, but they kept direction of the effort under Assembly control, thus usurping traditional executive powers. *Papers,* VI, 284–5, 392–6, 437–40; VII, 3–5, 25–8.

6. Franklin's militia bill provided for absolute exemption of Quakers and other conscientious objectors, voluntary enlistment, election of company officers by the ranks, and practically no military discipline. Altogether it was a most unusual piece of legislation, which Governor Morris and his friends proclaimed a "Solemn Farce," yet it was the first act establishing a military force ever passed in Quaker-controlled Pennsylvania. The Privy Council disallowed it on July 7, 1756. The text of the act and Franklin's argument in its favor, "A Dialogue between X, Y, and Z," first printed in *Pa. Gazette,* Dec. 18, 1755, are in *Papers,* VI, 266–73, 295–306.

7. Franklin and two other commissioners were in Northampton County, on the northeastern frontier, Dec. 18–31, 1755, planning defenses there. Then,

military Business, tho' I did not conceive myself well-qualified for it. He gave me a Commission with full Powers and a Parcel of blank Commissions for Officers, to be given to whom I thought fit. I had but little Difficulty in raising Men, having soon 560 under my Command. My Son who had in the preceding War been an Officer in the Army rais'd against Canada, was my Aid de Camp, and of great Use to me. The Indians had burnt Gnadenhut, a Village settled by the Moravians, and massacred the Inhabitants, but the Place was thought a good Situation for one of the Forts.[8] In order to march thither, I assembled the Companies at Bethlehem, the chief Establishment of those People. I was surprized to find it in so good a Posture of Defence. The Destruction of Gnadenhut had made them apprehend Danger. The principal Buildings were defended by a Stockade. They had purchased a Quantity of Arms and Ammunition from New York, and had even plac'd Quantities of small Paving Stones between the Windows of their high Stone Houses, for their Women to throw down upon the Heads of any Indians that should attempt to force into them. The armed Bretheren too, kept Watch, and reliev'd as methodically as in any Garrison Town. In Conversation with Bishop Spangenberg, I mention'd this my Surprize; for knowing they had obtain'd an Act of Parliament exempting them from military Duties in the Colonies, I had suppos'd they were consciencious[ly] scrupulous of bearing Arms.

---

after conferences with Morris in Reading, Franklin was given sole military and civil command in the county, Jan. 5, 1756, and returned there for about a month. Records and maps of his frontier service are in *Papers,* VI, 307–15, 339–83.

8. Indians destroyed Gnadenhütten (Huts of Grace), now Weissport, in the mountains about 25 miles above Bethlehem, on Nov. 24, 1755, and routed soldiers stationed there, Jan. 1, 1756. The Moravians (or Church of the United Brethren) had come to Pennsylvania, mostly from Saxony, in 1735. Their community life and mission work centered in Bethlehem, which they founded six years later.

He answer'd me, "That it was not one of their establish'd Principles; but that at the time of their obtaining that Act, it was thought to be a Principle with many of their People. On this Occasion, however, they to their Surprize found it adopted by but a few." It seems they were either deceiv'd in themselves, or deceiv'd the Parliament. But Common Sense aided by present Danger, will sometimes be too strong for whimsicall Opinions.

It was the Beginning of January when we set out upon this Business of Building Forts. I sent one Detachment towards the Minisinks,[9] with Instructions to erect one for the Security of that upper part of the Country; and another to the lower Part, with similar Instructions. And I concluded to go myself with the rest of my Force to Gnadenhut, where a Fort was tho't more immediately necessary. The Moravians procur'd me five Waggons for our Tools, Stores, Baggage, &c. Just before we left Bethlehem, Eleven Farmers who had been driven from their Plantations by the Indians, came to me requesting a supply of Fire Arms, that they might go back and fetch off their Cattle. I gave them each a Gun with suitable Ammunition. We had not march'd many Miles before it began to rain, and it continu'd raining all Day. There were no Habitations on the Road, to shelter us, till we arriv'd near Night, at the House of a German, where and in his Barn we were all huddled together as wet as Water could make us.[1] It was well we were not attack'd in our March, for Our Arms were of the most

9. The Delaware valley region between present Stroudsburg and Milford, Pa. Franklin's orders to Capt. John Van Etten to defend the area are in *Papers,* VI, 352–7.

1. Franklin's march from Bethlehem to Gnadenhütten took nearly four days, Jan. 15–18, 1756. His party stayed two nights at the place of Nicholas Uplinger, a German farmer and innkeeper who lived just beyond the Lehigh Water Gap in the Blue Mountains. They were held up there by this heavy winter rain, January 17, a damp and dreary fiftieth birthday for Franklin.

ordinary sort and our Men could not keep their Gunlocks dry. The Indians are dextrous in Contrivances for that purpose, which we had not. They met that Day the eleven poor Farmers above-mentioned and kill'd Ten of them. The one who escap'd inform'd that his and his Companions Guns would not go off, the Priming being wet with the Rain.[2]

The next Day being fair, we continued our March and arriv'd at the desolated Gnadenhut. There was a Saw Mill near, round which were left several Piles of Boards, with which we soon hutted ourselves; an Operation the more necessary at that inclement Season, as we had no Tents. Our first Work was to bury more effectually the Dead we found there, who had been half interr'd by the Country People. The next Morning our Fort was plann'd and mark'd out, the Circumference measuring 455 feet, which would require as many Palisades to be made of Trees one with another of a Foot Diameter each. Our Axes, of which we had 70 were immediately set to work, to cut down Trees; and our Men being dextrous in the Use of them, great Dispatch was made. Seeing the Trees fall so fast, I had the Curiosity to look at my Watch when two Men began to cut at a Pine. In 6 Minutes they had it upon the Ground; and I found it of 14 Inches Diameter. Each Pine made three Palisades of 18 Feet long, pointed at one End. While these were preparing, our other Men, dug a Trench all round of three feet deep in which the Palisades were to be planted, and our Waggons, the Body being taken off, and the fore and hind Wheels separated by taking out the Pin which united the two Parts of the Perch, we had 10 Carriages with two Horses each, to bring the Palisades from the Woods to the Spot. When they were set up, our Carpenters built a Stage of Boards all round within, about 6 Feet high, for the Men to stand on when to fire thro' the Loopholes. We had one swivel

2. Of this party of thirteen two escaped, one of whom, John Adam Huth (Hoeth), described the massacre vividly in *Pa. Gazette*, Jan. 29, 1756.

Gun which we mounted on one of the Angles; and fired it as soon as fix'd, to let the Indians know, if any were within hearing, that we had such Pieces; and thus our Fort, (if such a magnificent Name may be given to so miserable a Stockade) was finished in a Week, tho' it rain'd so hard every other Day that the Men could not work.[3]

This gave me occasion to observe, that when Men are employ'd they are best contented. For on the Days they work'd they were good-natur'd and chearful; and with the consciousness of having done a good Days work they spent the Evenings jollily; but on the idle Days they were mutinous and quarrelsome, finding fault with their Pork, the Bread, &c. and in continual ill-humour; which put me in mind of a Sea-Captain, whose Rule it was to keep his Men constantly at Work; and when his Mate once told him that they had done every thing, and there was nothing farther to employ them about; *O*, says he, *make them scour the Anchor.*

This kind of Fort, however contemptible, is a sufficient Defence against Indians who have no Cannon. Finding our selves now posted securely, and having a Place to retreat to on Occasion, we ventur'd out in Parties to scour the adjacent Country. We met with no Indians, but we found the Places on the neighbouring Hills where they had lain to watch our Proceedings. There was an Art in their Contrivance of these Places that seems worth mention. It being Winter, a Fire was necessary for them. But a common Fire on the Surface of the Ground would by its Light have discover'd their Position at a Distance. They had therefore dug Holes in the Ground about three feet Diameter, and some what deeper. We saw where they had with their Hatchets cut off the Charcoal from the Sides of burnt Logs lying in the Woods. With these Coals they had made small Fires in the Bottom of the Holes, and we observ'd among the Weeds and Grass the Prints of their Bodies made by their laying all round with their Legs hanging down in the Holes to

3. A diagram of this crude fortification is reproduced in *Papers*, VI, 367.

keep their Feet warm, which with them is an essential Point. This kind of Fire, so manag'd, could not discover them either by its Light, Flame, Sparks or even Smoke. It appear'd that their Number was not great, and it seems they saw we were too many to be attack'd by them with Prospect of Advantage.

We had for our Chaplain a zealous Presbyterian Minister, Mr. Beatty, who complain'd to me that the Men did not generally attend his Prayers and Exhortations. When they enlisted, they were promis'd, besides Pay and Provisions, a Gill of Rum a Day, which was punctually serv'd out to them half in the Morning and the other half in the Evening, and I observ'd they were as punctual in attending to receive it. Upon which I said to Mr. Beatty, "It is perhaps below the Dignity of your Profession to act as Steward of the Rum. But if you were to deal it out, and only just after Prayers, you would have them all about you." He lik'd the Thought, undertook the Office, and with the help of a few hands to measure out the Liquor executed it to Satisfaction; and never were Prayers more generally and more punctually attended. So that I thought this Method preferable to the Punishments inflicted by some military Laws for Non-Attendance on Divine Service.

I had hardly finish'd this Business, and got my Fort well stor'd with Provisions, when I receiv'd a Letter from the Governor, acquainting me that he had called the Assembly, and wish'd my Attendance there, if the Posture of Affairs on the Frontiers was such that my remaining there was no longer necessary. My Friends too of the Assembly pressing me by their Letters to be if possible at the Meeting, and my three intended Forts being now compleated,[4] and the Inhabitants contented to remain on their Farms under that Pro-

4. Franklin named the stockade he built Fort Allen; the others, built by parties sent out by him, were Fort Norris, about fifteen miles northeast, and one later called Fort Franklin, about the same distance in the opposite direction.

tection, I resolved to return. The more willingly as a New England Officer, Col. Clapham, experienc'd in Indian War, being on a Visit to our Establishment, consented to accept the Command. I gave him a Commission, and parading the Garrison had it read before them, and introduc'd him to them as an Officer who from his Skill in Military Affairs, was much more fit to command them than myself; and giving them a little Exhortation took my Leave. I was escorted as far as Bethlehem, where I rested a few Days, to recover from the Fatigue I had undergone.[5] The first Night being in a good Bed, I could hardly sleep, it was so different from my hard Lodging on the Floor of our Hut at Gnaden, wrapt only in a Blanket or two.

While at Bethlehem, I enquir'd a Little into the Practices of the Moravians. Some of them had accompanied me, and all were very kind to me. I found they work'd for a common Stock, eat at common Tables, and slept in common Dormitorys, great Numbers together. In the Dormitories I observ'd Loopholes at certain Distances all along just under the Cieling, which I thought judiciously plac'd for Change of Air. I was at their Church, where I was entertain'd with good Musick, the Organ being accompanied with Violins, Hautboys,[6] Flutes, Clarinets, &c. I understood that their Sermons were not usually preached to mix'd Congregations, of Men Women and Children, as is our common Practice; but that they assembled sometimes the married Men, at other times their Wives, then the Young Men, the young Women, and the little Children, each Division by itself. The Sermon I heard was to the latter, who came in and were plac'd in Rows on Benches, the Boys under the Conduct of a young Man their Tutor, and the Girls conducted by a

5. Franklin had stayed in Bethlehem, Jan. 7–15, 1756, preparing for his march to Gnadenhütten, but he was in a great hurry on his return, traveling all the way from Fort Allen to Philadelphia on February 4–5. He stopped in Bethlehem only overnight.

6. Oboes.

young Woman. The Discourse seem'd well adapted to their Capacities, and was delivered in a pleasing familiar Manner, coaxing them as it were to be good. They behav'd very orderly, but look'd pale and unhealthy, which made me suspect they were kept too much within-doors, or not allow'd sufficient Exercise. I enquir'd concerning the Moravian Marriages, whether the Report was true that they were by Lot? I was told that Lots were us'd only in particular Cases. That generally when a young Man found himself dispos'd to marry, he inform'd the Elders of his Class, who consulted the Elder Ladies that govern'd the young Women. As these Elders of the different Sexes were well acquainted with the Tempers and Dispositions of their respective Pupils, they could best judge what Matches were suitable, and their Judgments were generally acquiesc'd in. But if for example it should happen that two or three young Women were found to be *equally* proper for the young Man, the Lot was then recurr'd to. I objected, If the Matches are not made by the mutual Choice of the Parties, some of them may chance to be very unhappy. And so they may, answer'd my Informer, if you let the Parties chuse for themselves.—Which indeed I could not deny.

Being return'd to Philadelphia, I found the Association went on swimmingly, the Inhabitants that were not Quakers having pretty generally come into it, form'd themselves into Companies, and chosen their Captains, Lieutenants and Ensigns according to the new Law.[7] Dr. B.[8] visited me, and gave me an Account of the Pains he had taken to spread a general good Liking to the Law, and ascrib'd much to those Endeavours. I had had the Vanity to ascribe all to my Dialogue; However, not knowing but that he might be in

7. Actually, the election of militia officers, opposed by Governor Morris, caused great excitement and near riot in Philadelphia, but Franklin's associates had enough popular support generally to have their way. *Papers*, VI, 383–9.

8. Probably Dr. Thomas Bond.

the right, I let him enjoy his Opinion, which I take to be generally the best way in such Cases.

The Officers meeting chose me to be Colonel of the Regiment; which I this time accepted. I forget how many Companies we had, but we paraded about 1200 well looking Men, with a Company of Artillery who had been furnish'd with 6 brass Field Pieces, which they had become so expert in the Use of as to fire twelve times in a Minute. The first Time I review'd my Regiment, they accompanied me to my House, and would salute me with some Rounds fired before my Door, which shook down and broke several Glasses of my Electrical Apparatus. And my new Honour prov'd not much less brittle; for all our Commissions were soon after broke by a Repeal of the Law in England.[9]

During the short time of my Colonelship, being about to set out on a Journey to Virginia, the Officers of my Regiment took it into their heads that it would be proper for them to escort me out of town as far as the Lower Ferry. Just as I was getting on Horseback, they came to my door, between 30 and 40, mounted, and all in their Uniforms. I had not been previously acquainted with the Project, or I should have prevented it, being naturally averse to the assuming of State on any Occasion; and I was a good deal chagrin'd at their Appearance, as I could not avoid their accompanying me. What made it worse, was, that as soon as we began to move, they

9. Franklin's commission was issued on Feb. 23, 1756, the first review was on the 28th, and news of the disallowance of the Militia Act arrived in mid-October 1756. Franklin's political opponents viewed his parading less favorably; one reported that "The City is in an infinite distraction all owing to the Officers of the Militia puffed up and now solely directed by Colonel Franklin," while another questioned "Whether between 6 and 700 Men *and Boys*, a great Part of whom had never appeared in any former Muster, can with any Propriety be called a well trained Regiment of a Thousand Men?" *Papers*, VI, 409–11.

drew their Swords, and rode with them naked all the way. Somebody[1] wrote an Account of this to the Proprietor, and it gave him great Offence. No such Honour had been paid him when in the Province; nor to any of his Governors; and he said it was only proper to Princes of the Blood Royal; which may be true for aught I know, who was, and still am, ignorant of the Etiquette, in such Cases. This silly Affair however greatly increas'd his Rancour against me, which was before considerable, on account of my Conduct in the Assembly, respecting the Exemption of his Estate from Taxation, which I had always oppos'd very warmly, and not without severe Reflections on his Meanness and Injustice in contending for it. He accus'd me to the Ministry as being the great Obstacle to the King's Service, preventing by my Influence in the House the proper Forming of the Bills for raising Money; and he instanc'd this Parade with my Officers as a Proof of my having an Intention to take the Government of the Province out of his Hands by Force. He also apply'd to Sir Everard Fauckener, then Post Master General, to deprive me of my Office. But this had no other Effect, than to procure from Sir Everard a gentle Admonition.

Notwithstanding the continual Wrangle between the Governor and the House, in which I as a Member had so large a Share, there still subsisted a civil Intercourse between that Gentleman and myself, and we never had any personal Difference. I have sometimes since thought that his little or no Resentment against me for the Answers it was known I drew up to his Messages, might be the Effect of professional Habit, and that, being bred a Lawyer, he might consider us both as merely Advocates for contending Clients in a Suit, he for the Proprietaries and I for the Assembly. He would therefore sometimes call in a friendly way to advise with me on difficult Points, and sometimes, tho' not often, take my Advice.

1. Richard Peters.

We acted in Concert to supply Braddock's Army with Provisions, and when the shocking News arriv'd of his Defeat, the Governor sent in haste for me, to consult with him on Measures for preventing the Desertion of the back Counties. I forget now the Advice I gave, but I think it was, that Dunbar should be written to and prevail'd with if possible to post his Troops on the Frontiers for their Protection, till by Reinforcements from the Colonies he might be able to proceed on the Expedition. And after my Return from the Frontier, he would have had me undertake the Conduct of such an Expedition with Provincial Troops, for the Reduction of Fort Duquesne, Dunbar and his Men being otherwise employ'd; and he propos'd to commission me as General. I had not so good an Opinion of my military Abilities as he profess'd to have; and I believe his Professions must have exceeded his real Sentiments: but probably he might think that my Popularity would facilitate the Raising of the Men, and my Influence in Assembly the Grant of Money to pay them; and that perhaps without taxing the Proprietary Estate. Finding me not so forward to engage as he expected, the Project was dropt.[2] and he soon after left the Government, being superseded by Capt. Denny.

Before I proceed in relating the Part I had in public Affairs under this new Governor's Administration, it may not be amiss here to give some Account of the Rise and Progress of my Philosophical Reputation.

In 1746 being at Boston, I met there with a Dr. Spence,[3] who was lately arrived from Scotland, and show'd me some electric Experiments. They were imperfectly perform'd, as he was not very expert; but being on a Subject quite new to me, they equally surpriz'd and pleas'd me. Soon after my Return to Philadelphia, our

2. No other record of Morris' offer to Franklin is known and his plan for a renewed attack on Fort Duquesne came to nothing.

3. Archibald Spencer; the year was actually 1743.

Library Company receiv'd from Mr. Peter Colinson, F.R.S. of London a Present of a Glass Tube, with some Account of the Use of it in making such Experiments. I eagerly seized the Opportunity of repeating what I had seen at Boston, and by much Practice acquir'd great Readiness in performing those also which we had an Account of from England, adding a Number of new Ones.[4] I say much Practice, for my House was continually full for some time, with People who came to see these new Wonders. To divide a little this Incumbrance among my Friends, I caused a Number of similar Tubes to be blown at our Glass-House, with which they furnish'd themselves, so that we had at length several Performers. Among these the principal was Mr. Kinnersley, an ingenious Neighbour,[5] who being out of Business, I encouraged to undertake showing the Experiments for Money, and drew up for him two Lectures, in which the Experiments were rang'd in such Order and accompanied with Explanations in such Method, as that the foregoing should assist in Comprehending the following. He procur'd an elegant Ap-

4. In the early period of electrical investigation static electricity was usually produced for experimental purpose by rubbing a glass tube or globe with the hand or a piece of cloth or leather. It is uncertain just when the Library Company received Collinson's gift or when Franklin and his associates began to experiment with it. His friend James Logan, who lived a few miles outside Philadelphia, wrote him Feb. 23, 1747, that "yesterday was the first time that I ever heard of thy Electrical Experiments," and that he was greatly surprised by what he had heard. Franklin himself first mentioned his new activity in a letter to Collinson, March 28 of the same year, gratefully acknowledging that the Englishman's tube was what had "put several of us on making electrical experiments," and that "lately" this activity had "totally engrossed" his attention. Probably, therefore, he began his investigations sometime in 1746 or the winter of 1746–47. Long letters to Collinson of May 25 and July 28, 1747, on his and his associates experiments, were presented to the Royal Society, Jan. 21, 1748, and thereby introduced Franklin to English scientists. *Papers,* III, 110, 115–19, 126–35, 156–64.

5. The others were Thomas Hopkinson and Philip Syng.

paratus for the purpose, in which all the little Machines that I had roughly made for myself, were nicely form'd by Instrument-makers. His Lectures were well attended and gave great Satisfaction; and after some time he went thro' the Colonies exhibiting them in every capital Town, and pick'd up some Money. In the West India Islands indeed it was with Difficulty the Experiments could be made, from the general Moisture of the Air.

Oblig'd as we were to Mr. Colinson for his Present of the Tube, &c. I thought it right he should be inform'd of our Success in using it, and wrote him several Letters containing Accounts of our Experiments. He got them read in the Royal Society, where they were not at first thought worth so much Notice as to be printed in their Transactions. One Paper which I wrote for Mr. Kinnersley, on the Sameness of Lightning with Electricity, I sent to Dr. Mitchel, an Acquaintance of mine, and one of the Members also of that Society; who wrote me word that it had been read but was laught at by the Connoisseurs: The Papers however being shown to Dr. Fothergill, he thought them of too much value to be stifled, and advis'd the Printing of them. Mr. Collinson then gave them to Cave for publication in his Gentleman's Magazine; but he chose to print them separately in a Pamphlet, and Dr. Fothergill wrote the Preface.[6] Cave

6. In fact, many scientists in England recognized from the beginning that Franklin's experiments were important. Extracts from his 1747 letters were printed in the Royal Society's *Philosophical Transactions*, XLV (1748), 93–120, and the letter to Mitchell, read before the Royal Society and "Deservedly admired not only for the Clear Intelligent Stile, but also for the Novelty of the Subjects," was cited importantly in *ibid.*, XLVI (1749–50), 643. Edward Cave printed an article about Franklin's discoveries in *Gentleman's Magazine*, January 1750, and an extract from one of his letters in May. The pamphlet, the first edition of Franklin's basic scientific work, *Experiments and Observations on Electricity*, appeared in April 1751. With one exception (*Papers*, III, 472–3), all his major letters on electricity, 1747–53, were printed in this pamphlet or its supplements of 1753 and 1754; all are reprinted in *Papers* and

it seems judg'd rightly for his Profit; for by the Additions that arriv'd afterwards they swell'd to a Quarto Volume, which has had five Editions, and cost him nothing for Copy-money.

It was however some time before those Papers were much taken Notice of in England. A Copy of them happening to fall into the Hands of the Count de Buffon, a Philosopher deservedly of great Reputation in France, and indeed all over Europe he prevail'd with M. Dalibard to translate them into French, and they were printed at Paris. The Publication offended the Abbé Nollet, Preceptor in Natural Philosophy to the Royal Family, and an able Experimenter, who had form'd and publish'd a Theory of Electricity, which then had the general Vogue. He could not at first believe that such a Work came from America, and said it must have been fabricated by his Enemies at Paris, to decry his System. Afterwards having been assur'd that there really existed such a Person as Franklin of Philadelphia, which he had doubted, he wrote and published a Volume of Letters, chiefly address'd to me, defending his Theory, and denying the Verity of my Experiments and of the Positions deduc'd from them. I once purpos'd answering the Abbé, and actually began the Answer. But on Consideration that my Writings contain'd only a Description of Experiments, which any one might repeat and verify, and if not to be verify'd could not be defended; or of Observations, offer'd as Conjectures, and not delivered, dogmatically, therefore not laying me under any Obligation to defend them; and reflecting that a Dispute between two Persons writing in different Languages might be lengthened greatly by mis-translations, and thence misconceptions of one anothers Meaning, much of one of the Abbé's Letters being founded on an Error in the Translation; I concluded to let my Papers shift for themselves; believing it was

listed with page references in IV, 130, 461, and V, 435. Some later papers were included in the 1769 edition of *Experiments and Observations,* together with his writings on other scientific topics.

better to spend what time I could spare from public Business in making new Experiments, than in Disputing about those already made. I therefore never answer'd M. Nollet; and the Event gave me no Cause to repent my Silence; for my friend M. le Roy, of the Royal Academy of Sciences took up my Cause and refuted him, my Book was translated into the Italian, German and Latin Languages, and the Doctrine it contain'd was by degrees universally adopted by the Philosophers of Europe in preference to that of the Abbé, so that he liv'd to see himself the last of his Sect; except Mr. B—his Elève and immediate Disciple.[7]

What gave my Book the more sudden and general Celebrity, was the Success of one of its propos'd Experiments, made by Messrs. Dalibard and Delor, at Marly, for drawing Lightning from the Clouds. This engag'd the public Attention every where. M. Delor, who had an Apparatus for experimental Philosophy, and lectur'd in that Branch of Science, undertook to repeat what he call'd the *Philadelphia Experiments*, and after they were performed before the King and Court, all the Curious of Paris flocked to see them. I will not swell this Narrative with an Account of that capital Experiment, nor of the infinite Pleasure I receiv'd in the Success of a similar one I made soon after with a Kite at Philadelphia, as both are to be found in the Histories of Electricity.[8] Dr. Wright, an English Phy-

7. Nollet's book attacking Franklin is summarized in *Papers*, IV, 423–8. David Colden of New York and Giambatista Beccaria of Italy, as well as Dalibard and LeRoy, wrote effectively in his defense. *Ibid.*, V, 135–44, 395; VI, 97–101. Nollet's disciple was Mathurin-Jacques Brisson. Some of Franklin's electrical theories seem naïve and inadequate today, but, in the words of Nobel Prize winner Robert A. Millikan, they "laid the real foundation on which the whole superstructure of electrical theory and interpretation has been erected." Millikan included him in 1941 among "the fourteen most influential scientists who have lived since Copernicus was born in 1473."

8. The notable experiment at Marly-la-Ville, performed in essentially the manner Franklin had proposed in 1750, occurred on May 10, 1752; Guillaume

sician then at Paris, wrote to a Friend who was of the Royal Society an Account of the high Esteem my Experiments were in among the Learned abroad, and of their Wonder that my Writings had been so little noticed in England. The Society on this resum'd the Consideration of the Letters that had been read to them, and the celebrated Dr. Watson drew up a summary Account of them, and of all I had afterwards sent to England on the Subject, which he accompanied with some Praise of the Writer.[9] This Summary was then printed in their Transactions: And some Members of the Society in London, particularly the very ingenious Mr. Canton, having verified the Experiment of procuring Lightning from the Clouds by a Pointed Rod, and acquainting them with the Success, they soon made me more than Amends for the Slight with which they had before treated

---

Mazéas wrote the Royal Society of Louis XV's pleasure in the discoveries ten days later; and Franklin probably made his famous kite experiment in June 1752. *Papers,* IV, 302–10, 315–17. It is particularly disappointing that Franklin did not include here a full, first-hand account of his kite experiment. His statement of 1752 is very brief; the fullest report that survives is the one Joseph Priestley included in his *The History and Present State of Electricity* (London, 1767), based on information that Franklin had supplied him orally. *Papers,* IV, 360–9. Franklin had not carried out his own proposed experiment in 1750, soon after he first suggested it, because at that time he thought he needed to erect his conductor on a higher building than any then standing in Philadelphia. Apparently it was only later that he thought of using a kite.

9. Actually, Watson had read his "Account" to the Royal Society in June 1751, eleven months before Dalibard's successful experiment, but curiously he had failed to mention some of Franklin's most important ideas. especially his suggestions for protecting buildings from lightning and for proving experimentally whether clouds containing lightning are electrified. *Papers,* IV, 136–42. In contrast, Dalibard had immediately recognized the significance of the last suggestion, attempted it at the earliest possible moment, and so gained the priority.

me.[1] Without my having made any Application for that Honour, they chose me a Member, and voted that I should be excus'd the customary Payments, which would have amounted to twenty-five Guineas, and ever since have given me their Transactions gratis. They also presented me with the Gold Medal of Sir Godfrey Copley for the Year 1753, the Delivery of which was accompanied by a very handsome Speech of the President Lord Macclesfield, wherein I was highly honoured.[2]

Our new Governor, Capt. Denny, brought over for me the before mentioned Medal from the Royal Society, which he presented to me at an Entertainment given him by the City.[3] He accompanied it with very polite Expressions of his Esteem for me, having, as he said been long acquainted with my Character. After Dinner, when the Company as was customary at that time, were engag'd in Drinking, he took me aside into another Room, and acquainted me that he had been advis'd by his Friends in England to cultivate a Friendship with me, as one who was capable of giving him the best Advice, and of contributing most effectually to the making his Administration easy. That he therefore desired of all things to have a good Understanding with me; and he begg'd me to be assur'd of his Readiness on all Occasions to render me every

1. Benjamin Wilson and John Bevis also made experiments verifying Franklin's theory. *Papers,* IV, 390–2.

2. George Parker, Earl of Macclesfield, made the complimentary address before the Royal Society on Nov. 30, 1753, and Franklin was unanimously elected to the Society on April 29, 1756. *Papers,* V, 126–34; VI, 375–6.

3. The Rev. William Smith brought the medal to Franklin in May 1754, long before Governor Denny reached Philadelphia in August 1756. *Papers,* V, 331, 334. The "Entertainment" mentioned was probably the dinner given by the City Corporation to the new governor on August 22. Possibly Denny delivered the Royal Society's diploma of membership at this dinner and Franklin confused the two events in recollection.

Service that might be in his Power. He said much to me also of the Proprietor's good Dispositions towards the Province, and of the Advantage it might be to us all, and to me in particular, if the Opposition that had been so long continu'd to his Measures, were dropt, and Harmony restor'd between him and the People, in effecting which it was thought no one could be more serviceable than my self, and I might depend on adequate Acknowledgements and Recompences, &c. &c.

The Drinkers finding we did not return immediately to the Table, sent us a Decanter of Madeira, which the Governor made liberal Use of, and in proportion became more profuse of his Solicitations and Promises. My Answers were to this purpose, that my Circumstances, Thanks to God, were such as to make Proprietary Favours unnecessary to me; and that being a Member of the Assembly I could not possibly accept of any; that however I had no personal Enmity to the Proprietary, and that whenever the public Measures he propos'd should appear to be for the Good of the People, no one should espouse and forward them more zealously than myself, my past Opposition having been founded on this, that the Measures which had been urg'd were evidently intended to serve the Proprietary Interest with great Prejudice to that of the People. That I was much obliged to him (the Governor) for his Professions of Regard to me, and that he might rely on every thing in my Power to make his Administration as easy to him as possible, hoping at the same time that he had not brought with him the same unfortunate Instructions his Predecessor had been hamper'd with. On this he did not then explain himself. But when he afterwards came to do Business with the Assembly they appear'd again, the Disputes were renewed, and I was as active as ever in the Opposition, being the Penman first of the Request to have a Communication of the Instructions, and then of the Remarks upon them, which may be found in the Votes of the Time, and in the Historical Review I afterwards publish'd;[4] but between us personally no Enmity arose; we were often together, he was a Man of Letters, had seen much of the World, and was very entertaining and pleasing in Conversation. He gave me the first Information that my old Friend James Ralph was still alive, that he was esteem'd one of the best political Writers in England, had been employ'd in the Dispute between Prince Frederic and the King, and had obtain'd a Pension of Three Hundred a Year; that his Reputation was indeed small as a Poet, Pope having damn'd his Poetry in the Dunciad,[5] but his Prose was thought as good as any Man's.

The Assembly finally, finding the Proprietaries obstinately persisted in manacling their Deputies with Instructions inconsistent not only with the Privileges of the People, but with the Service of the Crown, resolv'd to petition the King against them, and appointed me their Agent to go over to England, to present and support the Petition.[6] The House had sent up a Bill to the Governor granting a Sum of Sixty Thousand Pounds for the King's Use, (£10,000 of which was subjected to the Orders of the then General Lord Loudon,) which the Governor absolutely refus'd to pass

4. The request to see the instructions and the long report to the Assembly of Sept. 23, 1756, condemning them are in *Papers*, VI, 496, 515–31. Richard Jackson's *An Historical Review of the Constitution and Government of Pennsylvania* was published in London with Franklin's assistance in May 1759.

5. Ralph defended some writers Pope had attacked in the first edition of the *Dunciad*, whereupon Pope added a couplet in the second edition:

> "Silence, ye Wolves! while Ralph to Cynthia howls,
> And makes Night hideous—Answer him ye Owls!"

He added a contemptuous footnote about "this low writer," "wholly illiterate," and scorned his recent poem, entitled "Night."

6. The Assembly protested the Proprietors' instructions on Sept. 16, 1756, and between Jan. 28 and Feb. 3, 1757, adopted unanimous resolves resulting in Franklin's appointment as agent in England. *Papers*, VI, 513–15; VII, 109–11.

in Compliance with his Instructions. I had agreed with Captain Morris of the Packet at New York for my Passage,[7] and my Stores were put on board, when Lord Loudon arriv'd at Philadelphia, expresly, as he told me to endeavour an Accomodation between the Governor and Assembly, that his Majesty's Service might not be obstructed by their Dissensions: Accordingly he desir'd the Governor and myself to meet him, that he might hear what was to be said on both sides.

We met and discuss'd the Business. In behalf of the Assembly I urg'd all the Arguments that may be found in the publick Papers of that Time, which were of my Writing, and are printed with the Minutes of the Assembly and the Governor pleaded his Instructions, the Bond he had given to observ them, and his Ruin if he disobey'd: Yet seem'd not unwilling to hazard himself if Lord Loudon would advise it. This his Lordship did not chuse to do, tho' I once thought I had nearly prevail'd with him to do it; but finally he rather chose to urge the Compliance of the Assembly; and he entreated me to use my Endeavours with them for that purpose; declaring he could spare none of the King's Troops for the Defence of our Frontiers, and that if we did not continue to provide for that Defence ourselves they must remain expos'd to the Enemy. I acquainted the House with what had pass'd, and presenting them with a Set of Resolutions I had drawn up, declaring our Rights, and that we did not relinquish our Claim to those Rights but only suspended the Exercise of them on this Occasion thro' *Force,* against which we protested, they at length agreed to drop that Bill and frame another conformable to the Proprietary Instructions. This of course the Governor pass'd, and I was then at Liberty to proceed on my Voyage: but in the meantime the Pacquet had sail'd with my

7. Capt. William Morris, master of the packet *Halifax,* is not further identified. The packets were fast vessels operated for the British government to carry mail and dispatches across the Atlantic.

Sea-Stores, which was some Loss to me, and my only Recompence was his Lordship's Thanks for my Service, all the Credit of obtaining the Accommodation falling to his Share.[8]

He set out for New York before me; and as the Time for dispatching the Pacquet Boats, was in his Disposition, and there were two then remaining there, one of which he said was to sail very soon, I requested to know the precise time, that I might not miss her by any Delay of mine. His Answer was, I have given out that she is to sail on Saturday next, but I may let you know, *entre nous*, that if you are there by Monday morning you will be in time, but do not delay longer. By some Accidental Hindrance at a Ferry, it was Monday Noon before I arrived, and I was much afraid she might have sailed as the Wind was fair, but I was soon made easy by the Information that she was still in the Harbour, and would not move till the next Day.

One would imagine that I was now on the very point of Departing for Europe. I thought so; but I was not then so well acquainted with his Lordship's Character, of which *Indecision* was one of the Strongest Features. I shall give some Instances. It was about the Beginning of April that I came to New York, and I think it was near the End of June before we sail'd.[9] There were then two of the

8. Franklin's summary of these events is badly scrambled. After several unsuccessful attempts to get a supply act which would include taxation of the proprietary estates, the Assembly yielded this major point and passed a tax bill exempting them, Jan. 29, 1757, but Denny rejected it for other reasons. The House adopted a strong remonstrance and voted to send Franklin to England to get the point settled for the future. So, when Loudoun arrived in Philadelphia, March 14, the Assembly had already made its concession on the bill and it was Denny, not the Assembly, on whom he brought effective pressure to give way. *Papers*, VI, 504–5; VII, 106–9, 145–53.

9. Franklin left Philadelphia on April 4, 1757, reached New York on the 8th, visited in New Jersey May 8–23, went on board the packet *General Wall* on June 5, sailed from Sandy Hook on the 20th, and departed from Loudoun's fleet shortly after June 23, 1757. *Papers*, VII, 174, gives a detailed chronology.

Pacquet Boats which had been long in Port, but were detain'd for the General's Letters, which were always to be ready to-morrow. Another Pacquet arriv'd and she too was detain'd, and before we sail'd a fourth was expected. Ours was the first to be dispatch'd, as having been there longest. Passengers were engag'd in all, and some extreamly impatient to be gone, and the Merchants uneasy about their Letters, and the Orders they had given for Insurance, (it being Wartime) and for Fall Goods. But their Anxiety avail'd nothing; his Lordships Letters were not ready. And yet whoever waited on him found him always at his Desk, Pen in hand, and concluded he must needs write abundantly. Going my self one Morning to pay my Respects, I found in his Antechamber one Innis,[1] a Messenger of Philadelphia, who had come from thence express, with a Pacquet from Governor Denny for the General. He deliver'd to me some Letters from my Friends there, which occasion'd my enquiring when he was to return and where he lodg'd, that I might send some Letters by him. He told me he was order'd to call to-morrow at nine for the General's Answer to the Governor, and should set off immediately. I put my Letters into his Hands the same Day. A Fortnight after I met him again in the same Place. So you are soon return'd, Innis! *Return'd;* No, I am not *gone* yet.—How so?—I have call'd here by Order every Morning these two Weeks past for his Lordship's Letter, and it is not yet ready.—Is it possible, when he is so great a Writer, for I see him constantly at his Scritore. Yes, says Innis, but he is like St. George on the Signs, *always on horse-back, and never rides on.* This Observation of the Messenger was it seems well founded; for when in England, I understood that Mr. Pitt gave it as one Reason for Removing this General, and sending Amherst and Wolf, *that the Ministers never heard from him, and could not know what he was doing.*

1. James Ennis.

This daily Expectation of Sailing, and all the three Packets going down to Sandy hook, to join the Fleet there, the Passengers thought it best to be on board, lest by a sudden Order the Ships should sail, and they be left behind. There if I remember right we were about Six Weeks, consuming our Sea Stores, and oblig'd to procure more. At length the Fleet sail'd, the General and all his Army on board, bound to Lewisburg with Intent to besiege and take that Fortress;[2] all the Packet Boats in Company, ordered to attend the General's Ship, ready to receive his Dispatches when those should be ready. We were out 5 Days before we got a Letter with Leave to part, and then our Ship quitted the Fleet and steered for England. The other two Packets he still detain'd, carry'd them with him to Halifax, where he staid some time to exercise the Men in sham Attacks upon sham Forts, then alter'd his Mind as to besieging Louisburg, and return'd to New York with all his Troops, together with the two Packets abovementioned and all their Passengers. During his Absence the French and Savages had taken Fort George on the Frontier of that Province, and the Savages had massacred many of the Garrison after Capitulation. I saw afterwards in London, Capt. Bonnell, who commanded one of those Packets. He told me, that when he had been detain'd a Month, he acquainted his Lordship that his Ship was grown foul, to a degree that must necessarily hinder her fast Sailing, a Point of consequence for a Packet Boat, and requested an Allowance of Time to heave her down and clean her Bottom. He was ask'd how long time that would require: He answer'd Three Days. The General reply'd, If you can do it in one Day, I give leave; otherwise not; for you must certainly sail the Day after to-morrow. So he never obtain'd leave tho' detain'd afterwards from day to day during full three Months.

2. Loudoun's forces gathered in Halifax during July 1757 for an assault on Louisbourg on Cape Breton Island, but bad weather, the lateness of the season, and the strength of the French prevented an attack. The army was

I saw also in London one of Bonell's Passengers, who was so enrag'd against his Lordship for deceiving and detaining him so long at New-York, and then carrying him to Halifax, and back again, that he swore he would sue him for Damages.[3] Whether he did or not I never heard; but as he represented the Injury to his Affairs it was very considerable. On the whole I then wonder'd much, how such a Man came to be entrusted with so important a Business as the Conduct of a great Army: but having since seen more of the great World, and the means of obtaining and Motives for giving Places and employments, my Wonder is diminished. General Shirley, on whom the Command of the Army devolved upon the Death of Braddock, would in my Opinion if continued in Place, have made a much better Campaign than that of Loudon in 1757, which was frivolous, expensive and disgraceful to our Nation beyond Conception: For tho' Shirley was not a bred Soldier, he was sensible and sagacious in himself, and attentive to good Advice from others, capable of forming judicious Plans, quick and active in carrying them into Execution.

Loudon, instead of defending the Colonies with his great Army, left them totally expos'd while he paraded it idly at Halifax, by which means Fort George was lost; besides he derang'd all our mercantile Operations, and distress'd our Trade by a long Embargo on the Exportation of Provisions, on pretence of keeping Supplies from being obtain'd by the Enemy, but in reality for beating down

---

back in New York on Aug. 31, 1757. Meanwhile, Loudoun's subordinates had behaved disgracefully during the French capture of Fort William Henry on Lake George (later rebuilt as Fort George) on August 9.

3. Here Franklin crossed out "and if he could not recover them, he would cut his Th." The angry man was Major Charles Craven, a passenger on Bonnell's packet, the *Harriott,* which, perhaps because of her sluggishness, was attacked and severely damaged by a French privateer, Nov. 11, 1757, during her long-delayed voyage to England.

their Price in Favour of the Contractors, in whose Profits it was said, perhaps from Suspicion only, he had a Share. And when at length the Embargo was taken off, by neglecting to send Notice of it to Charlestown, the Carolina Fleet was detain'd near three Months longer, whereby their Bottoms were so much damag'd by the Worm, that a great Part of them founder'd in the Passage home.[4] Shirley was I believe sincerely glad of being reliev'd from so burthensom a Charge as the Conduct of an Army must be to a Man unacquainted with military Business. I was at the Entertainment given by the City of New York, to Lord Loudon on his taking upon him the Command. Shirley, tho' thereby superseded, was present also. There was a great Company of Officers, Citizens and Strangers, and some Chairs having been borrowed in the Neighbourhood, there was one among them very low which fell to the Lot of Mr. Shirley. Perceiving it as I sat by him, I said, They have given you, Sir, too low a Seat. No Matter, says he, Mr. Franklin; I find *a low Seat* the easiest![5]

While I was, as aforemention'd, detain'd at New York, I receiv'd all the Accounts of the Provisions, &c. that I had furnish'd to Braddock, some of which Accounts could not sooner be obtain'd from the different Persons I had employ'd to assist in the Business. I presented them to Lord Loudon, desiring to be paid the Ballance. He caus'd them to be regularly examin'd by the proper Officer, who,

4. Loudoun imposed the embargo from March 2 to June 27, 1757, to insure that transports and supplies would be available for his Louisbourg expedition, as well as to keep provisions from the enemy. Loudoun did complain about the high prices his contractors were forced to pay, and of course he tried to keep them down, but there is no evidence that he profited personally from the embargo.

5. The entertainment took place on July 23, 1756, the evening of Loudoun's arrival in New York. At that time Shirley and Loudoun had begun a quarrel which became very bitter before Shirley left for England two months later, not in the least inclined to accept "a low Seat."

after comparing every Article with its Voucher, certified them to be right, and the Ballance due, for which his Lordship promis'd to give me an Order on the Paymaster. This, however, was put off from time to time, and tho' I called often for it by Appointment, I did not get it. At length, just before my Departure, he told me he had on better Consideration concluded not to mix his Accounts with those of his Predecessors. And you, says he, when in England, have only to exhibit your Accounts at the Treasury, and you will be paid immediately. I mention'd, but without Effect, the great and unexpected Expence I had been put to by being detain'd so long at N. York, as a Reason for my desiring to be presently paid; and on my observing that it was not right I should be put to any farther Trouble or Delay in obtaining the Money I had advanc'd, as I charg'd no Commissions for my Service, O, Sir, says he, you must not think of persuading us that you are no Gainer. We understand better those Affairs, and know that every one concern'd in supplying the Army finds means in the doing it to fill his own Pockets. I assur'd him that was not my Case, and that I had not pocketed a Farthing: but he appear'd clearly not to believe me; and indeed I have since learnt that immense Fortunes are often made in such Employments. As to my Ballance, I am not paid it to this Day, of which more hereafter.[6]

Our Captain of the Pacquet[7] had boasted much before we sail'd, of the Swiftness of his Ship. Unfortunately when we came to Sea,

6. Curiously, this story agrees more with Loudoun's contemporary report than with Franklin's to Speaker Norris. Loudoun noted that he would not pay because he wanted his accounts kept separate from those of Braddock and Shirley and because he thought Franklin's charge (£17 12*s.* 6*d.*) excessive. Franklin, on the other hand, reported Loudoun's final approval of the account, but to keep his affairs straight, the general asked, and Franklin agreed, that reimbursement be sought in England. *Papers,* VII, 226. There is no record that Franklin ever received payment in England.

7. Walter Lutwidge.

she proved the dullest of 96 Sail, to his no small Mortification. After many Conjectures respecting the Cause, when we were near another Ship almost as dull as ours, which however gain'd upon us, the Captain order'd all hands to come aft and stand as near the Ensign Staff as possible. We were, Passengers included, about forty Persons. While we stood there the Ship mended her Pace, and soon left our Neighbour far behind, which prov'd clearly what our Captain suspected, that she was loaded too much by the Head. The Casks of Water it seems had been all plac'd forward. These he therefore order'd to be remov'd farther aft; on which the Ship recover'd her Character, and prov'd the best Sailer in the Fleet. The Captain said she had once gone at the Rate of 13 Knots, which is accounted 13 Miles per hour.[8] We had on board as a Passenger Captain Kennedy[9] of the Navy, who contended that it was impossible, that no Ship ever sailed so fast, and that there must have been some Error in the Division of the Log-Line, or some Mistake in heaving the Log. A Wager ensu'd between the two Captains, to be decided when there should be sufficient Wind. Kennedy thereupon examin'd rigorously the Log-line and being satisfy'd with that, he determin'd to throw the Log himself. Accordingly some Days after when the Wind blew very fair and fresh, and the Captain of the Packet (Lutwidge) said he believ'd she then went at the Rate of 13 Knots, Kennedy made the Experiment, and own'd his Wager lost.

The above Fact I give for the sake of the following Observation. It has been remark'd as an Imperfection in the Art of Shipbuilding, that it can never be known 'till she is try'd, whether a new Ship will or will not be a good Sailer; for that the Model of a good sailing Ship has been exactly follow'd in the new One, which has

8. That is, 13 nautical miles, or not quite 17 land miles per hour.

9. Archibald Kennedy, Jr.

prov'd on the contrary remarkably dull. I apprehend this may be partly occasion'd by the different Opinions of Seamen respecting the Modes of lading, rigging and sailing of a Ship. Each has his System. And the same Vessel laden by the Judgment and Orders of one Captain shall sail better or worse than when by the Orders of another. Besides, it scarce ever happens that a Ship is form'd, fitted for the Sea, and sail'd by the same Person. One Man builds the Hull, another riggs her, a third lades and sails her. No one of these has the Advantage of knowing all the Ideas and Experience of the others, and therefore cannot draw just Conclusions from a Combination of the whole. Even in the simple Operation of Sailing when at Sea, I have often observ'd different Judgments in the Officers who commanded the successive Watches, the Wind being the same, One would have the Sails trimm'd sharper or flatter than another, so that they seem'd to have no certain Rule to govern by. Yet I think a Set of Experiments might be instituted, first to determine the most proper Form of the Hull for swift sailing; next the best Dimensions and properest Place for the Masts; then the Form and Quantity of Sails, and their Position as the Winds may be; and lastly the Disposition of her Lading. This is the Age of Experiments; and such a Set accurately made and combin'd would be of great Use. I am therefore persuaded that erelong some ingenious Philosopher will undertake it: to whom I wish Success.[1]

1. Though a landsman, Franklin was fascinated by this subject. In 1785, on the last of his eight ocean crossings and about three years before writing this part of his autobiography, he wrote a paper on Maritime Observations, the first part of which dealt with his theories for improving the speed of sailing vessels by reducing the size and increasing the number of the sails. His suggestions, while ingenious, have never found general acceptance, though in some measure they support the recognized advantages of fore-and-aft rig over square rig when sailing to windward.

We were several times chas'd on our Passage, but outsail'd every thing, and in thirty Days had Soundings.[2] We had a good Observation, and the Captain judg'd himself so near our Port, (Falmouth) that if we made a good Run in the Night we might be off the Mouth of that Harbour in the Morning, and by running in the Night might escape the Notice of the Enemy's Privateers, who often cruis'd near the Entrance of the Channel. Accordingly all the Sail was set that we could possibly make, and the Wind being very fresh and fair, we went right before it, and made great Way. The Captain after his Observation, shap'd his Course as he thought so as to pass wide of the Scilly Isles: but it seems there is sometimes a strong Indraught setting up St. George's Channel[3] which deceives Seamen, and caus'd the Loss of Sir Cloudsley Shovel's Squadron. This Indraught was probably the Cause of what happen'd to us. We had a Watchman plac'd in the Bow to whom they often call'd, *Look well out before, there;* and he as often answer'd *Aye, Aye!* But perhaps had his Eyes shut, and was half asleep at the time: they sometimes answering as is said mechanically: For he did not see a Light just before us, which had been hid by the Studding Sails from the Man at Helm and from the rest of the Watch; but by an accidental Yaw of the Ship was discover'd, and occasion'd a great Alarm, we being very near it, the light appearing to me as big as a Cart Wheel. It was Midnight, and Our Captain fast asleep. But

2. That is, had reached a point where bottom could be touched with a deep-sea lead line. Navigators knew, for example, that with a 240-foot line this was not possible until within about 60 miles west of the Scilly Islands, 25 miles off the southwest tip of England. Combined with a noontime observation of latitude, a sounding thus fixed a ship's position.

3. Between England and Ireland leading into the Irish Sea. A variable current across the mouth of the English Channel caused by strong west winds in the Bay of Biscay sometimes set sailing ships as much as fifty miles north of their dead-reckoning course.

Capt. Kennedy jumping upon Deck, and seeing the Danger, ordered the Ship to wear round, all Sails standing, An Operation dangerous to the Masts, but it carried us clear, and we escap'd Shipwreck, for we were running right upon the Rocks on which the Lighthouse was erected. This Deliverance impress'd me strongly with the Utility of Lighthouses, and made me resolve to encourage the building more of them in America, if I should live to return there.

In the Morning it was found by the Soundings, &c. that we were near our Port, but a thick Fog hid the Land from our Sight. About 9 a Clock the Fog began to rise, and seem'd to be lifted up from the Water like the Curtain at a Play-house, discovering underneath the Town of Falmouth, the Vessels in its Harbour, and the Fields that surrounded it. A most pleasing Spectacle to those who had been so long without any other Prospects, than the uniform View of a vacant Ocean! And it gave us the more Pleasure, as we were now freed from the Anxieties which the State of War occasion'd.

I set out immediately, with my Son for London, and we only stopt a little by the Way to view Stonehenge on Salisbury Plain, and Lord Pembroke's House and Gardens, with his very curious Antiquities at Wilton.[4]

We arriv'd in London the 27th of July 1757.

4. Wilton House, near Salisbury, the seat of the Herbert family, Earls of Pembroke. It had long been famous for its architecture, paintings, Roman statuary, and other "Antiquities," and for its magnificent gardens.

Part Four

As soon as I was settled in a Lodging Mr. Charles had provided for me, I went to visit Dr. Fothergill, to whom I was strongly recommended, and whose Counsel respecting my Proceedings I was advis'd to obtain. He was against an immediate Complaint to Government, and thought the Proprietaries should first be personally apply'd to, who might possibly be induc'd by the Interposition and Persuasion of some private Friends to accommodate Matters amicably. I then waited on my old Friend and Correspondent Mr. Peter Collinson, who told me that John Hanbury, the great Virginia Merchant, had requested to be informed when I should arrive, that he might carry me to Lord Granville's, who was then President of the Council, and wish'd to see me as soon as possible. I agreed to go with him the next Morning.

Accordingly Mr. Hanbury called for me and took me in his Carriage to that Nobleman's, who receiv'd me with great Civility; and after some Questions respecting the present State of Affairs in America, and Discourse thereupon, he said to me, "You Americans have wrong Ideas of the Nature of your Constitution; you contend that the King's Instructions to his Governors are not Laws, and think yourselves at Liberty to regard or disregard them at your own Discretion. But those Instructions are not like the Pocket Instructions given to a Minister going abroad, for regulating his Conduct in some trifling Point of Ceremony. They are first drawn up by Judges learned in the Laws; they are then considered, debated and perhaps amended in Council, after which they are signed by the King. They are then so far as relates to you, the *Law of the Land;* for THE KING IS THE LEGISLATOR OF THE COLONIES." I told his Lordship this was new Doctrine to me. I had always understood from our Charters, that our Laws were to be made by our Assemblies, to be presented indeed to the King for his Royal Assent, but that being once given the King could not repeal or alter them. And as the Assemblies could not make permanent Laws without his Assent, so neither could he make a Law for them without theirs. He assur'd me I was totally mistaken. I did not think so however. And his Lordship's Conversation having a little alarm'd me as to what might be the Sentiments of the Court concerning us, I wrote it down as soon as I return'd to my Lodgings.[1] I recollected that about 20 Years before, a Clause in a Bill brought into Parliament by the Ministry, had propos'd to make the King's Instructions Laws in the Colonies; but the Clause was thrown out by the Commons, for which we ador'd them as our Friends and Friends of Liberty, till by their Conduct towards us in 1765, it seem'd that they had refus'd that Point of Sovereignty to the King, only that they might reserve it for themselves.[2]

After some Days, Dr. Fothergill having spoken to the Proprietaries, they agreed to a Meeting with me at Mr. T. Penn's House in Spring Garden. The Conversation at first consisted of mutual Declarations of Disposition to reasonable Accommodation; but I suppose each Party had its own Ideas of what should be meant by *reasonable*. We then went into Consideration of our several Points of Complaint which I enumerated. The Proprietaries justify'd their Conduct as well as they could, and I the Assembly's. We now appeared very wide, and so far from each other in our Opinions, as to discourage all Hope of Agreement. However, it was concluded that

1. Franklin's notes are lost. His earlier accounts of the conversation, written in 1759 and 1772, give the same summary of Granville's remarks, but do not mention Franklin's reply.

2. In 1744 and again in 1749 Parliament had failed to pass bills offered to it which would have made royal instructions law in the colonies. The Stamp Act of 1765 extended parliamentary authority over the colonies into a new area and the Declaratory Act of 1766 asserted that this authority was unlimited.

I should give them the Heads of our Complaints in Writing, and they promis'd then to consider them.[3] I did so soon after; but they put the Paper into the Hands of their Solicitor Ferdinando John Paris, who manag'd for them all their Law Business in their great Suit with the neighbouring Proprietary of Maryland, Lord Baltimore, which had subsisted 70 Years,[4] and wrote for them all their Papers and Messages in their Dispute with the Assembly. He was a proud angry Man; and as I had occasionally in the Answers of the Assembly treated his Papers with some Severity, they being really weak in point of Argument, and haughty in Expression, he had conceiv'd a mortal Enmity to me, which discovering itself whenever we met, I declin'd the Proprietary's Proposal that he and I should discuss the Heads of Complaint between our two selves, and refus'd treating with any one but them. They then by his Advice put the Paper into the Hands of the Attorney and Solicitor General[5] for their Opinion and Counsel upon it, where it lay unanswered a Year wanting eight Days, during which time I made frequent Demands of an Answer from the Proprietaries but without obtaining any other than that they had not yet receiv'd the Opinion of the Attorney and Solicitor General: What it was when they did receive it I never learnt, for they did not communicate it to me,[6] but

3. Franklin submitted the "Heads of Complaint" to Thomas and Richard Penn on Aug. 20, 1757; *Papers*, VII, 248–52.

4. The dispute over the boundary between Maryland and Pennsylvania, settled, 1763–67, by the surveying of the Mason and Dixon Line.

5. Attorney General Charles Pratt and Solicitor General Charles Yorke.

6. Actually the Proprietors did send Franklin a copy of their answer (dated Nov. 27, 1758, and signed by F. J. Paris) to the "Heads of Complaint," though they did not furnish copies of the law officers' opinions nor of a letter to the Pa. Assembly (Nov. 28, 1758) containing strictures on Franklin's conduct. In response to his request (Nov. 28, 1758) for information needed to settle the tax dispute, the Proprietors contemptuously refused to have further dealings with him. These documents will be printed in *Papers*, VIII.

sent a long Message to the Assembly drawn and signed by Paris reciting my Paper, complaining of its want of Formality as a Rudeness on my part, and giving a flimsey Justification of their Conduct, adding that they should be willing to accomodate Matters, if the Assembly would send over *some Person of Candour* to treat with them for that purpose, intimating thereby that I was not such.[7]

The want of Formality or Rudeness, was probably my not having address'd the Paper to them with their assum'd Titles of true and absolute Proprietaries of the Province of Pensilvania, which I omitted as not thinking it necessary in a Paper the Intention of which was only to reduce to a Certainty by writing what in Conversation I had delivered *vivâ voce.* But during this Delay, the Assembly having prevail'd with Govr. Denny to pass an Act taxing the Proprietary Estate in common with the Estates of the People, which was the grand Point in Dispute, they omitted answering the Message.

7. Franklin and Thomas Penn quarreled bitterly during Franklin's first year in England. *Papers,* VII, 279–80, 285, 360–4, 366, 370, 372, 373–4. The agent reported that Penn talked "as a low Jockey might do when a Purchaser complained that He had cheated him in a Horse," while the Penns wrote that Franklin always looked "like a malicious V[illain]." Writing to a Pennsylvania Quaker, June 12, 1758, John Fothergill explained some of the difficulties: "B. Franklin has not yet been able to make much progress in his affairs. Reason is heard with fear: the fairest representations, are considered as the effects of superior art; and his reputation as a man, a philosopher and a statesman, only seem to render his station more difficult and perplexing: Such is the unhappy turn of mind, of most of those, who constitute the world of influence in this country. You must allow him time, and without repining. He is equally able and sollicitous to serve the province, but his obstructions are next to insurmountable: Great pains had been taken, and very successfully to render him odious and his integrity suspected, to those very persons to whom he must first apply. These suspicions can only be worn off by time, and prudence."

When this Act however came over, the Proprietaries counsell'd by Paris determin'd to oppose its receiving the Royal Assent. Accordingly they petition'd the King in Council, and a Hearing was appointed, in which two Lawyers were employ'd by them against the Act, and two by me in Support of it.[8] They alledg'd that the Act was intended to load the Proprietary Estate in order to spare those of the People, and that if it were suffer'd to continue in force, and the Proprietaries who were in Odium with the People, left to their Mercy in proportioning the Taxes, they would inevitably be ruined. We reply'd that the Act had no such Intention and would have no such Effect. That the Assessors were honest and discreet Men, under an Oath to assess fairly and equitably, and that any Advantage each of them might expect in lessening his own Tax by augmenting that of the Proprietaries was too trifling to induce them to perjure themselves. This is the purport of what I remember as urg'd by both Sides, except that we insisted strongly on the mischievous Consequences that must attend a Repeal; for that the Money, £100,000, being printed and given to the King's Use, expended in his Service, and now spread among the People, the Repeal would strike it dead in their Hands to the Ruin of many, and the total Discouragement of future Grants, and the Selfishness of the Proprietors in soliciting such a general Catastrophe, merely from a groundless Fear of their Estate being taxed too highly, was insisted on in the strongest Terms. On this Lord Mansfield, one of the

8. The hearings on the £100,000 Supply Act of 1759, taxing the proprietary estates, were held before the Privy Council committee, Aug. 27–28, 1760. The committee had before it a long report from the Board of Trade upholding the Proprietors' case and recommending disallowance of the Supply Act. The Board had reached this opinion after hearings in May 1760 at which Richard Jackson and William de Grey acted under Franklin's guidance as counsel for the Pennsylvania Assembly, and Charles Pratt and Charles Yorke were lawyers for the Proprietors. Franklin and Robert Charles appeared before the Privy Council committee, but its minutes do not name their counsel.

Council rose, and beckoning to me, took me into the Clerks' Chamber, while the Lawyers were pleading, and ask'd me if I was really of Opinion that no Injury would be done the Proprietary Estate in the Execution of the Act. I said, Certainly. Then says he, you can have little Objection to enter into an Engagement to assure that Point. I answer'd None at all. He then call'd in Paris,[9] and after some Discourse his Lordship's Proposition was accepted on both Sides; a Paper to the purpose was drawn up by the Clerk of the Council, which I sign'd with Mr. Charles, who was also an Agent of the Province for their ordinary Affairs; when Lord Mansfield return'd to the Council Chamber where finally the Law was allowed to pass. Some Changes were however recommended and we also engag'd they should be made by a subsequent Law; but the Assembly, did not think them necessary. For one Year's Tax having been levied by the Act, before the Order of Council arrived, they appointed a Committee to examine the Procedings of the Assessors, and On this Committee they put several particular Friends of the Proprietaries. After a full Enquiry they unanimously sign'd a Report that they found the Tax had been assess'd with perfect Equity.

The Assembly look'd on my entring into the first Part of the Engagement as an essential Service to the Province, since it secur'd the Credit of the Paper Money then spread over all the Country; and they gave me their Thanks in form when I return'd. But the Proprietaries were enrag'd at Governor Denny for having pass'd the Act, and turn'd him out, with Threats of suing him for Breach of Instructions which he had given Bond to observe. He however having done it [at] the Instance of the General and for his Majesty's Service, and having some powerful Interest at Court, despis'd the Threats, and they were never put in Execution.

9. Paris had died in December 1759; the Penns' new lawyer was Henry Wilmot.

Franklin's Outline

When Abel James wrote Franklin in 1782 that the original manuscript of the first part of the autobiography had come into his hands, he mentioned that with it "were Notes likewise in thy writing," and he enclosed a copy to help Franklin in his continuation. These "Notes" were an outline which Franklin had apparently set down soon after he began to write at Twyford in 1771. The original manuscript has not survived but what is almost certainly the copy James sent to France was acquired by John Bigelow with the manuscript autobiography in 1867. Probably Temple Franklin had given both to Le Veillard in 1791. It is printed here.[1]

Most of the text is in a clerical hand, but this part contains three emendations made later by Franklin. The portion at the end following the mention of the New Jersey Assembly was written by Franklin and must have been added at Passy. On the first page a vertical line extends from the top down through the word "Utility" in the notes about the Library. As this point corresponds with the end of Part One of the autobiography, Franklin must have drawn this line after receiving the copy to show the point he had reached while writing in 1771. Similarly, he later inserted a large closing bracket after "I am sent to England" to mark the end of Part Three.

Comparison with the text of the autobiography shows that Franklin apparently did not draw up this outline until he had begun to write at Twyford, because it begins only with mention of the Dogood letters,[2] *omitting the sections dealing with his ancestry and childhood. There*

1. Two variant copies of these notes also survive. One, in the hand of William Short, Thomas Jefferson's secretary in Paris, was made in 1786; the other, in Temple Franklin's hand and covering only the last third of the outline, was probably made some years later. They are described and discussed at length in Julian P. Boyd et al., eds., *The Papers of Thomas Jefferson*, IX (Princeton, 1954), 488–93.

2. See above, p. 67–8.

are also some variations in arrangement, indicating that he did not follow the outline precisely. The part not covered in the autobiography is of special interest, since it suggests the topics about which he had planned to write but never succeeded in treating.

My writing. Mrs. Dogoods Letters Differences arise between my Brother and me (his temper and mine) their Cause in general. His News Paper. The Prosecution he suffered. My Examination. Vote of Assembly. His Manner of evading it. Whereby I became free. My Attempt to get employ with other Printers. He prevents me. Our frequent pleadings before our Father. The final Breach. My Inducements to quit Boston. Manner of coming to a Resolution. My leaving him and going to New York. (return to eating Flesh.) thence to Pennsylvania. The Journey, and its Events on the Bay, at Amboy, the Road, meet with Dr. Brown. his Character. his great work. At Burlington. The Good Woman. On the River. My Arrival at Philada. First Meal and first Sleep. Money left. Employment. Lodging. First Acquaintance with my Afterwards Wife. with J. Ralph. with Keimer. their Characters. Osborne. Watson. The Governor takes Notice of me. the Occasion and Manner. his Character. Offers to set me up. My return to Boston. Voyage and Accidents. Reception. My Father dislikes the proposal. I return to New York and Philada. Governor Burnet. J. Collins. the Money for Vernon. The Governors Deceit. Collins not finding Employment goes to Barbados much in my Debt. Ralph and I go to England. Disappointment of Governors Letters. Col. French his Friend. Cornwallis's Letters. Cabbin. Denham. Hamilton, Arrival in England. Get Employment. Ralph not. He is an Expence to me. Adventures in England. Write a Pamphlet and print 100. Schemes. Lyons. Dr. Pemberton. My Diligence and yet poor thro Ralph. My Landlady. her Character. Wygate, Wilkes. Cibber. Plays. Books I borrowed. Preachers I heard. Redmayne. At Watts's—Temperance. Ghost. Conduct and Influence among the Men, persuaded by Mr. Denham to return with him to Philada. and be his Clerk. Our Voyage and Arrival. My resolutions in Writing. My Sickness. His Death. Found D. R married. Go to work again with Keimer. Terms. His ill Usage of me. My Resentment. Saying of Decow. My Friends at Burlington. Agreement with H. Meredith to set up in Partnership. Do so. Success with the Assembly. Hamiltons Friendship. Sewells History. Gazette. Paper Money. Webb. Writing Busy Body. Breintnal. Godfrey. his Character. Suit against us. Offer of my Friends Coleman and Grace. continue the Business and M. goes to Carolina. Pamphlet on Paper Money. Gazette from Keimer. Junto erected, its plan. Marry. Library erected. Manner of conducting the Project. Its plan and Utility.[3] Children. Almanack. the Use I made of it. Great Industry. Constant Study. Fathers Remark and Advice upon Diligence. Carolina Partnership. Learn French and German. Journey to Boston after 10 years. Affection of my Brother. His Death and leaving me his Son. Art of Virtue. Occasion. City Watch. amended. Post Office. Spotswood. Bradfords Behaviour. Clerk of Assembly. Lose one of my Sons. Project of subordinate Junto's. Write occasionally in the papers. Success in Business. Fire Companys. Engines. Go again to Boston in 1743. See Dr. Spence. Whitefield. My Connection with him. His Generosity to me. my returns. Church Differences. My part in them. Propose a College. not then prosecuted. Propose and establish a Philosophical Society. War. Electricity. my first knowledge of it. Partnership with D. Hall &c. Dispute in Assembly upon Defence. Project for it. Plain Truth. its Success. 10,000 Men raised and Disciplined. Lotteries. Battery built. New Castle. My Influence in the Council. Colours, Devices and Motto's. Ladies. Military Watch. Quakers. chosen of the common council. Put in the Commission of the Peace. Logan fond of me. his Library. Appointed post Master

3. The vertical line mentioned in the headnote stops here.

General. Chosen Assembly Man. Commissioner to treat with Indians at Carlisle and at Easton.[4] Project and establish Academy. Pamphlet on it. Journey to Boston. At Albany. Plan of Union of the Colonies. Copy of it. Remarks upon it. It fails and how. (Journey to Boston in 1754.) Disputes about it in our Assembly. My part in them. New Governor. Disputes with him. His Character and Sayings to me. Chosen Alderman. Project of Hospital. My Share in it. Its Success. Boxes. Made a Commissioner of the treasury. My Commission to defend the Frontier Counties. Raise Men and build Forts. Militia Law of my drawing. Made Colonel. Parade of my Officers. Offence to Proprietor. Assistance to Boston Ambassadors. Journey with Shirley &c. Meet with Braddock. Assistance to him. To the Officers of his Army. Furnish him with Forage. His Concessions to me and Character of me. Success of my Electrical Experiments. Medal sent me per Royal Society and Speech of President. Dennys Arrival and Courtship to me. his Character. My Service to the Army in the Affair of Quarters. Disputes about the Proprietors Taxes continued. Project for paving the City. I am sent to England.[5] Negociation there. Canada delenda est. My Pamphlet. Its reception and Effect. Projects drawn from me concerning the Conquest. Acquaintance made and their Services to me Mrs. S. Mr. Small. Sir John P. Mr. Wood. Sargent Strahan and others. their Characters. Doctorate from St. Andrews[6] Doctorate from Oxford. Journey to Scotland. Lord Leicester. Mr. Prat. De Grey. Jackson. State of Affairs in England. Delays. Event. Journey into Holland and Flanders. Agency from Maryland. Sons Appointment. My Return. Allowance and thanks. Journey to Boston. John Penn Governor. My Conduct towards him. The Paxton Murders. My

4. "and at Easton" is inserted in Franklin's hand.

5. The bracket mentioned in the headnote is inserted here.

6. Originally written "Edinburg," but "St. Andrews" is inserted below in Franklin's hand.

Pamphlet. Rioters march to Philada. Governor retires to my House. My Conduct. Sent out to the Insurgents—Turn them back. Little Thanks. Disputes revived. Resolutions against continuing under Proprietary Government. Another Pamphlet. Cool Thoughts. Sent again to England with Petition. Negociation there. Lord H. his Character. Agencies from New Jersey, Georgia, Massachusetts. Journey into Germany 1766. Civilities received there. Gottingen Observations. Ditto into France in 1767. Ditto in 1769. Entertainment there at the Academy. Introduced to the King and the Mesdames. Mad. Victoria and Mrs. Lamagnon. Duc de Chaulnes, M. Beaumont. Le Roy. Dalibard. Nollet. See Journals. Holland. Reprint my papers and add many. Books presented to me from[7] many Authors. My Book translated into French. Lightning Kite. various Discoveries. My Manner of prosecuting that Study. King of Denmark invites me to Dinner. Recollect my Fathers Proverb. Stamp Act. My Opposition to it. Recommendation of J. Hughes. Amendment of it. Examination in Parliament. Reputation it gave me. Caress'd by Ministry. Charles Townsends Act. Opposition to it. Stoves and Chimney plates. Armonica.[8] Acquaintance with Ambassadors. Russian Intimation. Writing in Newspapers. Glasses from Germany. Grant of Land in Nova Scotia. Sicknesses. Letters to America returned hither. the Consequences. Insurance Office. My Character. Costs me nothing to be civil to inferiors, a good deal to be submissive to superiors &c. &c.

Farce of perpetual Motion.
Writing for Jersey Assembly.[9]

7. Originally written "by," but corrected to "from," probably by James's copyist.

8. This word inserted in Franklin's hand.

9. These two lines, coming at the bottom of the third page, are the last in the hand of James's copyist. Franklin has written "verte" in the corner and the remaining notes, at the top of the fourth page, are in his hand in red ink.

Franklin's Outline

Hutchinson's Letters. Temple. Suit in Chancery, Abuse before the Privy Council. Lord Hillsborough's Character and Conduct. Lord Dartmouth. Negociation to prevent the War. Return to America. Bishop of St. Asaph. Congress, Assembly. Committee of Safety. Chevaux de Frize. Sent to Boston, to the Camp. To Canada. to Lord Howe. To France, Treaty, &c.

Biographical Notes

Assembled here in alphabetical order are brief sketches of all persons Franklin mentions in his autobiography, with two exceptions: (1) men or women whom it has been impossible to identify fully or on whom no information has been found other than what Franklin himself gives in the text; (2) those mentioned merely incidentally, such as authors of books Franklin read without ever coming into direct contact with the persons themselves. The symbol DAB or DNB at the end of a sketch indicates that an article on that person appears in Dictionary of American Biography *or* Dictionary of National Biography. *Useful full-length biographies or articles on a few individuals are also cited, but no attempt is made to list all sources from which information has been derived.*

ADAMS, MATTHEW (d. 1753), Boston merchant, book collector, one of the "Couranteers."

ALEXANDER, JAMES (1691–1756), a Jacobite descendant of the Earls of Stirling, fled from Scotland in 1715. He was a lawyer and politician who held offices in New York and New Jersey; also a mathematician and original member of the American Philosophical Society. His son William, who assumed the title of Lord Stirling (although the House of Lords disallowed his claim), was a prominent general in the American Army during the Revolution. *DAB.*

ALLEN, JOHN (d. 1750?), treasurer of the Western Division of New Jersey in 1730, judge of the Superior Court in the 1740s, sheriff of Hunterdon Co., 1750.

ALLEN, WILLIAM (1704–1780), merchant, public servant, chief justice, 1750–74. Born in Philadelphia, educated at Cambridge and the Middle Temple, he was Philadelphia's wealthiest citizen, leading philanthropist, social arbiter, and the political boss of the proprietary party. He assisted the artists Benjamin West and Charles Willson Peale, and also recommended Franklin for deputy postmaster general, later breaking with him over the issue of proprietary government. In 1776 he removed to England after fifty active and fruitful years service in the colony. *DAB.*

Biographical Notes

AMHERST, JEFFERY (1717–1797), British general, succeeded Loudoun as commander-in-chief in North America, 1758–63, and as titular governor of Virginia, 1759–68. He captured Louisbourg, 1758; Ticonderoga and Crown Point, 1759; and Montreal, 1760, ending French resistance in North America. He was made Knight of the Bath and received the thanks of Parliament, 1761, and was created Baron Amherst, 1776. Though he declined active command in America in that year, he was commander-in-chief in Great Britain in 1778 and again in 1793–95. *DAB, DNB.*

ANDREWS, JEDEDIAH (1674–1747?), A. B., Harvard, 1695, New England minister, recommended to Philadelphia Presbyterians by Increase Mather in 1698. He worked ably and energetically, especially opposing the Great Awakening. Hemphill became his assistant in 1733. Almost at the end of a long career he was suspended, accused of some "disgraceful act."

ANNIS, THOMAS, captain of the *London Hope,* on which Franklin sailed for London, Nov. 5, 1724.

BAIRD (BARD), PATRICK, surgeon, native Scot; Governor Keith's secretary; member of the Every Night Club; at several times secretary of the Provincial Council; appointed to visit sickly vessels, 1720. It is impossible to say which of several Scottish Patrick Bairds this particular one is; one authority has labeled him "the mysterious Dr. Baird of Philadelphia."

BALTIMORE, CHARLES CALVERT, 5TH BARON (1699–1751), proprietor of Maryland, held various offices in the royal household. He personally governed the province during a visit, 1732–33; M.P. 1734–51; F.R.S. The Penns began their "great Suit" against him in 1734, a decision was rendered in Chancery, 1750, but final settlement was reached only in 1767.

BALTIMORE, FREDERICK CALVERT, 6TH BARON (1731–1771), succeeded his father in the title and as proprietor of Maryland in 1751. Upon his death this "last and least worthy of the noble Calverts" bequeathed the province to an illegitimate son. *DNB.*

BASKETT, JOHN (d. 1742), master of the Stationers' Co., London, 1714–15. His Oxford Bible (1716–17) was typographically beautiful, but was called "a Baskett-full of printers errors." *DNB.*

Biographical Notes

BEATTY, CHARLES CLINTON (*c.* 1715–1772), fervent New Light Presbyterian, pastor of the Deep Run (Pa.) Church, successful exhorter of soldiers, later chaplain on the Forbes expedition against Ft. Duquesne. As a trustee of the College of New Jersey (Princeton), he visited England and the West Indies on fund-raising trips, dying in Barbados. *DAB*.

BENEZET, JOHN STEPHEN (1683–1751), well-to-do merchant and importer, came to Philadelphia in 1731 from London, where he had been a Huguenot refugee. He became a Quaker, then a Moravian, and was trustee of Whitefield's New Building and of the Charity School in Germantown.

BENGER, ELLIOTT (d. 1751), a Scot who emigrated to Virginia before 1728, entered the service of Col. Alexander Spotswood, and lived on his estate at New Post on the Rappahannock River near Fredericksburg. He married Spotswood's sister-in-law, and was appointed deputy postmaster general for North America, 1743.

BOND, PHINEAS. See immediately below.

BOND, THOMAS (1713–1784), physician, student in Paris and London, founder of the Pennsylvania Hospital, original member of the American Philosophical Society, trustee of the College, senior grand warden of Masons, first professor of clinical medicine in colonial America, did considerable service in organization of the army in 1777. *DAB*. His brother PHINEAS (1717–1773), another physician, was also active in the founding of the Hospital and in other civic activities. The Franklin family relied on one or the other of the brothers for medical service.

BONNELL, JOHN DOD, captain of the packet *Harriott*. He was wounded in action against a French privateer, Nov. 11, 1757, and in 1762 the postmasters general gave him and his ship's company £100 for their "gallant defense" against another privateer. He was then promoted to command an East India packet.

BRADDOCK, EDWARD (1695–1755), ensign in the British Army at fifteen, rising to major general in 1754; he landed in Virginia, 1755, as commander-in-chief with the widest powers ever given to a British officer in America. His initial objective was the capture of Fort Duquesne (Pittsburgh), but, without experience or even conception of wilderness warfare, and contemptuous of advice, he was defeated by French and Indians and fatally wounded in battle near the Monongahela River, July 9, 1755. *DAB; DNB;* Lee McCardell, *Ill-Starred General: Braddock of the Coldstream Guards* (Pittsburgh, 1958).

BRADFORD, ANDREW (1686–1742), son and partner of William Bradford; Franklin's competitor. He published the first Pennsylvania newspaper, *The American Weekly Mercury,* begun in 1719, as well as books, pamphlets, and almanacs; and was official printer to Pennsylvania. His nephew and adopted son William (also Franklin's competitor and printer of *The Pennsylvania Journal*) became the famous "patriot-printer" of the Revolution. *DAB;* Anna J. DeArmond, *Andrew Bradford, Colonial Journalist* (Newark, Del., 1949).

BRADFORD, WILLIAM (1663–1752), a pioneer American printer, father of Franklin's competitor Andrew, said to have come to Pennsylvania with William Penn. He displeased the Quaker leaders by printing some of George Keith's writings, was tried but not convicted, and in 1693 moved to New York, where he became royal printer. One of his apprentices was John Peter Zenger. *DAB.*

BREINTNALL, JOSEPH (d. 1746), Quaker, merchant, copyist, original member of the Junto, versifier; secretary of the Library Co., 1731–36; sheriff, 1735–38. He made prints of tree leaves, and devised an experiment to test the reflection of sun's rays with colored cloths. His papers on the Aurora Borealis and rattlesnake-bite appeared in the *Philosophical Transactions* of the Royal Society, and some of his Busy-Body letters in Bradford's *American Weekly Mercury.*

BRISSON, MATHURIN-JACQUES (1723–1806), scientist, succeeded his mentor Nollet in the chair of physics at the Collège de Navarre.

BROCKDEN (BROGDEN), CHARLES (1683–1769), came to Philadelphia in 1706 and held many offices, notably clerk and record keeper under the Proprietors and recorder of deeds for Philadelphia; a tireless drafter of legal documents. "Always on the wing" spiritually, he left the Anglican Church to become a Quaker, then a follower of Whitefield, and finally a Moravian.

BROWNE, JOHN (*c.* 1667–1737), physician and innkeeper of Burlington, N.J., educated in London, a prominent, erudite, and colorful freethinker to whom Franklin was attracted, and whose epitaph he may have written.

Biographical Notes

BROWNELL, GEORGE (d. after 1750), kept a writing and arithmetic school in Boston; then operated a drygoods store and kept a school in Philadelphia, where he was one of Franklin's customers.

BUFFON, GEORGES-LOUIS LECLERC, COMTE DE (1707–1788), French naturalist, director of the Jardin du Roi. His system of classification for animals is comparable in importance to that of Linnaeus for plants. His encyclopedic *Histoire naturelle* was the first great presentation of natural history in popular form. He was also interested in electricity and kept his English friends informed of French experiments. He and Franklin met in France.

BURNET, WILLIAM (1688–1729), son of Gilbert, the celebrated Bishop of Salisbury (see *DNB*). He was successful as governor of New York and New Jersey (1720–28), but his one year as governor of Massachusetts (1728–29) was taken up by a quarrel with the Assembly over a permanent salary. His library was one of the finest in the colonies. *DAB*.

BUSTILL, SAMUEL (d. 1742?), had fled to England in company with Daniel Coxe in 1716 because of difficulties with Governor Robert Hunter in New Jersey; he came back in 1720; served as clerk of the Grand Jury, 1728; deputy secretary, 1730; alderman of Burlington, 1734.

CANTON, JOHN (1718–1772), London schoolmaster, electrical scientist, F.R.S. By some of their experiments he and Franklin stimulated each other to further investigations. *DNB*.

CAVE, EDWARD (1691–1754), printer, journalist, founder and publisher of *The Gentleman's Magazine*, especially notable for the space it gave to American and scientific news. "Perhaps no single man received more favorable notice in its pages than Franklin." He also published *Experiments and Observations on Electricity*, 1751. *DNB;* C. Lennart Carlson, *The First Magazine: A History of the Gentleman's Magazine* (Providence, 1938).

CHARLES, ROBERT (d. 1770), had been secretary to Governor Gordon in Pennsylvania, where he formed a close friendship with Isaac Norris; he returned to England in 1739, became agent for New York, 1748, and for the Pennsylvania Assembly, 1752. He and Franklin shared the agency from 1757 to 1761, when Charles withdrew. His affairs as agent for New York so "bewildered and distressed [him] that he finally put an End to his Perplexities—by a Razor!"

Biographical Notes

CLAPHAM, WILLIAM (d. 1763), Indian fighter; after further service on the frontier he quarreled with his officers and the commissioners, resigned, and settled near Pittsburgh, where he was killed and scalped by the Indians.

CLIFTON, JOHN (d. 1755), lived in a large brick house at the southeast corner of Clifton (Drinker's) Alley and Second Street, where he kept an apothecary shop. At one time he ran the George Tavern at Arch and Second Streets. He was disowned by the Quakers for marrying a woman whose husband was believed living.

CLINTON, GEORGE (*c.*1686–1761), British naval officer; governor of New York, 1743–53. Indolent and dependent on local political advisers, he nevertheless achieved his ambition of returning to England a rich man (£80,000). His son, Sir Henry, was commander-in-chief of the British forces during part of the Revolution. *DAB.*

COLEMAN, WILLIAM (1704–1769), successful merchant, original member of the Junto. He held many civic and governmental posts, including that of associate justice of the Supreme Court, 1758–69. One of Franklin's closest friends, he helped him set up independently as a printer and was named executor in his will of 1757.

COLLINSON, PETER (1694–1768), London Quaker merchant, F.R.S., one of the most important people in Franklin's life. A man of wide interests, he was a noted botanist who corresponded with Linnaeus and with colonial scientists, especially the botanist John Bartram. He was a great help to the Library Co. of Philadelphia in getting books in its early years and was responsible for the first publication, 1751, of Franklin's *Experiments and Observations on Electricity*. He welcomed Franklin to London in 1757 and their friendship remained warm and enriching. *DNB;* Norman G. Brett-James, *The Life of Peter Collinson, F.R.S., F.S.A.* (London, [1926]).

CONWAY, HENRY SEYMOUR (1721–1795), brother of Lord Hertford, field marshal, secretary of state, 1765–68, cousin of Horace Walpole, with whom he had a strong and lifelong friendship. "No man of his time was so generally liked." He consistently opposed the war with the American colonies. *DNB.*

COOPER, JOSEPH (d. 1731?), Quaker, member of the New Jersey Assembly, and collector of Gloucester Co.

Biographical Notes

COPLEY, SIR GODFREY, baronet (*c.*1654–1709), member of Parliament, commissioner of accounts, F.R.S., with wide scientific interests; he made a valuable collection of prints and manuscripts. He was a friend of Sir Hans Sloane, to whose trust he bequeathed a fund for awards to be made by the Royal Society. These prizes were converted into medals in 1736. *DNB.*

CROGHAN, GEORGE (d. 1782), Indian interpreter and trader, land speculator, came from Ireland in 1741. Though chronically in debt, he was indispensable at Indian conferences, assisted Washington and Braddock, and became deputy superintendent of Indian affairs under Sir William Johnson. *DAB; DNB;* Nicholas B. Wainwright, *George Croghan Wilderness Diplomat* (Chapel Hill, 1959).

DALIBARD, THOMAS-FRANÇOIS (1703–1799), French physicist and botanist. After translating *Experiments and Observations on Electricity,* he arranged, and an assistant performed for the first time anywhere, May 10, 1752, Franklin's proposed experiment to prove the identity of lightning and electricity. He and Franklin corresponded and they met in Paris in 1767.

DECOW, ISAAC (d. before March, 1751), Quaker from Burlington Co., N.J., held various public offices, and became surveyor general in 1739.

DELOR, ——, "master of experimental philosophy," lectured on electricity in Paris, performed many of Franklin's experiments before King Louis XV, and repeated Franklin's suggested experiment to prove the identity of lightning and electricity in Paris a few days after Dalibard's achievement at Marly.

DENHAM, THOMAS (d. 1728), Philadelphia merchant, Franklin's benefactor, half-owner of the *Berkshire* on which Franklin returned from England. In his will he canceled the debt of £10 3*s.* 5*d.* due for passage.

DENNY, WILLIAM (1709–1765), A.B., Oxford, 1730, captain in the British Army, came to Pennsylvania as governor in 1756. Though Franklin here recalls no personal enmity, he did call the governor a Bashaw in the presence of his Council. The Indians wondered whether he was a man or a woman, the Quakers said, "Lord have mercy upon us," Secretary Peters called him "a triffler, weak of body," and his predecessor Morris said his only object seemed to be money. Unstable, bound by Proprietors' instructions, but dependent on the Assembly for salary and action, he could please neither party, and after disgusting everyone by virtually imprisoning his wife and abetting smugglers for pay, he was recalled in 1759, and finished out his life in ease and idleness.

DINWIDDIE, ROBERT (1693–1770), governor of Virginia, 1751–58. Born near Glasgow, he began a long and successful career in the colonial customs service in 1727, and as surveyor general for the Southern District in 1738 made his home in Virginia. His service as lieutenant governor and acting governor was distinguished by great energy and executive ability, especially in frontier and Indian affairs, but was marred by a quarrel with the Assembly over fees for land grants. *DAB*.

DUNBAR, THOMAS (d. 1767), colonel of the 48th Regiment of the British Army, on bad terms with General Braddock, he was in temporary command after Braddock's death. He was recalled after his misguided and panicky retreat to Philadelphia, resigned his regiment, and was appointed lieutenant governor of Gibraltar, 1755. He rose to major general, 1758, and lieutenant general, 1760, but was never again on active service.

EGREMONT, CHARLES WYNDHAM, 2D EARL OF (1710–1763), son of Sir William; succeeded to the earldom on the death of an uncle, 1750. As secretary of state for the Southern District, succeeding Pitt in 1761, he had charge of colonial affairs, which would bring him into contact with Franklin. His sister married George Grenville. *DNB*.

ENNIS, JAMES, courier in the service of the Pennsylvania government.

FAWKENER, SIR EVERARD (1684–1758), London merchant and official, ambassador to Turkey, secretary to the Duke of Cumberland, appointed joint postmaster general (with the Earl of Leicester) in 1745. *DNB*.

FISHER, MARY FRANKLIN (1673–1758) Benjamin's first cousin, daughter of his uncle Thomas. Franklin visited her at Wellingborough a few months before her death and found her "weak with age, . . . a smart, sensible woman . . . ," well-to-do, and living comfortably.

FISHER, RICHARD, of Wellingborough, husband of Franklin's cousin Mary.

FOLGER, PETER (1617–1690), Benjamin's grandfather, born in Norwich, Norfolk, migrated to Boston, 1635, to Martha's Vineyard, and to Nantucket,

1664. He married an indentured servant, Mary Morrill. He was a weaver, schoolmaster, miller, public official, and versifier, and founded a large and widespread American family. *DAB.*

FOSTER, JAMES (1697–1753), English dissenting clergyman, published four volumes of sermons. Inclined toward rationalism in his beliefs, he was regarded as one of the most eloquent preachers of his time. *DNB.*

FOTHERGILL, JOHN (1712–1780), M.D., Edinburgh, 1736; F.R.S., attended Franklin professionally in 1757. A strong Quaker, he was in constant touch with Friends in Pennsylvania and advised their withdrawal from the Assembly in 1756 because of the war with France. He wrote the preface for Franklin's *Experiments and Observations on Electricity,* 1751, and saw it through the press. He long sought a peaceful settlement of the disputes between the Pennsylvania Proprietors and the Assembly. In 1765 he gave Franklin a silver creampot engraved "Keep Bright the Chain," and as late as 1774 the two men were drawing up a scheme of reconciliation to submit to important persons on both sides of the ocean. Franklin wrote, "I can hardly conceive that a better man has ever lived." *DNB;* R.H. Fox, *Dr. John Fothergill and His Friends* (London, 1919).

FRANCIS, TENCH (d. 1758), attorney general, 1741–55, leading lawyer, came to America from Ireland about 1700 as attorney for Lord Baltimore. He moved from Maryland to Philadelphia in 1738 and was named attorney general in 1741. He was connected by marriage with most of the eminent families of Philadelphia, and was a trustee of the Academy. By 1756 he seems to have quarreled with William Allen, and was reported as being "no friend of the governor's party." *DAB.*

FRANKLIN, ABIAH FOLGER (1667–1752), Benjamin's mother. Only her children and her epitaph record details of her history. A memorial marks the site of her birth on Nantucket. Franklin tactfully and affectionately comforted her when she seemed worried about his "freethinking," and dutifully reported to her on her grandchildren.

FRANKLIN, ANN(E) CHILD (d. 1689), Josiah's first wife, born in Ecton and moved to Boston with her husband and three children; died a few days after the birth of her seventh baby.

Biographical Notes

FRANKLIN, ANN SMITH (1696–1763), wife of James, continued the printing business with her daughters and son after her husband's death and was one of Franklin's best customers for almanacs. She was colony printer for Rhode Island and published *The Newport Mercury*. She took Samuel Hall as partner, thus making another firm of Franklin and Hall.

FRANKLIN, BENJAMIN ("THE ELDER") (1650–1727), the uncle for whom Benjamin Franklin was named; London silk dyer; came to Boston in 1715, widowed, and having lost nine of his ten children; lived for four years with his brother Josiah's family.

FRANKLIN, DEBORAH READ ROGERS (1708–1774), married John Rogers, 1725, was deserted by him, and became Franklin's plain, sensible wife and competent helper in business. Though she could not share his intellectual or social life, he cherished her and was usually indulgent, affectionate, and generous. She did not accompany him on his two English missions, and she died, after a stroke, having not seen him for ten years. William reported "a very respectable number of the inhabitants" at her funeral.

FRANKLIN, FRANCIS FOLGER (1732–1736), son of Benjamin and Deborah. "The DELIGHT of all that knew him" his parents placed on his gravestone. Franklin wrote to his sister Jane in 1772 mentioning the boy, "whom I have seldom seen equall'd in anything, and whom to this Day I cannot think of without a Sigh."

FRANKLIN, JAMES (1697–1735), Benjamin's brother, learned the printer's trade in England. He brought back a press, types, and supplies, and started *The New England Courant*, 1721, a new and too lively kind of journalism for Boston. In about 1726 he went to Newport, where he published briefly the *Rhode-Island Gazette*, 1732–33, and became the public printer. His wife, daughters, and son carried on after his death. *DAB*.

FRANKLIN, JAMES, JR. (*c.*1730–1762), Benjamin's nephew, attended Philadelphia Academy with William Franklin before his apprenticeship with his uncle; he became his mother's partner about 1754. They started *The Newport Mercury*, 1758.

FRANKLIN, JOHN (1643–1691), Benjamin's uncle, dyer in Banbury, whose great-granddaughter Sarah (*c.*1753–1781) occasionally stayed with Franklin in London, 1766–70.

FRANKLIN, JOHN (1690–1756), Benjamin's favorite brother, moved to Rhode Island and set up as a soap boiler and candle maker. He was the originator of the "crown soap" so highly valued by the family. Subsequently he became postmaster of Boston and co-founder of a glass factory in Braintree. Benjamin had a flexible catheter made for him when he had a stone and suggested other treatment, but without success.

FRANKLIN, JOSIAH (1657–1745) Benjamin's father, silk dyer in Banbury before migrating to Boston in 1683, where he became a tallow chandler. By his first wife, Ann Child, he had seven children; by his second, Abiah Folger, Benjamin's mother, ten.

FRANKLIN, JOSIAH (1685–*c.*1715), Benjamin's half-brother; broke away from home and went to sea, returned after nine years, was finally lost at sea.

FRANKLIN, MARY. *See* FISHER, MARY FRANKLIN.

FRANKLIN, SAMUEL (b. 1684) Benjamin's first cousin, Boston cutler, son of Franklin's uncle Benjamin.

FRANKLIN, SAMUEL (1721–1775), Benjamin's first cousin once removed, Boston cutler, grandson of Benjamin "the Elder."

FRANKLIN (FRANKLYNE), THOMAS (fl. 1563–1573), Benjamin's great-great-grandfather, of Ecton, Northamptonshire; smith. Josiah Franklin wrote of him that "in his travels he went upon liking to a taylor; but he kept such a stingy house that he left him ... and came to a smith's house ... and he found good housekeeping there; he served and learned the trade of a smith."

FRANKLIN, THOMAS (1598–1682), Benjamin's grandfather, Ecton farmer and blacksmith. Benjamin's father, Josiah, wrote of him: "There were nine children of us who were happy in our parents, who took great care by their instructions and pious example to breed us up in a religious way."

FRANKLIN, THOMAS (1637–1702), Benjamin's uncle, Ecton schoolteacher, tobacco merchant, scrivener.

FRANKLIN, WILLIAM (*c.*1731–1813), son of Benjamin. In 1750 his father described him as "a tall proper Youth and much of a Beau." A close companion in many activities, he succeeded the older man as clerk of the Assembly and postmaster of Philadelphia, had a brief military career, went to

England with his father in 1757, and entered the Middle Temple to study law. He was appointed royal governor of New Jersey, 1762. They took opposite sides in the events leading to the Revolution; as a loyalist, William was arrested and confined in Connecticut, but was exchanged after two years, remained with the British Army in New York for nearly four years, and then went to England. A natural son, William Temple Franklin, was his grandfather's secretary in Paris during the war. Though there was an attempted reconciliation in 1785, Franklin almost wholly excluded William in his last will: "The part he acted against me in the late War, which is of public Notoriety, will account for my leaving him no more of an Estate he endeavoured to deprive me of." *DAB.*

FRENCH, JOHN (d. 1728), member of Governor Keith's council, 1717–26; had held many offices in the Lower Counties (Delaware): sheriff, register of wills, speaker of the Assembly.

GODFREY, THOMAS (1704–1749), glazier (he glazed the windows of Independence Hall), self-taught mathematician and astronomer, original member of the Junto. In 1730 he invented a new mariner's quadrant, known as Hadley's, for which the Royal Society gave him belated recognition. He was said to have had "a kind of natural or intuitive knowledge of the abstrusest parts of mathematics and astronomy." *DAB.*

GORDON, PATRICK (1664–1736), major in the British Army; governor of Pennsylvania, 1726–36. His term was relatively quiet after Keith's departure, perhaps because of his inexperience and dullness.

GRACE, ROBERT (1709–1766), proprietor of the Warwick Iron Works, which he got by marriage, and where Franklin's fireplaces were cast; an original member of the Junto, which met at his house, and director of the Library Co. He lent Franklin money to set up independently, refused payment of the debt, and Franklin in turn gave him the model of his fireplace to manufacture and sell without royalty. Grace rented his Market Street house to Franklin in 1739; here the "New Printing Office" was maintained for thirty-seven years and here the Franklin family lived until 1748.

GRANVILLE, JOHN CARTERET, FIRST EARL (1690–1763), long a power in British politics, was president of the Privy Council, 1751–63. He was married to Thomas Penn's sister-in-law. *DNB.*

Biographical Notes

HALIFAX, CHARLES MONTAGU, EARL OF (1661–1715) native of Northamptonshire, public official, patron of literature, F.R.S. (president, 1695–98). Created first Baron Halifax of Halifax, 1700; Earl of Halifax, 1714. *DNB.* Possibly, though not probably, Franklin's reference may have been instead to George Savile, Marquis of Halifax (1633–1695). *DNB.*

HALL, DAVID (1714–1772), born in Edinburgh, journeyman with Watts (where Franklin had worked) in London, then with William Strahan, who sent him to Franklin in 1744. Instead of setting Hall up in the West Indies, as he had intended, Franklin made him his foreman and then his partner, 1748, and their close relationship lasted until Hall's death. When their partnership terminated, Hall formed a new connection with William Sellers, and the firm of Hall and Sellers, continued by his sons, lasted until 1807. *DAB.*

HAMILTON, ANDREW (*c.*1676–1741), lawyer and officeholder. A powerful, able, and controversial figure in Pennsylvania, politically independent, he was speaker of the Assembly, 1729–33, 1734–39. His most famous legal case was his successful defense of John Peter Zenger when tried for seditious libel in New York, 1735. Franklin regarded him as a most "useful" friend and, in turn, actively supported him and on his death published an admiring and laudatory obituary. *DAB.*

HAMILTON, JAMES (*c.*1710–1783), son of Andrew, held many public offices in Pennsylvania, including the governorship in 1748–54 and 1759–63. Among his other activities he was trustee of the Library Co. and College, a Mason, and member of the American Philosophical Society. He refused to support the Hospital, fearing its domination by Quakers. Franklin reported "we esteem him a benevolent and upright as well as a sensible Man," and public business frequently brought them together, but they were often opposed politically and seem not to have been close friends. *DAB.*

HANBURY, JOHN (1700–1758), important and well-connected London Quaker, "the greatest tobacco merchant of his day, perhaps in the world." In association with John Thomlinson he was money contractor for the British armies in North America.

HARRY, DAVID (1708–1760), printer, born in Radnor, Pa., of a Welsh Quaker family; apprenticed to Keimer, who sold out to him in 1730. He followed Keimer to Barbados, probably after the death of his wife in December 1731. He had apparently returned to Philadelphia by 1756, and he died there.

HEMPHILL, SAMUEL, Presbyterian minister from Ireland, received by the Synod of Philadelphia in 1734 as assistant to Andrews. To explain and urge the eternal laws of morality, he said, was "not only a truly Christian, but beyond comparison the most useful Method of Preaching." He attracted large audiences, disturbed Andrews by his unorthodox beliefs and probably made him jealous (Andrews considered Hemphill's congregations as "Free-thinkers, Deists and Nothings"), and had to defend himself against charges of heresies tending toward deism. He was suspended, after which he drifted away into obscurity.

HERTFORD, FRANCIS SEYMOUR CONWAY, MARQUIS OF (1719–1794), K.G., privy councilor, ambassador extraordinary to France, lord lieutenant of Ireland; cousin of Horace Walpole. *DNB*.

HOCKLEY, RICHARD (d. 1774), merchant, agent and receiver general for the Penns, served in the Assembly, 1748–52; well connected socially, made gifts to the Library Co.

HOLLAND, SAMUEL, printer, journeyman in Franklin's shop, 1746–48, succeeded another of Franklin's former journeymen in Lancaster, Pa., 1752, and, first with a partner, then independently, printed the *Lancastersche Zeitung*, 1752–53. In the latter year he entered into an agreement to rent a press and types from Franklin.

HOMES, ROBERT (d. before 1743), husband of Franklin's sister Mary, ship captain in the coastal trade.

HOPKINSON, THOMAS (1709–1751), lawyer, came to America before 1731 as agent for London firms; took part in many public activities and held numerous judicial offices; member of the Junto. He was the first president of the American Philosophical Society, and one of Franklin's colleagues in electrical experiments.

HOUSE, GEORGE, shoemaker, original member of the Union Fire Co., 1736, overseer of the poor, 1746.

HUME, DAVID (1711–1776), Scottish philosopher and historian. He probably met Franklin in London in 1758–59 and their friendship was strengthened when Franklin visited Edinburgh the following summer and again in 1771. His enlightened and tolerant skepticism made their relationship particularly congenial. He wrote Franklin in 1762: "America has sent us many good things, gold, silver, sugar, tobacco, indigo, &c.: but you are the first philosopher, and indeed the first great man of letters for whom we are beholden to her." *DNB*.

HUNTER, WILLIAM (d. 1761), printer of Williamsburg, Va., and Franklin's agreeable colleague as deputy postmaster general; he was in poor health during much of their joint service. He published *The Virginia Gazette*, almanacs, and Washington's 1753 journal. Franklin took charge of his natural son's education.

ISTED, AMBROSE (1718–1781), succeeded his father Thomas as lord of the manor of Ecton in 1731. He was an intimate friend of Lord Halifax, president of the Board of Trade, and is described by Halifax's secretary, the dramatist Richard Cumberland, as a most amiable character.

JAMES, ABEL (*c.*1726–1790), prominent Philadelphia Quaker merchant, promoter, with Franklin, of silk culture in Pennsylvania, member of the American Philosophical Society, head of the firm of James and Drinker, which nearly suffered a Philadelphia Tea Party: a consignment was shipped to him in 1773, he hesitated about receiving it, and was "visited" by angry citizens in a tar-and-feather mood. He guaranteed by his word, his property, and his daughter, that the tea would not be landed. He was one of the executors of Mrs. Joseph Galloway's estate, 1782, and it may have been through this means that he got possession of the first part of Franklin's autobiography.

JOHNSTON, WILLIAM, deputy paymaster general of the British army in North America, escaped after Braddock's defeat with a military chest and papers.

KEIMER, SAMUEL (*c.*1688–1742), printer; in London he first joined, then disavowed, the group of religious enthusiasts known as the French Prophets, and spent long terms in prison for debt and for seditious publications. Deserting his wife, he moved to Philadelphia in 1722 and took Franklin on as a journeyman in 1723. Failing in business there, he went to Barbados in 1730, where he was equally unsuccessful. Unconventional in his beliefs and habits and intractable personally, he was nevertheless useful as printer of English works for the American market. *DAB; DNB;* Stephen Bloore, "Samuel Keimer," *Pa. Mag. of Hist. and Biog.*, LIV (1930), 255–87; C. Lennart Carlson, "Samuel Keimer," *ibid.*, LXI (1937), 357–86.

KEITH, GEORGE (1638–1716), Quaker leader and missionary; headmaster (1689) of what is now the William Penn Charter School in Philadelphia. He quarreled violently with other Quaker leaders, established a schismatic group, and was "disowned." Returning to England, where he was ordained as an Anglican clergyman, he resumed missionary work in the colonies for more than two years before accepting a rectory in England. *DAB, DNB.*

KEITH, SIR WILLIAM, Baronet (1680–1749), governor of Pennsylvania, 1717–26, after previous service as surveyor of the customs for the southern colonies. He was dismissed by the Proprietors for siding with the Assembly, in which he then won a seat. He returned to England, 1728, wrote on colonial affairs, was finally imprisoned for debt, and died in the Old Bailey. *DAB.*

KENNEDY, ARCHIBALD (1685–1763), member of the New York Council, collector of customs; descendant of a noble Scottish family (Cassillis); wrote several important pamphlets on Indian and other colonial affairs. A successful speculator in land, he once owned Bedloe's Island, on which the Statue of Liberty now stands, and sold it to New York City for a quarantine station at a profit of 900 percent. *DAB.*

KENNEDY, ARCHIBALD, JR. (d. 1794), son of the above, captain, Royal Navy, 1757. He succeeded a cousin as the 11th Earl of Cassillis, 1792.

KINNERSLEY, EBENEZER (1711–1778), ordained a Baptist clergyman but never pastor of a church, master of the English School in the Academy of Philadelphia, lecturer on electricity, Franklin's principal associate in electrical experiments. His first lecture, dated 1752, is printed in I. Bernard Cohen, ed., *Benjamin Franklin's Experiments* (Cambridge, Mass., 1941), pp. 409–21; the second has not been found. Joseph Priestley wrote, 1767, "if he continue his electrical enquiries, his name, after that of his friend [Franklin], will be second to few in the history of electricity." *DAB.*

LAWRENCE, THOMAS (1689–1754), born in New York, merchant, city official, provincial councilor, trustee of the Academy, lieutenant colonel of the Philadelphia City Regiment.

LE ROY, JEAN-BAPTISTE (1720–1800), physicist and member of a family of French scientists. He invented the first practical generator and perfected the lightning rod and the hydrometer. Franklin first met him while visiting Paris in 1767 and procured his election to the American Philosophical Society in 1773. During Franklin's residence in France an intimate friendship developed between him and the Le Roy family, and the two men shared interest in such matters as mesmerism and the sanitation of prisons and hospitals.

LOGAN, JAMES (1674–1751), scholar, Quaker statesman, whom Franklin revered, came to Philadelphia, 1699, with William Penn and was for over a half century a leading political figure and the Penns' trusted agent. His intellectual and scientific interests brought him the attention of Linnaeus and other Europeans, and he was the foremost classicist in the colonies. He left his library of 3000 volumes, considered the finest in America, for the benefit of the people of Philadelphia. Franklin was one of the original trustees. *DAB; DNB;* Frederick B. Tolles, *James Logan and the Culture of Provincial America* (Boston, 1957).

LOUDOUN, JOHN CAMPBELL, 4TH EARL OF (1705–1782), major general; one of the representative peers of Scotland in the House of Lords; F.R.S. He served in Europe and in the suppression of the Rebellion of 1745 before coming to America to succeed Braddock and Shirley as commander-in-chief, 1756, and was titular governor of Virginia, 1756–59, but never actually administered the colony. Pitt removed him from his command after the abortive Louisbourg expedition. Franklin's opinion of him after their first conference was somewhat different from that expressed here: "[I am] extreamly pleas'd with him. I think there cannot be a fitter Person for the Service he is engaged in." *DAB; DNB;* Stanley Pargellis, *Lord Loudoun in North America* (New Haven, 1933).

LUTWIDGE, WALTER (d. 1761), captain of the packet *General Wall* which took Franklin to England, died of wounds received in a battle with a French privateer.

LYONS, WILLIAM, surgeon, author of *The Infallibility, Dignity, and Excellency of Humane Judgment . . .* (London, 1719). In the fourth edition (1724) he added an appendix called "A Dissertation on Liberty and Necessity," which has been erroneously described as a reply to Franklin's pamphlet with the same title, printed the next year.

MACCLESFIELD, GEORGE PARKER, 2D EARL OF (1697–1764), astronomer, mathematician, F.R.S. (president, 1752–64), largely responsible for the calendar change of 1752, had his own observatory and laboratory, for which he designed apparatus. *DNB.*

MANDEVILLE, BERNARD (1670?–1733), Dutch physician, philosopher, and satirist; M.D., Leyden, 1691; practiced medicine in London; best known for his *Fable of the Bees, or Private Vices, Public Benefits*, 1714. *DNB.*

MANSFIELD, WILLIAM MURRAY, BARON (1705–1793), defender of the royal prerogative, chief justice of the King's Bench, 1756–88; perhaps England's greatest jurist in the eighteenth century. As a politician, he supported the coercive measures against the colonies. He was raised to the peerage in 1756, and advanced to an earldom in 1776. *DNB.*

MARTIN, DAVID (d. 1751), native of Ireland, came to America on a scheme for making potash; marshal of Trenton, N.J., and sheriff of Hunterdon Co., N.J.; first rector of the Academy of Philadelphia, 1750, and Franklin's principal antagonist at chess. Whether he was the chess-player with whom Franklin learned Italian is uncertain.

MATHER, COTTON (1663–1728), minister of the Second (Congregational) Church, Boston; writer; somewhat more liberal than his father Increase. Interested in science (F.R.S.), he was a pioneer advocate of inoculation against smallpox. Franklin rejected his theological orthodoxy but accepted the social ethic implicit in the *Essays to do Good.* His *Magnalia Christi Americana* (1702) is a still useful ecclesiastical history of early New England. *DAB.*

MAUGRIDGE, WILLIAM (d. 1766), carpenter, original member of the Junto and Library Co. He was related by marriage to Daniel Boone's father, bought his farm, and in 1762 mortgaged it to Franklin, who finally received payment from Maugridge's daughter.

MEREDITH, HUGH (*c.*1697–*c.*1749), printer; fellow employee of Franklin at Keimer's, then his partner; original member of the Junto. Some years after moving to North Carolina he returned to Philadelphia, and Franklin continued trying to help him, but in 1749 noted that he "went out again with a Parcel of Books, &c. which I trusted him with amounting to about £30. Since which I have not seen him nor received any thing from him."

MEREDITH, SIMON (d. 1745?), early Welsh settler in Chester Co., Pa., father of Hugh; as late as 1739 he sought a loan for his son from Franklin.

MICKLE, SAMUEL (*c.*1694–1765), Philadelphia merchant, common councilor from 1732 until his death. With all his "croaking," he took title to 1250 acres of land in Pennsylvania between 1731 and 1736.

MITCHELL, JOHN (d. 1768), physician, naturalist, mapmaker, F.R.S., came to Virginia about 1720 and traveled widely in America. He published a number of scientific and medical papers. His *Map of the British and French Dominions in North America,* 1755, used in the peace negotiations of 1782–83, has been called the most important map in American history, and was the subject of Franklin's last surviving letter (to Thomas Jefferson, April 8, 1790). *DAB, DNB.*

MORRIS, JAMES (1707–1751), prominent Quaker, assemblyman, trustee of the Loan Office, member of the Union Fire Co., and the Library Co.

MORRIS, ROBERT HUNTER (*c.*1700–1764), New York born, had a long public career beginning in New Jersey, where he served as chief justice, 1738–64, under appointment of his father, Governor Lewis Morris. As governor of Pennsylvania, 1754–56, he quarreled zestfully with the Assembly over paper money, defense, and the taxing of the proprietary estates. Though, according to Franklin, their personal relationship was pleasant, Morris once wrote that "He [Franklin] has nothing in view but to serve himself ... however he may give another turn to what he says and does"; and Franklin described Morris as "half a mad Man." *DAB.*

NEWTON, SIR ISAAC (1642–1727), the great mathematician, astronomer, and natural philosopher. Among his major contributions are the idea of universal gravitation and the mechanical principles explaining the motions of celestial bodies, basic theories of light and color, and the invention of "fluxions" (differential calculus), also independently invented by Leibniz. He was fellow of Trinity College, Cambridge, 1667; Lucasian professor, 1669, fellow of the Royal Society, 1672, president, 1703–28; warden of the mint, 1696, master of the mint, 1699; knighted, 1705. *DNB.*

NOBLE, THOMAS (d. 1746), wealthy New York merchant, friend of Jonathan Edwards and George Whitefield. A zealous Moravian, he left most of his large estate to the community at Bethlehem, Pa.

NOLLET, JEAN-ANTOINE (1700–1770), principal electrical scientist of France, F.R.S., director of the Académie des Sciences, instructor of the Dauphin in science, opponent and detractor of Franklin's theories. The two men did not meet in Paris in 1767.

NORRIS, ISAAC (1701–1766), wealthy merchant, book collector, nonpacifist Quaker, antiproprietary leader in the Assembly, speaker, 1750–64; attended the Carlisle Treaty of 1753 and the Albany Congress of 1754 with Franklin. *DAB.*

ONION, STEPHEN (d. 1754), Maryland businessman, came to America with the Russells, established the Principio Iron Works, the first in Maryland, which was confiscated during the Revolution.

ORME, ROBERT (d. 1790?), captain, Braddock's aide-de-camp and favorite. He offered 60 guineas for volunteers to help move the wounded and deserted general; the two who responded were Americans: George Croghan and George Washington. Orme returned to England and resigned his commission in 1756, possibly as the result of a scandal in his private life.

OSBORNE, CHARLES, clerk in Charles Brockden's office, one of Franklin's early Philadelphia companions, later "of more or less prominence in the town."

PALMER, JOHN (*c.*1612–1679), rector of Ecton, 1641–79; archdeacon of Northamptonshire, 1665–79; uncle Thomas Franklin witnessed his will.

PALMER, SAMUEL (d. 1732), London printer of *The Grub Street Journal*, supervisor of a private press set up by the royal family at St. James's, 1731. At the time of his death he had published several parts of *The General History of Printing*, left incomplete. "A good printer, but a bad historian, ignorant, careless and inaccurate." *DNB.*

PARIS, FERDINAND JOHN (d. 1759), solicitor specializing in colonial affairs, legal advisor to the Penns, shrewd, energetic, skilled in exploiting every technicality. Franklin found him a formidable opponent. His high fees were famous ("Ferdinando Parisian accounts"), a trait Poor Richard found characteristic of lawyers. William Franklin wrote, Dec. 28, 1759: "Paris is now no more, and it may be some Time before he [Penn] can find another Person infamous enough to do his Dirty work."

PARKER, JAMES (*c.*1714–1770), New York journalist, printer in New York, New Jersey, and Connecticut, one of the ablest in colonial America. He established *The New-York Weekly Post-Boy,* 1743, later changing the name to *New-York Gazette.* He was a close and trusted friend of Franklin, who appointed him comptroller of the American postal system before going to England in 1757. Upon the dissolution of the partnership of Franklin and Hall, 1766, he audited and settled their accounts. *DAB.*

PARSONS, WILLIAM (1701–1757), shoemaker, scrivener, surveyor general, 1741–48, and co-founder, with Nicholas Scull, of Easton, 1752, where he held various public offices. He was politically aligned with the proprietary party. He attended Indian conferences, and was a major under Franklin's command on the frontier. In Philadelphia, he was an original member of the Junto and the American Philosophical Society, and librarian of the Library Co., 1734–46. After long association Franklin characterized him as prosperous but always fretting.

PEARSON, ISAAC (d. 1749?), silversmith and clockmaker, Quaker, member of the New Jersey Assembly from Salem, clerk of the Council of Proprietors, 1730.

PEMBERTON, HENRY (1694–1771), physician, writer, F.R.S., employed by Newton to superintend publication of the third edition of the *Principia.* In 1728 he published *A View of Sir I. Newton. DNB.*

PENN, JOHN (1729–1795), son of Richard and grandson of William, the founder of Pennsylvania; he resided there, 1752–55, was a member of the Provincial Council and commissioner to the Albany Congress, 1754. He served as governor from 1763 to 1771, when he inherited his father's share of the proprietorship, and again from 1773 to 1776, when proprietary authority ended, but continued to live in Philadelphia until his death. *DAB, DNB.*

PENN, THOMAS (1702–1775), Proprietor of Pennsylvania, resident, 1732–41, absentee after that. The son of William the founder, after the death of his brother John (1746) he owned three-fourths of the proprietary interest, and his brother Richard, who owned the remainder, took little part in decision making. Thomas departed from Quaker belief and habit, but restored the family fortunes. He was an energetic and often generous administrator, yet alienated the Assembly by his policies and seeming avarice. He and Franklin quarreled violently over the taxation of proprietary estates and in England became bitter enemies. *DAB, DNB.*

Biographical Notes

PENN, WILLIAM (1644–1718), Quaker founder and Proprietor of Pennsylvania, and one of the early Proprietors of West New Jersey. He visited Pennsylvania twice, 1682–84 and 1699–1701. Before leaving for the second time he granted the Charter of 1701, which established the political system under which Pennsylvania was governed until the Revolution. *DAB, DNB.*

PETERS, RICHARD (*c.*1704–1776), Anglican clergyman and scholar, came to America, 1734, where he held many offices, notably provincial secretary for the Proprietors, president of the Academy trustees, rector of Christ Church and St. Peter's. His interest in the College and Academy was second only to Franklin's, and they were close friends until they became leaders of opposing political factions. When Franklin left for England he complained of Peters' injustice in supplanting him at the Academy, and Peters wrote: "I am afraid that B.F. whose face at Times turns white as the driven Snow, with the Extreams of Wrath may assert Facts not true.... I have a very high Opinion of B.F.'s virtue and uncorrupted honesty, but party Zeal throws down all the poles of Truth and Candour and lays all the Soul waste to Temptation without knowing or suspecting it." As the Proprietors' principal informant on local affairs, his letters to England present a totally different view of Pennsylvania politics than does Franklin's autobiography. *DAB;* Hubertis Cummings, *Richard Peters* (Phila., 1944).

PITT, WILLIAM (1708–1778), the great statesman who led Great Britain during the Seven Years' War, was secretary of state and in effect prime minister, 1756–61. He was created Earl of Chatham, 1766. Though Franklin first found him "inaccessible," they both worked desperately in 1774–75 to avoid the break between the colonies and Great Britain. To Franklin Pitt was "that truly great Man," and Pitt ranked Franklin "with our Boyles and Newtons ... an Honour, not to the English Nation only, but to Human Nature." *DNB.*

POTTS, STEPHEN (d. 1758), Franklin's fellow employee at Keimer's, original member of the Junto, bookseller, later a tavernkeeper. Franklin's ledgers indicate extensive business with him between 1733 and 1757. Upon hearing of his death Franklin noted that he was an odd character, "a Wit that seldom acted wisely ... in the midst of Poverty, ever laughing!"

POWNALL, THOMAS (1722–1805), A.B., Cambridge, 1743, came to New York in 1753 as secretary to Governor Osborne, who committed suicide almost at once. At a loose end, Pownall traveled among the colonies as a sort of unofficial observer for the British government; began a lifelong friendship with Franklin on a visit to Philadelphia; was a guest at the Albany Congress, 1754; and held the nominal office of lieutenant governor of New Jersey, 1755–57. He became secretary to Lord Loudoun, 1756, and was governor of Massachusetts, 1757–60, serving ably and energetically and winning the approval of the popular party. After his return to England he published, 1764 and five later editions, *The Administration of the Colonies,* which showed a broad understanding of the colonial point of view. As a member of Parliament he was a friend of the American cause. *DAB; DNB;* John A. Schutz, *Thomas Pownall* (Glendale, Cal., 1951).

PRATT, CHARLES (1714–1794), lawyer and jurist, became attorney general under Pitt; 1757; was knighted and appointed chief justice of the Common Pleas, 1761, and lord chancellor, 1766–70; raised to the peerage as Baron Camden, 1765, and made Earl Camden, 1786. Franklin found him in 1759 a "Stanch Friend to Liberty"; he opposed the Stamp Act a few years later. *DNB.*

QUINCY, JOSIAH (1710–1784), A.B., Harvard, 1728, Boston merchant, public official. The capture of a Spanish treasure ship and governmental contracts combined to make his firm the wealthiest in Massachusetts. He was an active Son of Liberty. His lawyer son Josiah, Jr. (1744–1775), who was also a friend and correspondent of Franklin, joined with John Adams to defend the British soldiers indicted for the Boston Massacre, though his father expostulated with him for helping "those criminals."

RALPH, JAMES (d. 1762), ambitious but undisciplined writer and would-be poet, another of the charming companions and beloved ne'er-do-wells of Franklin's youth. His verse was unsuccessful, but he did collaborate with Henry Fielding as dramatist and journalist and wrote a good history of England. He became so effective a political writer in the interest of leaders out of office that the ministry paid him £300 a year not to write. He and Franklin renewed their friendship in London in 1757, where he helped in Franklin's propaganda activities. *DAB, DNB.*

READ, DEBORAH. *See* FRANKLIN, DEBORAH READ ROGERS.

READ, JAMES (1718–1793), lawyer and clerk, Franklin's neighbor and rival bookseller, husband of Deborah Franklin's second cousin. After his failure to replace Franklin as clerk of the Assembly, he moved to Reading, where he continued to hold one public office after another.

READ, JOHN (1677–1724), Deborah's father. Born in London, a carpenter by trade, settled in Birmingham after his marriage in 1701, but had moved to Philadelphia with his wife and one or more children by 1711, when he bought property on Market Street. Financial difficulties (probably caused by the "very Knave" William Riddlesden) may have been the reason for his mortgaging this property shortly before his death, thereby causing his widow additional loss.

READ, SARAH WHITE (1675–1761), Deborah's mother. Born in Birmingham, daughter of Joseph and Deborah (Cash) White, she married John Read in 1701. Of her seven children, John, Deborah, and Frances attained adulthood. During her widowhood she helped support herself and children by making and selling medicines and salves. At her death Franklin wrote: "I cannot charge myself with having ever fail'd in one Instance of Duty to her during the many Years that she call'd me Son."

RIDDLESDEN, WILLIAM VANHAESDONCK (d. before 1733), alias William Cornwallis, an attorney, had been transported to Maryland as a felon; apparently lived for a time in Philadelphia. He engaged widely in fraudulent transactions in Maryland and New Jersey lands, one of his victims being John Read, Deborah's father. He returned to England, 1722–23, was imprisoned, but released on giving bond to go back to America. A Maryland Assembly act described him as "a Person of a matchless Character in Infamy."

ROBERTS, HUGH (*c.*1706–1786), merchant, son of the mayor of Philadelphia, wealthy and well connected. One of Franklin's close friends—they were associated in the Junto, the Pennsylvania Hospital, the Library, American Philosophical Society, the Union Fire Co., and, in 1751–52, in the Assembly.

ROBERTS, JAMES (*c.*1669–1754), eminent London printer and book publisher; master of the Stationers' Co., 1729–31.

ROGERS, JOHN, potter, married Deborah Read, perhaps bigamously, Aug. 5, 1725; absconded December 1727, taking with him a Negro lad. His reported death in the West Indies remained unconfirmed in Philadelphia.

ROSE, AQUILA (*c.*1695–1723), poet, Andrew Bradford's journeyman, operator of a ferry over the Schuylkill, father of Joseph, Franklin's apprentice. *DAB.*

ROSE, JOSEPH, son of Aquila, seems to have become Franklin's foreman by 1741. He published his father's *Poems on Several Occasions* in 1741.

RUSSELL, WILLIAM OF THOMAS, of Onion and Russell. Two generations of the family, each including a William and a Thomas, established the Principio Iron Works in Maryland with Stephen Onion. William Russell, Jr. (1740–1818) befriended American prisoners in England during the Revolution, later came to America, and became a close friend of Washington.

SCULL, NICHOLAS (1687–1761), surveyor, original member of the Junto, versifier, mapmaker, Indian interpreter, sheriff, 1744–46, and later aligned politically with the Proprietors, becoming surveyor general in 1748. He acquired large land holdings, and was, with William Parsons, a founder of Easton, 1752.

SHARPE, HORATIO (1718–1790), proprietary governor of Maryland, 1753–69; formerly an officer in the marines and the British Army serving in the West Indies. He was energetic in colonial defense and well liked in the colony, but quarreled with his Assembly, as did the governors of neighboring Pennsylvania, over the taxation of proprietary estates. *DAB.*

SHIRLEY, WILLIAM (1694–1771), London barrister before coming to Boston, where after holding various offices he became a successful governor, serving from 1741 to 1757. His part in the capture of Louisbourg made him something of a popular hero. He was interested, with Franklin, in colonial union, and succeeded Braddock as commander-in-chief until Loudoun, who disliked him intensely, replaced him in 1756. He was governor of the Bahamas, 1758–67. Though a place-hunter and careless about his military accounts, he was able, tactful, and honest. *DAB; DNB;* John A. Schutz, *William Shirley King's Governor of Massachusetts* (Chapel Hill, N.C., 1961).

SHIRLEY, WILLIAM, JR. (1721–1755), eldest son of the Massachusetts governor; naval officer in Boston, agent for his father in England; and military secretary to Braddock. He was killed in Braddock's defeat.

SHOVELL, SIR CLOWDISLEY (1650–1707), British admiral. He died when his flagship and two other ships were lost in the Scilly Islands. *DNB.*

SLOANE, SIR HANS (1660–1753), physician, antiquarian, botanist, secretary of the Royal Society, successor to Newton as president, 1727; also president of the Royal College of Physicians. He was created a baronet in 1716. Sloane bequeathed his natural history and manuscript collections to the nation; these and certain others provided the nucleus of the British Museum in 1754. *DNB;* G.R. de Beer, *Hans Sloane and the British Museum* (London, 1953).

SPANGENBERG, AUGUSTUS GOTTLIEB (1704–1792), German-born Moravian bishop, lived in America, 1735–62. He organized the Moravian missions in the colonies and was regarded in Europe as the great authority on American missions. Franklin was grateful during his own service on the frontier for Spangenberg's aid in defense. *DAB.*

SPENCER, ARCHIBALD (*c.*1698–1760), Edinburgh male midwife, in America an itinerant lecturer on electricity whom Franklin met in Boston in 1743, where he was giving a "Course of Experimental Philosophy." He lectured in Philadelphia the following year and subsequently in the South. Later he was ordained an Anglican clergyman and served a parish in Maryland. His first name has often, but erroneously, been given as Adam.

SPOTSWOOD, ALEXANDER (1676–1740), colonel in the British Army, energetic lieutenant governor and acting governor of Virginia, 1710–22, greatly concerned with Indian policy, defense, and western settlement. He was appointed deputy postmaster general of North America in 1730 and extended and increased the efficiency of the system. *DAB; DNB;* Leonidas Dodson, *Alexander Spotswood, Governor of Colonial Virginia, 1710-1722* (Phila., 1932).

SYNG, PHILIP (1703–1789) came from Ireland in 1714; silversmith (his inkstand was used at the signing of the Declaration of Independence and Constitution), an original member of the Junto, and member of many civic organizations. He engraved the seals for the Library Co., and the Philadelphia Contributionship, and joined with Franklin in electrical experiments. *DAB.*

TAYLOR, ABRAHAM (*c.*1703–1772), merchant, emigrated to Philadelphia about 1724; alderman, deputy collector of customs. He became a provincial councilor, 1741, but was removed from office, 1751, for quarreling with the Proprietors over land claims and supporting Lord Baltimore on the Pennsylvania-Maryland boundary dispute. He was elected colonel of the Association regiment, 1747–48. He returned to England, 1762.

TENNENT, GILBERT (1703–1764), one of a well known family of Presbyterian clergymen who came from Ireland about 1718; M.A., Yale, 1725, licensed in Philadelphia the same year, he was pastor in New Brunswick, N.J., 1726–43, then for the rest of his life of the newly organized Presbyterian Church in Philadelphia. A friend and co-worker with Whitefield, his spirited and stormy leadership in the Great Awakening helped produce the schism between Old Light and New Light Presbyterians. *DAB.*

THOMAS, GEORGE (*c.*1695–1774), born in Antigua, served in the Assembly and Council of the Leeward Islands, and came to Pennsylvania as governor, 1738–47, where, though he quarreled with the Assembly and the Quakers, he was energetic and generally successful, especially in dealing with the Indians. He was also royal governor of the Leeward Islands, 1753–1766, and was created a baronet upon retirement. *DAB.*

TIMOTHY, ELIZABETH (d. 1757), widow of Lewis, conducted the press left by her husband until their son Peter came of age, 1741.

TIMOTHY (TIMOTHÉE), LEWIS (LOUIS) (d. 1738), son of a French Huguenot refugee, came from Holland to Philadelphia, 1731, taught French, and was Franklin's editor of the *Philadelphische Zeitung* as well as journeyman. He was librarian of the Library Co., 1732. In Charleston he resumed publication of his predecessor Whitmarsh's *South-Carolina Gazette. DAB.*

TIMOTHY, PETER (d. 1781) succeeded his father Lewis as printer to the colony, and later to the state, of South Carolina; an able, intelligent, and patriotic printer and editor. His widow Ann succeeded him until his son Benjamin Franklin Timothy took over in 1792. Hennig Cohen, *The South-Carolina Gazette, 1732-1775* (Columbia, S.C., 1953).

VAUGHAN, BENJAMIN (1751–1835), diplomat, merchant, agriculturist. Born in Jamaica, educated in England; his long friendship with Franklin began in London before the American Revolution. He edited the first general collection of Franklin's works, 1779. Sympathetic with the colonies and often employed by Lord Shelburne on confidential missions, he was sent to France, 1782, to assist unofficially in the peace negotiations. He became actively interested in the French Revolution, settled in France, escaped from the Terror, and then moved to America, 1796, retiring from politics but engaging in writing and in agricultural experiments on his Maine farm. *DAB, DNB.*

VERNON, SAMUEL (1683–1737), silversmith, public official in Rhode Island, father of Thomas Vernon, whom Franklin "repaid" with a commission as postmaster of Newport, 1754. *DAB.*

WATSON, JOSEPH (d. 1728?), clerk in Charles Brockden's office, one of Franklin's early Philadelphia companions; probably the first husband of Frances Read, Deborah's sister. Christ Church records show that on Jan. 10, 1728, Rebecca, daughter of Joseph and Frances Watson, was baptized at the age of three months.

WATSON, WILLIAM (1715–1787), physician, naturalist, F.R.S. (one of those who nominated Franklin for membership, 1756); an indefatigable pioneer in electrical studies, he published some 58 papers, was knighted, 1786. *DNB.*

WATTS, JOHN (*c.*1678–1763), head of one of the most important London printing houses, located in Wild Court, three-quarters of a mile west of Bartholomew Close where Franklin first worked. Several eminent printers worked there as young men. Watts was also a patron of William Caslon and lent him £100 to make his start as a designer and founder of printing types.

WEBB, GEORGE (b. *c.*1709), matriculated at Balliol College, Oxford, July 18, 1724; original Junto member; Franklin and Meredith published his *Batchelor's Hall*, 1731.

WHITEFIELD, GEORGE (1714–1770), strenuous and successful evangelist, joined the Wesley movement while at Oxford, and was ordained an Anglican priest in 1739, soon beginning his open-air preaching in England. He made seven journeys to America, founded an orphanage in Georgia, preached up and down the colonies, attracting unprecedented numbers of auditors wherever he went. He was more responsible than any other one man for starting the "Great Awakening," the first major religious revival in America. Conservative in doctrine and belief, he was radical and emotional in his methods, and aroused bitter antagonism among many of the clergymen of the chief denominations in both England and the colonies. Though he was never able to win Franklin over to his own religious practices and beliefs, the two remained warm friends. *DAB; DNB;* Stuart C. Henry, *George Whitefield: Wayfaring Witness* (N.Y., 1957).

WHITMARSH, THOMAS (d. 1733), became Franklin's journeyman about 1729. He was a Mason in St. John's Lodge. The South Carolina Assembly induced him to move there in 1731. Franklin as silent partner supplied him with printing equipment and Whitmarsh founded *The South-Carolina Gazette* in Charleston the next year.

WIGATE (WYGATE), JOHN, worked with Franklin at Watts's in London, where a warm friendship developed. He was well educated for a printer; served as clerk on Christopher Middleton's vessel searching for the Northwest Passage, 1741–42.

WILCOX, JOHN (fl. 1721–1762), London bookseller; probably the man who was elected a warden of the Stationers' Co. in an insurrectionary movement, 1762.

WILKS, ROBERT (1665?–1732), London actor, associated with management of the Haymarket Theatre and later of the Drury Lane in its heyday. He played hundreds of roles, including Hamlet and Lear, but excelled in comedy. *DNB.*

WOHLFAHRT (WELFARE), MICHAEL (1687–1741), "Brother Agonius" in the pietist community at Ephrata, came frequently to Philadelphia to exhort the Quaker Yearly Meeting. Franklin printed the sermon he was not allowed to give there in 1734.

WOLFE, JAMES (1727–1759), British major general. The son of an army officer, he was commissioned at the age of fourteen and saw extended active service on the Continent and against the Jacobite rebels in Scotland before he was twenty-one. He commanded the forces sent up the St. Lawrence against Quebec and was killed at his moment of victory over Montcalm on the Plains of Abraham. *DNB.*

WRIGHT, EDWARD (d. 1761), English physician, microscopist, F.R.S.; defended, against Buffon, the historicity of the Biblical deluge; published *Conjecture on the Course of Thunder* (Paris, 1756).

WYNDHAM, SIR WILLIAM, 3D BARONET (1687–1740), prominent political figure in England. A high Tory with Jacobite leanings and a mouthpiece for Bolingbroke, he sparred for many years with Robert Walpole. *DNB.*

YORKE, CHARLES (1722–1770), lawyer and jurist, with a brilliant career in Parliament, became solicitor general, 1756, attorney general, 1762, and was named lord chancellor and offered a peerage three days before his death. Franklin found him "wholly and strongly tinctured with high Notions of the [royal] Prerogative." *DNB.*

Franklin Chronology

PERIOD OF THE AUTOBIOGRAPHY, PARTS ONE, TWO, THREE, 1706–1757

1706

January 17: Benjamin Franklin born in Boston (Jan. 6, 1705, Old Style).

1718?

Apprenticed to his brother James, a printer.

1722

April 2: First Silence Dogood paper published in *New England Courant.*

1723

February 11: *New England Courant* appears over Benjamin's name following brother's troubles with the authorities.

September–October: Runs away to Philadelphia; soon begins working for Samuel Keimer.

1724

November 5: Sails for England; while there works in Palmer's and Watts's printing offices.

1725

Writes and prints *A Dissertation on Liberty and Necessity.*

1726

July 21: Sails from London, arriving at Philadelphia Oct. 11.

1726–27

Employed as Denham's clerk; works for Keimer.

1727

The Junto formed.

1728

Forms printing partnership with Hugh Meredith.

Chronology

1729

April 3: Publishes pamphlet on paper currency.
October 3: Franklin and Meredith take over *The Pennsylvania Gazette* from Keimer.

1730

January 29: Franklin and Meredith appointed printers to the Assembly.
July 14: Partnership with Meredith dissolved.
September 1: Takes Deborah Read to wife.

1731?

William Franklin born.

1731

November 8: First meeting of directors of the Library Company.

1732

October 20: Francis Folger Franklin born.
December 19: First *Poor Richard: An Almanack* (for 1733) published.

1735

April–September: Defends heterodox preacher, Samuel Hemphill.

1736

October 15: Appointed clerk of the Assembly.
November 21: Francis Folger Franklin dies.
December 7: Union Fire Company formed.

1737

October 5: Opens his accounts as postmaster of Philadelphia, serving until 1753.

1739

November 2: George Whitefield visits Philadelphia for first time.

1739–40

Invents Pennsylvania fireplace ("Franklin stove").

Chronology

1741

January–June: Publishes *The General Magazine.*

1743

May 14: Publishes *Proposal for Promoting Useful Knowledge,* which leads to formation of American Philosophical Society.

May–June: In Boston, meets Dr. Archibald Spencer and witnesses electrical experiments.

August 31: Sarah Franklin born.

1747

March 28: First mention occurs of his electrical experiments.

November 24: The Association formed for defense of Pennsylvania.

1748

January 1: Forms 18-year partnership with David Hall; retires from active printing business.

October 4: Elected member of Philadelphia Common Council.

1749

[October]: Publishes *Proposals Relating to the Education of Youth in Pensilvania.*

November 13: Elected president of trustees of Academy of Philadelphia (later Academy and College of Philadelphia, now University of Pennsylvania); serves as president until 1756, then continues as trustee until death.

1751

April: His *Experiments and Observations on Electricity,* Part I, published in London; supplements (Parts II and III) published in 1753 and 1754; five editions through 1774.

May 11: Pennsylvania Hospital chartered.

August 13: Takes seat as member of Assembly from Philadelphia.

October 1: Elected alderman of Philadelphia.

1752

March 25: Fire insurance company ("The Philadelphia Contributionship") founded, Franklin president.

May 10: Dalibard performs Franklin's suggested lightning experiment in France.

June?: Performs kite experiment in Philadelphia (account published Oct. 19).

1753

July 25: Receives honorary A.M. degree from Harvard.

August 10: Appointed deputy postmaster general of North America jointly with William Hunter.

September 12: Receives honorary M.A. degree from Yale.

November 30: Royal Society of London confers Copley Medal on Franklin.

1754

June 19–July 11: Attends Albany Congress, which adopts Plan of Union based largely on his proposals.

1755

April–May: Active in supplying General Braddock with horses, wagons, and provisions, for first major campaign of French and Indian War.

June 30: Elected president of Managers of Pennsylvania Hospital.

December 18–31: In Northampton County with other commissioners, organizing defense against Indians.

1756

January 7–February 5: In command in Northampton County; builds three forts across the mountains.

February 24: Commissioned colonel of Philadelphia militia regiment.

April 20: Receives honorary M.A. degree from College of William and Mary.

April 29: Elected Fellow of the Royal Society.

1757

February 3: Appointed Assembly agent to go to England.

June 20–July 17: On voyage to England with son William; while at sea composes preface to *Poor Richard* for 1758, later best known as "The Way to Wealth."

July 27: Arrives in London; takes lodgings a few days later with Mrs. Margaret Stevenson in Craven St.

Chronology

FIRST MISSION TO ENGLAND, 1757–1762

Purpose: To negotiate with the Pennsylvania Proprietors, Thomas and Richard Penn, and with officials of the British government on behalf of the Assembly concerning its disputes with the Proprietors, especially on the issue of taxing proprietary estates in common with other property.

1757

August 13–20: Begins negotiations with Penns, which are protracted until August 1760, when the central issue is settled by the Privy Council largely in favor of the Assembly position.

September–November: Seriously ill in his Craven St. lodgings.

1758

Sponsors Richard Jackson's *Historical Review of the Constitution and Government of Pensylvania* (published in 1759) in defense of the Assembly.

Summer: With William visits Franklin and Read ancestral homes and relatives in Ecton, Banbury, and Birmingham.

1759

February 12: Receives honorary LL.D. degree from University of St. Andrews (thereafter generally addressed as "Doctor Franklin").

August–October: With William visits northern England and Scotland, establishing warm friendships with the Scottish intellectual circle of Hume, Kames, Robertson, Dick, Cullen; is granted freedom of the city of Edinburgh (Sept. 5), of Glasgow (Sept. 19), and of the burgh of St. Andrews (Oct. 2).

1760

April 17: Publishes *The Interest of Great Britain Considered* (the "Canada Pamphlet") arguing for British retention of Canada after the war instead of Guadeloupe.

August 27–28: Hearings by Privy Council Committee in which Assembly agents win main point permitting taxation of proprietary estates, but on condition of indemnifying Proprietors if Assembly fails to pass stipulated legislation.

September–October: With William visits Coventry, Cheshire, Wales, Bristol, and Bath.

December 8: Takes seat for first time as member of the Council of the Royal Society; serves again 1765, 1766, 1772.

1761

August–September: With son William and Richard Jackson visits Flanders and Holland, returning to London in time to see coronation procession of George III (Sept. 22).

1762

April 30: Receives honorary D.C.L. degree from Oxford University, William receiving honorary M.A. degree at same time.

July 13: Describes his new musical instrument, the glass armonica.

August 24?: Sails from Portsmouth for Philadelphia.

September 4: William Franklin marries Elizabeth Downes.

September 9: William Franklin commissioned royal governor of New Jersey (assumes office Feb. 25, 1763).

PHILADELPHIA, 1762–1764

1762

November 1: Benjamin Franklin arrives home in Philadelphia.

1763

Early this year work begins on building a new house for Franklin family in a court off Market St. (between Third and Fourth Sts.); construction so slow that Deborah and Sally move in only in May 1765 after Franklin has gone back to England.

April–May: On about four weeks' trip to Virginia on post-office business.

June 8?–November 5: In New Jersey, New York, and New England on post-office business; suffers two bad falls on the trip; daughter Sarah with him most of the journey.

December: Western Indian uprisings inflame Pennsylvania frontiersmen against all Indians. The "Paxton Boys" attack and massacre friendly Indians on Conestoga Manor (Dec. 14) and the rest of the group at Lancaster (Dec. 27).

1764

January 30?: Franklin publishes *A Narrative of the Late Massacres* denouncing the unchristian behavior of the Indian-haters and calling for just treatment.

February 3: "Paxton Boys" march on Philadelphia to seize friendly Indians guarded there; Franklin organizes volunteer defenders of the city; at governor's request goes with a few other leaders to meet rioters; persuades them to disperse.

April 12: Publishes *Cool Thoughts on the Present Situation of Public Affairs* urging that the King assume government of Pennsylvania, indemnifying the Proprietors.

May 26: Elected speaker of the Assembly, his predecessor having resigned because of illness.

October 1: After a scurrilous campaign, Franklin is narrowly defeated for reelection to the Assembly from Philadelphia, though his party wins majority in the House. First defeat after 13 consecutive elections; his Assembly career now terminates.

October 26: Elected, 19 to 11, Assembly agent to go again to England.

November 9: Sails for England, leaving behind his wife Deborah, who, as before, refuses to cross the ocean and whom he never sees again.

SECOND MISSION TO ENGLAND, 1764–1775

Purpose: To persuade the British officials to end proprietary government of Pennsylvania, assuming direct control by the Crown. He is later also appointed agent for Georgia (1768), the New Jersey House of Representatives (1769), and the Massachusetts House of Representatives (1770). As the controversies between the colonies and Great Britain intensify, he becomes increasingly recognized as the leading spokesman in Great Britain for the colonial point of view.

1764

December 10: Arrives in London after quick but stormy passage; resumes lodgings with Mrs. Stevenson at Craven St.

1765

February 2: With other colonial agents, confers with George Grenville on the proposed Stamp Act; secretly suggests, with Thomas Pownall, a currency plan as a possible substitute.

March 22: Stamp Act passed, to go into effect Nov. 1. Though opposing it, Franklin fails to sense the depth of American hostility and expects colonial compliance; he shortly makes the major political mistake of his career by nominating his friend John Hughes for appointment as stamp distributor for Pennsylvania. Violently criticized at home, Franklin is even accused of having framed the act himself; his popularity reaches its lowest point. Quietly, however, during the remainder of this year he works for repeal.

1766

January: Publishes anonymously in London papers several pieces directly or indirectly advocating repeal of the Stamp Act.

February 6: Printing partnership with David Hall expires; a major source of private income is thereby closed off.

February 13: Examined before House of Commons on repeal; an adroit and brilliant statement of the colonial position, printed and spread about as American propaganda.

March 18: Stamp Act repealed; Declaratory Act passed.

June 14–August 13: On long journey through Germany with Sir John Pringle, the Queen's physician, meeting men of literary and scientific interests. Both men elected members of the Royal Society of Sciences at Göttingen (July 19).

1767

July 2: Townshend Duty Act passed.

August 28–October 8: On journey to Paris with Pringle; presented to Louis XV; meets Dalibard and many of the French scientists and physiocrats, including Dubourg, the Le Roys, Mirabeau, and Quesnay.

October 29: Daughter Sarah marries Richard Bache, Philadelphia merchant.

1768

January 7: Prints in *London Chronicle* his "Causes of the American Discontents before 1768"; continues to contribute pieces on colonial affairs to London journals during this and the following years.

April 11: Appointed agent of the province of Georgia.

October 1: Dines with King Christian VII of Denmark, who is visiting London.

1769

January 2: Elected president of American Philosophical Society (reelected annually during his life).

January–February: Fourth edition of his *Experiments and Observations on Electricity* published, greatly expanded to include his scientific papers on a wide variety of topics in addition to electricity.

June–December: With English and American promoters organizes land company (Vandalia) to seek grants in Ohio Valley.

July 14–August 23: Makes second journey to France.

November 8: Appointed agent of New Jersey House of Representatives.

1770

April: Townshend duties repealed, except that on tea.

October 24: Appointed agent of Massachusetts House of Representatives.

1771

January 16: Waits on Lord Hillsborough, secretary of state for the colonies, to inform him of Massachusetts appointment and is rebuffed.

June: Spends a week at Twyford, home of Bishop Shipley.

July 30–August 13: Spends two weeks at Twyford; writes first part of autobiography.

August 25–November 30?: On journey to Ireland and Scotland, his longest trip during English residence; cordially entertained in Dublin; guest of Lord Hillsborough near Belfast, of David Hume in Edinburgh, and of other Scottish friends. At Preston, Lancashire home of Bache family, meets his son-in-law Richard Bache (in England on business) for first time; they return to London together.

1772

June 5: Appears with Samuel Wharton to present Vandalia Land Company claims before Privy Council Committee. The grant, though approved by committee, is never completed.

June–July: Visits northwest England; climbs mountains in Lake Country and descends into mine under the sea.

August–December: Dartmouth succeeds Hillsborough as colonial secretary; Franklin more optimistic on American affairs and finds own position pleasant: "Nothing can be more agreeable. . . . I hope for less embarrassment from the new ministry. . . . I seldom dine at home in the winter and could spend the whole summer in the country-houses of inviting friends, if I chose it. . . . The King too has lately been heard to speak of me with great regard, but a violent longing for home sometimes seizes me."

August 16: Elected to French Academy of Sciences, one of only eight foreign members.

August 21–27: Draws report of Royal Society for Board of Ordnance on protection of powder magazines from lightning.

October 8–24: Visits country home of Sir Francis Dashwood (Lord Le Despenser), one of the postmasters general, escaping the turmoil at home while his landlady, Mrs. Stevenson, moves their establishment to a neighboring house on Craven St.

December 2: Sends the "Hutchinson letters" (urging a firm hand and use of armed force, if necessary, in America) to Massachusetts Committee of Correspondence; gives early warning of East India Company's financial difficulties.

1773

May 10: Tea Act passed, making possible sharply lowered price for East India Company tea in competition with smuggled Dutch tea.

May–July: Warns Dartmouth that the colonies will not yield, and advises colonies that the King and ministry are determined and that Americans can hope for redress only if they remain firm and united.

Summer: Jacques Barbeu Dubourg publishes in Paris his translation of an enlarged edition of Franklin's works.

August 21: Sends Dartmouth the Massachusetts petition for removal of Governor Hutchinson.

September: Publishes "Rules by Which a Great Empire May be Reduced to a Small One" (Sept. 11), "Edict by the King of Prussia" (Sept. 22), satirical attacks on British policy.

October: Preface to "Abridgment of Book of Common Prayer" (with Lord Le Despencer); conducts experiments at Portsmouth on the effects of oil on rough water.

December 16: Boston Tea Party (news published in London Jan. 22).

Chronology

1774

January 29: Called before Privy Council Committee on the Massachusetts petition; viciously attacked by Solicitor General Wedderburn for role in "Hutchinson letters" affair, but stands silent throughout; petition rejected.

January 31: Dismissed as deputy postmaster general.

March–June: Coercive Acts passed: Boston Port Act, March 31; Massachusetts Government Act and Administration of Justice Act, May 20; Quartering Act, June 2.

July 28: "God knows my Heart, I would not accept the best Office the King has to bestow, while such Tyrannic Measures are taking against my Country." (To sister Jane Mecom).

August: On invitation, calls on Lord Chatham to discuss American crisis; stresses to Chatham, and later to other Opposition leaders, firmness and unity of Americans.

September 30: Recommends Thomas Paine, "an ingenious, worthy young man," to friends in Philadelphia.

December: Influential Quakers and Lords Hyde and Howe, acting as intermediaries for ministry, begin secret discussions with Franklin, seeking basis for settlement of colonial crisis; at their request Franklin prepares 17-point proposal for mutual concessions (Dec. 6). He also confers with Lord Chatham and other Opposition leaders.

December 19: Deborah Franklin dies in Philadelphia.

1775

January–March: Further extended discussions fail to find a solution; Chatham consults Franklin (Jan. 31) on a proposed plan, which he presents to House of Lords (Feb. 1) but which is there rejected with bitter personal attack on Franklin, who is present as Chatham's guest. Ministers send word to Franklin through intermediaries that his proposal contains totally unacceptable provisions. By about March 1 Franklin has virtually given up hope of peaceful settlement.

March 20: Leaves London for Portsmouth; sails for Philadelphia, March 22; on voyage writes "An Account of Negotiations in London."

Chronology

IN AMERICA, 1775–1776

1775

May 5: Lands at Philadelphia; learns of battles of Lexington and Concord.

May 6: Chosen delegate to Second Continental Congress.

May 10: Attends opening session of Congress; during following months is appointed to numerous committees, including those on posts, "Olive Branch Petition," manufacture of gunpowder, the Secret Committee (to procure arms, etc., Sept. 19); the Committee of Secret Correspondence (foreign affairs, Nov. 29).

June 30: Appointed to Pennsylvania Committee of Safety (president, July 3) which met every morning "at six . . . till nearly nine."

July 21: Submits draft Articles of Confederation for United Colonies.

July 26: Elected postmaster general by Congress.

October 4–November 13: As one of a committee of three members of Congress visits Washington's camp at Cambridge to confer on maintenance and regulation of the Continental Army.

1776

March 25–May 30: With Samuel Chase and Charles Carroll of Carrollton, accompanied by Father John Carroll, on futile mission to Montreal to persuade French Canadians to join revolting colonies against Great Britain. Franklin (now 70) worn out by this dangerous and difficult journey.

June 11: On committee with Thomas Jefferson, John Adams, Roger Sherman, and Robert R. Livingston to prepare Declaration of Independence. Later suggests minor changes in Jefferson's draft.

June 12: With John Adams and others on committee to prepare plan of treaties with foreign powers. "Plan of 1776" (adopted Sept. 17) becomes model for future trade policy and commercial treaties.

July 2: Richard Henry Lee's motion "That these United Colonies are, and, of right ought to be, Free and Independent States; . . ." passed, Franklin voting in favor.

July 4: Declaration of Independence adopted.

July 8: Elected delegate to Pennsylvania Constitutional Convention; presides at opening, July 15; later attendance somewhat limited by duties in Congress.

September 9–13: With John Adams and Edward Rutledge journeys to Staten Island to hear Lord Howe's proposals for settlement of conflict; no agreement found possible.

September 26: Appointed with Silas Deane and Thomas Jefferson commissioners to the court of France; upon Jefferson's declining appointment for family reasons, Arthur Lee appointed in his place (Oct. 22).

October 1: Arranges with Robert Morris for reception of first shipment of French aid, sent through Beaumarchais, under strict secrecy.

October 26: Sails for France on Congress warship *Reprisal,* Lambert Wickes captain, accompanied by two grandsons, William Temple Franklin (aged 16) and Benjamin Franklin Bache (aged 7).

FRANCE, 1776–1785

Purposes of mission: initially, to secure treaties of commerce and alliance with France and French aid in money and supplies; later, to negotiate treaty of peace with Great Britain; thereafter to negotiate treaties of amity and commerce with other powers. Other responsibilities: procurement and shipment of supplies for American army, assistance to American naval vessels in French waters, commissioning of privateers, adjudication of prizes, promoting the exchange and repatriation of American prisoners of war, and continuously, fostering the sympathy and support of the French people for American cause.

At the start the American commissioners are Franklin, Silas Deane (already in France), and Arthur Lee (arrived from London, Dec. 22, 1776). John Adams arrives to replace Deane (recalled), April 8, 1778. Franklin is appointed sole minister plenipotentiary to court of France, Sept. 14, 1778 (presents credentials, March 23, 1779). Adams appointed minister plenipotentiary to negotiate treaties of peace and commerce with Great Britain, Sept. 27, 1779, but Congress adds Franklin, John Jay, Henry Laurens, and Thomas Jefferson to Adams for this purpose, June 13, 14, 1781. Jefferson never serves. Congress names Adams, Franklin, and Jefferson joint commissioners to negotiate treaties of amity and commerce with foreign powers, May 7, 12, June 3, 1784.

1776

December 3: Lands at Auray, France; reaches Paris, Dec. 21.

December 23: Franklin, Deane, and Lee request audience with Comte de Vergennes, French foreign minister; meet him Dec. 28 and negotiations begin.

1777

January–February: Franklin lionized in Paris; attends meeting of French Academy of Science; visits famous salon of Mme. du Deffand; dines with Duc de La Rochefoucauld and other notables.

January 14: Commissioners assured of French support, receiving first secret subsidies.

March 2: By this date Franklin is established at Passy, a village two miles from Paris, in a comfortable house "with a large garden to walk in," part of estate of Hôtel de Valentinois, the property of Donatien Le Ray de Chaumont. Deane lives there with him, but Lee resides elsewhere. Franklin soon sets up small private press there, on which are printed papers and forms used in his public business and light essays (his "Bagatelles").

December 4: News of Burgoyne's surrender at Saratoga (Oct. 17) arrives and spurs negotiations leading to French alliance.

1778

During this year Jean Antoine Houdon executes his famous bust of Franklin. A widely circulated epigram, attributed to Turgot, declares: *Eripuit caelo fulmen sceptrumque tyrannis* ("He seized the lightning from Heaven and the scepter from tyrants"). Portraits, medallions, and engravings of Franklin become highly popular in France.

January 16: Franklin and Deane issue instructions to John Paul Jones, then of the *Ranger*, for cruise in British waters.

January 28: Commissioners report French grant of six million livres for the year, payable quarterly.

February 6: Treaties of alliance and of amity and commerce with France signed (ratified by Congress, May 4); American commissioners formally and publicly presented to Louis XVI on March 20.

April 7: Assists in initiation of Voltaire in Masonic Lodge of the Nine Sisters; by audience demand, publicly embraces Voltaire at meeting of French Academy of Sciences, April 29.

April 9: John Adams, replacing Deane as commissioner, takes up residence with Franklin at Passy. Lee has been feuding with Franklin and Deane.

Though recognizing Franklin's great reputation and popularity, Adams gradually comes to believe him too inattentive to business and too favorable to French rather than American interests.

June 17: Anglo-French hostilities begin.

1779

February 12: Franklin receives notice of appointment as sole minister plenipotentiary at court of France; illness prevents his presenting credentials until March 23.

March 10: Issues directive to armed ships in European waters recommending free passage to England for Capt. James Cook's expedition returning from scientific voyage to Pacific. For this courtesy the Royal Society awarded him in 1784 one of the medals struck in honor of Cook and the British Admiralty presented him a copy of Cook's *Voyage to the Pacific.*

Spring, summer, fall: Occupied in supplying American armies, paying bills, securing more aid; suggests in letters home that Americans might do more to raise their own funds; comments (Oct. 11) that France is "the civilest Nation upon Earth. . . . 'Tis a delightful People to live with."

June 21: Spain declares war on Great Britain.

September 23: John Paul Jones in *Bonhomme Richard* defeats *Serapis.*

December: Despite the war, Benjamin Vaughan publishes in London *Political, Miscellaneous, and Philosophical Pieces; . . . Written by Benj. Franklin, LL.D. and F.R.S.,* the first general compilation to consist chiefly of his nonscientific writings.

1780

February 9–July 27: Adams again in Paris with powers to negotiate peace with Great Britain and secure loan and treaty from Holland; mutual antagonism between him and Vergennes aggravates Franklin's struggle to secure funds to meet Congressional drafts, pay bills, and secure shipments of supplies.

March–July: Deeply involved in bitter controversy between John Paul Jones and Pierre Landais, a half-mad Frenchman in American naval service, over command of frigate *Alliance,* Franklin supporting Jones, and Lee, still in France, supporting Landais. During Jones's absence Landais seizes *Alliance* and sails for America taking Lee, whom Franklin calls "the most malicious Enemy I ever had," and who is intent on disgracing Franklin at home and forcing his recall.

June 27: In rare moment of deep depression Franklin writes a relative: "I have been too long in hot Water, plagu'd almost to Death with the Passions, Vagaries, and ill Humours and Madnesses of other People. I must have a little Repose."

October 2: Hopes for Spanish loan, recognition, and alliance, but rejects any surrender of American claims to the Mississippi as a price.

1781

February–August: France considers possibility of negotiating peace terms unfavorable to United States through mediation of Russia and Austria.

March 10: Vergennes informs Franklin of proposed mediation and asks that Congress send instructions thereon. Franklin replies that Adams is the man appointed to negotiate peace and probably already has instructions.

March 12: Asks Congress to relieve him as minister and appoint a replacement, pleading age (75) and ill health. "I have been engag'd in publick Affairs, and enjoy'd public Confidence in some Shape or other, during the long term of fifty Years, an honour sufficient to satisfy any reasonable Ambition."

June 13, 14: Congress appoints Franklin, Jay, Laurens, and Jefferson to join with Adams as commissioners to negotiate peace. New instructions to commissioners requiring them to act only with the knowledge and concurrence of France. No formal action taken on Franklin's request to retire. He learns of the new commission Aug. 15.

November 19, 11 P.M.: Vergennes sends Franklin news of Cornwallis' surrender at Yorktown, Oct. 19.

1782

March–June: Begins informal peace negotiations with British emissaries, acting alone; suggests, April 20–22, that Adams (then at The Hague) and Jay (then in Madrid) join him in Paris (Laurens, captured at sea, is a prisoner in England). Chief British negotiator with Americans is Richard Oswald.

June 23: Jay arrives to join in negotiations.

July 10: Franklin suggests to Oswald "necessary" terms without having communicated them to Vergennes.

July–October: Franklin and Jay stand out for recognition of American independence as prior condition for formal negotiation; wording of a new commission for Oswald, Sept. 21, constructively achieves this. Draft article for treaty prepared and sent to England without communication to Vergennes.

October 26: Adams arrives in Paris and joins negotiations.

November 28: Laurens arrives, having been exchanged for Cornwallis.

November 30: Oswald and American commissioners sign preliminary articles of peace.

December 15–17: Vergennes complains of American neglect; Franklin diplomatically admits impropriety and expresses American gratitude to France.

December 20: Franklin is assured of French loan of six million livres for 1783.

1783

January 20: Franklin and Adams present at signing of Anglo-French and Anglo-Spanish preliminary articles, upon which Anglo-American articles come into effect and commissioners declare armistice.

March–July: Arranges to publish in French the American State Constitutions with the Articles of Confederation and the treaties with France, Sweden, and the Netherlands.

April 3: Treaty of amity and commerce with Sweden signed.

April–August: Negotiations with British envoy, David Hartley, for a commercial treaty and for changes in peace treaty come to nothing.

July 1783–July 1784: Franklin consulted by Papal Nuncio in Paris on procedure of organization of Roman Catholic Church in United States; suggests John Carroll (an associate on 1776 mission to Canada), who is appointed, July 9, 1784, superior (prefect apostolic).

August–December: A series of experimental balloon ascensions fascinate Franklin, who reports on them in letters to scientific friends; witnesses two of the first manned flights (Nov. 21, Dec. 1).

September 3: Definitive treaty of peace between Great Britain and United States (same terms as preliminary articles) signed in Paris by Hartley, Adams, Franklin, and Jay.

1784

May 12: Formal ratification of peace treaty with Great Britain exchanged; the next day Franklin renews his request for release from post.

July–August: Receives commissions and instructions to negotiate (with Adams and Jefferson) treaties of amity and commerce with European nations and Barbary States (23 powers in all); Jefferson arrives, Aug. 6; Adams arrives, Aug. 13; commissioners begin joint work, Aug. 30; but only treaty with Prussia is ready for signature before Franklin leaves France.

December 2: Mary ("Polly") Stevenson Hewson, daughter of his English landlady, and her children arrive to spend winter with Franklin.

During this year writes Part Two of autobiography.

1785

May 2: Jefferson receives his appointment as minister to France succeeding Franklin, now permitted to come home.

July 12: Franklin leaves Passy; because of painful condition resulting from bladder stone, is carried in one of Queen Marie Antoinette's litters borne by Spanish mules; arrives at Southampton, England, July 24; visited there by son William (reconciliation is formal only), by Bishop and Mrs. Shipley and daughter Catherine, and by other friends; sails for Philadelphia, July 28. On voyage writes "Maritime Observations," "On the Causes and Cure of Smoky Chimneys," and "Description of a New Stove for Burning of Pitcoal, and Consuming all Its Smoke."

THE FINAL YEARS, 1785–1790

1785

September 14: Lands at Philadelphia; greeted by cannon salutes, pealing bells, and large crowd of cheering Philadelphians; during next few days is presented with addresses of congratulation and welcome by the Assembly, University, other civic bodies and organizations.

October 11: Elected member of Supreme Executive Council of Pennsylvania (3-year term); elected its president, Oct. 18, and reelected annually during his membership.

1786

Finds his Market St. house (occupied also by Richard and Sarah Bache and six children) too cramped, so builds large addition, including dining room to seat 24 and impressive library to house his 4000 or more books.

Chronology

1787

February 9: Society for Political Enquiries founded, Franklin first president; it usually meets at his house.

April 23: Pennsylvania Society for Promoting the Abolition of Slavery reorganized (first founded 1775), Franklin elected president.

May 16: Entertains Washington and other Convention delegates at dinner.

May 28–September 17: A Pennsylvania delegate to Federal Constitutional Convention: "I attended the Business of it 5 Hours in every Day from the Beginning. . . . You may judge from thence, that my Health continues."

June 28: Moves that sessions of Convention be opened with prayer; motion dropped for fear it would lead to rumors of dissensions.

July 3: Moves in Grand Committee acceptance of "The Great Compromise" on representation; approved by committee; voted by Convention July 16.

September 17: Makes the closing speech at Convention, urging every member to "doubt a little of his infallibility" and permit unanimous approval of Constitution.

November 14: Agrees to publication of his final Convention speech, which is reprinted over fifty times during ratification controversy.

1788

July 17: Makes last will and testament; adds codicil, June 23, 1789, making famous bequests to Boston and Philadelphia.

August: Begins writing Part Three of autobiography.

October 14: Ends service as president of Supreme Executive Council and thereby terminates his public career.

1789

September 16: Congratulates Washington "on the growing Strength of our New Government under your Administration. For my own personal Ease, I should have died two Years ago, but tho' those Years have been spent in excruciating Pain, I am pleas'd that I have liv'd them, since they have brought me to see our present Situation."

November 2, 13: Sends copies of Parts One, Two, and Three of autobiography to friends in England and France.

1790

February 3: His last public document: signs as president of Pennsylvania Abolition Society petition to Congress against slavery and the slave trade.

March 9: Restates to Ezra Stiles his lifelong religious creed: a belief in one God, the Creator, who is best served by "doing good to his other Children"; immortality of the human soul, to be "treated with Justice in another Life respecting its Conduct in this"; Jesus' system of morals and his religion, as he left them, "the best the World ever saw or is likely to see," though since somewhat corrupted; some doubts as to the divinity of Jesus, "tho' it is a Question I do not dogmatize upon, having never studied it, and think it needless to busy myself with it now, when I expect soon an Opportunity of knowing the Truth with less Trouble."

April 8: His last letter and final public service: replies to Secretary of State Jefferson's query on northeast boundary as settled at Paris by Peace Commissioners; sends his own copy of the Mitchell map used there.

April 17, evening: Benjamin Franklin dies quietly, aged 84 years, 3 months.

Selected Bibliography

Among the hundreds of books and articles about Franklin, his writings, activities, and contributions, the following are particularly useful. Bibliographies and footnote references in many of them will guide readers to other works on appropriate topics.

A. FRANKLIN'S WRITINGS

Leonard W. Labaree, William B. Willcox, Claude A. Lopez, Barbara B. Oberg, and Ellen R. Cohn, et al., eds., *The Papers of Benjamin Franklin* (37 vols. to date, New Haven and London, 1959—). A comprehensive edition of Franklin's writings; includes letters received as well as those written. The volumes published so far document Franklin's life to 1782.

Albert Henry Smyth, ed., *The Writings of Benjamin Franklin* (10 vols., New York, 1905–7). The most extensive previous collection of Franklin's personal and public papers; includes few letters written to him.

J. A. Leo Lemay, ed., *Writings* (New York, 1987). The best one-volume collection of Franklin's miscellaneous writings.

J. A. Leo Lemay and P. M. Zall, eds., *The Autobiography of Benjamin Franklin: A Genetic Text* (Knoxville, 1981). A meticulous critical edition that documents Franklin's changes, cancellations, and additions to the text.

I. Bernard Cohen, ed., *Benjamin Franklin's Experiments: A New Edition of Franklin's Experiments and Observations on Electricity* (Cambridge, Mass., 1941). A reprint of the 5th edition of 1774, omitting the non-electrical papers; the introduction contains the most complete historical and critical study of Franklin's discoveries in electricity.

B. BIOGRAPHIES

H. W. Brands, *The First American: The Life and Times of Benjamin Franklin* (New York, 2000). A comprehensive popular biography.

J. A. Leo Lemay, "Benjamin Franklin," *American National Biography* (24 vols., New York and Oxford, 1999), VIII, 382–95. The best brief sketch by a leading contemporary expert on Franklin. Supersedes Becker's article in the *Dictionary of American Biography.*

Edmund S. Morgan, *Benjamin Franklin* (New Haven and London, 2002). An insightful, compact, and beautifully written biographical study.

Carl Van Doren, *Benjamin Franklin* (New York, 1938). The best full-length biography.

C. SPECIAL STUDIES

Alfred Owen Aldridge, *Franklin and His French Contemporaries* (New York, 1957). Franklin's literary, intellectual, and social relations; reputation; and influence in France. Not entirely reliable.

I. Bernard Cohen, *Franklin and Newton: An Inquiry into Speculative Newtonian Experimental Science and Franklin's Work in Electricity as an Example Thereof* (Philadelphia, 1956). Massive scholarly treatment of the development of physical science in the eighteenth century and of Franklin's place in scientific thought as well as in practical application. *Benjamin Franklin's Science* (Cambridge, Mass., 1990), a collection of essays by the same author, considers the relationship between Franklin's scientific interests and other aspects of his career.

Paul W. Conner, *Poor Richard's Politics* (New York, 1965). An unsurpassed study of Franklin's political thought.

Claude-Anne Lopez, *Mon Cher Papa: Franklin and the Ladies of Paris* (New Haven and London, 1966). An unsurpassed study of Franklin's social circle during his nine-year diplomatic mission to France.

Claude-Anne Lopez and Eugenia W. Herbert, *The Private Franklin: The Man and His Family* (New York, 1975). The classic account of Franklin's family life and friendships.

Robert Middlekauff, *Benjamin Franklin and His Enemies* (Berkeley, 1996). A study of Franklin's strained relationships with his political foes as well as with his Loyalist son William.

C. William Miller, *Benjamin Franklin's Philadelphia Printing, 1728–1766: A Descriptive Bibliography* (Philadelphia, 1974). Annotated bibliography of all works known to have been published by Franklin during his Philadelphia printing career.

Antonio Pace, *Benjamin Franklin and Italy* (Philadelphia, 1958). Franklin's relations with Italian scholars and his influence on Italian political thought and culture.

Charles Coleman Sellers, *Benjamin Franklin in Portraiture* (New Haven and London, 1962). Thorough and scholarly study of the paintings, sculpture, and engravings, with a catalogue of artists; extensively illustrated; also valuable for the background and Franklin's circle of friends.

Gerald Stourzh, *Benjamin Franklin and American Foreign Policy* (Chicago, 1954). The most complete analysis of Franklin's role in shaping foreign policy, as well as the political and economic ideas upon which his thinking was based.

D. RELATED TOPICS

Carl and Jessica Bridenbaugh, *Rebels and Gentlemen: Philadelphia in the Age of Franklin* (New York, 1942). Classic account of eighteenth-century Philadelphia, a city that both shaped and was shaped by Franklin.

Jonathan R. Dull, *A Diplomatic History of the American Revolution* (New Haven and London, 1985). Sets the American Revolution in the context of eighteenth-century European diplomacy and warfare.

James H. Hutson, *Pennsylvania Politics, 1746–1770: The Movement for Royal Government and Its Consequences* (Princeton, 1972). The American background to Franklin's early political career.

Michael G. Kammen, *A Rope of Sand: The Colonial Agents, British Politics, and the American Revolution* (Ithaca, N.Y., 1968). The standard study of Franklin and his fellow lobbyists' activities in Britain on the eve of the Revolution.

Index

Académie Royale des Sciences, mentioned, 244
Academy, Phila., BF proposes, 181–2; founding of, 192–3; subscription for, 193; trustees elected, 193; moves to New Building, 193–5; incorporated, 195; Peters replaces BF as president of trustees, 196 n
Account of the New-Invented Pennsylvania Fire Places, published, 191
Accounts, financial, importance of keeping well, 172–3
Acrostic, by Uncle Benjamin, 49
Adams, John: on BF's lack of order, 156 n
Adams, Matthew: lends books to BF, 59; biographical note, 273
Addison, Joseph: autobiography compared to, 14; BF copies style of, 61 n; *Cato* quoted, 153
Aix-la-Chapelle, Treaty of, Phila. learns of, 182 n
Albany Congress: Pa. Assembly approves delegation to, 209; account of, 209–11
Albany Plan of Union: BF projects, 209–10; passage, 210; rejected, 210–1, 216; BF defends, 211–2
Alderman, Phila., BF elected, 196
Alexander, James: approves Plan of Union, 210; biographical note, 273
Alexandria, Va., Braddock lands at, 216
Allen, John: BF meets, 113; biographical note, 273
Allen, William: to get cannon from N.Y., 184; biographical note, 273
Allen, Fort, construction of, 233–4
Almanac. *See Poor Richard's Almanack.*
Almanacs, sold by printers, 141
Amboy, N.J., BF sails to, 71
America, colonial: habits and values, compared with England, 16; parliament to tax, for defense, 211
American Philosophical Society, founding of, 182
American Revolution: Vaughan on, 139; peace treaty signed, 141 n; BF papers lost in, 161; taxation as cause of, 211; French troops in, 226
American Weekly Mercury, Bradford prints, 119. *See also* Bradford, Andrew.
Amherst, Jeffrey: Pitt sends to America, 251; biographical note, 274
Ancestry: BF's interest in, 43; BF's account of, 45–52; BF traces at Ecton, 46 n. *See also* Franklin family.
Andrews, Jedediah: sermons do not inspire BF, 147–8; biographical note, 274
Anecdotes and aphorisms: of family Bible, 50; on helpful wife, 144–5; the speckled ax, 157; in *Poor Richard*, 164; "empty sack," 164; on favors, 172; on Penn's pacifism, 188; Dunkers on changing "truth," 190–1; of men in fog, 191; Indians and rum, 199; on keeping busy, 234; bringing men to prayers with rum, 235; on Loudoun's inactivity, 250–2
Annis, Thomas: BF to sail to England with, 87; biographical note, 274
Antigua, partnerships at, 181 n
Anti-Semitism, BF wrongly charged with 146–7 n
Aphorisms. *See* Anecdotes and aphorisms.
Appearance, BF: on arriving at Phila., 75; becomes more respectable to Deborah, 79; on return to Boston, 81; of industry and frugality, 125–6

Index

Aristotle, *Ethics*, mentioned, 1
Arnauld, Antoine, *Logic: or the Art of Thinking*, BF reads, 64
Arnold, Matthew, on 18th century writing, 3
Articles of Belief and Acts of Religion, BF composes, 148
Art of Virtue: BF's intention to write, replaced by section in autobiography, 23; Vaughan on, 135, 136, 140; incorporated in autobiography, 148 n; book on, projected, 157; never written, 158
Asbestos purse, BF sells to Sloane, 97–8
Assembly, Pa.: BF and Meredith official printers to, 121; passes paper-money bill, 124, 230; BF prints money for, 124; BF clerk of, 171, 185; fails to create militia, 182; Quaker majority, 185, 188–9; votes aid for New England, 189, 214–6; Quaker influence declines, 191; contributes to Academy, 195; BF elected to, 196, 197; BF defeated for, 197 n; assists Pa. Hospital, 200–1; provides for paving and lighting Phila. streets, 203; approves delegation to Albany Congress, 209; rejects Plan of Union, 212; Morris and, 213; and taxation of proprietary estates, 214, 239, 240, 248–9, 264; wary of Braddock, 216; gives provisions to Braddock's officers, 221–2; accepts Proprietors' donation in lieu of tax, 229–30; BF called to attend meeting, 235; disputes with Denny, 247–8; sends BF to England, 248; declares its rights, 249; Loudoun tries to reconcile with governor, 249; BF draws up complaints of, 263; Penns request BF's replacement by, 263–4; Penns reply to complaints of, 265 n; settlement with Penns, 266; thanks BF, 266
Association: organized, 182–3; officers chosen, 183; parishioners urged to join, 185. *See also* Militia.
Astrology, Parson's interest in, 117
Authors read, quoted, or mentioned by BF (alphabetically arranged): Addison, 61–2, 153; Arnauld, 64; Browne, 73; Bunyan, 57, 72; Burton, 57–8; Cicero, 153; Cocker, 63; Collins, 64; Cotton, 74; Crouch, 58; Defoe, 58, 72; Dillon, 66; Dryden, 114, 211; Folger, 51–2; Greenwood, 64; Locke, 64; Mandeville 97; Mather, 51, 58; Newton, 97; Nicole, 64; Nollet, 243–4; Pemberton, 97; Plutarch, 58; Pope, 65–6, 91, 114, 248; Pythagoras, 151; Ralph 91, 248; Richardson, 72; Rose 78; Seller, 64; Sewel, 118; Shaftesbury, 64; Steele, 61 n; Sturmy, 64; Thévenot, 104; Thomson, 154; Tryon, 63, 87; Vergil, 74; Xenophon, 64; Young, 98–9
Autobiography, BF: in literary tradition, 1–4; peculiarly American qualities, 4–6; inaccuracies in, 6–7; vividness, 7–8; style, 8–9; account of writing of, 21–6; the manuscript described, 25; publication history, 26–38; form of present publication, 38–9; purpose of, 43; James and Vaughan urge completion, 133–40; outline of, James tends to BF, 134, 267
Ax, speckled, anecdote, 156

Bache, B. F.: BF uses as secretary, 26; makes copies of autobiography, 28; as "improver" of BF MS, 32–3
Bache, Richard, marries Sarah Franklin, 144
Bacon, Francis, methods of, 14
Baird, Dr. Patrick: Keith's secretary, 92; praises BF's industry, 119; biographical note, 274
Baltimore, Charles Calvert, 5th Baron: Penns' suit against, 263; biographical note, 274
Baltimore, Frederick Calvert, 6th Baron, biographical note, 274
Banbury, BF and son at, 43 n, 46 n
Band Club, formed, 171
Barbados, Keimer and Harry at, 126

Index

Bartholomew Close, mentioned, 96
Bartram, John, and founding of American Philosophical Society, 182 n
Baskett, John: mentioned, 93; biographical note, 274
Batson's Coffee House, London, BF at, 97
Battery, Association, for defense of Phila., 183–4
Beatty, Charles: method of getting soldiers to prayers, 235; biographical note, 275
Beccaria, Giambatista, defends BF, 244 n
Becker, Carl, quoted on BF, 14–5
Beer, BF prefers water at work, 99
Benezet, John Stephen: unable to entertain Whitefield, 178; biographical note, 275
Benger, Elliott: BF succeeds as postmaster general, 208; biographical note, 275
Bethlehem, Pa.: defenses at, 231; founded, 231 n; BF marches from, 232; BF at, 236–7
Bevis, John, verifies BF's electrical theories, 245, 246 n
Bible: autobiography compared to vividness of, 19; secretly read by BF's ancestors, 50; Browne's travesty of, 74; friendly hoax on 18th Psalm, 90–1; quoted, 144, 147, 153, 158
Bigelow, John: locates, acquires, and publishes autobiography, 34–5; accuracy of edition of, 35
Birmingham, England, BF and son at, 46 n
Biscay, Bay of, navigation near, 258 n
Blackbeard. *See* Teach, Edward.
Blackfriars, BF swims to, 104, 105
Block Island, mentioned, 87
Board of Trade: and Albany Congress, 209; rejects Albany Plan of Union, 210–1; supports Proprietors, 265 n
Bond, Phineas: prepares to celebrate Braddock's victory, 228–9; biographical note, 275
Bond, Thomas: and Pa. Hospital, 199; prepares to celebrate Braddock's victory, 228–9; promotes Phila. militia, 237–8; biographical note, 275
Bonnell, John Dod: on Loudoun's Louisbourg campaign, 252; biographical note, 275
Books: BF sells, 125; printers sell, 141. *See also* Authors; Reading.
Boston, Mass.: Uncle Benjamin moves to, 48; BF born in, 51; newspapers in, 66–7; BF leaves, 71; BF unwilling to return to, 79; BF tempted to return to, 111; booksellers in, 141; BF visits, 81, 169, 211, 212, 240–1; Whitefield in, 178; cannon procured from, 184; electrical experiments at, 240
Boston News Letter, first American paper, 66–7
Boyle, Robert, establishes lecture series, 113 n
Boyle's lectures, BF reads sermons delivered at, 113
Braddock, Edward: expedition of, 211 n; arrives in America, 216; BF at camp of, 217, 221; asks BF to procure wagons, 217; advances money for wagons, 221; grateful for aid, 222; pays BF, 222; plans campaign, 223; characterized, 223–4; defeat of, 224–5, 229, 240; death of, 226; welcomed in colonies, 226 n; praises BF, 227; and enlistment of servants, 227–8; Shirley succeeds, 253; biographical note, 275–6. *See also* French and Indian War; Wagons.
Bradford, Andrew: sends BF to Keimer, 77; BF's host in Phila., 77, 79; Keimer fears competition of, 112; prints poor newspaper, 119; "Busy Body" essays for paper of, 120; loses Pa. official business, 121; prints paper money, 124 n; unfair competition by, 126–7; on prospects in printing business, 127; newspaper declines, 172; replaced as postmaster, 172; biographical note, 276
Bradford, William: in Keith quarrel, 71; BF seeks work with, 71; sends BF to

Phila., 71; introduces BF to Keimer, 77; as printer, 78–9; biographical note, 276
Breintnall, Joseph: member of Junto, characterized, 117; procures Quakers' business for BF and Meredith, 118; writes "Busy Body" essays, 120; helps BF with legal forms, 125; biographical note, 276
Brisson, Mathurin-Jacques: defends Nollet, 244; biographical note, 276
British Army, behavior of troops of, 226
Brockden, Charles: BF's friends employed by, 89; draws up Library Co. articles, 130, 142; comments on Library Co. future, 142–3; biographical note, 276
Brooks, Philips, *Biography*, quoted, 19
Browne, John: BF at inn of, 73–4; biographical note, 276
Brownell, George: BF attends school of, 53; biographical note, 277
Bruce, William C., *Benjamin Franklin Self-Revealed*, cited, 19 n
Buffon, Georges-Louis Le Clerc, Comte de: introduces *Exper. and Obser.* in France, 243; biographical note, 277
Buisson, Jacques: publishes autobiography in French, 27; text retranslated into English, 27
Bunyan, John: autobiography compared to writing of, 14; BF buys works of, 57; BF sees Dutch copy of *Pilgrim's Progress*, 72; dialogue in, 72
Burlington, N.J.: located, 73 n; BF at, 74; BF makes friends at, 112–13
Burnet, Gilbert, mentioned, 85
Burnet, William: shows civility to BF, 85; BF reports dispute of, 121; biographical note, 277
Burton, Robert (Richard), BF buys works of, 57–8
Bustill, Samuel: BF meets, 113; biographical note, 277
"Busy Body" essays, BF and Breintnall write, 120
"Caelia Shortface," pseudonym, 120 n
Caesar, Julius, writings of, mentioned, 135
Calendar change, of 1752, 47 n
Canton, John: experiments with lightning, 245; biographical note, 277
Carlisle, Pa., BF helps negotiate treaty at, 197–9
Catholicism. *See* Roman Catholicism.
Cave, Edward: publishes *Exper. and Obser.*, 242–3; biographical note, 277
Cellini, Benevenuto, *Autobiography*, quoted, 14
"Chapel" laws, BF revises at Watts, 101
Chapmen's books, BF sells, 125
Charity: BF contributes to all sects, 146; for Whitefield's orphanage, 177–8; BF advises on solicitation, 201–2
Charles II, Franklin family during reign of, 50
Charles, Robert: finds lodging for BF, 261; appears before Privy Council committee, 265; signs settlement with Penns, 266; biographical note, 277
Charleston, S.C.: Timothée in, 166; Loudoun detains fleet at, 254
Chastity, in BF's list of virtues, 150
Chaucer, Geoffrey, *Canterbury Tales*, franklin in, 45 n
Cheapside, London, alehouse in, 97
Checkley, John, at *Courant* office, 67 n
Chelsea, BF swims at, 104, 105
Chelsea College, BF visits, 103
Chess, learning Italian with, 168
Christian VI, King of Denmark, BF dines with, 144
Cicero, *Tusculan Disputations*, quoted, 153
Clapham, William: commands on frontier, 236; biographical note, 278
Clarke, Samuel, lecture of, 113 n
Cleaning, of streets, 202–3, 204–7
Cleanliness, in BF's list of virtues, 150
Clifton, John: introduces street lamp in Phila., 203; biographical note, 278
Clinton, George: supplies cannon, 184; biographical note, 278

Index

Clubs. *See* Band, Every Night, Friday, Junto, Union, Vine, Witty.
Cocker, Edward, arithmetic book, BF studies, 63
Cod, as argument against vegetarianism, 87–8
Coffeehouses. *See* Batson's; Saltero's.
Colden, David, defends BF's electrical theories, 244 n
Coleman, William: member of Junto, characterized, 118; helps BF financially, 122–3; biographical note, 278
Collins, Anthony, BF reads deistic works of, 64
Collins, John: debates with, 60–1; arranges BF's escape, 71; BF confides whereabouts to, 79; to join BF in N.Y., 82; library of, 82–3; BF meets in N.Y., 84; addiction to drink and gambling, 84–6; BF weary of, 85–6; in debt to BF, 85, 86; goes to Barbados, 86; BF converts to deism, 114
Collinson, Peter: sends glass tube to Library Co., 241; letters to, on electrical experiments, 242; arranges publication of *Exper. and Obser.*, 242; BF visits, 261; biographical note, 278
Colonial union: impossibility of, 216 n. *See also* Albany Plan of Union.
Common Council, Phila., BF elected to, 196
Congregationalism, and Presbyterianism, 145–6 n
Congress, U.S., appoints BF minister to France, 141 n
Connecticut, BF visits, 209
Constables, responsible for city watch, 173
Constitutional Convention, BF at, 24; falsely reputed speech at, 146–7 n
Contentment, related to work, 234
Conversation: spoiled by disputes, 60; humility in, 66, 158–9; reading improves, 112, 130–1; Junto meetings improve, 118; trifling, to be avoided, 149
Conway, Henry Seymour: Hume secretary of, 227; biographical note, 278
Cooper, Joseph: BF meets, 113: biographical note, 278
Cooper's Creek, N.J., BF spends night at, 74–5
Copernicus, BF ranked with, 244 n
Copley, Sir Godfrey, baronet, biographical note, 279
Copley Medal, BF receives, 246
Copper-plate press, BF contrives, 112
Cotton, Charles, writes doggerel on Vergil, 74
Council, Pa.: consults BF on defense, 184; BF intimate with, 185; versus Assembly, 189; and Carlisle Treaty, 197–8
Courtship: "promises" exchanged with Deborah Read, 92; BF courts Godfreys' relative, 127–8; BF resumes, with Deborah, 128–9. *See also* Franklin, Deborah Read.
Crane, Verner W., on Farrand's "restoration," 37 n
Craven, Charles, and Loudoun's delays, 253 n
Creed, BF's, 146, 162
Croghan, George: in Braddock's campaign, 223; biographical note, 279
Croker, John, Frances Reed marries, 128 n
Crouch, Nathaniel, Burton a pseudonym of, 58 n
Cumberland County, Pa., BF advertises for wagons in, 219
Cumberland, Fort, located, 218 n. *See also* Wills's Creek.
Currency, paper: Keimer and BF print for N.J., 112; needed in Pa., 123–4; BF pamphlet on, 124; BF prints for Pa., 124; Bradford prints, 124 n; gradually increased in Pa., 124–5; BF prints for Del., 125; royal orders on, 215 n; lack of, 220; BF secures credit of, 266

Dalibard, Thomas-François: translates *Exper. and Obser.*, 243; conducts lightning experiment, 244; defends BF's

electrical theories, 244 n; adopts idea of lightning rod, 245 n; biographical note, 279
Daylight Saving Time, BF anticipates, 207 n
Debate: in conversation, 60–1; BF's method of, 64–5, 88; in Junto, 117; humility in, sought, 159; success in, 160; Morris enjoys, 212–3
Debts. *See* Finances.
Declaration of Independence, nature of autobiography helps to explain, 16
Declaratory Act, and parliamentary authority, 262 n
Decow, Isaac: BF meets, 113; biographical note, 279
Defense: Pa. lacks provision for, 181–2; Dunbar asked to provide, 225–6; taxation to provide for, 229; BF's activities on frontier, 230–6; BF gives guns to farmers, 232; forts built, 233–4, 235 n; Morris asks Dunbar to maintain, 240; Loudoun leaves to Assembly, 249. *See also* Association; Militia.
Defoe, Daniel: compared with BF, 16; BF reads, 58; BF quotes *Essay on Projects,* 60 n; BF on dialogue in, 72
Deism (freethinking): BF accepts, 113–15; does not improve conduct, 114
Delaware, BF official printer for, 125
Delor, ——, conducts electrical experiment, 244; biographical note, 279
Democracy, in Albany Plan, 210
Denham, Thomas: BF's shipmate to England, 93; enlightens BF on Keith, 94; advises return to Pa., 104; characterized, 104; pays his debts, 104–5; hires BF as clerk, 105; illness and death, 107; BF protégé of, 107; BF legatee of, 107; biographical note, 279
Denny, William: and taxation of proprietary estates, 214, 264; replaces Morris as governor, 240; welcomed to Phila., 246; asks BF's advice and cooperation, 246–7; relations with BF, 247–8; disputes with Assembly, 247–8; brings word of Ralph, 248; Loudoun tries to reconcile, with Assembly, 249; Loudoun forces, to sign supply bill, 250 n; sends messages to Loudoun, 251; dismissed, 266; biographical note, 279–80
Denonville, Marquis de, defeated by Seneca, 223 n
"Dialogue between X, Y, and Z": BF writes, 230; promotes Phila. militia, 237–8
Dinwiddie, Robert, asks Dunbar to defend frontier, 225–6; biographical note, 280
Dissertation on Liberty and Necessity, BF writes, prints, and later regrets, 96, 114
Dogood. *See* Silence Dogood.
Dominica, BF founds press at, 181 n
Douglass, William, at *Courant* office, 67 n
Dowry, BF expects, 127
Dress. *See* Appearance.
Drink, drinking: the drunken Dutchman, 72–3; Collins addicted to, 84–6; BF drinks water, not beer, at work, 99; Meredith addicted to, 108, 111, 120, 122; of constables, 173; Indians drunk at Carlisle, 198–9; liquor traded to Indians, 199 n; brings soldiers to prayers, 235. See also Beer; Madeira wine; Rum; Temperance; Water.
Dryden, John: *Oedipus,* quoted, 114; translation of Juvenal, quoted, 211
Duke Street, London, BF lodges in, 101
Dunbar, Thomas: reports subalterns lack stores, 221; grateful for stores, 222; retreats to Phila., 225, 227; and enlistment of servants, 227; Morris asks, to defend frontier, 240; biographical note, 280
Dunkers, modesty in asserting beliefs, 190–1
Duquesne, Fort: Braddock's objective, 223; Bonds prepare to celebrate taking of, 228; BF proposed to lead expedition against, 240
Durno, J., pirates Pa. fireplace, 192 n

Index

Ecton, England: BF and son visit relatives at, 43 n; 46 n; Franklin family at, 45–50; Uncle Thomas in, 47
Edinburgh, Scotland, breeds disputatious men, 60
Edinburgh Review, review of autobiography quoted, 16–7
Education: BF's schooling, 52–3; of women, 60–1, 166; BF's independent study, 63–4, 143–4; BF as example of self-education, 136; BF uses Sundays for study, 145–6; value of almanacs to, 164; BF learns languages, 168–9; teaching of languages, 168–9. *See also* Academy.
Edward VI, and Protestantism, 50 n
Egremont, Charles Wyndham, 2nd Earl of: asks BF to teach swimming, 106; biographical note, 280
Electricity: BF begins experiments with, 196, 241; honors to BF for discoveries in, 209, 245–6; Spenser's experiments in, 240–1; apparatus broken by militia salute, 238; early method of generating static, 241 n; Kinnersley's lectures on, 241–2; lightning identified with, 242; experiments with, in France, 244. *See also Experiments and Observations on Electricity;* Royal Society.
Elizabeth, Queen, and Protestantism, 50 n
Embargo, Loudoun imposes, 253–4
England, BF's first visit to, 93–106; second visit, 261–6. *See also* Great Britain.
English Channel, navigation dangerous, 258
Engraving, BF performs, 110
Ennis, James: and Loudoun's delays, 251; biographical note, 280
Epitaph: BF's, for himself, 44 n; for parents, 56
Erratum, BF's metaphorical use of term, 43 n, 70, 86, 96 (2), 99, 122, 129
Europe, *Exper. and Obser.* accepted in, 244
Every Night Club, members pessimistic about BF's success, 119
Experiments. *See* Electricity; Science; Navigation.
Experiments and Observations on Electricity: published, 242; editions of, 242–3 n; not widely noticed in England, 243; translated into French, 243; Nollet attacks, 243; translated into Italian, German, and Latin, 244; accepted in Europe, 244; summary read to Royal Society, 245

Falmouth, England, BF at, 259
Farrand, Max: publishes Parallel Text, 35; attempts restoration of text, 35–6
Fast, BF writes proclamation for, 184–5
Father Abraham: pseudonym in 1758 almanac, 164
Faulkner, William, *The Sound and the Fury,* autobiography contrasted with, 21
Favors, aphorism on, 172
Fawkener, Sir Everard: admonishes BF, 239; biographical note, 280
Federal Constitutional Convention: BF at, 24; speech at, forged, 146–7 n
Finances, business: S. Meredith offers loan for partnership, 111; rent for printing shop, 115; from first printing customer, 116; Coleman and Grace finance BF, 122, 123; BF pays debts, 125; importance of reputation for, 126; debts necessitate industry, 143–4; almanac highly profitable, 164; partnership with Timothée, 166; income from *Pa. Gaz.,* 172; partnership with Hall, 195; income from post office, 208
Finances, personal: assets on entering Phila., 75; on visiting Boston, 82; misuse of Vernon's money, 85, 86; cost of London lodgings, 95, 102; Ralph's debts to BF, 95, 99, 106; poverty in London, 96; BF lends to workmen at Watts's, 100; wages under Denham, 105; legacy from Denham, 107; debt to Vernon, 110; paid, 122; debts necessi-

tate industry, 143–4; growing income, 180–1; involved in wagon affair, 221, 228, 254–5
Fire, protection against, 174–5
Fisher, Mary Franklin: lives in family house at Ecton, 46; BF inherits from, 46 n; biographical note, 280
Fisher, Richard: mentioned, 46; biographical note, 280
Fleet, Thomas, at *Courant* office, 67 n
Folger, Abiah, marries Josiah Franklin, 51. *See also* Franklin, Abiah Folger.
Folger, Peter: Cotton Mather praises, 51; poem of, 51–2; biographical note, 280–1
Folger family, account of, 51–2
Food, BF: indifference to, 55; buys gingerbread, 74; dines on ox cheek, 74; buys bread on arriving at Phila., 75–6. *See also* Vegetarianism.
Food, general: diet of London workmen, 99–100; at London lodging, 102; family eats simply, 145; Assembly supplies, for Dunbar's officers, 221–2. *See also* Temperance; Vegetarianism.
Fortescue, Sir John, on origin of Franklin name, 45 n
Forts. *See* Allen; Cumberland; Duquesne; Franklin; Frontenac; George; Niagara; Norris.
Foster, James: Hemphill uses sermons of, 167; biographical note, 281
Fothergill, John: plan to clean London streets proposed to, 204; and publication of *Exper. and Obser.*, 242; advises BF in dispute with Proprietors, 261; arranges BF meeting with Proprietors, 262; on BF as diplomat, 264 n; biographical note, 281
France, French: BF leaves, 141 n; King George's War, 182; in American Revolution, 226; reception of *Exper. and Obser.* in, 243; electrical experiments in, 243–4; take Ft. George, 252. *See also* French and Indian War.
Francis, Tench: and Academy constitution, 193; defeats BF in election, 197 n; biographical note, 281
Francklyne, Thomas: conceals Bible, 50; biographical note, 283
Franklin, Abiah Folger: good health of, 56; epitaph of, 56; tries to reconcile sons, 82; biographical note, 281
Franklin, Ann Child: children of, 51; biographical note, 281
Franklin, Ann Smith: succeeds husband in business, 169; biographical note, 282
Franklin, Benjamin (uncle): relates family history, 45–7; eldest son follows his trade, 46; account of, 48–50; books of, found in London, 49; relates story of family Bible, 50; becomes Nonconformist, 50; gives BF volumes of sermons, 53; son of, a cutler in Boston, 57; biographical note, 282
Franklin, Deborah Read: BF visits English relatives of, 46 n; sends food to BF, 55 n; sees BF entering Phila., 76; BF appears more respectable to, 79; BF courts, 89; BF's promises to, 92; BF forgets in London, 96; unsuccessful marriage to Rogers, 106–7; BF regrets conduct toward, 114; BF courts again and marries, 128–9; as helpmate, 129, 145; buys silver spoon for BF, 145; biographical note, 282
Franklin, Francis Folger: short life of, 144 n; death of, 170; biographical note, 282
Franklin, James: takes BF as apprentice, 58–9; relations with BF, 59, 68, 69; owns volumes of *Spectator*, 61 n; pays BF's board, 63; prints *New-England Courant*, 66–7; prints BF's "Dogood" essays, 67–8; imprisoned, 69; newspaper censored, 69–70; BF leaves shop of, 70; holds grudge against BF, 81–2; aided by father, 82 n; no reconciliation with, 83; BF reconciled with, 169; death of, 169; BF repays, 170; biographical note, 282

Index

Franklin, James, Jr.: BF educates and apprentices, 169; biographical note, 282

Franklin, John (uncle): Josiah F. apprenticed to, 46; mentioned, 48; biographical note, 282

Franklin, John (brother): marries and moves to Rhode Island, 57; BF visits, 83; biographical note, 283

Franklin, Josiah (father): on origin of Franklin name, 45 n; eldest son follows his trade, 46; becomes Nonconformist, 50; early life of, 51; destines BF for church, 52; and BF's education, 53; forbids BF to become seaman, 53; BF works for, 53, 57; disciplines BF, 54; qualities of, 54–5; good health of, 56; epitaph, 56; suggests trades for BF, 57; library of, 58; decides to make BF a printer, 58; discourages BF's writing poetry, 60; criticizes BF's prose style, 61; mediates disputes between sons, 68; declines Keith's proposal, 81, 82; aid to son James, 82 n; approves BF's return to Phila., 83; and BF's religion, 113; BF away from guidance of, 115; BF fulfills intention of, 143; quotes Bible on diligence, 144; biographical note, 283

Franklin, Josiah, Jr. (brother): lost at sea, 51 n; runs away to sea, 57; biographical note, 283

Franklin, Mary. *See* Fisher, Mary Franklin

Franklin, Samuel: BF tries trade of, 57; biographical note, 283

Franklin, Samuel, Jr.: lives in Boston, 48; biographical note, 283

Franklin, Sarah: education of, 60 n; birth and marriage of, 144 n

Franklin, Thomas (grandfather): account of, 46; biographical note, 283

Franklin, Thomas (uncle): lives in family house at Ecton, 46; account of, 47–8; compared to BF, 47–8; biographical note, 283

Franklin, William: autobiography addressed to, 22, 43; estranged from father, 22; accompanies BF to Ecton and Banbury, 43 n; compares BF with Uncle Thomas, 47–8; with BF in Scotland, 119; birth and nickname, 144 n; appointed clerk of Assembly, 197; with BF at Braddock's camp, 216, 221–2; helps procure wagons, 219; lists supplies for officers, 221–2; military experience of, 222 n, 231; BF's aide on frontier, 231; with BF in England, 259; biographical note, 283–4

Franklin, William Temple: BF's literary legatee, 26; confers with Le Veillard on autobiography, 26; delays publication of works, 30; edition described, 30–2; uses Stuber's life of BF, 31 n; as "improver" of BF text, 31–2; copy of outline in hand of, 267 n

Franklin family: history of, 45–50; religion of, 50–1; surprised by BF's return, 81; anecdotes of, omitted from later parts of autobiography, 133; BF's children and descendants, 144 n

Franklin & Hall, successful partnership formed, 195

Franklin & Meredith: open printing shop, 115; print Quaker history, 118; usefulness of Junto to, 118–9; official printers of Assembly, 121; sued for debt, 122; partnership ended, 123

Franklin, Fort, built, 235 n

Franklin name, origin of, 45

Franklin stove. *See* Pennsylvania fireplace

Frederick, Prince, dispute with George II, 248

Frederick, Md.: Braddock at, 216; BF at, 221

Free and Easy. *See* Society of the Free and Easy

Freedom of Speech, and *Courant*, 70 n

French, John: promises to assist BF, 80; helps BF at Newcastle, 93; biographical note, 284

French and Indian War: inflation during,

125; necessitates colonial union, 209; begun, 214; colonial strength in, 216 n; British intentions prior to, 227; Loudoun's campaign against Louisbourg, 252, 253–4; French take Fort George, 253. *See also* Amherst; Braddock; Defense; Loudoun; Shirley; Wagons.
French language: BF learns, 168; *Exper. and Obser.* translated into, 243
French Prophets, Keimer a member of, 79
French Revolution, precedes Temple Franklin publication, 30
Freud, Sigmund, writings, BF's contrasted with, 21
Friendship, usefulness of, 113
Frontenac, Fort, in Braddock's plans, 223
Frugality: vegetarianism and, 63; BF practices, 79, 144, 145; Josiah Franklin on, 83; importance of, 125–6; BF's practices, 145; in BF's list of virtues, 149, 151; he attributes success to, 157; in Soc. of Free and Easy, 163; *Poor Richard* preaches, 164

Galloway, Joseph: BF leaves papers with, 23; remains loyalist, 23; defeated for Assembly, 197 n
Galloway, Mrs. Joseph, possessed autobiography MS, 23
Gambling: Collins addicted to, 84; Meredith addicted to, 122
Generosity: BF's, to relatives, 46 n; among the poor, BF on, 75
Gentleman's Magazine, and publication of BF electrical papers, 242
George II: BF presented to, 144 n; to be petitioned regarding Proprietors, 248; dispute with Prince Frederick, 248
George III, BF presented to, 144 n
George, Fort, French capture, 252, 253
Georgia, Whitefield orphanage in, 177–8
German: printers of, in Phila., 181 n; fast proclamation translated into, 185; *Exper. and Obser.* translated into, 244
Germantown, Benezet moves to, 178
Gibelin, Jacques, translation of autobiography attributed to, 27 n
Gloucester, Eng., Webb's youth at, 109
Gnadenhütten: Indians attack, 231; BF builds fort at, 232–3
God: BF thanks for success, 43; attributes of, 114; BF's belief in, 146, 162; blesses BF, 157. *See also* Deism; Religion.
Godfrey, Thomas: family lives with BF and Meredith, 115, 127; member of Junto, characterized, 117; neglects work to study mathematics, 127; biographical note, 284
Godfrey, Mrs. Thomas, attempts matchmaking for BF, 127–8
Gordon, Patrick: succeeds Keith as governor, 106; biographical note, 284
Gospel of work. *See* Aphorisms; Industry; Puritanism; Virtues.
Grace, Robert, member of Junto characterized, 117–8; helps BF financially, 122–3; Junto meets in house of, 130; BF rents house of, 130 n; builds Pa. fireplace, 191; biographical note, 284
Granary Burying Ground, Boston, BF's parents buried at, 56 n
Granville, John Carteret, 1st Earl: BF meets, 261; on instructions to governors, 261–2; biographical note, 284
Gravesend, BF sails from, 106
Great Awakening, at Phila., 175–6. *See also* Religion; Whitefield, George.
Great Britain: literary fashions in, compared with America, 16; as source of books for colonies, 141; in Wars of Jenkins' Ear and Austrian Succession, 182; cannon ordered from, 184; Academy contributions from, 195; rejects Albany Plan of Union, 216; BF's hostility toward, 216 n; opposition to Proprietors in, 229; electrical experiments in, 241; reception of *Exper. and Obser.* in, 245; Pa. Assembly sends BF to, 248. *See also* England.
Greek, and teaching of languages, 169

Index

Greenwood, James, BF reads *English Grammar*, 64
Grey, William de, presents Assembly's case to Privy Council, 265 n

Hadley's quadrant, Godfrey invents, 117
Halifax, Charles Montagu, Earl of: patron of Uncle Thomas, 47; biographical note, 285
Halifax, Nova Scotia, Loudoun sails to, 252, 253
Halkett, Sir Peter, grateful to BF for provisions, 222
Hall, David: becomes BF's partner, 195; biographical note, 285
Hamilton, Andrew: intended voyage to England, 93; Riddlesden letter shown to, 94; conspiracy against, 94; BF's patron, 121; gets printing orders for BF, 125; biographical note, 285
Hamilton, James: intended voyage to England, 93; signs Academy subscription, 193 n; incorporates Academy, 195; appoints BF justice of peace, 196; proposes Carlisle Treaty, 197; and Albany Congress, 209; approves Plan of Union, 212; replaced as governor, 212; biographical note, 285
Hanbury, John: introduces BF to Granville, 261; biographical note, 285
Happiness: BF thanks God for, 45; from small things, 207
Harcourt. *See* Hertford.
Harry, David: employed by Keimer, 108; buys out Keimer, loses business, and goes to Barbados, 126; mentioned, 127; biographical note, 285
Harvard College, honorary degree from, 208–9
"Heads of Complaint," Penn requests, 262–3. *See also* Proprietors.
Health: on drinking water for fever, 73; BF neglects exercise in London, 99; BF has pleurisy, 107; passions endanger, 128; and temperance, 157; inoculation and, 170. *See also* Pennsylvania Hospital.
Hemphill, Samuel: controversy over, 167–8; biographical note, 286
Henry VIII, mentioned, 50 n
Herbert of Cherbury, Lord, *Autobiography*, quoted, 14
Hertford, Francis Seymour Conway, Marquis of: Hume secretary to, 227; biographical note, 286
History: BF reads, 58; observations on reading, 161–2; a record of errors, 211
Hoax, on Osborne, 90–1
Hobbes, Thomas, autobiography compared with, 20
Hockley, Richard, receiver general: ordered to pay Proprietor's gift, 229; biographical note, 286
Holland, Samuel: partnership with, 181 n; biographical note, 286
Holland, education of women in, 166
Homes, Robert: urges BF to return to Boston, 79; fails to write family about BF, 81; supports BF's ambition, 82; advises BF on career, 107–8; biographical note, 286
Honors: Harvard and Yale degrees, 209; Fellow of Royal Society, 245–6; Copley Medal, 246
Hopkinson, Thomas: and money for Georgia orphanage, 177–8; experiments with electricity, 241 n; biographical note, 286
Horns (London alehouse), BF at, 97
House, George: brings customer to BF & Meredith, 115–6; biographical note, 286
Household: names of BF's children, 144; live simply, 145; daily schedule, 154; electrical experiments in, 241
Hume, David: religion of, 113 n; tells BF of Braddock's praise, 227; biographical note, 286–7
Humility: BF expresses, 45; in disputes, 64–6, 158–9; usefulness of, 143; in BF's list of virtues, 150; added to list

Index

after Quaker's criticism, 158–9; difficult to distinguish appearance and reality, 159; difficult to acquire, 160; BF embarrassed at regimental escort, 238–9. *See also* Modesty.
Hunter, William; appointed postmaster general, 208; biographical note, 287
Huntington Library, MS. now at, 36
Hutchinson letters, BF and publication of, 208 n
Huth (Hoeth), John Adam, escapes Indian massacre, 233 n

Immortality, in BF's creed, 146, 162
Indians: Carlisle Treaty with, 197–9; drunk, at Carlisle, 198–9; at Albany Congress, 209; Braddock's opinion of, 223, 224; fighting techniques of, 224; defeat Braddock, 224–5; attack Gnadenhütten, 231; conversion of, 231 n; craftiness of, 233; fortifications against, 234, 235 n; take Fort George, 252. *See also* Iroquois; French and Indian War; Seneca
Industry: useless if not honest, 54; BF practices, 79; Josiah Franklin on, 83; brings Franklin & Meredith credit, 119; Baird praises BF's, 119; importance of, 119, 143–4; importance of appearance of, 125–6; Bible quoted on, 144; Deborah Franklin's, 145; in BF's list of virtues, 149, 151; he attributes success to, 157; in Soc. of the Free and Easy, 164; in *Poor Richard,* 164
Innis. *See* Ennis.
Inoculation, BF's son dies without, 170 n
Instructions, proprietary, disputes over, 247–8
Inventions: copper-plate press, 112; Godfrey invents quadrant, 117; Pennsylvania fireplace, 191–2; BF on patents for, 192; magic squares and circles, 197; street lamp, 203–4. *See also* Daylight Saving Time; Matching gifts.
Ireland: Hemphill from, 167; revenue from post office of, 208; navigation near, 258 n
Iroquois: chiefs at Albany, 209; grievances, 209 n. *See also* Seneca.
Isted, Ambrose: owns Franklin house at Ecton, 46; biographical note, 287
Italian: BF learns via chess, 168; *Exper. and Obser.* translated into, 244

Jackson, Richard: *Historical Review . . . of Pennsylvania* describes disputes with Denny, 248 n; presents Assembly's case to Privy Council, 265 n
James, Abel: has first part of autobiography MS, 23–4, 134, 267; letter from, 133–4; biographical note, 287
James, Thomas, type cast by, 110
Jefferson, Thomas: is loaned copies of papers on autobiography, 133 n; on BF as a speaker, 160 n
Jeffrey, Francis, review of autobiography quoted, 16–7
Jesus: BF on moral system of, 13; humility of, to be imitated, 149; in Whitefield letter, 178
Jews, BF's relations with, 146–7 n
John ——: Irish workman at Keimer's, 108; runs away, 109
Johnson, Samuel (1709–1784), on *Spectator* style, 61 n
Johnston, William: has money for wagons, 228; biographical note, 287
Journal Book, plan of life in, 114
Journal of a Voyage, BF writes at sea, 106
Joyce, James, *Ulysses,* autobiography contrasted with, 21
Junto: Mather and formation of, 58 n; formed, 116; rules of, 116–7, 118; first members, 117–8; usefulness of, to Franklin & Meredith, 118–9; discusses paper money, 124; helps form Library Co., 130; members pool books, 130, 141–2, 182; papers reprinted in *Pa. Gazette,* 165; organizes subordinate clubs, 170–1; and city watch, 173;

hears proposal on fire companies, 174; mentioned, 177; members help found Academy, 192–3
Justice: in BF's list of virtues, 150; he attributes public confidence to, 157
Justice of the Peace: BF appointed, 196; BF feels unqualified as, 197
Juvenal, *Satire X*, quoted, 211

Keimer, Samuel: BF applies for job with, 77; qualifications as printer, 78–9; characterized, 78–9, 112–3; surprised at Keith's interest in BF, 80; BF's relations with, 88; gluttony of, 89; business improved, 107; offers job, 108; reputation in London, 108; unable to teach apprentices, 109; religion of, 109; quarrels with BF, 110–1; weak financial condition, 111; fears Bradford competition, 112; BF resumes work with, 112; BF and Meredith leave, 115; prints for Quakers, 118; starts newspaper ahead of BF, 120; "Busy Body" ridicules, 120; sells business and moves to Barbados, 126; mentioned, 119, 127; biographical note, 287
Keith, George: confused with Sir William, 32, 36; Bradford involved in controversy of, 71; biographical note, 288
Keith, Sir William: confused with George, 32, 36; promises of, to BF, 80–2, 86, 92; letter to Josiah F., 82; BF misjudges character, 87; fails to keep promises, 92–5; characterized, 94–5; in conspiracy against Hamilton, 94; career, 95; replaced by Gordon, 106; avoids BF, 106; a freethinker, 114; biographical note, 288
Kennedy, Archibald: approves Plan of Union, 210; biographical note, 288
Kennedy, Archibald, Jr.: sails with BF to England, 256; saves ship, 258–9; biographical note, 288
Kinnersley, Ebenezer: lectures on electricity, 241–2; biographical note, 288
Kite experiment, BF performs, 244. *See also* Electricity.

Lady's Magazine, The, publishes autobiography, 28
Lampooning, BF inclined to, 83
Lancaster, Pa.: BF at, 217; BF advertises for wagons at, 218
Lancaster County, Pa.: wagons needed in, 219; enlistment of servants in, 227
Languages: BF studies, 168; method of teaching, 168–9
Latin: BF learns, 168; comments on study of, 168–9; *Exper. and Obser.* translated into, 244
Lawrence, Thomas: lieut. col. of militia, 183; to get cannon from N.Y., 184; biographical note, 288
Lecky, William E. H., *History of England,* quoted, 19–20
Legal forms, BF sells, 125
Leisure: spent with friends, 79; spent talking with Collins, 84; in daily schedule, 154; BF retires from business, 195. *See also* Reading.
LeRoy, Jean-Baptiste: defends BF's electrical theories, 244 n; biographical note, 288–9
Le Veillard, Louis Guillaume: gets copy of autobiography, 25, 26; asked for comments, 26; Temple Franklin asks to seal autobiography, 26; as source of French translation, 27; Temple Franklin trades copies of autobiography with, 28; translates autobiography, 34; death of, 34; translates Uncle Benjamin verses, 48 n; gets copies of James letter and BF outline, 133; lends these to Jefferson, 133 n
Liberty and Necessity. See Dissertation on Liberty and Necessity.
Libraries, subscription, growth of, in colonies, 130–1
Library Company of Phila.: organized, 130, 141; incorporated, 130, 143; imi-

tated, 130, 142; opens, 142; annual fee, 142; Collinson sends glass tube to, 241
Lighthouses, utility of, 259
Light House Tragedy, BF writes ballad called, 59
Lighting: of streets, 203–4; improved street lamps, 204
Lightning: identified with electricity, 242; French experiments with, 244; kite experiment, 244; Cannon experiments with, 245
Lightning rod, Dalibard and, 245 n
Lincoln's Inn Fields, Watts printing house in, 99
Liquor. *See* Drink and drinking.
Little Britain, London: BF lodges in, 95, 97; BF leaves, 101
Loan Office, and aid for Mass., 215–6
Locke, John, *Essay Concerning Human Understanding*, BF reads, praises, 64
Logan, James: supports defensive war, 187–8; characterized, 188 n; on BF's electrical experiments, 241 n; biographical note, 289
Logic, Keimer wants to exploit BF's, 88
London: Uncle Benjamin apprentice in, 48; BF arrives in, 93, 259; tires of, 105; leaves, 106; BF meets Whitefield in, 179; street lamps in, 204; proposal for cleaning streets in, 204–7; inhabitants sleep by day, live by night, 207
Long Island, BF at, 72
Lottery: for battery, 183; Union Fire Co. buys tickets, 186; Logan buys tickets, 187
Loudoun, John Campbell, 4th Earl of: supply bill for, 248–9; unable to defend frontier, 249; tries to reconcile Assembly and governor, 249, 250 n; characterized, 250–2; delays BF's sailing, 250–3; forces Denny to sign supply bill, 250 n, 266; Denny sends messages to, 251; campaign against Louisbourg, 252, 253–4; embargoes colonial trade, 253–4; N.Y. honors, 254; takes command, 254; delays settlement of wagon account, 254–5; quarrels with Shirley, 254 n; biographical note, 289
Louis XV: BF presented to, 144 n; witnesses electrical experiments, 244
Louis XVI, BF presented to, 144 n
Louisbourg, Canada: aid to garrison of, 189; Loudoun's abortive campaign against, 252, 253–4
Lucas, F. L.: on style of autobiography, 18 n
Lutwidge, Walter: BF sails to England with, 256; Kennedy saves ship of, 258–9; biographical note, 289
Lyons, William: introduces BF to London friends, 97; biographical note, 289

Macclesfield, George Parker, Earl of: praises BF, 246; biographical note, 289–90
Madeira wine: Denny drinks with BF, 247; increases Clinton's generosity, 280
Magic squares and circles, BF constructs, 197
Mandeville, Bernard: BF meets, 97; biographical note, 290
Mansfield, William Murray, Baron: arbitrates dispute between Assembly and Penns, 265–6; biographical note, 290
Mark Twain. *See* Clemens, Samuel L.
Marly-la-Ville, France, kite experiment performed at, 244 n
Marriage: BF considers, 127–8; customs, 128 n; to Deborah Read, 129; Pa. laws on, 129 n; Moravian customs, 237
"Martha Careful," pseudonym, 120 n
Martin, David: plays chess with BF, 168 n; biographical note, 290
Marx, Karl, writings, BF's contrasted with, 21
Mary, Queen, mentioned, 50
Maryland, boundary dispute with Pa., 263 n
Mason-Dixon Line, settles boundary dispute, 263 n

Index

Massachusetts: James F. and General Court of, 69; political dispute in, 121; aid for, in Crown Point attack, 214–6

Matching gifts, BF devises system of, 200–1

Mathematics: Godfrey learned in, 117, 127; Parsons learned in, 117

Mather, Cotton: *Corderius Americanus* mentioned, 13; praises Folger, 51; *Essays to Do Good*, 58; biographical note, 290

Mather, Samuel, letter to, quoted, 18

Maugridge, William, member of Junto, characterized, 117; biographical note, 290

Maxims. *See* Anecdotes and Aphorisms.

Mazéas, Guillaume, on French experiments, 244–5 n

McGuffey, William H., uses autobiography, 10

Mecom, Benjamin, partnership with, 181 n

Mecom, Jane, mentioned, 51 n

Melville, Herman: Israel Potter, quoted, 20

Meredith, Hugh: employed by Keimer, 108; partnership with BF planned, 111–2; persuades BF to work for Keimer, 112; member of Juno, 117; contributes little to partnership, 120; addicted to drinking and gambling, 122; ends partnership with BF, 123; goes to No. Car., 123; writes pieces for BF, 123; biographical note, 290. *See also* Franklin & Meredith.

Meredith, Simon: sets up son with BF, 111; fails to provide backing, 122; biographical note, 290

Metaphysics. *See* Religion.

Mickle, Samuel: predicts ruin for Phila., 116; biographical note, 291

Mikveh Israel, Congregation, BF contributes to, 146–7 n

Milford, Pa., mentioned, 232 n

Militia: Assembly fails to establish, 182; Association of volunteers (1747–48), 182–5; organized in Phila. (1755–56), 237–8; BF elected colonel, 238; pays honors to BF, 238–9; criticized, 238 n. *See also* Association.

Militia Act: BF draws and gets passed, 230; disallowed, 238

Millikan, Robert A., on BF as scientist, 244 n

Mill Pond, young BF plays at, 54

Minisinks, defense of, 232

Mitchell, John: on reception of BF electrical letter by Royal Soc., 242; biographical note, 291

Moderation, in BF's list of virtues, 150

Modest Enquiry into the Nature and Necessity of a Paper Currency, A: BF writes, 124

Modesty, in speech, BF commends, 66. *See also* Humility.

Mohammedanism, might be preached in Phila., 176

Money. *See* Currency, paper.

Money Bills: Assembly objects to amendment, 229; passed, 230; BF accused of obstructing, 239; Denny vetoes, 248–9

Monongahela, Battle of, 224–6

Morality: BF's early views on, 113–5; Junto discusses, 116–7; creeds fail to promote, 146. *See also* Project for Attaining Moral Perfection; Virtue.

Moravians: Indians attack, 231; set up defenses, 231; pacifism of, 231–2; migration to America, 231 n; missionary activities, 231 n; provide supplies for BF, 232; practices described, 236–7

Morgan, J. Pierpont, receives MS outline, 35

Morris, James: opposes buying lottery tickets, 186–7; biographical note, 291

Morris, Robert Hunter: BF confers with, 212; love of disputation, 212–3; relations with BF, 213–4; vetoes act to aid Mass., 215; asks Dunbar to defend frontier, 225–6, 240; calls for tax for defense, 229; sends BF to frontier, 230–1; confers with BF at Reading, 231 n; recalls BF from frontier, 235;

personal relations with, 239; would make BF a general, 240; leaves Pa., 240; biographical note, 291
Morris, William, BF engages passage with, 249
Mufti of Constantinople, mentioned, 176
Mugridge, Donald H., on Farrand's "restoration," 36 n
Music of Moravians, BF describes, 236

Nantucket Island, Folgers at, 51–2 n
Napoleon, overthrow of, precedes Temple Franklin publication, 30
Natural philosophy. *See* Science.
Navigation: BF studies, 64; of packet, 255–6; experiments suggested, 256–7; on approach to England, 258
New Building: erected in Phila., 176; Association meeting in, 183; taken over by Academy, 193–5; BF becomes trustee of, 194
Newcastle, Del., BF at, 92. *See also* Delaware.
New England: currency inflation in, 124; BF familiar with fasts in, 184; seeks aid to attack French, 189; BF visits, 208–9
New-England Courant: James F. prints, 66–7; BF's file of, 67 n; BF contributions to, 68; appears under BF's name, 69; censored, 69–70
New Haven, press founded at, 181 n
New Jersey: Keimer and BF print money for, 112; BF meets assemblymen of, 112–3
Newport: BF visits, 83, 169
Newspaper: BF plans to start, 119–20; Bradford's characterized, 199; Keimer starts, but sells out to BF, 120
Newspapers: early American, 66–7; Webb writes for, 109; editorial policies of *Pa. Gazette,* 165. *See also American Weekly Mercury;* Bradford, Andrew; *New-England Courant; Pennsylvania Gazette.*
Newton, Sir Isaac: objectivity mirrored in autobiography, 14; world-view of, as influence on BF, 21; BF hoped to meet, 97; biographical note, 291
New York (city): BF escapes to, 71; BF crosses harbor, 72; BF in, 84, 210, 212, 250; books not sold in, 141; BF meets Morris in, 212; Loudoun sails to, 252; honors Loudoun, 254
New York (province): cannon procured from, 184; Mass. seeks aid from, 214; Moravians get arms from, 231
Niagara, Fort, in Braddock's plans, 223
Nicole, Pierre, *Logic: or the Art of Thinking,* BF reads, 64
Noble, Thomas: as trustee of New Building, 194; biographical note, 291
Nollet, Abbé Jean-Antoine: attacks *Exper. and Obser.,* 243–4; refuted, 244; biographical note, 291–2
Norris, Isaac: friendship with, 171–2; at Carlisle Treaty, 198; at Albany Congress, 209; and Plan of Union, 212; biographical note, 292
Norris, Fort, built, 235 n
Northampton, England, Uncle Thomas in, 47
Northampton County, Pa., BF in command in, 230–1 n
North Carolina, Meredith goes to and describes, 123
"Nun," in Duke St. lodgings, 102–3

Observations on Reading History, text, 161–2
Offices, public, held by BF in Phila., 196
Office-seeking, BF denies, 185
Onion, Stephen: BF sails to England with, 93; biographical note, 292
Order: in BF's list of virtues, 149, 151, 154; he never attains, 155–6
Orme, Robert: mortally wounded, 226; biographical note, 292
Osborne, Charles: BF friendship with, 89–92; promises posthumous visit, 91–2; biographical note, 292

Index

Outline of autobiography: James sends copy to BF, 24, 134; Bigelow acquires James copy, 35; description, 267–8; text, 268–72

Oxford, Webb attends, 108–9

Palmer, John: patron of Uncle Thomas, 47; biographical note, 292

Palmer, Samuel: employs BF, 96; BF leaves, 99; biographical note, 292

Paper money. *See* Currency, paper.

Paris, Ferdinand John: represents Proprietors on Heads of Complaint, 263–4; characterized, 263; requests BF's replacement, 264; and dispute over tax on proprietary estates, 266; death of, 266 n; biographical note, 292

Paris, France, electrical experiments at, 244

Parker, James: partnership with, 181 n; biographical note, 292–3

Parker, Theodore, on autobiography, 19

Parliament: exempts Moravians from military service, 231; on instructions to governors, 262

Parsons, J., publishes autobiography in English, 28

Parsons, Talcott, writings, BF's contrasted with, 21

Parsons, William: member of Junto, 117; biographical note, 293

Partnerships, BF forms, 181. *See also* Franklin & Hall; Franklin & Meredith; Hall, David; Holland, Samuel; Mecom, Benjamin; Meredith, Hugh; Parker, James; Smith, Thomas; Timothée, Louis.

Passy, France, autobiography resumed at, 141

Paternoster Row, London, mentioned, 95

Paving, of streets, 202–3

Pearson, Isaac: BF meets, 113; biographical note, 293

Pemberton, Henry: BF meets, 97; biographical note, 293

Pembroke, Earl of, BF visits house and gardens of, 259

Penn, John: at Albany Congress, 209; biographical note, 293. *See also* Proprietors.

Penn, Thomas: annoyed at BF's popularity, 239; opposes BF in England, 239; makes advances to BF, 247; BF meets Proprietors at house of, 262; BF quarrels with, 264 n; biographical note, 293. *See also* Proprietors.

Penn, William: *Fruits of a Father's Love*, mentioned, 13; pacifist principles of, 188; characterized, 188 n; biographical note, 294

Pennsylvania: prospers under Keith, 95; Denham advises return to, 104; BF anticipates return to, 105; newspapers, 121; paper currency, 123–5; scarcity of bookshops, 141; religions, 146; lacks militia and academy, 181; proclaims fast, 184; aids New England to attack French, 189; delegation to Albany Congress, 209; taxation of Proprietors' estates, 214, 215 n, 229, 240, 248–9, 263, 265, 266; Mass. seeks aid from, 214; wagons for Braddock in, 217; boundary dispute with Md., 263 n. *See also* Defense.

Pennsylvania fireplace: invented, 191; design of, 191–2 n; BF declines to patent, 192

Pennsylvania Gazette: prints piece on literary style, 20; publication begins, 120 n; makes BF known, 121; high quality of, 121; has prominent subscribers, 121; postriders bribed to carry, 127; instructional purpose, 165; no personal abuse in, 165; defends Hemphill, 167; and postmastership, 172; profit from, 180–1

Pennsylvania Hospital: idea conceived by Bond, 199; BF solicits for, 199–200; establishment, 199–201; Assembly aids, 200–1; cornerstone inscription, 201 n

Index

Pennsylvania, University of, academy and college becomes, 195, 196 n

Perfection, moral. *See* Project for Attaining Moral Perfection.

Perkins, William, *A Treatise of the Vocations,* cited, 13

Peter Parley. *See* Goodrich, Samuel.

Peters, Richard: proposed as academy head, 182; on proclamation of fast, 184; replaces BF as president of Academy trustees, 196 n; at Carlisle Treaty, 198 n; at Albany Congress, 209; reports BF's militia escort, 239; biographical note, 294

Philadelphia: BF's first arrival at, 75–7; building sites located, 75 n; Keimer sets up press at, 77; BF becomes acquainted in, 79; BF on life in, 81–2; departure from, 92; changes before BF's return, 106; BF returns to, from Burlington, 115; Mickle predicts ruin for, 116; decline of economy, 124; Bradford and BF only printers in, 126; few books sold in, 141; few readers in, 142; city watch, 173; fire companies, 175; New Building, 176; Association for defense of, 182–7; hospital established in, 199–201; paving and cleaning streets, 202–3; street lamps, 203–4; Dunbar retreats to, 225–6, 227; BF returns to, 237; near riot in, 237 n; kite experiment at, 244; welcomes Denny, 246. *See also* Public affairs.

Philanthropy. *See* Charity.

Philosophy, natural. *See* Science.

Pilgrim's Progress. See Bunyan, John.

Pitt, William: removes Loudoun, 251; biographical note, 294

Plan of Conduct, BF composes at sea, 106

Plain Truth, published, 182–3

Plutarch, *Parallel Lives:* mentioned, 13; BF reads; 58; autobiography compared to, 139

Poetry: by Uncle Benjamin, 48–9 n; BF writes ballads, 59; father discourages, 60; by Browne on Bible, 74; by Cotton on Vergil, 74; BF and friends write and criticize, 90–1; Pope ridicules Ralph's, 91, 248; BF urges Ralph to give up writing, 98–9; printers sell ballads, 141

Politics, Junto discusses, 116–17. *See also* Public affairs.

Poor Richard's Almanack: BF begins, 163; described, 164; Father Abraham's speech in, 164

Pope, Alexander: autobiography debt to methods of, 14; *Essay on Criticism* quoted, 65–6; ridicules Ralph, 91, 248; *Essay on Man* quoted, 114

Port Royal, Messrs. du. *See* Arnauld, Antoine; Nicole, Pierre.

Post office: Bradford uses, in newspaper competition, 126–7; BF becomes Phila. postmaster, 172; BF appointed comptroller, 208; appointed deputy postmaster general, 208; successful operation, 208; Penn seeks BF's removal, 239

Potts, Stephen: employed by Keimer, 108; member of Junto, 117; biographical note, 294

Pownall, Thomas: seeks N.Y. aid for Mass., 214; biographical note, 294–5

Pratt, Charles: reviews Heads of Complaint, 265; presents Proprietors' case to Privy Council, 265 n; biographical note, 295

Prayer: BF composes for private use, 148, 153; chaplain gets soldiers to attend, 235

Presbyterian Church. *See* Andrews, Jedediah; Hemphill, Samuel; Second Presbyterian Church.

Presbyterianism, BF rejects some dogmas of, 145–6

Press, printing: Keimer's "shattered," 78; BF contrives, for copper-plate work, 112; BF and Meredith order from England, 111–2. *See also* Printing.

Price, Richard: to comment on autobiography, 26; proposed editor of BF works, 29; death of, 29

Pride, to be controlled, 158–9, 160
Priestley, Joseph, recounts kite experiment, 245 n
Printing: provides metaphor for autobiography, 43 n; Keimer tests BF's ability, 77; Bradford's and Keimer's qualifications, 78–9; Keith offers to help BF in business, 80, 87, 92; father refuses to set BF up, 82; BF lists equipment for, 87 n; BF at Palmer's, 96; BF at Watts's, 99; chapel laws at Watts's, 101; BF gives up, 105; Keimer's business improves, 107; BF resumes work with Keimer, 108; BF casts type, does engraving, makes ink, 110; equipment to be ordered from London, 111; BF builds copper-plate press, 112; equipment arrives from London, 115; of Quaker history, 118–9; BF gets Assembly business, 121, 171; for Pa. and Del. 125; Bradford discouraging on, 127; BF retires from, 195. *See also* Finances, business; Newspapers; Partnerships
Privy Council: disallows Militia Bill, 230 n; hears arguments of Penns and Assembly, 265
Project for Attaining Moral Perfection: described, 148–60; to be practised by Society of Free and Easy, 162–3
Proposals relating to the Education of Youth, published, 193
Proprietors of Pa.: BF negotiations with, as agent, 24; Keith disregards instructions of, 95; Peters secretary to, 182; solicited for cannon, 184; contribute to Academy, 195; instructions cause disputes, 212; taxation of estates of, 214, 215 n, 229, 240, 248–9, 263, 265, 266; donate £5000 for defense, 229; BF's first conference with, 262–3; sue Lord Baltimore, 263; BF's quarrel with, 264 n; dismiss Denny, 266. *See also* Heads of Complaint; Penn, John; Penn, Thomas; Penn, William.
Protestantism, in Franklin family, 50
Proverbs. *See* Anecdotes and aphorisms.
Providence, saves BF from dangers of youth, 115
Public affairs: BF's basis for success in, 159–60; self-interest as factor in, 161; beginning of BF interest in, 173; BF occupied with, after retirement, 196; campaigning, 197 n; BF a provincial commissioner, 230; building frontier forts, 230–6; BF pens Assembly message, 247–8; agency in London, 261–3; civic improvements, 196–208; colonial defense, 216–36; agency to England, 248, 261–6. *See also* Academy; Albany Plan of Union; Association; Defense; Fire protection; Library Co.; Post office.
Punning, Grace enjoys, 118
Pythagoras, advises self-examination, 151

Quadrant, Godfrey invents, 117
Quakers: BF's account of, considered, 19; BF sleeps in meetinghouse of, 76; Franklin & Meredith print for, 118; attitude toward defense, 182, 185–91; permit subterfuges, 189–90; position in Assembly, 185, 188–9, 191; leave public offices, 191; and Albany Plan, 212 n; BF sides with, 214; exempted from militia, 230; mentioned, 237
Quincy, Josiah: seeks Pa. aid for Mass., 214–6; BF writes address for, 215; thanks Assembly, 216; biographical note, 295
Ralph, James: BF's Phila. friendship with, 89–92; as poet, 90–1, 98; Pope attacks, 91, 248; accompanies BF to England, 92; with BF in London, 95–6, 98; fails to find career in London, 95; borrows from BF, 95; *Liberty and Necessity* dedicated to, 96; teaches school, 98; uses BF's name, 98; mistress, 98–9; refuses to pay debts to BF, 99; BF reviews relations with, 106; BF converts to deism, 114; Denny reports on later career, 248; biographical note, 295

Index

Rationalizing, BF on, 88
Read, Deborah. *See* Franklin, Deborah Read.
Read, James: asks BF to resign clerkship, 185; biographical note, 295–6
Read, John: BF passes house of, 76; lodges with, 79; half ruined by Riddlesden, 94; biographical note, 296
Read, Sarah White: cool to BF's courtship of Deborah, 89; biographical note, 296
Reading, Pa., BF and Morris confer at, 231 n
Reading, BF: as a child, 57–8; as an apprentice, 59–64; on religion, 64, 113–4; Bunyan, Defoe, and Richardson, 72; with friends, 79; arrangements for, in London, 97; BF and Wygate read together, 103; in London, 106; has two days a week for, 109; conversation improved by, 112; his sole diversion, 126, 143; moral virtues vary in, 149; in daily schedule, 154. *See also* Authors; Education.
Reading, general: Collins' library, 82–3; Burnet and BF discuss, 85; of Junto members, 118; educates Americans to defend privileges, 130–1; few readers in Phila., 142; becomes fashionable, 142; raises cultural level in colonies, 142. *See also* Junto; Library Co. of Phila.
Reason, versus "inclination," 148
Recorder, BF defeated for election as, 197 n
Reed, Frances, marriages of, 128 n
Religion: of Franklin and Folger families, 50–2; Folger on liberty of, 52; BF prefers reading to public worship, 63; BF becomes a "doubter," 64; BF indiscreet about, 71; of Dr. Browne, 74; Keimer and BF plan sect, 88; Keimer's, 79, 88, 109, 112–3; BF observes Lents, 89; of BF's early Phila. friends, 89–90; *Liberty and Necessity* on, 96, 114; BF's views on, 113–5; BF's upbringing, 145–6; BF's creed, 146, 162; BF respects and contributes to all sects, 146; possible utility of, 147; prefers private worship, 147–8; his private ritual, 148; in Project for Attaining Moral Perfection, 157–8; BF gives up church attendance, 168; soldiers' attendance at prayers, 235. *See also* Deism; Dunkers; Great Awakening; Hemphill, Samuel; Moravians; Quakers; Roman Catholicism; Whitefield, George.
Renouard, Jules, publishes BF writings, 34 n
Residences, BF: final home in Phila., 75 n; with Read, 79; in Little Britain, London, 95, 97; in Duke St., London, 101–2; in Market St., Phila., 115; in Grace's house, 130 n; in Race St., Phila., 196 n; near Jersey Market, Phila., 202; in Craven St., London, 205 n, 261
Resolution, in BF's list of virtues, 149, 151
Revolution, American. *See* American Revolution.
Rhode Island, French troops in, 226. *See also* Newport.
Richardson, Samuel, BF on dialogue in, 72
Riddlesden, Walter Vanhaesdonck: knavery of, 94; biographical note, 296
Roberts, Hugh: member of Junto, 118 n; biographical note, 296
Roberts, James: does not hire Ralph, 95; biographical note, 296
Robinson, G. G. J. and J., publish autobiography, 28–9
Rogers, John; Deborah Read marries, 107; status of her marriage to, 129; biographical note, 296
Roman Catholicism: Franklin family opposes, 50; of BF's landlady and tenant, 102–3
Roscommon, Wentworth Dillon, Earl of, *Essay on Translated Verse*, BF quotes, criticizes, 66
Rose, Aquila: death of, 71; Keimer eulogizes, 78; son apprenticed to BF, 125; biographical note, 296

Index

Rose, Joseph: apprenticed to BF, 125; biographical note, 297
Rousseau, Jean Jacques, compared with BF, 15–6
Royal Academy of Sciences. *See* Académie Royale des Sciences.
Royal Society: BF's letters read to, 241 n, 242; on identity of lightning and electricity, 242; praises BF, 242 n; revises view of *Exper. and Obser.*, 244–5; prints summary of *Exper. and Obser.*, 245; learns of French experiments, 245 n; elects BF, 245–6; presents him with Copley Medal, 246
Rum: as Great Spirit's gift to Indians, 199; used to bring soldiers to prayers, 235
Russel, William or Thomas: BF sails to England with, 93; biographical note, 297

Sabbatarianism, of Keimer, 88, 109
Sack, empty, aphorism on, 164
St. Andrews, Scotland, BF and son in, 119
St. Clair (Sinclair), Sir John, and wagons, 221
St. George's Channel, problem of navigation in, 258
Salisbury Plain, BF at, 259
Saltero's coffeehouse, curiosities at, 103–4
Sancho Panza, cited, 213–4
Sandy Hook, N.J., fleet gathers at, 252
Saturday Evening Post, not founded by BF, 120 n
Saunders, Richard, pseudonym in almanac, 163
Schedule, BF's, for each day, 154
Schools. *See* Education.
Science: Junto discusses, 116–7; BF studies, 240–1; BF's importance in development of, 244 n; maritime experiments suggested, 256–7. *See also* Electricity.
Scilly Islands, and navigation, 258
Scotland, BF and son in, 119
Scott, Sir Walter, autobiography compared with, 19
Scull, Nicholas: member of Junto, characterized, 117; biographical note, 297
Second Presbyterian Church, Phila., BF's advice on raising funds for, 201–2
Self-interest, influence of, in public affairs, 161
Seller, John, *An Epitome of the Art of Navigation*, BF studies, 64
Seneca, defeat French army, 223 n
Servants, enlistment of, 227
Seven Years' War. *See* French and Indian War.
Sewel, William, *The History of the Quakers*, Franklin & Meredith print part of, 118 n
Shaftesbury, Anthony Ashley Cooper, 3d Earl of, BF reads works on religion by, 64
Shakespeare, William, autobiography compared with, 19
Sharp, James, on improving Pa. fireplace, 192 n
Sharpe, Horatio: asks Dunbar to defend frontier, 225–6; biographical note, 297
Shaving, advantages of doing oneself, 207
Shipley, Jonathan: letter to, quoted, 14; autobiography begun during visit with, 21, 43
Ships, need for experiments in design of, 257
Shirley, William: BF discusses Plan of Union with, 211; orders payment for wagons, 228; succeeds Braddock, 228 n, 253; abilities of, 253–4; prefers "low Seat," 254; quarrels with Loudoun, 254 n; biographical note, 297
Shirley, William, Jr.: killed, 225; papers of, in French hands, 226–7; biographical note, 297
Short, William, makes copies of James letter and BF outline, 133 n, 267 n
Shorthand system, invented by Uncle Benjamin, 48–9

Index

Shovel, Sir Cloudsley: squadron lost, 258; biographical note, 297
Silence, in BF's list of virtues, 149–51, 152
Silence Dogood essays, writing of, 67–8
Sincerity: in BF's list of virtues, 150, 151; public confidence attributed to, 157
Six Nations. *See* Iroquois.
Sloane, Sir Hans: BF sells asbestos purse to, 97; biographical note, 297–8
Smallpox, death of son from, 170
Smith, William, brings Copley Medal to BF, 246 n
Smith, Thomas, partnership with, 181 n
Some Account of the Pennsylvania Hospital, published, 200 n
Society of the Free and Easy, proposed, 161–3
Socrates; BF imitates debating method, 64–5, 88, 165; humility of, to be imitated, 150
Spanish, BF learns, 168
Spain, in War of Jenkins' Ear, 182
Spangenberg, Augustus G.: on Moravian pacifism, 231–2; biographical note, 298
Speech: BF's limitations in, 91, 160; Whitefield's effectiveness, 179–80
Spencer, Archibald: BF buys electrical apparatus of, 196; electrical experiments of, 240; biographical note, 298
Spectator, The: model of good writing, 61–2; Ralph imitates, 95
Spotswood, Alexander: appoints BF postmaster, 172; biographical note, 298
Stamp Act, and parliamentary authority, 262 n
Stationer's shop, BF opens, 125
Stationery, sold by printers, 141
Steele, Richard, BF copies style of, 61 n
Stevenson, Margaret, BF lives in house of, 205 n
Stevenson, Mary (Polly), BF and education of, 60 n
Stonehenge, BF visits, 259
Streets: paving and cleaning, 202–3, 204–7; lighting, 203–4
Stroudsburg, Pa., mentioned, 232 n
Stuber, Henry: writes biography of BF, 29; reprinted, 29–30; Temple Franklin uses his life of BF, 31 n
Sturmy, Samuel, *The Mariner's Magazine*, BF studies, 64
Style, literary, BF's principles of, 20
Success: industry leads to, 119; humility contributes to, 143
Sunday, BF's study day, 62–3. *See also* Sabbatarianism.
Supreme Executive Council, Pa., BF elected president, 24
Swimming: BF expert at, 53–4; BF's exploits in London, 103–4; Wyndham asks BF to teach sons, 105; BF tempted to open school for, 106
Synagogue, BF contributes to paying debt on, 146–7 n
Syng, Philip: member of Junto, 118 n; in Union Fire Co., 175 n, 189–90; experiments with electricity, 241 n; biographical note, 298
Tacitus, Cornelius, writings of, mentioned, 135
Tax, taxation: for city watch, 173; parliamentary, for colonial defense, 211; led to Revolution, 211; of proprietary estates, *see* Proprietors.
Taylor, Abraham: militia colonel, 183 n; to get cannon from N.Y., 184; biographical note, 298
Teach, Edward (Blackbeard), BF writes ballad on, 59
Temperance: and study, 63; in BF's list of virtues, 149–50, 152; health attributed to, 157
Tennent, Gilbert: consults BF on building church, 201; biographical note, 298–9
Theater, BF and Ralph attend in London, 96, 106
Thévenot, Melchisédeck de, *The Art of Swimming*, BF practices from, 104
Thomas, George: signs Library Co. charter, 143 n; requests militia law, 182; consults BF on defense, 184; urges As-

Index

sembly aid to New England, 189; biographical note, 299
Thomson, James, *The Seasons*, BF uses prayer from, 154
Timothée, Elizabeth: succeeds husband in business, 166; biographical note, 299
Timothée, Louis: set up as printer in Charleston, 166; death of, 166; partnership with, 181 n; biographical note, 299
Timothy, Peter: established as printer, 166; biographical note, 299
Toleration: BF's, to all sects, 146; in Phila. New Building, 176
Tranquility, in BF's list of virtues, 150
Travels, BF: to Ecton and Banbury (1758), 43, 46 n; escape to N.Y. (1723), 70–1; 87–8; N.Y. to Phila. (1723), 71–5; to Boston (1724), 81; Boston to Phila. (1724), 83–6; to London (1724), 92–3; BF and Wygate consider European trip, 104; to Phila. (1726), 106; to Scotland (1759), 119; to Boston (1733), 169; to New England (1753), 208–9; to Albany (1754), 210; to Boston (1754), 211, 212; to N.Y. (1754), 213; to Braddock's headquarters (1775), 216–7; to Lancaster (1755), 217; to Pa. frontier (1755–6), 231–6; to Virginia (1756), 238–9, to Boston (1743), 240–1; to N.Y. (1757), 250; to England (1757), 255–9; sightseeing in England, 259
Treaty of Peace, signing of, frees BF to resume autobiography, 24
Trenton, N.J., Dunbar to return servants to, 227
Trevose, BF papers left at, scattered, 23
Tyron, Thomas, *The Way to Health*, on vegetarianism, 63, 87
Tube, electrical, presented to Library Co., 241, 242
Twyford, England, BF begins autobiography at, 21, 43
Type: BF improvises method of casting, 110; pied, incident of, 119. *See also* Printing.
Uplinger, Nicholas, BF's company stays at farm of, 232 n
Union, colonial, impossibility of, 216 n. *See also* Albany Plan of Union.
Union Fire Co: organized, 174; imitated, 174–5; buys lottery tickets, 186–7, 189
Union Club, formed, 171
United Party for Virtue. *See* Society of the Free and Easy.
Universal Asylum, The, publishes Stuber's life of BF, 30–1

Van Doren, Carl, *Benjamin Franklin*, quoted, 21
Van Etten, John, ordered to defend Minisinks, 232 n
Vanity: a comfort of life, 44; BF accused of, 68; sacrifice of, useful, 143
Vaughan, Benjamin: urges continuation of autobiography, 18, 24, 133, 135–40; copy sent to, for comments, 26; mentioned, 27, 28, 29; makes retranslation, 29; BF letter to, quoted, 33–4 n; biographical note, 299
Vegetarianism: BF adopts, 63; forsakes, 87–8; persuades Keimer to practice, 88–9; economy of, 89
Vergil, Cotton's travesty of, 74
Vernon, Samuel: BF to collect debt for, 83; collected, 85; BF's misuse of money of, 86, 87, 110, 114; reminds BF of debt, 121–2; BF repays, 122; biographical note, 299
Verse. *See* Poetry.
Vine Club, formed, 171
Virginia: French troops in, 226; Spotswood governor of, 172, journey to, 238–9
Virtue(s): important in human relations, 114; rewarded in after life, 146, 162; BF's list of, 149–50; exercises for practice of, 151–5; practical necessity of, 158; as habit, 165. *See also: Art of Virtue;* Project for Attaining Moral Perfection; individual virtues by name.

Index

Wagons: BF procures for Braddock, 217–21; text of advertisement for, 218–21; bond given for, 221; BF praised for providing, 227; financial settlement for, 228, 254–5. *See also* Braddock; French and Indian War.

Walpole, Horace, publishes Lord Herbert's autobiography, 14

War: Uncle Benjamin's verses on, 48; events of, subject to uncertainty, 228–9. *See also* American Revolution; French and Indian War; War of Austrian Succession; War of Jenkins' Ear.

War of the Austrian Succession: defense of Phila. during, 182–5; W. Franklin in, 231

War of Jenkins' Ear, mentioned, 182

Watch, city: improvements needed, 173; reformed, 174 n

Water, BF prefers, to beer at work, 99

Watson, Joseph, BF friendship with, 89–92; marries Frances Read, 128 n; biographical note, 300

Watson, William: summarizes *Exper. and Obser.*, 245; ignores idea of lightning rod, 245 n; biographical note, 300

Watts, John: BF works at printing house of, 99–101; biographical note, 300

"Way to Wealth, The": in *Poor Richard*, 164; widely reprinted, 164

Webb, George: employed by Keimer, 108; early career, 109; member of Junto, 117; seeks job with BF, 119; betrays BF's plans, 120; biographical note, 300

Wedderburn, Alexander, abuses BF before Privy Council committee, 208 n

Weissport, Pa., mentioned, 231 n

Welfare. *See* Wohlfahrt, Michael.

West Indies: Osborne success in, 91–2; BF to be sent to, 105; Rogers goes to, 107; electrical experiments in, 242. *See also* Antigua; Barbados; Dominica.

Westminster, England, proposal for cleaning streets in, 206

Whitefield, George: impact of, in Phila., 175–6; New Building erected for, 176; Georgia orphanage of, 176–8; effect of oratory, 177–8; BF prints works, 178; relations with BF, 178–9; powerful voice and delivery, 179–80; critics, 180; mentioned, 194; followers build church, 201; biographical note, 300

Whitmarsh, Thomas: BF hires, 125; sets up as printer, 166 n; biographical note, 300

Wilcox, John: lends BF books, 97; biographical note, 301

Wilks, Robert: dissuades Ralph from acting career, 95; biographical note, 301

William Henry, Fort. *See* George, Fort

Wills's Creek, Braddock's supply depot, 218

Wilmot, Henry, represents Penns, 266 n

Wilson, Benjamin, verifies BF's electrical theories, 245, 246 n

Wilson, Woodrow, on autobiography, 17–8

Wilton House, England, BF at, 259

Witty Club, Gloucester, Webb a member, 109

Wohlfahrt, Michael: on Dunkers, 190–1; biographical note, 301

Wolfe, James: sent to America, 251; biographical note, 301

Wollaston, William, *The Religion of Nature Delineated*, BF answers, 96

Women: education of, 60–1, 166; BF and "strumpets," 83; intrigues with, 115 n, 128

Woolman, John, compared with BF, 15–6

Worship, BF's private liturgy for, 148

Worthylake, George, ballad on, 59

Wright, Edward: praises BF, 244–5; biographical note, 301

Writing: BF's principles of style, 20; father criticizes BF's, 61; spelling and punctuation standards, 61 n; BF's method of improving, 61–2; BF on dialogue in Bunyan, Defoe, Richardson, 72; required by Junto, 117; skill in, pays off, 121, 124

Wygate, John: BF's friendship with, 103; proposes European travel with BF, 104; biographical note, 301
Wyndham, Sir William: asks BF to teach sons to swim, 105; biographical note, 301

Xenophon, *Memorabilia* mentioned, 13, 64

Yale College, honorary degree from, 209
York County, Pa., BF advertises for wagons in, 219
Yorke, Charles: reviews Heads of Complaint, 265; presents Proprietors' case before Privy Council, 265 n; biographical note, 301
Young, Edward, *Love of Fame*, BF copies satire from, 98–9
Youth, influence of autobiography on, 134, 136